# UNDERSTANDING
## and COUNSELING
## the ALCOHOLIC

Howard J. Clinebell, Jr.

# UNDERSTANDING
# and COUNSELING
# the ALCOHOLIC

## Through Religion and Psychology

*Revised and Enlarged Edition*

ABINGDON PRESS

*Nashville*

UNDERSTANDING AND COUNSELING THE ALCOHOLIC: REVISED

MANUFACTURED BY THE PARTHENON PRESS AT
NASHVILLE, TENNESSEE, UNITED STATES OF AMERICA

# Foreword

That Howard Clinebell has unusual understanding of the alcoholic and his problems becomes crystal clear as one reads this book. First published in 1956, it quickly won a place for itself as one of the best books in the field. Revising and enlarging this work has vastly increased its usefulness, to the point that people working in the field can ill afford to be without it; and people who become interested and want to learn will find it "must" reading.

For Howard Clinebell, now professor of pastoral counseling at the School of Theology, Claremont, California, does not limit his book to the special area he knows so well. He has provided first a broad and well-informed survey of our current knowledge about the disease of alcoholism and its victims, and followed this with many practical suggestions on how to help alcoholics. His interest embraces education and its role both in bringing the alcoholic to treatment and in prevention. Finally, he has included much of the history of the whole alcoholism movement.

Dr. Clinebell's background and vocation naturally ensure that the role of religion in both the treatment and the prevention of alcoholism shall have full attention. Many may be unaware of just how important a role this has been, and still is today. While ministers will benefit especially from a study of this book, others who work with alcoholics—doctors, psychologists, nurses, social workers, counselors, and employers, as well as families and friends—should find their effectiveness greatly enhanced if they will take advantage of Dr. Clinebell's expertise as expressed here.

Perhaps most important is the attitude that pervades the book. Howard Clinebell clearly *likes* alcoholics. He does not confuse the condition of illness with the person who has it. His concern is always for that person and his potential as a human being, once he can be freed from the entangling web of his terrible compulsion. This, in my opinion, is the reason Dr. Clinebell has been able to help so many alcoholics to recover.

It is my hope that his readers will imbibe at least some of his understanding, compassion, and caring. If they do, countless sick alcoholics will have a chance to get well.

MARTY MANN
Founder-Consultant
National Council on Alcoholism

# Preface

This book was written for those who want help in dealing with alcoholism, one of the most pressing and perplexing problems of our day. It is aimed at helping the individual who is confronted with such practical problems as what to teach concerning alcoholism and how to handle the alcoholic who comes seeking counsel. Specifically, it is designed to be an aid to the person who wishes to apply religious resources more effectively to the problem of alcoholism.

Parts I and II have as their purpose the undergirding of such practical *action* with *adequate understanding*. Action in the area of alcoholism, when it lacks a solid foundation of understanding, tends to be misdirected and ineffective. On the other hand, action which possesses such a foundation can be realistic and effective. Part I presents the scientific facts concerning alcoholism in a synoptic manner, describing the various factors in the etiology and development of this complex illness. Knowledge of such facts is essential as preparation for both realistic prevention and effective treatment of the sickness. The presentation of the scientific facts is particularly necessary because of the amount of propagandistic literature, with little foundation in objective fact, which has been produced on the subjects of alcohol and alcoholism.

Part II aims at helping the reader to profit by the experience of those religious groups which have been especially concerned with helping alcoholics. It presents three varied types of religious approaches to alcoholism, with an evaluation of the strength and weakness of each, together with a psychological analysis of how each operates. Chapter 6 is in a sense a summary of Part II, showing the unique contributions of religious, as contrasted with nonreligious, approaches to alcoholism. It also describes the dynamics of the process by which religion can provide a psychological and spiritual substitute for alcohol, and thus become a solution to the problem of alcoholism. Part II is actually a study in the psychology of applied religion. By this I mean that its focus is

7

not religion in general or in the abstract, but religion as it is applied to one concrete area of human tragedy.

The fundamental orientation throughout Parts I and II is practical, rather than theoretical. The question which is always in view is this: How are these facts relevant to the work of one who is confronted with the problems of applying the insights of psychology and religion more effectively to the sickness called alcoholism?

Part III aims at applying the understanding of alcoholism gained in Part I and the understanding of religious approaches to the problem gained in Part II, to the work of the pastor. To the extent that it is successful in achieving this aim, it will have value for any person wishing to help an alcoholic by the use of therapeutic religion. Chapter 7 attempts to clarify some of the issues involved in the question which is a stumbling block to many clergymen: What is the ethical problem in alcoholism? Chapters 8, 9, and 10 deal with the important matter of counseling alcoholics. Chapters 11 and 12 focus on counseling the families of alcoholics, and helping to prevent alcoholism, respectively. And Chapter 13 discusses the role of the church in dealing with alcoholism.

It is important to point out that this is not a study of either the ethics of social drinking or of the problems which arise from the moderate use of alcoholic beverages in our mechanized and socially complicated culture. This is not to deny either the existence or the importance of such problems. But to lump all the diverse problems associated with alcohol into one cauldron is to brew the stew of confusion rather than to distill clarification and understanding. So, this book limits itself to one problem area. It is not a book about *alcohol* but about the sickness called *alcoholism*.

How did this book come to be written? The material on which Parts I and II are based was taken from the findings of the writer's doctoral dissertation at Columbia University, entitled "Some Religious Approaches to the Problem of Alcoholism." *

This material, presented here in abbreviated form, is the result of a research program extending over a period of six years. Part III consists essentially of the practical implications for the religious worker of the research findings. Several of the chapters in Part III include some salient findings of a questionnaire which was mailed to all clergymen who attended the Yale Summer School of Alcohol Studies during the first seven years of its operation.

An explanation of certain terms and abbreviations is in order. The terms "Yale School" and "Yale ministers" refer to the Yale University Summer School of Alcohol Studies (the school has subsequently been transferred to Rutgers University) and the ministers who attended that school, respec-

---

* Anyone wishing to refer to the original dissertation will find it on file in the microfilm library at Columbia University and in the Library of Congress, Mic. A54-1859.

tively. The initials "QJSA" refer to *The Quarterly Journal of Studies on Alcohol,* the most authoritative journal in the field of alcohol and alcoholism, formerly published at Yale and now at Rutgers University. The term "interviewee" refers to the alcoholics whom I interviewed as a part of my doctoral research. "AA" is an accepted abbreviation for Alcoholics Anonymous.

I feel a profound sense of gratitude to the individuals who contributed directly and indirectly to this study. Horace L. Friess, of Columbia University, was chairman of the committee which guided the doctoral research program. As such he gave generously of his time, scholarly insight, and friendly encouragement. The other committee members, Paul Tillich, Carney Landis, and David E. Roberts, now deceased, are remembered appreciatively for their valuable counsel and guidance. For whatever understanding I may possess concerning the dynamics of interpersonal relations, I must acknowledge my indebtedness to the faculty of the William Alanson White Institute of Psychiatry, Psychoanalysis and Psychology. The intellectual stimulation and interchange of ideas in the student-faculty seminar on religion and health at Columbia proved to be most helpful to me in the general area of psychology and religion. To the faculty of the 1949 Yale Summer School I am grateful for an orientation in the general field of alcohol and alcoholism. For their helpful suggestions at various points in my study, I would like to express thanks to Selden D. Bacon, of Rutgers and Yvelin Gardner of the National Council on Alcoholism; the help of two pioneers in the field of alcoholism research and treatment, the late E. M. Jellinek and the late Harry M. Tiebout, is remembered with gratitude.

A group of the most generous contributors to this study must remain anonymous. They are the scores of alcoholics whom I heard and talked with at AA meetings and elsewhere, and particularly the seventy-nine who supplied information concerning nearly every aspect of their lives as they willingly allowed themselves to be interviewed. The interviews averaged about three hours in length and covered the following areas: early home life, educational, vocational and marital backgrounds, prealcoholic drinking and the developmental pattern of their alcoholism, experience in AA (or in other therapies), and self-analysis. Data derived from these interviews supplied much of the material for Part I, nearly all the AA chapter, and considerable material for several of the other chapters. The interviewees were obtained largely through the cooperation of Bill W., one of the co-founders of AA, and through the direct contact work of Bob H., former head of the New York AA intergroup organization. My debt to these two men and to the interviewees is clearly evident. Whatever realism and authenticity this study may have so far as alcoholism is concerned is due in considerable measure to the willing self-revelation of the alcoholics who were interviewed. Bob H. also rendered invaluable service by reading the manuscript. His counsel was particularly helpful because of his vantage point "inside" the problem of alcoholism. Bill W. also supplied historical information on AA and checked the historical section of the AA chapter for accuracy. I feel indebted to the 146 Yale ministers who returned the questionnaires I sent to them. Their investment of time resulted in a major contribution to Part III. I am also grateful to those leaders of the Salvation Army and the various rescue missions who cooperated by answering my endless questions concerning their approaches to alcoholism.

I would like to acknowledge the permission granted me by the General Service Board of Alcoholics Anonymous to use the selections I have quoted from *Alcoholics Anonymous* and from the A. A. *Grapevine*, and also the permission granted me by the *Quarterly Journal of Studies on Alcohol* to use the passages I have quoted from that journal and from *Alcohol, Science and Society*.

A number of leaders in the field of alcoholism were of major help in the process of completing the revised edition of the book. Yvelin Gardner of N.C.A. and Milton A. Maxwell of the Rutgers School of Alcohol Studies were generous in supplying information from their comprehensive knowledge of the contemporary alcoholism scene. Ruth Fox, Medical Director of N.C.A., gave invaluable assistance in providing information about current medical and psychotherapeutic therapies. Thomas Richards, a leader in work with homeless alcoholics, provided information about recent developments in that area; and Gus Hewlett of the North American Association of Alcoholism Programs did the same for the new federal program in the alcoholism field. Helpful staff members at both AA's General Service Office and the Al-Anon Family Group Headquarters supplied answers to my numerous questions about recent developments in their respective groups. I welcome this opportunity to acknowledge my appreciation to these busy people for their much-needed help.

Finally, it is a pleasure to express my gratitude to my wife for her patience and help with the various phases of the development of the book, including the revision.

When the first edition was published, I expressed my hope in the preface that it would be of sufficient value to individuals who were facing the perplexing problems of helping alcoholics that it would justify the investment of countless hours and insights by the many individuals whose help made the book possible. To those persons, I am pleased to be able to report that their investments have proved to be of worth to many people who are working with alcoholics. The continued use of the book has led to this revised edition. It has been particularly gratifying that a positive response has come not only from those who counsel with alcoholics, but also from alcoholics and their families. Interest has been evidenced in such faraway places as Australia,

Ireland, South America, and Africa. The opportunity to revise the volume is welcome since it allows me to incorporate both some of the key developments which have occurred in the past decade and changes in my own approach to counseling with alcoholics and their families. I have also added a chapter outlining the church's role in this area.

And so, again, I re-launch this book with the hope that it will continue to be of use to those who are in the front lines of treating and preventing the illness called alcoholism.

HOWARD J. CLINEBELL, JR.
Claremont, California

11

# Contents

# PART I

# UNDERSTANDING
# the PROBLEM
# of ALCOHOLISM

# 1

# What Is an Alcoholic?

Have you ever known an alcoholic? Have you ever tried to help such a person? Almost everyone reading this page can answer the first question in the affirmative. Many can do the same for the second. For few problems are as widespread as alcoholism. Directly or indirectly, most adults have had some experience with this perplexing sickness. It may have touched one's immediate family; or it may have been experienced in an employee, a fellow worker, a friend or the friend of a friend, a distant relative, or a chance acquaintance. In a survey conducted in the state of Washington, 72 percent of the sample population had known at least one alcoholic.[1] Of these, 40.5 percent had been related as close friends or relatives of the alcoholic they had known.

Anyone whose work brings him into intimate touch with people is painfully acquainted with the problem of alcoholism. Ministers, physicians, psychotherapists, social workers, and others whose work includes helping people in trouble have the problem thrust at them many times in the course of their professional activity. As I think back over my own professional experience, I am impressed by the variety of such encounters. I think, for example, of Mr. K., who stopped after choir practice to chat and during the conversation worked around to unburdening his soul of the grim story of his wife's recent spree. I think of Mrs. L., who phoned to ask if I could help persuade her alcoholic husband to see a psychiatrist. I think of Bill, a member of the youth group, who came to tell of the trouble his family had been having with an alcoholic uncle who, though abstinent in AA, continued to be difficult to live with. I think of Joe, a promising young man of twenty-nine, who saw that his drinking was out of hand and, in desperation, appealed for help. I think of Mr. B., a respectably dressed stranger who came to the parsonage door with a convincing story about needing a loan to redeem his tools which he had been forced to pawn during a prolonged illness. On investigation, his story proved to be a clever alcoholic ruse. I

17

think of Mr. P., a business executive and church member, who after many years of periodic binges had been happily sober in AA for three years. I think of Mr. L., talented artist and frequent patron of the city hospital's alcoholic ward, who could not admit that he had an alcoholic problem. I think of Mac, a member of another religious faith, who used to knock on my door every few weeks, asking for a "loan." (I had made the mistake of following the course of least resistance and had given him a small sum on the first occasion.) Each time Mac came, he looked more like death—a condition toward which he was slipping with tragic alacrity. I think of Bert, a young man from a disturbed home, who consistently arrived at senior youth meetings with alcohol on his breath. I think of Mrs. R., a parishioner whom I felt sure was having serious trouble with alcohol, but who was expert on hiding the fact from everyone including herself. Any clergyman, physician, or social worker could duplicate and double this list.

As I write, I think of these and others who have crossed my path bearing an alcoholic cross. I think of the times I have felt completely helpless in the face of this problem—the times I have failed—the feelings of frustration that have accompanied the failures. I also recall the satisfaction that has attended the experiences in which I have been able to make even a meager contribution toward bettering a tragic situation.

Few problems have been so baffling in nature as alcoholism. Until recent years, little has been known about either the causes or cures of alcoholism. Much of what had been written had been of a propagandistic nature with only a flimsy foundation of objective facts. Many of the so-called cures were relatively ineffective. In some cases they were outright deceptions involving despicable exploitation of human misery. An atmosphere of hopelessness has clung to the problem. For many, it still clings. In the Washington state survey mentioned above, 53.3 percent of the sample population had never known an alcoholic who had recovered.

Alcoholism is still a baffling problem, but developments in recent years have brought the dawning of a new hope. A dozen or more scientific disciplines have focused their research eyes on the problem, bringing new understanding. Most important of all, from the standpoint of the alcoholic and his family, is the hope engendered by the wonderful success of AA.

There is no area of human suffering in which religion has given a more convincing demonstration of its therapeutic power than in the problem of alcoholism. For a long time it has been recognized that religion has tremendous resources for dealing with the problem. In his classic sermons on intemperance [2] published in 1827, Lyman Beecher made it clear that some sort of religious experience was the best hope for the alcoholic. Even those who had no professional interest in religion often shared this view. Around 1930 the director of a large chemical company in America sought help for his alcoholism from the famous Swiss psychoanalyst Carl Gustav Jung. Dr. Jung went over his case very carefully and then told him that nothing but a religious conversion could give him any lasting help. The man returned to America where he received help in the Oxford Group Movement. Interestingly enough, he later became one of the "pre-founders" of an amazing group that has given us the most convincing evidence of the therapeutic effectiveness of religion—Alcoholics Anonymous. This group has reclaimed from the scrap heap of society more than 375,000 "hopeless" alcoholics.

Our task in this volume will be to explore the ways in which religious resources may be used with greatest effectiveness in dealing with alcoholism. By implication, we may throw some light on religion as a resource for dealing with other human problems.

### Recognizing the Problem

Whatever the problem, effective treatment depends on accurate recognition and diagnosis. For this reason the first concern of those who would help alcoholics is to recognize and understand the problem. Some time ago I attended a dinner and was seated beside a guest who plied me with questions concerning alcoholism. During the conversation she raised this problem: "I am concerned about a friend who seems to me to be drinking too much. How can I tell whether or not he is an alcoholic?" In answering her query I pointed out that it is often difficult or even impossible to be absolutely certain that a given person is afflicted with the alcoholic sickness, but that there is a useful rule of thumb which often gives one a valid clue. Put in the form of a question, it is this: *Does the person's drinking frequently or continuously interfere with his social relations, his role in the family, his job, his finances, or his health?* If so, the chances are that that person is an alcoholic or on the verge of becoming one.

This simple test question can be rephrased as a useful definition of what is meant by the term "alcoholic" in this book. *An alcoholic is anyone whose drinking interferes frequently or continuously with any of his important life adjustments and interpersonal relationships.*

This definition points to the essential nature of alcoholic drinking which distinguishes it from other kinds of drinking behavior. If a drinker who is not an alcoholic finds that his drinking is interfering with his work, for instance, he will reduce his consumption. In contrast, the alcoholic will usually not even recognize the causal relation between his drinking and his job trouble; rather he will project the blame for his trouble on others. He cannot recognize the real cause of his difficulty because alcohol is very important to him. To recognize it as the offender would threaten the center around which he has organized his life. Even if he suspects that alcohol is a cause of his trouble, he will not be able to reduce his consumption for any extended period. This is because his drinking is gradually becoming compulsive. He is driven by forces beyond his rational control. For reasons not completely known, he is losing the power of choice when alcohol is involved. The old phrase "driven to drink" can be accurately applied to him. He is driven by powerful forces within himself. Once he begins to drink, he usually will not be able to stop until he is "broke," unconscious, or until his digestive system revolts and refuses to take any more alcohol. An alcoholic, then, is a person for whom one drink frequently touches off a chain reaction leading to drinking that is excessive in the sense that it hampers his interpersonal life. It should be noted that some alcoholics are able to control their drinking for a considerable period before it results in a binge.

There are other indications which may be useful in recognizing incipient alcoholism. Anyone who uses alcohol as a persistent means of interpersonal adjustment—who drinks regularly to allow himself to be more aggressive in his work or less shy at social functions—is in danger. He may be near the intangible line that separates nonpathological from compulsive drinking. Again, anyone whose drinking behavior is in defiance of the standards of the group from which he derives his sense of belonging is suspect, so far as alcoholism is concerned. Sneaking drinks and drinking alone are two examples of such defiance. The fact that alcohol is more important to him than it should be is shown by the fact that he is willing to risk rejection by his in-group in order to satisfy his drinking demands.

Frequent drunkenness would seem to be the most obvious indication of alcoholism. A word of caution is in order. All alcoholism is attended by drunkenness, but not all drunkenness is indicative of alcoholism. Alcoholism and drunkenness are not synonymous. For example, what has been called "rough recreational drinking" was much more common during frontier days than today. Almost every weekend "the boys" would assemble to get and stay roaring drunk. This was the accepted social pattern among some frontier groups, and although there was a great deal of this kind of drunkenness, there was probably less alcoholism than there is today. This is not to suggest rough recreational drinking as a solution to alcoholism, but simply to show that drunkenness is not always a symptom of alcoholism. It is indicative of alcoholism when it interferes with interpersonal functioning, or is in defiance of the drinking mores of one's group. Either of these indicates that the drinking is to a degree compulsive. Obviously a person who has a susceptibility to alcoholism will be more apt to become afflicted in a social group that encourages heavy drinking and drunkenness.

It is wise to remember that the alcoholic himself is often the last person to recognize that his drinking is a problem. And yet, those who specialize in helping people are sometimes asked to suggest aids to self-recognition of alcoholism. The literature of AA suggests:

We do not like to pronounce any individual an alcoholic, but you can quickly diagnose yourself. Step over to the nearest barroom and try some controlled drinking. Try to drink and stop abruptly. Try it more than once. It will not take long for you to decide, if you are honest with yourself about it. It may be worth a bad case of jitters if you get a full knowledge of your condition.[3]

The point of this experiment is that an alcoholic usually cannot control his drinking for more than a few successive occasions. (For this experiment to be reasonably conclusive, the person should be able to stop after one or two drinks for at least a month.)

The late Robert V. Seliger, a psychiatrist who worked extensively with alcoholics, offered this checklist:

## ARE YOU AN ALCOHOLIC?

To answer this question, ask yourself the following questions and answer them as honestly as you can.

1. Do you lose time from work due to drinking?
2. Is drinking making your home life unhappy?
3. Do you drink because you are shy with other people?
4. Is drinking affecting your reputation?
5. Have you ever felt remorse after drinking?
6. Have you gotten into financial difficulties as a result of drinking?
7. Do you turn to lower companions and an inferior environment when drinking?
8. Does your drinking make you careless of your family's welfare?
9. Has your ambition decreased since drinking?
10. Do you crave a drink at a definite time daily?
11. Do you want a drink the next morning?
12. Does drinking cause you to have difficulty sleeping?
13. Has your efficiency decreased since drinking?
14. Is drinking jeopardizing your job or business?
15. Do you drink to escape from worries or troubles?
16. Do you drink alone?
17. Have you ever had a complete loss of memory as a result of drinking?
18. Has your physician ever treated you for drinking?
19. Do you drink to build up your self-confidence?
20. Have you ever been to a hospital or institution on account of drinking? [4]

"Yes" answers to even a few questions such as these constitute a warning that trouble may be ahead. There are two weaknesses to any scheme of self-recognition such as this. For one thing the alcoholic is often a master in self-deception and, as such, he does not recognize alcohol as the cause of the troubles listed. For another, the alcoholic may use such a list in a negative fashion. For example, I remember a woman who had had a serious alcoholic problem for years but who rationalized that she was not an alcoholic because she never drank in the morning.

## Types of Alcoholics

One important reason why alcoholism is frequently difficult to recognize is that every case is different. There is a baffling variety of types and degrees of the disorder, so that if one uses any generalization as an infallible touchstone, he will be led astray in dealing with individuals. Some sample case histories taken from the author's files will highlight this point. Names and other identifying data have been altered to preserve anonymity; the essentials, however, are unchanged.

Sidney L. was born in a midwestern city forty-seven years ago. His father was mean-tempered and harshly authoritarian. His mother died when Sidney was sixteen. He left school in the seventh grade and worked at a series of unskilled jobs. He began drinking at fourteen; his drinking was abnormal from the beginning. He began to drink in the mornings when he was twenty-three. In a few years he had become the neighborhood drunk and was spending a substantial share of his time "on the bum" living on Skid Rows around the country. At thirty he was sent to a state hospital for his alcoholism. Between then and forty-three he was in the state hospital eleven times. Between hospitalizations he lived in Salvation Army homes, missions, and public parks. He drank whatever was available, including rubbing alcohol and "smoke" (wood alcohol). He deteriorated physically, mentally, and morally. He suffered alcoholic hallucinations. At forty-three he was pronounced "a hopeless chronic alcoholic—a menace to himself and society." He says, "I was living the life of oblivion. I had to beg to live. I was as helpless as a one-year-old baby." He wanted to die but did not have the nerve to take his own life.

Alcoholics of Sidney's type can be recognized readily from their grossly asocial behavior. The Skid Row alcoholic who becomes open to help is sometimes called a "low-bottom" alcoholic, indicating that he has reached a low point of social disintegration.

Although the low-bottom alcoholic has provided the stereotype of what all alcoholics are supposed to be like, he represents less than one tenth of the total alcoholic population. In contrast to this group the vast majority of alcoholics are not living on Skid Row and are still able to hold jobs and live

22

with their families. Such an alcoholic is "dragging his anchor" because of his drinking. He is less adequate as a father and husband, as well as less efficient in his work than he would otherwise be. He may have an above-average amount of absenteeism and is usually tired and run-down. Alcoholics who become open to help at this level of minimal social disintegration are called "high-bottom" or "high-high-bottom" alcoholics. Such alcoholics are the most difficult to recognize simply because alcohol has not cut them off from normal social intercourse, even though it is giving them trouble. The National Council on Alcoholism has estimated that "at least 85 per cent of alcoholics are 'hidden' in factories, offices and homes in large and small communities throughout the country." [5] All too frequently the alcoholic remains hidden until the final stages of his sickness.

The following case is illustrative of the high-bottom type:

William B., forty-five, was born in a small town in a western state. His parents both hated liquor and would not allow it in the house. William was valedictorian of his high-school class and graduated Phi Beta Kappa from college. He had the first drink when he was a senior in college. He drank very little during law school. Following graduation his drinking consisted of an occasional social cocktail. When he was thirty-three he began daily social drinking, following the example of an admired senior partner. He liked the boost alcohol gave his self-confidence. Gradually his drinking increased in volume. By the age of forty-one he began to feel caught in a "squirrel-cage" of drinking throughout the day. His remorse was intense because he was using money he could ill afford to spend on alcohol. In spite of his heavy drinking, he did not experience severe hangovers and did not miss a single day at work because of drinking. He did reach the point, however, at which he could hardly force himself to work. He would sit in his office and think about liquor. He became desperate when liquor began to lose its effect. At this point he contacted AA and had been sober for eight months at the time of the interview.

William B. had not lost his job, his home, or his wife; yet he had been drinking alcoholically for two years before he came into AA.

Both Sidney and William were "steady" alcoholics in that they drank heavily nearly every day. In contrast, the "periodic" alcoholic is one who is abstinent for periods ranging from a few days to several months between the times when a wave of craving hits him and he goes on a bender. The case of Henry P., a low-bottom alcoholic, is illustrative of the "periodic." It might be well to point out that periodics probably appear most frequently among high-bottom alcoholics, however.

Henry began drinking during Prohibition at the age of fifteen. By the time he was eighteen he was having trouble controlling the length of his bouts with

23

alcohol. He left school after his junior year in high school to take a job. By the age of twenty he had worked his way up to an executive position. He held this position until twenty-seven when he was fired because of his drinking. Of his drinking pattern he says, "I would be dry for a couple of months, then a terrible urge would come over me like a wave and I'd disappear for weeks on a bender. I'd come home finally with all my money gone." One drink never interested him. His disintegration was rapid in all departments of his life. By the age of thirty-nine he was living in doorways on a Skid Row. He was jailed repeatedly; twice he tried to take his life. Finally a judge suggested he go to AA. He had been sober for four years (after twenty years of problem drinking) at the time of the interview and had established a successful business.

It is axiomatic among students of alcoholism that the sickness is no respecter of persons. It can happen to anyone, regardless of age, sex, occupation, education, social or national background. On the subject of age, for example, it is interesting that there was an age range of from twenty-eight to seventy among the alcoholics interviewed by the writer. There are almost endless variations in the pattern by which the addiction develops. Some alcoholics, for example, embark on their addiction after extended periods of controlled or social drinking, often at a time of personal crisis. The case of Mary P. illustrates this type:

Mary P., age forty-four, was born in a southern state. There was a great deal of conflict between her parents. Her father died when she was twelve. Her mother is described as "very nervous and neurotic—a cold, straight-laced person who didn't like people." Mary was an only child. She had few friends her own age. Often she got her way by means of temper tantrums. At seventeen she left home, "to get away from mother," and went to a large city to work. At twenty she married a man twelve years her senior who proved to be an alcoholic. The marriage lasted four years. She had begun drinking at the age of nineteen to give herself courage for social situations. When Mary was about thirty-five, she suffered the shock of a disappointment in love. After fifteen years of uneventful social drinking, she began to drink excessively. She began to drink alone and in the morning. After a while she began to hallucinate and even attempted to jump from a window when the ambulance arrived to take her to the city hospital. Of her drinking she says, "It was escapism—the realities were too unpleasant." At the time of the interview, Mary had been sober for nearly three years in AA.

Many alcoholics embark on their pathological drinking from what seems like a relatively adequate psychological adjustment. About an equal number are quite obviously disturbed personalities. Those who begin addictive drinking early in life, or with no period of social drinking, are often of the latter type. Take Rita K., age twenty-eight, for example:

Rita was born in an eastern city. Her father was a weak sort of man who was nagged and dominated by his wife. Of her father Rita says, "He never really cared about me." Her mother is described as "a destructive bitch who was opposed to spanking but who nagged instead." Rita still feels sick inside when she thinks of her mother telling her at age eight that she was egocentric and silly. Later her mother predicted that she was going to become a prostitute. Rita was extremely shy and unhappy during her erratic childhood. She suffered from terrible guilt concerning masturbation. For days she went without saying more than a few words to anyone. She recalls, "I couldn't get along with anyone." After college she held a series of jobs, following which she enlisted in the army. Six months later she was given a medical discharge with a diagnosis of dementia praecox. There seems to be considerable doubt about the accuracy of the diagnosis. She has been to a series of psychiatrists and has been "diagnosed as everything." Rita began to drink when she was fifteen. She found she was able to flirt after a few drinks. Before she was sixteen she was getting drunk at every opportunity. She says, "I always liked to get drunk; it was the only purpose of drinking for me. My drinking was a problem to me from the start." At the time of the interview Rita had been sober for about four months. Concerning her drinking as related to her psychological problems, she said, "Drinking is not my only problem, but it's my first one now."

Rita has come to the valid insight that she must learn to live without alcohol if she is to be in a position to work on her psychological problems. Like Henry P., Rita is a periodic alcoholic.

Of the various classifications of alcoholics by types, the best-known is that devised by the late E. M. Jellinek, father of scientific alcoholism research. Acquaintance with this typology will help alert the clergyman to the multiple forms in which the illness can occur. Jellinek began with a broad operational definition: alcoholism is "any use of alcoholic beverages that causes any damage to the individual or society or both." [6] He then went on to identify five types:

*Alpha alcoholism* is a purely psychological dependence on alcohol to relieve pain—emotional or bodily. Drinking damages interpersonal relationships, but there is no loss of control or other evidence of physiological addiction. Some students prefer to use "problem drinking" rather than alcoholism in describing this nonaddicted excessive drinking, since there is apparently no loss of the ability to control the intake of alcohol. The clergyman often encounters such problem drinking in those marital difficulties in which excessive (but noncompulsive) drinking both reflects and intensifies the pain in the relationships. If the marital conflict can be reduced, this type of drinking usually diminishes and comes within nondestructive limits.

*Beta alcoholism* is characterized by such nutritional deficiency diseases as gastritis, cirrhosis of the liver, and polyneuropathy, without loss of control, withdrawal, or other addictive manifestations. It tends to occur in certain hard-drinking social groups in which there are poor nutritional habits. Damage is primarily physiological, with reduced life expectancy, reduced earning capacity, and reduced family stability resulting. The pastor may encounter this problem in social and economically disadvantaged groups. The nutritional deficiency diseases may also occur in the three following types of alcoholism.

*Gamma alcoholism,* the type from which the vast majority of American alcoholics suffer, is synonymous with "steady alcoholism." Like the Delta and Epsilon types, it involves a true physiological addiction. Loss of control, craving, increased tissue tolerance to alcohol, and withdrawal symptoms are present. It is the most destructive type, progressively impairing all areas of the person's functioning, including his health. It has been estimated that 85 percent of AA members are Gamma alcoholics.

*Delta alcoholism,* often called "plateau alcoholism," is identified by the need to maintain a certain minimum level of inebriation much of the time, rather than consistently seeking the maximum impact of alcohol on the central nervous system, as the Gamma alcoholic tends to do. This type is found among Skid Row alcoholics who may ration their supply in order to distribute its effects over a longer time. It is prevalent among French alcoholics, and it is probably much more common than has been suspected among women alcoholics in the U.S. Characteristically, the person "nips" on alcohol a considerable part of the day; he maintains an "all-day glow," but may seldom become obviously intoxicated. Because of this and the fact that, unlike Gamma alcoholism, social disintegration tends to occur subtly and gradually, the Delta alcoholic is often able to hide his problem for many years.

*Epsilon alcoholism* is the "periodic" form of the problem, in which the person is usually abstinent between binges. Although relatively little is known scientifically about this type, it is probable that it occurs in persons subject to manic-depressive mood swings. The individual may begin a binge when he feels the skid into painful depression beginning.[7]

As Jellinek recognized, there is nothing absolute about this (or any) typology. The same individual may slip from one type into another—e.g., from Alpha or Beta into Gamma; or from Epsilon into Gamma. There may be other types or patterns of alcoholism not yet identified. The value of this typology for the pastor is that of emphasizing the existence of alcoholisms and identifying those forms which he may encounter in his work.

The word "alcoholic" will be used in this book to refer only to the three addictive types—steady, plateau, and periodic (Gamma, Delta, and Epsilon)—in which loss of control is a crucial factor which must be faced in counseling. The special problems of counseling with "problem drinkers" (Alpha alcoholics) will be discussed briefly in Chapter 9.

## Terms Related to the Subject of Alcoholism

Before proceeding, let us glance at some of the terms which we will use and which one is likely to encounter in the general literature on alcoholism. We have defined "alcoholic" and by inference "alcoholism." The term "problem drinker" may refer to a nonaddicted excessive drinker (alpha alcoholism), or it is sometimes used as a synonym for "alcoholic" as defined previously. In counseling and educational work, "problem drinker" often is a valuable substitute for the term "alcoholic." This is true in those cases in which "alcoholic" is a stumbling block for the person or persons involved because of their preconceived stereotype concerning the term. "Alcohol addict" is roughly synonymous with "alcoholic" (Gamma, Delta, or Epsilon types) and is useful to keep in mind, in that it conveys a sense of the intensity of the compulsion involved. "Chronic alcoholism" usually refers to the advanced stages of the illness. It is during these stages that medical and psychiatric "complications" frequently occur.

These complications are the physical and psychological diseases resulting directly or indirectly from the prolonged excessive use of alcohol. They include polyneuropathy, pellagra, cirrhosis of the liver, Korsakoff's psychosis, delirium tremens, acute alcoholic hallucinosis, and others. Such complications are suffered by one out of four alcoholics in our country. An alcoholic who is so afflicted is in need of immediate medical attention and often hospitalization.

The terms "high bottom" and "low bottom" refer, as has been suggested, to the degree of social disintegration that has occurred by the time the person "hits bottom" or becomes open to help. These terms are so completely relative as to be of limited usefulness except when describing those at the two extremes. Steady and periodic alcoholics occur among both high- and low-bottom alcoholics, although it seems likely that a much smaller proportion of low-bottom alcoholics are periodics than is true among high-bottom alcoholics.

## How Alcoholism Develops

It is essential that we know something of the developmental pattern of alcoholism. It is important from a practical standpoint that one be able to recognize alcoholism at various stages. Early detection and treatment are as vital in this as in any other sickness. Knowledge of the danger signals or the early symptoms can be a valuable asset to a counselor. On the other hand, if we are to understand how religion meets the problem, we must know as much as possible about the problem. What experiences has the alcoholic been through, and how does he feel when he finally turns to a religious group for help? Again it is worth repeating for emphasis that no two alcoholics are alike and that all generalizations, therefore, are somewhat dangerous. However, it is true that there is a certain pattern of experiences which is characteristic of many, though not all, alcoholics. We need to know more about this pattern.

Let us, therefore, trace the path by which the "glass crutch" develops and crumbles. The most systematic study of this process is that done by the late E. M. Jellinek, as reported in "Phases in the Drinking History of Alcoholics: Analysis of a Survey Conducted by the *Grapevine*, Official Organ of Alcoholics Anonymous." [8] Here is a summary of Jellinek's findings concerning thirty-four kinds of characteristic alcoholic behavior and the average ages at which each first occurred:

## THE ADDICTIVE PATTERN

| Characteristic Alcoholic Behavior | Number Reporting (out of 98) | Average or Mean Age (of first occurrence) |
|---|---|---|
| 1. Getting drunk | 98 | 18.8 |
| 2. Blackouts | 89 | 25.2 |
| 3. Sneaking drinks | 89 | 25.9 |
| 4. Week-end drunks | 74 | 27.2 |
| 5. Loss of control | 95 | 27.6 |
| 6. Extravagant behavior | 77 | 27.6 |
| 7. Rationalization | 81 | 29.2 |
| 8. Losing friends | 63 | 29.7 |
| 9. Morning drinks | 91 | 29.9 |
| 10. Indifference to quality (liquor) | 84 | 30.0 |
| 11. Losing working time | 90 | 30.4 |
| 12. Midweek drunks | 78 | 30.4 |
| 13. Family disapproval | 95 | 30.5 |
| 14. Losing advancements (on job) | 56 | 30.6 |
| 15. Go on water wagon | 80 | 30.7 |
| 16. Losing job | 56 | 30.9 |
| 17. Daytime drunks | 85 | 31.0 |
| 18. Solitary drinking | 87 | 31.2 |
| 19. Antisocial behavior | 60 | 31.3 |
| 20. Benders | 89 | 31.8 |
| 21. Remorse | 91 | 32.2 |
| 22. Protecting supply (of liquor) | 77 | 32.5 |
| 23. Tremors | 90 | 32.7 |
| 24. Changing drinking pattern | 73 | 32.7 |
| 25. Fears | 72 | 32.9 |
| 26. Resentment | 69 | 33.1 |
| 27. Seeking psychiatric advice | 53 | 35.0 |
| 28. Sedatives | 60 | 35.5 |

| | | |
|---|---|---|
| 29. Felt religious need | 60 | 35.7 |
| 30. Seeking medical advice | 80 | 35.8 |
| 31. Hospitalization | 60 | 36.8 |
| 32. Admit to self inability to control | 98 | 38.1 |
| 33. Admit to others inability to control | 91 | 39.5 |
| 34. Reached lowest point (hit bottom) | 97 | 40.7 |

It is important for the person who is interested in helping alcoholics to keep this list of forms of characteristic alcoholic behavior in mind, remembering that no single form of behavior except "getting drunk" applied to all the alcoholics reporting. Because these thirty-four forms of behavior are of common occurrence among alcoholics, they constitute a useful guide, not only in identifying an individual as an alcoholic, but in helping to ascertain approximately at what stage he has arrived in his sickness. However, the order and average age of first occurrence varies tremendously from one alcoholic to another. For this reason, the list should not be used in a mechanical fashion. With this in mind, we will utilize the list, supplemented by case-history material collected by the author, to follow the drinking history of "Mr. X," a statistically average alcoholic. To repeat for emphasis, no person exactly like Mr. X exists. Every alcoholic is an individual, and therefore his alcoholism develops according to a unique pattern. However, there is a certain general pattern of development which applies, with modifications, to many alcoholics. To trace this general pattern is now our task.

Mr. X begins drinking at about sixteen and one-half when he becomes a part of a group for whom drinking is a folkway. (Only about 10 percent of alcoholics begin as solitary drinkers.) He is about eighteen and one-half when he first becomes intoxicated. If his need for the effects of alcohol had been relatively more intense, he might have become intoxicated on the occasion of his first drink. One alcoholic of this type said, "I never liked the taste of liquor; I would get in the half-world of alcohol and want to stay there, even in the early years."

X represents the majority of alcoholics who become addicted following a period of what appears to be normal drinking. Long before it gives him trouble, however, X's drinking is abnormal. Alcohol is a social lubricant, and X needs a lot of lubrication. At the time X only knows that he "feels good" when he drinks—more adequate and self-confident. Someday, in retrospect, he may say with one of the interviewees, "My drinking was alcoholic from the beginning because it meant too much to me." This was a danger signal which he could not recognize.

According to Marty Mann in her book, New Primer on Alcoholism,[9] the major psychological symptom of the early stage of alcoholism is growing dependence on alcohol. X is gradually using alcohol more and more as a means of interpersonal adjustment. He is experiencing its "pampering" effects. He begins to feel that he is not at his best unless he is "fortified." He drinks at the slightest provocation—when he feels depressed or elated, when he has a success or failure in his work, to help him sleep, and to combat the "tired feeling" (which is increasingly present). He organizes his life more and more around his drinking times during the day.

X has good competitive resources and a strong success drive. In spite of his drinking, he does well in his work. Occasionally, when something has irritated him, he gets very drunk. But he is still able to control the occasions and general length of drunkenness. His drinking is not yet a symptom of the full-blown disease of alcoholism.

X's tolerance for alcohol is increasing, i.e., he must drink more to get the same effect. After a period of particularly heavy consumption at around twenty-five, a new symptom appears. X "pulls a blank." He awakens the morning after a party to make the frightening discovery that he remembers nothing that happened after a certain point the night before. His friends assure him that he did not pass out and that his behavior was about as usual. This temporary amnesia disturbs X, and he vows with himself to "take it easy on the hard stuff." Among students of alcoholism it is believed that the occurrence of a blackout may indicate that a new process—possibly a physiological one—has begun. About 90 percent of alcoholics have them. Blackouts can be considered danger signals in that they occur approximately three times as commonly among prealcoholics as among drinkers who will not become alcoholics.

There are other omens of approaching alcoholism in X's behavior. He *sneaks drinks.* At parties X slips out to the kitchen for an extra one. He may drink before he goes to a party, just to be sure he has enough. He *gulps drinks.* Everyone else drinks too slowly for him. He may begin carrying a secret supply. He *lies about his drinking.* He becomes defensive about how much he drinks. He lies to himself to hide the fact that his drinking is not the same as his friends'. He may feel some remorse about an embarrassing episode and promise himself to go "on the wagon" when his work lets up. Alcohol is beginning to cause him trouble.

One day when X is around twenty-seven and one-half, he drops into his favorite gin mill for his usual two drinks before supper. Against his conscious intention he "winds up cockeyed." He is mystified by his own lack of control, but he rationalizes that he has been under special strain lately. Before long X is consistently drinking more than he intends. About the same time (two years after his first blackout) X's Friday night drunks expand to include the entire weekend. He has "lost control." It is noteworthy that loss of control usually occurs so gradually as to be imperceptible. The person first loses control of the amount he drinks and second of the occasion of excessive drinking. He begins to experience a craving for alcohol. Once he begins to drink, he often cannot stop. This fact determines the course of his alcoholism. He could probably still stop drinking at this point if he were aware of his need for help and could find it. But X rationalizes each experience of excess. He convinces himself (via spurious reasoning) that external circumstances cause his excess and that he can stop when he "really wants to." Lacking awareness of the nature of his problem, X starts on the search for the secret of controlled drinking. To learn the magic formula for "drinking like a gentleman" becomes almost an obsession. The search leads in one direction for an alcoholic—downward.

As we saw in the case of Mary P., some environmental crisis may coincide with the onset of addiction. In the case of X, who represents the majority, no reason is apparent for his "crossing the line" into uncontrollable drinking. Perhaps it is simply that the inner pressures which have been gradually accumulating have surpassed the critical load.

Whatever the cause, X is now drinking compulsively. He is literally getting drunk against his intention. For reasons which we shall examine subsequently, he is blind to his condition. He defends himself by an elaborate system of alibis and self-deception from the truth that his drinking is out of control. He is caught in the talons of a compulsion that determines his behavior from a subconscious level—below the rational or volitional activities of his mind. Yet he continues to believe that his problem is a matter of external circumstances ("A wife like mine would drive anyone to drink.") or of "bracing up and using a little more will power."

In the early years of his drinking, alcohol had been a neurotic solution to the problem of X's interpersonal inadequacy. Now the solution has also become a problem. X is now *drinking to overcome the pain caused by previous drinking*. This use of alcohol marks the beginning of the actual addiction. A vicious cycle is established. To the extent that X regards his trouble as a matter of weak willpower, he thinks of himself as a moral jellyfish. The resultant guilt over his alcoholic behavior causes him additional psychological pain and internal chaos. So X increases the consumption of his favorite pain-killer, alcohol.

The vicious cycle of addiction also operates on the physiological level. One gray morning when X is about thirty, he is in such bad shape that he can't navigate. His nerves are playing "Chopsticks," and there are drums in his head. Through the fog comes the dim recollection of hearing someone once say, "Only the hair of the dog that bit you can cure a bad hangover." So he pours himself a double shot and drinks it as he sits on the edge of the bed. He manages to keep it down, and by the time he has finished a cigarette, things begin to look better. He has found the quick, but disastrous, cure for all hang-

31

overs. He is now using alcohol as a self-prescribed medicine to cure the symptoms induced by previous drinking. The *morning drink* becomes standard practice. This is regarded as an almost sure sign that the person is in trouble.

X's addiction spreads like a cancer, gradually disrupting the various departments of his life. At this point it is well to remember that many alcoholics become disorganized in one area but maintain stability in other areas of their lives. For example, one may continue to hold his job even though his social and domestic life is completely disrupted. This fact often confuses the one who is attempting to identify alcoholism in a particular case. Let us say that X represents the case in which alcoholism gradually creeps into all areas of life. His inner life has already been hit by the spiraling fears and resentments of compulsive drinking. This inner chaos is now reflected in his homelife. His trying, irrational, egocentric behavior gives rise to a continuous round of quarrels, sprees, promises, ad infinitum. Of the author's male interviewees, 65 percent had been divorced at least once. In many other cases, the spouse remained, in spite of everything, as a masochistic leaning-post for the alcoholic.

About the same time (age thirty), X's vocational life is hit. He loses time from his work because of hangovers. Even when he is there physically, he is half absent mentally. As a result he is bypassed when advancements come. This gives him added reason to drink. Finally his boss has had enough. X quits in righteous indignation (just before he is fired) and gets roaring drunk.

Alcohol strikes his social life about the same time. Well-meaning friends plead: "You've got everything to live for. Why don't you cut down for the kids' sake?" or "Can't you see what you're doing to yourself? Try sticking to beer." The more he drinks, the less he cares about his friends, except for an easy "touch." The friends gradually disappear. Then X has his first bitter taste of the "penal treatment" for alcoholism. He lands in jail for drunken and disorderly conduct. He is pushed around by the police. (Hopefully, there is a growing number of courts which refer alcoholics to some treatment facilities. May their tribe increase!) The humiliation of all his experiences—at home, on the job, with his friends, and with the law—adds fuel to the flame of X's motive for drinking. X now drinks to anesthetize the sense of failure, guilt, and isolation resulting from his drinking behavior. He is trapped in a vicious cycle of drinking to overcome the effects of drinking—the "squirrel cage" of alcoholism.

What has happened to X? His excessive drinking was originally a symptom of his interpersonal inadequacy. Now the symptom has gone berserk and created what, in terms of therapy, is another disease entity. This "runaway symptom" [10] must be halted if X is to be salvaged.

After the age of thirty, statistically average alcoholic X's disintegration moves rapidly. He now organizes his life around drinking. He plans his day in terms of it. He becomes increasingly indifferent to the quality of his liquor. At about the age of thirty-one he begins to have drunks in the daytime and during the middle of the week. This shows that his compulsion is driving him with greater force so that he becomes intoxicated at the times which are least socially acceptable. At about the same age X begins to manifest the *social isolation* which is typical of alcoholics. Solitary or "lone wolf" drinking is one expression. Antisocial acts—aggressive, often malicious behavior—are another. These indicate that the inhibiting power of social sanctions is weakening as X withdraws from normal society. Antisocial acts are his way of striking back at a rejecting society, as well as securing punishment which his guilt makes him crave. Each experience of interpersonal pain drives him deeper into his isolation and thickens his defensive shell of alcoholic grandiosity. This shell makes him difficult to reach with help. He lives more in the private world in which illusory "successes" compensate for real failures.

Social isolation is accelerated by the onset of benders, which provide ample opportunity for brooding and self-pity. His binges usually last as long as he can get liquor or keep it on his stomach. Jellinek once pointed out that "a man who stays drunk for days without regard to family, work and other duties commits such a gross violation of all cultural standards that his action cannot be a matter of choice unless his is a psychopathic constitution." [11] For this reason the onset of benders may be regarded as the beginning of the acute phase of alcoholism.

The end of each bender brings a horror-filled hangover. Of this, Marty Mann says, "The widely experienced hangover of the nonalcoholic drinker is but a pale approximation of the epic horror known to the alcoholic . . . an all-encompassing onslaught on himself." [12] One of the interviewees described such hangover: "You feel like you're falling apart. Your whole body cries out for alcohol. You shake and shake." The important things to remember is that during or following such hangovers, the alcoholic's defenses may be beaten down enough by the experience to render him open to receiving help.

Following a painful hangover, X may try a series of self-help plans. He *goes on the wagon.* He manages to remain abstinent for several weeks, but he is filled with self-pity and is socially unbearable. A speaker at an AA meeting recalled, "My wife said to me, 'You've been dry for three months but you're the same s.o.b. you've always been.' " X's period on the water wagon ends in a humpty-dumpty act in the form of a long spree. Then he tries *changing his pattern of drinking* to find the secret of control. He decides that it must be the fourth drink that causes him to lose control, or certain kinds of drinks that cause him trouble. He changes his brand or drinks only with his left hand. When all experiments fail, he tries *changing geographic location.* "After all," he rationalizes, "wouldn't New York make anybody want to get drunk?" So he moves to the country and gets drunk in the village saloon.

33

By the age of thirty-two, X is beset with nameless fears. Blackouts occur on nearly every drunk. On one bender he finds himself in a cheap hotel in a city eight hundred miles from home. He has no recollection of how he got there. About two years after his benders begin, X starts to show the "personality change" which is so typical that some students of alcoholism have labeled it the "alcoholic syndrome." Before his addiction X had been known as a good-natured fellow, honest and reasonably unselfish. Now he has become mean and selfish, watching the dire effects of his drinking on his family with apparent indifference. Freud once wrote (in *Totem and Taboo*), "Neurotics live in a special world in which only the 'neurotic standard of currency' counts." This is also true of alcoholics. X begins to live in a world in which only the alcoholic standard of currency has any value. Extramural values like honesty have less and less meaning. He will lie and steal (even from close friends, if he still has any) to achieve his one value—his pearl of great price—alcohol. He will pawn his coat in the middle of the winter. As one alcoholic put it, "For me alcohol was a necessity; my coat wasn't."

X invests amazing ingenuity in protecting his supply, hiding bottles on ropes out the window and in the water closet of the toilet. If conventional beverage alcohol is denied him, he will turn to hair tonic, vanilla, and even Sterno to get his alcohol. Drinking is no longer an option with him; he must drink to live.

By about thirty-five, X is desperate enough to seek help. Approximately two thirds of Jellinek's cases reported feeling a religious need. X may begin to pray. The usual gist of his prayers is, "Get me off this hook, and I'll never do it again." Along with X's other relationships, his relation to organized religion has disintegrated. If he is a Protestant, he probably began to get away from his church about the time he started having blackouts; if he is a Catholic, this avoidance behavior occurred somewhat later. In his desperation X may become a religious "taster"—now Unity, now Christian Science, now his wife's church. He may go to see one or more clergymen—to placate his wife, make an easy touch, or because he feels a genuine religious need. He may prefer a minister who does not know him although this depends on the nature of his previous relationship to clergymen.

At about the same age that X seeks religious help, he may also try psychiatric and medical help. The doctor tells him that he has a bad liver and must give up alcohol. This warning may effect a brief sobriety, or he may walk out of the doctor's office into the nearest bar like a rebellious child. At the age of thirty-seven, after a protracted binge, X has his first hospitalization for alcoholism (although the doctor may have to register him under some other diagnostic label to get him into an unenlightened hospital). If the hospital is enlightened, so far as alcoholism is concerned, he will receive medication for acute intoxication and vitamin therapy, to make up for the vitamin deficiency caused by the weeks of "drinking his meals." In addition, he may be visited by members of AA who have a working relationship with the hospital administration. If the hospital merely "dries him out" and treats his physical condition, without giving attention to the underlying trouble, X will be drunk within a few hours, days, or weeks after release. As the months stagger past, X lands in a series of sanitariums, rest homes, and "cure" establishments. Sixty-nine percent of the author's male interviewees had been hospitalized; six of these forty-one had been in thirty times or more.

The failure of each attempt to get help plunges X deeper into the dismal morass of advanced alcoholism. He drinks around the clock. Every moment of partial sobriety is filled with irrational thoughts and fears. One alcoholic said, "I was a façade with a puddle of fear behind." He loses all sense of time. The need for alcohol provides the only continuity in his life. The withdrawal of alcohol at any time brings all the tortures of hell. His jitters are now best described as "leaps." The pleasant sedative effect of his early drinking is now gone. As one alcoholic puts it, "I just tipped back the bottle and skidded into oblivion." More and more alcohol is required to produce blessed oblivion. So he may begin to use "goof balls" (barbiturates) to enhance the waning effects of alcohol. If he does, he has added another layer to his complex problem. He may become addicted to drugs as well as alcohol.*

As his reality situation becomes increasingly grim, X requires an increasingly grandiose self-concept to protect his alcoholic ego. This picture of himself can be maintained only by longer flights into the reality-denying world of alcoholic fantasy. His prealcoholic inferiority feelings are now grounded in reality. He is not only unemployed; he is practically unemployable. Fears of the future form a vicious alliance with terrible remorse (usually hidden from others) about the past. X feels that nobody understands him. His inner conflicts have grown to almost complete paralysis. Even little tasks like tying his shoelaces become impossible without a drink. Two hands are required to get the glass of whiskey to his lips. He hides himself in cheap hotels—drinking, drinking, drinking—until he is taken to the city hospital in alcoholic delirium. He feels cornered—trapped like a rat.

By this time X may be a physical wreck. His face may be bloated, his eyeballs yellow. His endocrine and metabolic systems are apt to be acutely disturbed. His steps are uncertain. His hands tremble. There is a vacant expression in his eyes. However, the extent of physical disturbance which some alcoholics can hide even in the advanced stages of the illness is often amazing.

* AA regards the abuse of barbiturates and tranquilizers as a major hazard for alcoholics. See "Tranquilizers, Sedatives, and the Alcoholic" (AA World Service, 1959). One danger is derived from the mutually reinforcing effects of alcohol and these drugs, resulting in accidental and potentially fatal overdoses.

At the age of thirty-eight and one-half, Xs' alibi or rationalization system, by which he has for so long defended his ego, begins to crumble. He stands before the (to him) humiliating truth that he is unable to control his drinking. The fact that has been painfully obvious to others for a long time is now forced upon him. He is licked, and he knows it. In spite of this it takes another year or more for him to admit to others that he cannot control his drinking.

At about forty, X reaches his "bottom." This is a matter of emotional bankruptcy and does not necessarily involve living on Skid Row. Having hit bottom, X is what one student of alcoholism has called a "ripe alcoholic." For the first time he is really open to outside help. If none is available, he may attempt suicide. What brings X to his bottom? Perhaps a specific and crushing humiliation. Perhaps the fact that liquor—his god—has let him down by losing its effect. Perhaps some physical illness tips the scales in his psychic economy so that it becomes more painful to drink than not to drink. In many cases there are no obvious causes. Whether or not there is a precipitant, the feeling most commonly described is, "I was sick of myself and wanted to die."

Within a few years after this there comes a fork in X's path. He must find help or risk going under. Going under means a "wet brain" (one of the alcoholic psychoses) and the booby hatch, Skid Row, and a welfare grave. Or, he may go on for years teetering on the brink of destruction.

Many of the alcoholics who come to religious groups and leaders for help have gone through something like the course which we have traced. Many others who come in contact with ministers are of the hidden type—men and women who are holding jobs and living with their families. One of the stereotypes which has been very slow in becoming dislodged from our thinking is that alcoholism is synonymous with extreme social disruption or deterioration. Actually the ability of many alcoholics to maintain stability in some areas of their lives over extended periods is quite amazing. Some alcoholics who come for help have paused for years at one stage or another of the developmental pattern. Others have gone through the stages described with greater rapidity. Some may have had entirely different developmental patterns. Because a person does not fit the typical pattern does not mean that he is not an alcoholic. If his drinking interferes with any of his basic interpersonal relationships, then he is an alcoholic.

Some of the alcoholics interviewed by the author were fortunate. They reached their "bottom" long before they had come to the level of physical, mental, moral, and religious disintegration described in Mr. X. Some had actually "gone under" and then had come back via a religious solution. In either case—high-bottom or low—they were desperate and defeated when they found a religious solution. Otherwise they would not have been able to accept help.

## The Woman Alcoholic

The problem of the woman alcoholic has received increased attention in recent years, particularly by those who treat alcoholism and are impressed with the substantial numbers of women seeking help. To what extent this reflects a "greater rate of emergence of formerly hidden alcoholism among women" [13] and to what extent a rise in the number of women alcoholics (associated with the increase of women drinkers since World War II) is not really known.

In a study by psychologist Edith S. Lisansky, forty-six women alcoholics and fifty-five men alcoholics were compared.[14] All of them came to Connecticut alcoholism outpatient clinics voluntarily. The male and female groups were found to be approximately the same in social class, age, education, and ethnic background. Marital disruption was prevalent among both groups (and to a similar extent). Alcoholism in a parent, sibling, or a spouse was more common among the women alcoholics than among the men. Thirty-five percent of the women, but only 9 percent of the men, reported alcoholism in their spouses. Apparently alcoholics tend to attract alcoholics to some extent. Lisansky found that the average woman alcoholic had begun to drink later and had lost control of her drinking later than the average male alcoholic. Only about half as many men as women could point to a specific life crisis which seemed to precipitate excessive drinking—e.g. divorce, death of a parent, an uphappy love affair. The study showed that a "significantly greater proportion of women alcoholics drink alone, presumably at home. Frequently reported patterns were going to bed at night with a bottle and sipping at home during the day." [15] Significantly, the women sought help sooner after the beginning of addictive drinking than did the men. This may be due either to a telescoping of the stages of the illness or to less resistance to seeking help on the part of the woman alcoholic, perhaps both.

Probably because they tended to drink alone and at home, in a "plateau" pattern, the women in the study had a markedly lower rate of arrests and mental hospital commitments than the men. It is likely that "respectable" hidden (or semihidden) women alcoholics who stay out of difficulty in the community constitute the vast majority of female alcoholics. This does not mean that the plight of women alcoholics is less tragic than that of male alcoholics. In some ways, it is more tragic in its devasting impact on the emotional health of the family organism. One experienced therapist with alcoholics declares:

Many women alcoholics start drinking when their husbands leave for work in the morning and their children are off to school. Yet, somehow, they manage to pull themselves together to get the evening meal on the table. The discovery of their illness . . . waits for months or even years while the guilt and the fear and the loneliness torment them.[16]

Several students of the problem have said that women alcoholics show much greater personality abnormality than do male alcoholics. Clinical evidence is often cited which seems to support this view. The inference drawn from this is that women alcoholics are generally more difficult to treat than are male alcoholics. Lisansky makes an important observation about this:

As a rule, women alcoholics, like men, are not seen in clinics or hospitals until the drinking problem has gone on for some years. It is likely that the social consequences of the drinking problem, i.e., family breakup, job dismissal, rejection by friends and associates, and general social disapproval, are greater for the woman alcoholic who is known as such. The woman patient who appears at a clinic or hospital after years of uncontrolled drinking could therefore conceivably be a more disturbed individual than her male counterpart as a result of her alcoholism and its socially punishing consequences, and not because she was initially, in her prealcoholic personality, a more disturbed individual.[17]

The Lisansky study compared the women outpatient clinic patients with a group of women alcoholics who had been committed to a state farm for various offenses. Striking differences between the social background of the two groups were found. The state farm group showed more psychopathology, greater marital disruption, less drinking alone, and four times the sexual promiscuity associated with drinking, as compared with the clinic group. Lisansky concludes that at least two subgroups must be distinguished among "women alcoholics"—the "respectable" woman whose drinking is relatively concealed and the woman alcoholic whose drinking makes her an obvious problem to society and not just to herself and her family. It is possible, Lisansky speculates, that there are other subgroups—e.g. unmarried middle-aged women who become alcoholic because of feelings of loneliness and diminished self-esteem.

## The Size and Cost of the Problem of Alcoholism

Of the approximately eighty million adults in the United States who drink—about seventy-one percent of the adult population [18]—between five and six million can be considered "alcoholics" by our definition. The National Council on Alcoholism estimates six and one-half million, whereas the Rutgers University Center of Alcohol Studies holds that our most reliable evidence points to an estimate close to five million.[19] For every female alcoholic in the U.S.A., there are between four and five male alcoholics.[20] The Rutgers Center put the 1965 estimates at 4,200,000 male alcoholics and 800,000 female alcoholics.[21] Of every one hundred males who drink, nine and one-half are alcoholics. For every one hundred adults in the United States, 4.2 are alcoholics. The rates vary greatly from one geographical region and state to another, within the country. For example, Nevada with 6.6 alcoholics per one hundred adults, and California with 6.4 stand in sharp contrast to Idaho with 1.9 and Alabama with 1.8. Variations of alcoholism rates among countries are also striking.[22] France has the highest rate with 5.7 alcoholics per one hundred adults.

There seems to be no evidence of a substantial rise in the rate of alcoholism [23] either among drinkers or in the total adult population since 1948. But there has been an enormous expansion of the total number of drinkers since 1940—a rise of thirty-seven million. This increase reflects both the expansion of the population and the rise in the percentage of those who use alcohol. Thus, without a marked rise in the rate of alcoholism, the total number of alcoholics nearly doubled between 1940 and 1966 (from 2,600,000 to 5,000,000 plus).

It is striking to note that alcoholism is more than five times more prevalent than cancer. Psychiatrist Karl Menninger has stated that the alcoholics in the United States constitute our largest single mental health problem. In speaking at the annual meeting of the National Council of Churches' Department of Pastoral Services, he said, "Nothing looms as large on the horizon. Every day we see horrifying examples of men and women who drink up every penny they own and make serious critical errors in judgment that affect you and me. It is a problem which is taking a tremendous mental, social and physical toll." [24]

The economic, social, and cultural costs of alcoholism are staggering in their dimensions. The economic liability of having a large proportion of 4.25 million adult males out of fully productive relationship with the community is gigantic. The illness most frequently reaches its full-blown form between ages thirty-five and fifty, normally a time of maximum productivity. The estimated two million employed alcoholics probably cost industry a billion dollars annually in absenteeism, high accident rates, and inefficiency. When AA had only sixty thousand members, they had an estimated annual earning capacity of $150,000,000. In New York City, where there are at least 200,000 alcoholics, the annual loss of wages due to this sickness is estimated at $50,000,000. Family relief costs each year, in New York City, due to alcoholism, are approximately $2,600,000.[25] Twenty-two percent of male first admissions to mental hospitals in 1964 were given the diagnosis of alcoholism.

There are other less tangible costs. Untreated alcoholism takes twelve years off the life expectancy of its victims and makes their later years a kind of living death by crushing potentialities for constructive relationships. The social costs of this, though impossible to measure, are astronomical. The pain and destructiveness are certainly not limited to the alcoholics themselves. Around each alcoholic there is what has been fittingly termed a "circle of tragedy" composed of all those whose lives are in close touch with his. The total number of persons involved in these circles has been estimated at twenty million by Marty Mann, director of the National Council on Alcoholism. Obviously the psychological damage to the children of alcoholics is impossible to estimate. Or take the cultural costs. For every artist who appears to be more creative when under the influence there are probably a dozen who "drink their poems," their symphonies, their novels, and their plays. In his book *The Other Side of the Bottle*,[26] Dwight Anderson gives us a poignant example of this facet of the tragedy of alcoholism. He points out that the familiar words "All the world is sad and dreary, everywhere I roam," reflect the pathos of the alcoholic's inner world. Their author died in the alcoholic ward of New York's Bellevue Hospital at the age of thirty-eight. In his pocket was a torn piece of paper on which were penciled the words for a song, "Dear friends and gentle hearts," a lyric which might have been loved like "Jeanie with the Light Brown Hair." The story of alcoholism is replete with such might-have-beens.

## Summary

In this chapter we have given what can be considered a working definition of alcoholism : A person is an alcoholic if one or more of his major adjustments in living—health, vocational, social, or marital—is periodically or continuously hampered by drinking. We have described the types and developmental pattern of alcoholism from the beginning when alcohol is a neurotic solution to interpersonal problems, to the point at which the solution itself becomes the chief problem. We have discussed the problem of the woman alcoholic. Lastly, we have described the size and seriousness of the problem. Let us now examine the causes of alcoholism.

## REFERENCES

1. M. A. Maxwell, "Drinking Behavior in the State of Washington," *QJSA*, XIII (June, 1952), 236.

2. *Six Sermons on the Nature, Origin, Signs, Evils and Remedy of Intemperance* (New York: American Tract Society, 1827).

3. Alcoholics Anonymous, *The Story of How Many Thousands of Men and Women Have Recovered from Alcoholism* (New York: Works Publishing, 1950), p. 43.

4. "How to Help an Alcoholic, A Brief Medical Summarization with Practical Suggestions and Tests" (Columbus, Ohio: School and College Service, 1951).

5. From "Alcoholism: A Major Health Problem, A Major Public Responsibility," report of the National Committee on Alcoholism presented to the Annual Meeting on March 18, 1955.

6. *The Disease Concept of Alcoholism* (New Haven: Hillhouse Press, 1960), p. 35.

7. See *ibid.*, pp. 36-41, for a discussion of these five types.

8. *QJSA*, VII (June, 1946), 8-9.

9. (New York: Holt, Rinehart & Winston, 1950), p. 24.

10. For this highly descriptive term, I am indebted to the late Harry Tiebout, a psychiatrist who did a great deal of work with alcoholics.

11. *QJSA*, VII (June, 1946), p. 72.

12. *New Primer on Alcoholism*, p. 40.

13. Mark Keller and Vera Efron, "The Prevalence of Alcoholism," *QJSA*, XVI (December, 1955), 631-32.

14. Edith S. Lisansky, "Alcoholism in Women: Social and Psychological Concomitants," *QJSA*, XVIII (December, 1957), No. 4, 588-623.

15. *Ibid.*, p. 605.

16. Genevieve Burton in "The Woman Alcoholic," *The Evening Bulletin* (Philadelphia), October 18, 1966, p. 19.

17. "Alcoholism in Women," p. 590.

18. Harold A. Mulford, "Drinking and Deviant Drinking, U.S.A., 1963," *QJSA*, XXV (December, 1964), No. 4, 639. Based on a survey done by the National Opinion Research Center showing that 79 percent of the U.S. males and 63 percent of the U.S. females drink. (A 1946 survey showed that 75 percent of males and 56 percent of females drank.) Mark Keller of Rutgers estimates that the total drinking population, including the fifteen to twenty-one age group, was 93½ million in 1965. A national survey conducted in 1964-65 showed that 68 percent of adults drink. The difference between this figure and the 71 percent figure of the 1963 survey may reflect sampling variation rather than a change in drinking practices.

19. Mark Keller, Lecture at the 1966 Rutgers Summer School of Alcohol Studies, "Trends in Drinking and Trends in Alcoholism, with a Critique of Statistics and Statwistics."

20. The National Council on Alcoholism estimates that there are four male alcoholics to every female alcoholic; the Rutgers Center puts the ratio at 5.3 to 1, in 1965 (see Keller lecture).

21. See Keller lecture.

22. Accurate comparisons of alcoholism rates in different countries are extremely difficult to make because of wide variations in the way vital statistics are collected and recorded in this field. Data on deaths from cirrhosis of the liver (per 100,000 of the population) are available, e.g. Australia—5.0%; Austria—15.6%; Belgium—8.2%; Canada—5.2%; Denmark—6.4%; England—2.6%; France—31.9%; W. Germany—12.4%; Italy—13.9%; Israel—3.3%; Japan—8.6%; Netherlands—3.4%; Sweden—4.4%; Switzerland—13.1%; U.S.A.—10.2%. "Jellinek's formula," by which alcoholism rates in this country are estimated, is based on the assumption that there is a significant and relatively constant correlation between deaths from cirrhosis of the liver and alcoholism. No direct inference about *international* alcoholism rates should be drawn from comparing cirrhosis of the liver mortality rates, however, since the variations in the relationship between these rates and alcoholism rates, from country to country, are not known. The above figures can only be taken as suggestive. The figures are from *Epidemiological and Vital Statistics Report*, XI, No. 4 (Geneva: World Health Organization, 1958), 136-38.

23. Mark Keller, "The Definition of Alcoholism & the Estimate of Its Prevalance" in *Society, Culture, and Drinking Patterns*, ed. by David J. Pittman and Charles R. Snyder (New York: John Wiley & Sons, 1962), p. 326.

24. *The Clipsheet*, Methodist Board of Temperance, Washington, D.C., July 25, 1955.

25. From a study conducted by the Committee on Alcoholism of the Welfare and Health Council of New York in 1952.

26. (New York: A. A. Wyn, 1950), p. 28.

# 2

# What Are the Causes of Alcoholism?

Both the ethical and the therapeutic approachs to the problem of alcoholism must be based on an understanding of alcohol, drinking, and the physiology and psychology of the human being. Many of those who attempt to control alcoholism are like those who attempted to control lightning without knowledge of electricity.
—Selden D. Bacon, lecturing at the Yale
Summer School of Alcohol Studies, 1948

An acquaintance with the facts concerning the causes of alcoholism is a prerequisite to any effective preventive or therapeutic action. Careful examination of the findings of the sciences is important in dealing with any social problem. It is especially so in an area so befogged by misinformation as the one under consideration.

What are the causes of alcoholism? Nobody knows in any complete or final sense. Alcoholism is, at least to a degree, a "cryptogenic" disease—a disease of which the basic roots or cause are hidden. A great deal is known, however. It behooves us to take advantage of the available knowledge to form a working hypothesis for dealing realistically with the problem. At the same time, a spirit of tentativeness is indicated since tomorrow's findings may easily render today's conceptions obsolete.

At the present stage of research it is impossible to point to any single or simple cause of alcoholism. On the contrary, the research findings indicate forcefully that alcoholism is a complex disease in which a variety of factors play a role. The late Carney Landis, from the perspective of a research psychologist, wrote: "If there is any human disorder which can be truly said to be of multiple etiology, it is alcoholism in all its diverse forms." [1] The following types of causative factors seem to be involved in alcoholism: physiological, psychological, cultural, philosophical, and religious. While all of these factors will not operate equally on every level, a combination of one or more will be

42

found at work on each of three levels: (1) factors which make one vulnerable to alcoholism; (2) factors which determine the selection of alcoholism as a symptom, as over against all the other types of psychopathological symptoms; and (3) factors which cause alcoholism to be self-perpetuating once it has reached a certain point. The last of these levels is particularly important because it will deal with the problem of why the alcoholic is usually unable to accept help early in the development of his sickness.

### Level One: The "Soil of Addiction"

Fundamentally, the alcoholic is not sick because he drinks but . . . he drinks because he is sick, and then becomes doubly sick.—Carroll A. Wise [2]

Why is it that of the eighty million people in our country who use alcohol, at least seventy-four million do *not* become alcoholics? This question leads inevitably to the search for some Achilles' heel which renders 6 percent of drinkers vulnerable to alcoholism. Inasmuch as 94 percent do not become addicted, alcoholism cannot be considered simply a property of alcohol. There must, therefore, be some "soil of addiction" which is receptive to the seeds of the problem.

There are those who would deny that any special soil of addiction is necessary. One writer quotes Robert Fleming as saying, "Any normal human being can get caught in the vicious downward spiral of alcohol addiction, if he drinks enough liquor over a long enough period of time." [3] This point of view, which regards alcohol as the basic cause of alcoholism, was reflected in the thinking of the alcoholic who said, "The only reason I know why I became an alcoholic was that I drank too damn much whiskey." It should be emphasized that this view is shared by only a small minority.

According to this school of thought the process by which one becomes an alcoholic is simple and direct. A person begins to drink in compliance with social pressures. One drink leads to two, two to three, etc. Each occasion leads to another of increasing intensity as one comes under the sway of the "habit-forming properties" of alcohol. The reason why the 94 percent of drinkers have not become alcoholics is that they haven't been at it long enough.

This conception of the etiology of alcoholism is descriptive of what happens in the case of some drinkers, namely alcoholics. It is descriptive, but not explanatory. It falls into an oversimplification which leads to the fallacious identification of one factor as the sole cause of alcoholism. It does not answer the question posed by this illustration, given by Dwight Anderson. Stephen Foster died, as we have described, at the age of thirty-eight. His appearance was that of an old man. His life was burned out by alcoholism. In contrast, his contemporary, Dan Emmett, author of "Dixie," drank a limited amount

43

nearly every day of his adult life and lived, still drinking, to the age of eighty-four. Both musicians were amply exposed to the "habit-forming properties" of alcohol. Why is it that Emmett drank all his life without becoming addicted, whereas alcoholism had ravaged Foster's life at thirty-eight?

The cogency of the belief that alcoholism is the simple result of drinking alcohol is even more seriously challenged by certain subcultural studies. In a nationwide survey sponsored by the State University of Iowa [4] it was found that by religious groups abstinence is practiced as follows:

> Protestant  . . . . . . . . . . . . 37%
> Roman Catholic  . . . . . . . . 11
> Jewish  . . . . . . . . . . . . . . . . 10

If alcohol were the primary cause of alcoholism, the Jewish group could be expected to have a high rate, since 90 percent of American Jews drink. The striking fact is that the Jewish rate is much lower than that of any other religious or ethnic group in the country, with the one exception of Americans of Chinese descent. Sociologist Charles R. Snyder summarizes the matter:

> In terms of percentages, there are probably more users of alcoholic beverages in the Jewish group than in any other major religio-ethnic group in America. Yet as has been shown repeatedly both in this country and abroad, rates of alcoholism and other drinking pathologies for Jews are very low.[5]

Do drinkers become addicted merely by acquiring the habit, with no preliminary pathology (i.e., soil of addiction)? What do the scientists who have studied the problem most intensively have to say? The late E. M. Jellinek, pioneer in alcoholism research at Yale University and later with the World Health Organization, once stated:

> Repetition alone won't produce addiction. It only comes when there is a motive for repeating. Alcohol is not habit-forming in the sense that a drug like morphine is. Rather than calling alcohol a habit-forming drug, it is more accurate to say that it is a substance that lends itself to those who form compulsive habits easily. The alcoholic reaction is atypical, not universal. It is the reaction of a minority of people, not a property of alcohol.[6]

Jellinek's observation that alcohol lends itself to those who form compulsive habits easily suggests that alcohol has certain pharmacological properties which render its use hazardous to those with addiction-prone personalities. It is noteworthy that in 1955 the World Health Organization Committee on Alcohol and Alcoholism designated alcohol as a drug intermediate (in kind and degree) between "habit-forming drugs" and "addiction-producing drugs."

In a more recent statement by a WHO committee, the distinction between habituating and addictive drugs was superceded by one term—"drugs dependence." Alcoholism is one of numerous forms of drug dependence.

Even if we accept the fact that pharmacologically alcohol has certain properties which tend to induce dependence, we must still explain why only certain people become dependent, habituated, or addicted. The weight of evidence, then, seems to be on the side of those who hold to the view expressed by Carroll A. Wise, of Garrett Theological Seminary "The belief that the excessive use of alcohol is simply a matter of habit is no longer scientifically tenable." [7]

Two kinds of cases tend to confuse the issue regarding the existence of a soil of addiction. One is the sudden onset of addictive drinking after years of social drinking. The case of Mary P, cited in Chapter 1, comes to mind. Another is the case of Mrs. Sandra R. For twenty years she drank socially. Alcohol posed no special problem for her. Then the news came that her oldest son had been killed. Immediately her drinking became pathological. Long months after the first awful pain of grief had passed, she continued to shut herself in her room with her bottle. To the casual observer Mrs. R.'s addictive drinking was caused by the trauma. This explanation, however, is incomplete in that it ignores the thousands of other mothers who were social drinkers, lost sons, and did not become alcoholics. In such cases one must always distinguish between the precipitating crisis and the basic cause.

The second type of confusing case is that represented by Oliver M., who in the midst of a successful business career begins to drink addictively. Oliver is known to his friends to be, as one of them put it, "as normal as the next guy." His load of responsibilities and worries is apparently no heavier than that of his nonalcoholic neighbors. Only by looking behind the scenes of Oliver's life can one make any sense out of his strange behavior. Here one discovers two factors that are important: (1) the ability of the psychic organism to carry a terrific load of inner conflicts over long periods of time and yet to present an adjustment to the world (and even to one's conscious self) that hides the inner chaos; (2) the discrepancy between our culture's definition of "success" and "normal"—which in our "Babbitt" culture is often a sort of standardized neurosis—and real integrated emotional health. Henry David Thoreau was probably thinking of the "successful" farmers of Concord when he observed, "The mass of men lead lives of quiet desperation." [8] Often one's desperation is so quiet that even the person himself is aware of only a vague, nameless restlessness. If one bears this in mind, then it is valid to say that "normal" people can become alcoholics. However, it is well to remember the opinion expressed by Giorgio Lolli, former medical director of the Yale Plan Clinic for Alcoholics, who states: "There is practically no case of alcohol addiction isolated from other neurotic disorders and bodily illnesses." [9]

In other words, the evidence seems to point to the fact that *alcoholism comes in people, not in bottles.* We must look within people for the underlying causes. The scientists who have been doing this may be divided into two schools of thought: those who emphasize the physiological factors in the soil of addiction and those who emphasize the sociopsychological.

Let us examine the evidence for a *physiological* soil of addiction. The idea that the alcoholic is "allergic" to alcohol was suggested by William Silkworth in 1937 and has since been given wide distribution by the literature and members of AA. E. M. Jellinek stated that a definitive experimental study in 1952 "entirely refuted the allergy hypothesis." [10] Although the alcoholic is not allergic to alcohol in the literal, medical sense (comparable to an allergy to ragweed pollen, for example), he certainly has a "psychological allergy" to alcohol in that he cannot use it without disastrous results. Thus, the figurative use of "alcoholism is an allergy," in counseling and in AA Twelfth Step work, is a useful way of briefing the alcoholic on his condition.

The often-used analogy between diabetes and alcoholism, although useful in counseling, is not based on a strict physiological comparability. In diabetes, pancreatic dysfunction interferes with the metabolism of sugar, producing "a physiologically noxious accumulation of sugar in the organism." [11] According to Jellinek, there is no evidence that the metabolism of alcohol is impaired in the alcoholic, neither the absorption nor the oxidation of alcohol being different in addictive and small users. [12]

Two major physiological hypotheses—the endocrinological and the nutritional—have been advanced by scientists in the alcoholism field. James J. Smith, representing the endocrinological view, reports on research done at Bellevue Medical Center in New York City. "Our laboratory and clinical studies of alcoholics during the past several years have convinced us that alcoholism is a metabolic disease." [13] Studies at Bellevue have shown that disturbances or deficiencies of the pituitary-adrenal-gonadal triad of endocrine glands are present in many alcoholics. Addressing the New York State Medical Society, Smith said: "These observations led us to explore the possibility that the alcoholic's problem was caused by disturbance of bodily chemistry." [14] This exploration apparently led Smith and his co-workers to the conviction that the alcoholic suffers from an abnormal endocrine system which predisposes him to alcoholism.

Leopold E. Wexberg, director of the Alcoholics Rehabilitation Program, District of Columbia, gives us this critique of Smith's theory:

Smith emphatically states his conviction that alcoholism is a metabolic disease. No one familiar with the signs and symptoms . . . can challenge this statement. . . .

It is an entirely different matter, however, to believe—as Smith apparently does —that . . . the alcoholic possesses a metabolic individuality which *predisposes* to addiction. Nowhere in Smith's article, and nowhere else in the literature, to our knowledge, have facts been brought out to support this theory.[15]

Wexberg goes on to point out that the pathological changes in metabolic and endocrine systems that are fairly common among alcoholics may be the *result* of years of excess, rather than the cause. This is the point at which the disagreement between the physiological and psychological school focuses.

Closely related to the physiological explanation of alcoholism is the question of heredity. Investigators have long been impressed by the fact that alcoholism has a much higher incidence in some families than in others. Of the 79 alcoholics interviewed by the author, 50 reported having alcoholics on their family tree. Twenty-seven reported alcoholic parents. Jellinek combined a number of studies embracing a total of 4,372 alcoholics and found that 52 percent had an alcoholic parent. The normal expectancy of alcoholism among children of alcoholics is between 20 and 30 percent as contrasted with an expectancy of approximately 4 percent for the adult population at large.

What is the explanation for this? R. J. Williams' "genetotrophic" theory of alcoholic etiology holds that certain individuals have inherited metabolic patterns which result in nutritional deficiencies which give rise to a craving for alcohol. Studies with white rats have shown, according to Williams, that some inbred strains have a consistently greater preference for spiked milk than do other strains. Other competent researchers have pointed to certain weaknesses in these experiments. So the question cannot be settled at the present stage of our knowledge.*

More important for our purposes is a study by Anne Roe of a group of 36 children of alcoholic parents who were separated from their parents and reared by nonalcoholic foster parents. At the time of the study they had reached the age of 21 or over. A control group of children born of normal parents but also raised in foster homes was used for comparison. Roe summarizes her findings:

As regards their present adjustment, there are no significant differences between the groups, and there are as many seriously maladjusted among the normal-parentage group as there are among the alcoholic-parentage group. . . . The children

---

* Based on his nutritional-deficiency theory, Williams has developed a form of therapy based on a balanced diet plus special high-vitamin supplementary nutrients. No one would question the need of many alcoholics for vitamin therapy and good diet. That the Williams' approach constitutes an adequate therapy for most alcoholics, however, is rejected by the vast majority of therapists. (For a critical review of the various physiological theories of alcoholism, see E. M. Jellinek *The Disease Concept of Alcoholism*, pp. 82-115. A description of Williams' approach is found in his book, *Alcoholism, the Nutritional Approach*.[16])

47

of alcoholic parentage . . . cannot be said to have turned out as expected on the basis of any hypothesis of hereditary taint.[17]

She points out that none of the children of alcoholic parents is alcoholic and that only three use alcohol regularly. The fact that so few use alcohol now and, more important, that most of them have established adequate personal lives would seem to give good reason to expect that few, if any, would become alcoholics.

In the light of this study, it is simply not justified to consign the problem of alcoholism to the category of heredity, with somber implications of hopelessness. The transmission of alcoholism from parents to child would seem to be a question of social rather than biological heredity. In fact, the emotionally insecure atmosphere of an alcoholic home tends to produce a high rate of all forms of social pathology. In the case of the approximately 8 percent of inebriates who are mental defectives, heredity plays an important role. Its role is not in the transmission of inebriate tendencies, but of the mental inadequacy of which the drinking is purely symptomatic.

Having granted that the existence of a physiological soil of addiction is still a moot question, let us turn to the evidence for a *psychosocial vulnerability* to alcoholism. This view holds that the alcoholic is emotionally sick even before he begins to drink; he is vulnerable because he possesses a damaged personality. To use Carroll Wise's words again, "He drinks because he is sick and then becomes doubly sick." His drinking is a symptom of his inner problems.

What evidence is there that alcoholics were psychologically inadequate before they began to use alcohol? Here the author's interview material will be useful. This material throws light on the characteristics of the parents and the childhood of the alcoholics, thus allowing us to delve back into the period before they began to drink.

Let us begin with the recognition that children have certain basic psychological needs or hungers analogous to their nutritional needs. To the extent that these needs are satisfied in the home, the child's personality grows strong and healthy in its ability to live a satisfying life in relation to others. To the extent that emotional malnutrition exists, personality stunting, immaturity, and interpersonal inadequacy result.

As is true in the case of physical nutrition, deprivation of adequate emotional food is the most damaging in the earliest years of life, when growth is the most rapid and personality the most plastic. Many psychologists believe that the foundations of subsequent health or illness are laid during the first few years of life. This general point of view concerning psychic needs of hungers is widely accepted by social scientists. Dorothy Walter Baruch gives us an excellent discussion of the nature of these needs in her outstanding book

48

on rearing emotionally healthy children entitled *New Ways in Discipline, You and Your Child Today:*

> What are the emotional foods that every human being must have regardless of age? What are the basic emotional requirements that must come to every small infant, to every growing child, to every adult?
>
> In the first place, there must be *affection* and a lot of it. Real down-to-earth, sincere loving. The kind that carries conviction through body-warmth, through touch, through the good, mellow ring of the voice, through the fond look that says as clearly as words, "I love you because you are you."
>
> Closely allied with being loved should come the sure knowledge of *belonging, of being wanted,* the glow of knowing oneself to be a part of some bigger whole. Our town, our school, our work, our family—all bring the sound of togetherness, of being united with others, not isolated or alone.
>
> Every human being needs also to have the nourishment of *pleasure that comes through the senses.* Color, balanced form and beauty to meet the eye, har nonious sounds to meet the ear. The hearty enjoyment of touch and taste and smell. And finally, the realization that the pleasurable sensations of sex can be right and fine and a part of the spirit as well as of the body.
>
> Everyone must feel that he is capable of achievement. He needs to develop the ultimate conviction, strong within him, that he can do things, that he is adequate to meet life's demands. He needs also the satisfaction of knowing that he can gain from others *recognition* for what he does.
>
> And most important, each and every one of us must have *acceptance* and *understanding.* We need desperately to be able to share our thoughts and feelings with some one person, or several, who really understands. . . . We yearn for the deep relief of knowing that we can be ourselves with honest freedom, secure in knowledge that says, "This person is *with* me. He *accepts* how I feel!" [18]

The interviews showed that of the seventy-six parental constellations [19] described by the interviewees, seventy-one showed the presence in a marked degree of those attitudes and practices on the part of the parents which tend to deprive children of the adequate satisfaction of these basic emotional needs! Of these seventy-one inadequate homes, forty-four were obviously so; the remaining twenty-seven showed fewer or better disguised inadequacies, and would probably be described by the casual observer as "normal" homes. In five of the seventy-six homes, no apparent inadequacy was found.

Among the inadequate homes were found twenty-seven cases of parental alcoholism, producing twenty-one home situations in which unity was seriously disturbed or nonexistent. Twenty-three other alcoholics reported broken homes—divorce, "emotional divorce" (i.e., constant strife), or the death of a parent when the child was under eighteen. In other words, 57 percent of the alcoholics came from broken homes. In addition, four alcoholics reported psychotic parents. In one case the father was an alcoholic and the mother a drug addict.

49

Even if one makes generous allowances, as one must do, for distortions in the data due to emotional blindspots in the interviewees, the striking impression is still intact: Generally speaking, these alcoholics came from disturbed and inadequate homes! What is important here is not the percentages themselves, but the general evidence which is supported by them that many alcoholics come from such homes.

The homes of the alcoholics showed four main types of parental attitudes and behavior which make for the traumatization and emotional deprivation of a child's personality: *authoritarianism, success-worship, moralism,* and *overt rejection.* As we shall see, the first three types actually amount to *covert* rejection of the child's basic needs.

The most frequent parental characteristic was what psychoanalyst Erich Fromm has described as "irrational authoritarianism." This is the kind of authority that is based not on competence but solely on superior power. Fifty-six of the alcoholics, or 72 percent, described this in one or both parents.

In the father this most often took the direct "Papa is all" form. In the mothers it took the more indirect form of dominance through overprotection, the benevolent matriarch type. A frequent pattern was that in which the male child of a stern father formed an unhealthy indentification with an overprotective mother. Authoritarianism denies fulfillment of the child's need for unqualified love by making acceptance contingent on obedience. It denies the fulfillment of the need for gradually increasing autonomy by making him a puppet of the parents. Severe inferiority feelings are the result.

In some cases the descriptions of parental authoritarianism gave evidence of sadism and emotional rejection. Here are some samples from interviews with male alcoholics:

Tom R. recalled: "Father had a killing temper . . . practically killed me when he got mad. I didn't know him very well . . . didn't like him. . . . I lost interest in things early in life."

Frank P. said concerning his father: "My Dad was a big shot in town. I was just someone who happened to come along. There was fear of the head of the house . . . strict discipline . . . he hit us with his big mit."

Just as the authoritarian parent makes love contingent on obedience, the success-worshiping parent makes it contingent on the child's ability to feed the parental ego by his success. The presence of this factor among the parents of the alcoholics was exceeded in frequency only by authoritarianism. Of the seventy-seven who provided data, thirty-three reported homes in which success-worship was a prominent factor. This took various forms—excessive ambition for the child in terms of financial success, position, and educational attainment were all common. It is interesting that only four of the thirty-three were females. This points to the fact that the cult of success exerts greater pressure on boys in our culture than on girls. The cultural expectations for girls are in a different direction.

Success-worship deprives the child of his need for self-direction. It saddles him with parent-chosen goals which are usually impossibly perfectionistic (since they are derived from the parents' own frustrations) and completely out of touch with the realities of the child's abilities and inclinations. A child soon internalizes his parents' excessive goals and becomes his own slavedriver.

The case of alcoholic Frederick N., age fifty-four, illustrates the effects of a combination of authoritarian overprotection and success-worship:

Fred describes his parents in glowing terms. "My father was a very successful banker, a Phi Beta Kappa in college. He often called my attention to how successful my grandfather had been. I was closer to him than my mother. She was a very unusual person—widely traveled and cosmopolitan. She was the family disciplinarian, but there were few spankings because I was a good boy. I was taught that I was better than other folks."

Concerning his childhood he says: "I was an only child and the only link in both sides of the family chain. Consequently I was closely guarded. . . . My parents wanted me to win scholarships and study to become a great doctor. I was the prime disappointment of their lives. Goals and standards were set for me. They made all the decisions. I lost heart very early because I couldn't measure up. Everything became distasteful to me. I did only what was necessary."

Fred began to drink at the age of twelve with a group of boys. His parents got him out of repeated jams in college resulting from his drinking. Finally he dropped out of college because of his drinking and got a job in a mill. This was a crushing blow to his parents' dreams. Twenty years of periodic binges followed. Of his drinking he says, "My deep inadequacy was lost in alcohol. I could feel I was anybody when I was drinking."

In retrospect, as a result of insight gained from psychiatric help, Fred says, "Had I grown up differently and had been allowed to find my own level, I wouldn't have had the terrific sense of disappointment as early as twenty-one. No matter what I did it was so far short of what they had in mind for me, it didn't seem like an achievement."

Moralism is the word used to describe the behavior of the parent who unwittingly projects puritanical attitudes onto the child. Moralism results in strong feelings of guilt and inhibition concerning bodily drives and hostile feelings. As a result the child grows up emotionally handicapped in the areas of sex and normal aggression. A parent who is compulsively "moral" because of guilt feelings will project impossibly perfectionistic standards on the child. The child will feel that he must earn the all-important love of the parent by being a "good" child. Since the standards of parental expectation are perfectionistic, the child can never really feel accepted. He can, therefore, never accept such vital areas of himself as his bodily drives and normal negative feelings.

51

Twenty-nine of the seventy-seven alcoholics mentioned strong traits of puritanism in describing their parents. Roger L., age thirty-eight, one year of college, illustrates the destructive effects of puritanism, success-worship, and overt authoritarianism:

Roger says: "My father was very stern. I was deathly afraid of him. If I did something that was wrong, he wouldn't talk to me, just beat me. My mother was very much like my father—I never got much love from her. She had a feeling that she shouldn't get too close to me. She was a very righteous person, very moral. My terrific standards come from this, I think."

Concerning his childhood, Roger recalls: "I was shy and aloof, never comfortable with people. I was very weak and never wanted to fight with other boys. My father beat me for walking away from fights. He beat me for petty stealing. Never praised me. Would say, 'Why can't you be like other boys?' I had three sisters and one brother. I was the black sheep—very dull in school—deathly afraid of reciting. I was beaten for not being a good student. I took a business course in college because my father wanted me to follow him; I really wanted to be a surgeon—a great surgeon. Always wanted to be something great."

Both Roger's parents were adamantly against alcohol. He began to drink at eighteen and got drunk the first time he drank. He dropped out of college because of drinking. He says, "I had no period of social drinking. It was no fun. I used it to escape from my problems from the beginning." Roger worked for a time as a salesman. "I drank to sell. Couldn't sell anything without alcohol in me—afraid of people in general—never able to hold a job for long because of my drinking." After a discharge without honor from the army because of drinking, Roger lived on various Skid Rows for several years. Just prior to his discharge he had married a woman seven years older than himself. He says, "I was looking for the maternal care I had missed." Roger's guilt about sexual matters proved too strong, and they were divorced after six months. Although he has been sober for three years in AA, Roger still can't forgive himself for sexual deviations during his drinking. The success worship and puritanism of his parents are still reflected in statements such as: "I push myself entirely too much—makes me unhappy. I condemn myself when I do wrong, feel I'm cutting myself off from God. My standards are too high. Always concerned about whether I'm doing right. If I can't be almost perfect I don't expect anything good to happen to me."

Roger's parents rejected him by their crude authoritarianism, moralism, and success-worship. In many of the cases of those interviewed, the parental errors were not so obvious. In others, the rejection was even more overt.

Up to this point we have been discussing inadequacies in the parents of the alcoholics. Is there concrete evidence that these inadequacies actually affected the alcoholics adversely? Is there evidence of serious maladjustment in the childhood and adolescence of the alcoholics, even before they began drinking? Here again, the impression is striking. Of the seventy-seven cases in which this kind of data was available, only ten were lacking in evidence of a disturbed childhood. Behavior difficulties, evidences of low self-esteem, and unhappy memories of childhood were a constant refrain in the interviews. Here are some sample recollections from the interviews with five different male Alcoholics: "I was three years behind in school—life a hell on earth, no kid's life." "I had few playmates. There was no love in our home. My big desire was to get away." "I lived in a shell as a kid, felt different and confused." "I was alone as a boy. I was left-handed, and my father forced me to use my right. I stuttered terribly, and the nuns made fun of me." "I never got along with people."

Low self-esteem during childhood was indicated by the following: A total of fifty-four of the interviewees said, in effect, that they had "inferiority complexes," were "very shy," or felt "lonely." This is approximately 70 percent of the total number interviewed. These samples give the tone of the recollections. One said, "I was shy, fearful—had nightmares of a big snake." Another recalled, "I was timid as far back as I can remember—thought of myself as 'nasty self.' Always expected to fail." A third put it this way, "I had no close friends—felt alone and inferior. Never had any self-confidence."

The weight of evidence seems to be that a high percentage of alcoholics are emotionally disturbed even before they begin drinking. The soil of addiction is prepared by the inadequacies of their lives. Numerous psychological tests have shown that, although many alcoholics are able to function with remarkable social adequacy when they are not drinking, they make their social adjustment in spite of their inner conflicts. In the case of those who do not adjust well, the effect of the inner conflicts is quite obvious. These inner conflicts, which are a carry-over from unsatisfactory childhoods, constitute an essential part of the soil of addiction.

A knowledge of the psychological problems and attributes which are typical of many alcoholics can be of tremendous practical importance to anyone who wishes to help them. The following have been mentioned repeatedly in reports of psychological studies of alcoholics: (1) a high level of anxiety in interpersonal relationships, (2) emotional immaturity, (3) ambivalence toward authority, (4) low frustration tolerance, (5) grandiosity, (6) low self-esteem, (7) feelings of isolation, (8) perfectionism, (9) guilt, (10) compulsiveness. These psychological attributes are often present in enlarged proportions when the person is in the nightmare of active alcoholism. That they are not entirely the result of prolonged excessive drinking is indicated by the fact that the attributes are present in many alcoholics before they begin excessive drinking and persist in diminished form long after sobriety has been achieved.

Many of the alcoholics interviewed gave evidence of continuing inner conflict and anxiety. About half mentioned depression and mood swings as being severe enough to bother them. Thirty-five described themselves as "the nervous type" (or some equivalent term). Twenty-six complained of chronic insomnia and fatigue. Twenty spoke of "nervous stomach," including nine cases of ulcers, several of which had developed since they had been sober. Referring to his anxiety, one male alcoholic said, "I feel like there's a rattlesnake in me breeding venom." What do the psychological tests show? Bühler and Lefever, in "A Rorschach Study on the Psychological Characteristics of Alcoholics," report the "presence of high anxiety and apprehension." [20] Florence Halpern [21] mentions uncertainty, irritability, depression, and tension as evidence that her subjects experience considerable anxiety.

We have seen ample evidence of conditions in the emotional climate of the early lives of the alcoholics which give rise to inner conflicts. For example, authoritarianism does so by forcing the child to choose between security and autonomy, both of which he needs. *Emotional immaturity,* a phrase one hears in many an AA meeting, is the result of this conflict. The individual's emotional or interpersonal development is stunted on a level incommensurate with his chronological age. He continues to respond in childish fashion long after he has left the age when such was appropriate.

One symptom of this failure to grow up emotionally is the continuance of childhood or adolescent *ambivalence toward authority.* As Giorgio Lolli has pointed out, the conflict between dependence and independence is almost universal among alcoholics. An alcoholic will often form a very dependent relationship (in counseling, for example) and then keenly resent his own dependency. This conflict often operates in the alcoholic's marital relationship, where he will marry a dominant, mothering woman (who protects him to an absurd degree) and then so resent the dependency as to turn the marriage into a civil war.

*Low frustration tolerance* is another characteristic of many alcoholics which makes counseling difficult. The alcoholic tends to escape from any frustration or tension into the world of alcohol. Reporting on their Rorschach study, Bühler and Lefever say: "Statistically, the most significant and most consistent trait is the alcoholic's incapacity to stand strain or tension." [22] Inability to tolerate frustration is normal in children. Anything that impairs a child's security can render him hypersensitive to frustration throughout his life.

*Grandiosity,* another common alcoholic trait, is especially evident in the defiant, self-inflating behavior during active alcoholism, when the alcoholic seems to "organize the universe around the perpendicular pronoun," as one of them put it. Harry Tiebout (now deceased), a psychiatrist who studied this attribute, referred to the "king complex." A king is a special kind of person who can't be frustrated. The alcoholic's grandiosity is a mechanism for defending, in an immature way, his hypersensitive ego. Grandiosity, again, is a symptom of emotional stunting or immaturity. In order to maintain his grandiose image of himself, the person must shut himself off from interpersonal reality by what Tiebout called the "alcoholic shell." This shell makes the establishment of a real therapeutic relationship in counseling a difficult matter. To relax his defensive shell and fully accept help would be the equivalent of surrendering his "idealized image" (to use Karen Horney's phrase) of himself. The image cannot be surrendered because it reflects the person's feelings of what he *must be* in order to be worthwhile. Perfectionism, a common complaint of alcoholics, is dynamically related to the maintenance of the grandiose ego image. It is important to remember that this process is not amenable to conscious control.

That the ego defenses of the alcoholic are not an effective psychological solution is clear. Take the problem of alcoholic depression. It was Augustine, a man of immense introspective insight, who said, "Pride is known by its despondency as well as its arrogance." The shell of an unrealistic image of self may protect one from some of the discomforts of interpersonal life, but it also cuts one off from vital satisfactions. One alcoholic, viewing in retrospect his grandiose isolation, said, "I felt so far removed from common garden-variety people that there wasn't any place for me." Thirty-four of the interviewees (44 percent) reported feelings of *isolation* and *loneliness*, a majority tracing their feelings throughout their lives. A typical comment was, "I can't feel warm toward people."

*Perfectionism* is actually a form of self-punishment. Inevitable failure, resulting from perfectionistic goals, is followed by extreme *guilt*. For many alcoholics guilt is a persistent problem. As one put it, "There's some kind of guilt complex with most of us alcoholics." A very articulate alcoholic wrote: "I was crucified on the bitter angle guilt cuts across the rigid upright of every American's puritanism." [23] We have already seen the roots of this guilt.

When discussing the subject of guilt, it is well to bear in mind that an appreciable percentage of alcoholics comes from the clinical group known as "psychopathic personalities," who are unable to experience either guilt or responsibility. In AA these are known as "phonies." These unfortunate persons can give any counselor grey hair unless he is alert to the situation.

The grandiosity of the alcoholic is a defense against his own real feelings of *low self-esteem*. The alcoholic's outwardly self-enamored behavior is a mask for his shaky self-regard. This fact can be all-important in counseling procedures. Because of his low self-esteem the alcoholic is hypersensitive to criticism and will often misinterpret the behavior of others as rejection. Low self-esteem gives rise to anxiety in interpersonal relationships.

Insecurity and low self-esteem are two of the effects of parental alcoholism. A female alcoholic said: "My father was a periodic alcoholic. This was a disgrace in our little town. . . . He felt he was lord and master. We were all afraid of him. . . . Mother thought sex was a terrible thing." The community's ostracism, the father's authoritarianism, and the mother's puritanism combined in this case to produce a child who grew up feeling "self-conscious and inferior ... I was different. I lived in a shell."

The general psychological maladjustment suffered by alcoholics is reflected, in many cases, in their sexual maladjustment. For example, a study of seventy-nine alcoholics by Jacob Levine showed that a decided majority had either diminished or nonexistent interest in heterosexual relationships.[24] The orthodox psychoanalytic hypothesis regarding alcoholism is that the alcoholic has a basic homosexual problem, usually unconscious, of which the alcoholism is an expression. Although many alcoholics are sexually maladjusted and some homosexual, it seems likely that these sexual problems are more adequately understood as *symptoms*, like the person's alcoholism, of underlying personality problems. However, one who is counseling alcoholics should bear in mind that their sexual problems may complicate and aggravate their alcoholic problems, and vice versa.

A significant longitudinal (before-and-after) study of alcoholics was made by sociologists William and Joan McCord, and reported in *Origins of Alcoholism*.[25] For ten years, beginning in 1935, records were kept on the family relationships of 650 boys as a part of the Cambridge-Somerville delinquency prevention project. A follow-up study of 510 of these, in 1956, revealed that approximately 10 percent of the group, now in their early thirties, had become alcoholics. The differences in the family backgrounds of those who did and those who did not become alcoholics were then compared by the McCords. They conclude: "The major force which seemed to lead a person under heavy stress to express his anxiety in alcoholism was the erratic frustration of his dependency desires" (in childhood).[26] They found that a lower percentage of the boys who had experienced overt rejection by their mothers eventually became alcoholics than those whose mothers were *alternatively loving and rejecting*. (The overtly rejected produced a higher percentage of criminal behavior.) One third of the sons of the highly ambivalent mothers had become alcoholics in their thirties!

As Pavlov and others demonstrated, the erratic, unpredictable alternation between frustration and satisfaction of a need enhances the strength of that need. The McCords reason that the prealcoholic is involved in an endless quest to satisfy intense dependency needs which, in our culture, are unacceptable to the self-image of males. It is noteworthy that the lowest rates of alcoholism, in their study, were among persons raised in homes which seemed to satisfy dependency needs. Concerning the overall pattern of the prealcoholic homes, the McCords state: "The typical alcoholic, as a child, underwent a variety of experiences that heightened inner stress, intensified his desire for love, and produced a distorted self-image." [27]

The general conclusions of the psychological studies in the field of alcoholism show that there can be little doubt that psychological maladjustment is an important part of the soil of addiction. Two studies, for example, are conclusive on the point that behind the addiction there is an emotionally warped personality. Halpern reports: "It can be stated at the outset that not one of the Rorschach Test records obtained from the forty-seven subjects could be considered a normal one. In all of them was evidence of emotional disturbances." [28] Charles C. Hewitt summarizes his findings, in "A Personality Study of Alcohol Addiction," as follows: "Alcohol addiction, in the group studied in this survey, seems to be associated, with but few exceptions, with deep personality disorders. Even those exceptions are doubtless more apparent than real." [29]

The assumption that *all* alcoholics have major underlying personality disorders which cause their alcoholism was sharply challenged by E. M. Jellinek. He stated that generalizations about alcoholics are often based on a biased population—namely those who seek psychiatric help *because* they have serious personality disorders. He reports that many nonneurotic alcoholic addicts with only minor psychological vulnerabilities have been seen, especially in the viticulture countries. He concludes: "The contention that neurosis is a sine qua non of 'alcoholism' cannot be accepted." [30] However, the evidence seems clear that the vast majority of American alcoholics *do* suffer from relatively severe personality disorders which provide the soil in which the seed of addiction takes easy root when the person begins to drink. This is particularly true in those groups in which the heavy use of alcohol is not regarded as normal behavior. The greater the pressure to drink in a given group, the less the degree of psychological vulnerability required to become addicted.

One will not fully understand alcohol as a problem until one sees it as a "solution." For the alcoholic, alcohol serves as a magic but tragic solution to his personality problems. Because of his inner conflicts he is motivated by an intense need for the kind of satisfactions which alcohol can give. Let us examine the way in which alcohol "solves" the personality problems of the typical alcoholic. The alcoholic's inner conflicts and anxiety cause intense psychic pain. Alcohol is a cheap, easily obtainable pain-killer. The physiologists classify it as an anesthetic. Various experiments on animals have shown that alcohol reduces the awareness of pain produced by neurotic conflicts. The classic example is the experiment on cats by J. H. Masserman and K. S. Yum. The experimenters induced a neurosis in the cats by creating a conflict between their fear of pain and their need for food. The animals became thoroughly neurotic, losing all interest in normal cat-satisfactions. But when they were given an injection of alcohol, they were suddenly able to perform normally. Their neurotic conflict had been anesthetized. Soon they became addicted to spiked milk which they had ignored completely before their neurosis. Only when the neurosis was alleviated by reconditioning could their feline addiction be broken.[31] It is pertinent to note that anthropologist

Donald Horton says, after a study of many cultures, "The primary function of alcoholic beverages in all societies is the reduction of anxiety." [32]

Alcohol "solves" the problem of the alcoholic's emotional immaturity by allowing him to regress psychologically to a level at which he can feel comfortable. Sober adult life demands too much for the immature individual, so he slips back via the Bacchus-trail to a level where the demands are minimal. Alcohol honors his low frustration tolerance by allowing him an easy way to escape frustrating situations. At the childish level to which he regresses under alcohol, adult responsibility vanishes and he can revel in the infantile grandiosity of the early stages of life.

Alcohol serves as a "solution" to the alcoholic's *guilt, low self-esteem, isolation,* and *perfectionism* by depressing his self-critique. The alcoholic's overweening conscience is relaxed by alcohol, and it ceases plaguing him for the time being. Further, the prolonged excessive use of alcohol serves to insure the social censure which registers as punishment with the masochistic alcoholic and thus helps him atone for his guilt. For the alcoholic with a rigid, puritanical conscience, alcohol allows behavior otherwise forbidden by his conscience. As has been said, "The superego is soluble in alcohol." Alcohol reduces the burden of repressed feelings by relaxing the mechanism of repression. A male alcoholic said, "The only time I had a temper was when I reached a certain point in a drunk." At other times he had pushed all hostile feelings out of consciousness by means of repression. Alcohol "solves" the alcoholic's conflict concerning authority by allowing him to rebel temporarily against those upon whom he is actually becoming increasingly dependent. An understanding of the dynamics involved here is exceedingly important in counseling with families of alcoholics.

The alcoholic's deep inferiority feelings are temporarily relieved by alcohol. For the time he can feel perfectly successful. As one alcoholic put it, "With a pint you can feel like you're president." Thus perfectionism is satisfied in the grandiose, illusory world of alcohol. The widespread use of alcohol as a social lubricant is an indication of its power to "solve" the problem of interpersonal isolation, a painful problem for the alcoholic. It allows him to accept himself temporarily and therefore to feel closeness to others.

The McCords, in the study cited above, point out that alcohol is highly functional in the psychic economy of an intensely dependent male who cannot accept his dependency needs and strivings. Simultaneously, alcohol facilitates closeness and a kind of pseudo-dependency on others, and yet it permits the person to reinforce his defensive self-image of rugged virility by "drinking like a man." In their view, it is when the self-image of the strong, independent he-man breaks down, through the effects of prolonged excessive drinking, that alcoholism develops.

The tragedy of the use of alcohol as a solution to the interpersonal problems of living is twofold. For one thing, the solution is illusory. It can be maintained only so long as the anesthetic is present in the body. For another, the solution carries the seeds of its own destruction. As we have seen, the use of this solution intensifies the very problems to which it has served as an illusory answer. But, however tragic and unsatisfactory in the long run, alcohol gives a temporary answer to the pain and problems of the alcoholic. It does so in a relatively effortless way and, as such, fits his emotional immaturity.

## Level Two: Factors Leading to the Selection of the Symptom

Why is it that of all the maladjusted persons who drink, only certain ones develop alcoholism? Or, why is it that a given individual's psychic economy unconsciously turns to alcoholism from among all the possible symptoms? Here we are in the baffling area of "symptom choice" in which little is actually certain. It is clear, however, that the choice is below the level of consciousness in the individual.

Some exponents of the biochemical conception of the etiology of alcoholism, such as R. J. Williams, mentioned earlier, claim that there is a metabolic peculiarity that specifically predisposes certain persons to alcoholism. This explanation has not been adequately substantiated as yet. Even if there are biochemical or metabolic factors in the underlying causes of alcoholism, it seems unlikely that they would be such as to specifically predispose to alcoholism. The fact that some drug addicts switch from morphine to alcohol and back, as the supply of one or the other becomes inaccessible, seems to belie the existence of a specific physical predisposing factor.

Moving over into the psychological realm to look for an answer to our question, we find that there are a few students of alcoholism who believe that there is a unique "alcoholic personality," a distinctive syndrome of psychological attributes which predisposes to alcoholism. Tiebout held to this view although he pointed out that the distinctive factors have not as yet been isolated. In contrast, most researchers emphasize the heterogeneity of alcoholic personalities. Thirty-seven reports of organized research on the personality characteristics of chronic alcoholics were surveyed by E. H. Sutherland and his associates. They concluded that there is not satisfactory evidence that justifies the belief that emotionally disturbed persons of one type are more likely to become alcoholics than those of another type.[33] It is well to remember that the personality traits and conflicts discussed previously as of common occurrence among alcoholics also occur among nonalcoholic neurotics. It is a healthy thing to recall that the alcoholic's conflicts are structured by the culture in which he lives, and that they are shared to a degree by even the so-called normal individuals within that culture, including those who write books about alcoholics and those who try to help them.

59

Sociocultural factors seem to be of first importance in determining the selection of alcoholism as a symptom. The *availability* and *attractiveness* of alcohol as a means of interpersonal adjustment certainly influence the "choice" of an alcoholic symptom, as against other symptoms. The importance of availability is emphasized by the statistics on alcoholism during Prohibition. They show that there was a substantial drop in the rate of chronic alcoholism during the decade of 1920-30. According to Jellinek, this drop was the result of

the greater inaccessibility of liquor during the years 1915-19 during which more and more states introduced prohibition, and the per capita rate of alcohol consumption dropped by twenty-two percent compared with the period 1910-14. And since the bootleg supply was insufficient and unorganized in these years, many alcoholics were checked in their course.[34]

This statement becomes intelligible if one remembers that chronic alcoholism rates are the product of excessive drinking several years before the rates are given.

The availability of alcohol does play a role in the causation of alcoholism on the level of symptom choice. Obviously, the person with underlying pathology will have many opportunities to "solve" his problem alcoholically when alcohol is thrust at him from all sides. If alcohol is relatively less available, he will tend to utilize other neurotic solutions.

A very important factor is the manner in which social attitudes determine the desirability or attractiveness of using alcohol as a means of personality adjustment. Here we return to the Jewish subcultural group and ask the postponed question: Why is it that the Jews, among whom drinking is so widespread, have an infinitesimally low rate of alcoholism?

Fortunately for us there have been a number of intensive studies of this problem. Some have advanced the theory that the strong family and ingroup ties of the Jewish culture provide a more secure childhood than in other groups, thus producing less need for artificial escape. Though this seems plausible at first glance, the statistics do not support it. Abraham Myerson, a student of the problem, points out that Jews have their full share of neuroses and psychoses of the depressive type.[35] R. F. Bales adds that Jews have a high rate of drug addiction.[36]

What about a physiological explanation of the low Jewish alcoholism rate? Charles R. Snyder observes: "The heterogeneity of Jews in terms of physical or racial characteristics casts doubt upon any kind of bio-racial explanation. This doubt is considerably strengthened by the failure of science to uncover any specific hereditary mechanisms sufficient to account for drinking pathologies." [37]

The most cogent explanation of the Jewish rate is that of cultural controls on inebriety. The Jewish child encounters the moderate use of alcohol from his earliest years. One study of Jewish children showed that 91 percent of those between five and seven had been introduced to alcoholic beverages and that most of them considered it just another food to like or dislike.[38] Sociologists say that the attitudes and behavior learned during the earliest years have the strongest controlling influence on a person's later behavior. The Jewish child acquires strong inner controls as to the proper role of alcohol in one's life. Since it is a part of his life from early years, there is little chance that alcohol can be used as a symbol of revolt against authority during adolescence.

The use of alcohol is closely integrated with the whole religio-social web of the Jewish community. Since the ingroup ties are strong, the sanctioning power on the individual in the group is also strong. The one Jewish alcoholic interviewed by the author told of the unbearable guilt he experienced at thirty-two when he began to defy group sanctions by drinking alone. For a Jew the use of wine is closely associated with religious ceremonials. As Bales puts it, "In the Jewish culture wine stands for a whole complex of sacred things. Wine is variously alluded to as 'the word of God' and 'the commandment of the Lord.' " [39] To use wine to excess is to abuse something sacred.

The Jewish culture has strong sanctions against drunkenness. As Myerson says, "To be a drunkard is to cease being a Jew." [40] Immanuel Kant attributed the low rate of drunkenness among Jews (as well as among clergymen and women) to their weak social position. Throughout history Jews have been surrounded by hostile and stronger groups so that drunkenness on the part of any individual endangers the whole group. If a Jew, with his pent-up rage against the oppressor, should become intoxicated and vent his repressed feeling, the entire Jewish group might suffer. This Kantian explanation is probably the historic reason for the existence of strong sanctions against drunkenness.

A Jew may be very neurotic, but the chances are that he will not be an alcoholic. To be such would be to suffer rejection by his group. Thus the Jewish community makes alcoholism undesirable as a symptom.[41]

In contrast, the American scene as a whole has no unified attitudes toward either drinking or drunkenness. The young non-Jewish American finds himself in the midst of a sea of attitudinal crosscurrents, the most dangerous of which encourage the frenzied search for thrills and the use of alcohol as a symbol of "being a man." Harvard sociologist Robert F. Bales has stated that the rate of alcoholism will tend to rise when a society by its attitude "positively suggests drinking to the individual as a means of relieving his inner tensions." [42] There are pressures in American life which do exactly this by identifying alcohol with gracious living, with a sense of warm fellowship, and with being emancipated and sophisticated. Alcohol employed as a frequent means of interpersonal adaptation often becomes a "glass crutch."

In order to understand the extent and complexity of the confusion which exists in our country on the matter of attitudes toward alcohol, it is necessary to examine the relationships between these attitudes and the class and ethnic structure of our society. An excellent discussion of these relationships as they developed historically in our country is found in Chapters I and II of *Drinking in College* by Robert Straus and Selden D. Bacon. The confusion of attitudes which exists in our society at large is both reflected and intensified by the conflict of attitudes within the churches on the subject. Think of the gulf that separates the fundamental attitudes toward drinking of a certain upper-class Episcopal church with its occasional "sherry parties" after services from the attitudes of a middle-class Baptist church with its annual "temperance speaker." In their study mentioned above, Straus and Bacon write:

American church groups are in sharp disagreement, sometimes in open conflict, as to both the nature of the problem and what should be done about it. Although all agree that drunkenness is a problem, many feel that the real difficulty is drinking and that abstinence, whether achieved by persuasion or force, is the only answer. Over 40 million Americans belong to church groups that hold the latter belief. About an equal number belong to sects holding other views. There are groups within the sects on both sides which disagree with the stand taken by the majority: there are total abstinence groups in churches which do not stand for total abstinence; there are "moderation" groups in churches which stand for total abstinence. Nor do the conflict and confusion stop at this point. There are individual churches which clearly fail to adhere to the denominational policy. Perhaps most significant of all, large numbers of individual members of total abstinence churches, who otherwise accept their religion and participate in its activities, reject their church's policy on this matter in thought or action, sometimes quite openly. . . . Major denominations have formally changed their policies in the last decade. . . . Bitter antagonisms have even flared openly at formal meetings.[43]

The confusion of basic philosophy concerning alcohol is caused in part by the marked differences in attitudes toward alcohol on the part of the various socioeconomic classes in our country. Straus and Bacon, for example, in their study of over 15,000 college students, found that the incidence of abstention from alcohol on the part of the parents decreased in each category as they moved from lower to higher family income. (Since the study was of parents of college students it is probable that it did not include a proportional sampling of the lowest classes on the socioeconomic scale.) Imitation of the drinking habits of the upper classes is one important factor in influencing the drinking patterns of the middle classes. Such imitation is thus a part of the whole picture of social climbing in our country. There are other factors at work which tend to make the militant temperance movement predominantly a middle-class concern. Though there is widespread discontent among this class with the one-track approach of the movement, there is as yet no recognized position which has developed as an acceptable alternative. The differences in general class background of various denominations tend to influence the approach which their members and leaders take toward alcoholics. Compare the attitudes of the so-called temperance churches, for example, with that of the Episcopal Church where an understanding exists on the part of those members taking Antabuse that they will not be expected to take the wine in the service, but will be allowed to take only the wafer.

Social class differences in drinking patterns constitute significant, though not fully understood, influences on the development of pathological drinking behavior. Therefore, these differences must be taken into account both in the understanding of the sociocultural factors in the causation of alcoholism and in its prevention. At the Yale Summer School of Alcohol Studies in 1943, social anthropologist John Dollard delivered a lecture on "Drinking Mores of the Social Classes." His analysis, though frankly speculative and provisional, was widely accepted as authoritative. Since it has served as a point of departure for most subsequent studies, it may be useful to present its basic ideas:

In the Upper classes, drinking is not a moral issue. People at the top of our social structure drink a good deal; both sexes drink. Men and women drink in the same groups, in party style. There are, however, certain stiff controls here which do not exist in some of the Lower classes. One is condemned in the Upper classes, not for drinking, not for drunkenness, but for antisocial behavior while drunk. Fighting is taboo; aggressive behavior is heavily penalized even when expressed only in verbal assaults.

It is crucial to recognize the attitude of the Upper classes toward drinking because behavior patterns tend to shift downward in our society. Middle groups are likely to become tolerant and, perhaps, ultimately imitate the customs of the topmost groups into which they, as individuals, would like to move. It might be said that the failure of Prohibition legislation lay in our social class system, for the highest people socially did not taboo drinking and their social customs were stronger than legislative controls.

In the Lower-Upper class we have the "cocktail set" who drink a good bit more recklessly than the people in the old families of the Upper-Upper class. The new families of wealth are in a rather insecure, frustrating position. They are constantly comparing themselves with the families who socially "own" the territory in which they live. . . . Realizing that their great-grandfather was "just a butcher," rather than a powerful landowner, they suffer from a helpless feeling of inadequacy. Parental controls are weak and the scars from social competition painful, so Lower-Upper young people may try to escape from social discomforts by drunkenness. . . .

In the Upper-Middle class we have a strong evaluation of wealth and talent, and, ordinary, moral values have restraint. However, the apparent nearness to the Upper classes and partial identification with this group have some effect on the drinking habits in the Upper-Middle class. In general, the men drink on social occasions, at their poker games, and at casual gatherings in friends' houses, but

63

Upper-Middle class women rarely drink. Drinking is not customary in mixed groups. Evidently, Upper-Middles have a neutral attitude toward drinking.

In the Lower-Middle class we would expect to find, with both sexes, a very strong taboo on drinking. Lower-Middle people value highly the traits of respectability which differentiates them from the Lower group. They emphasize this by rejecting the customs found in the Lower classes . . . Lower-Middle men and women are the most stringent in exerting social control over drinking.

In the Upper-Lower class, which is the chief labor group, there is much more drinking. The Upper-Lowers do not have the same taboos as the Lower Middles, but they do have some occupational restraints. A railway workman, for example, will tend to have an occupational taboo on drinking in some situations. In general the Upper-Lowers drink at home and in the taverns, which provide a kind of club for Lower-class people. But if they are to be mobile into Lower-Middle class, they have to change such habits.

Lower-class persons usually become openly aggressive when drinking because they have not been trained to exercise the control of aggression that is demanded of those at the top. In the Lower class, it is not a disgrace to get drunk and fight even if this behavior has dangerous consequences. A Lower-class man may be aggressive in the family toward wife and children. This group does not have the "drink like a gentleman" taboo. Differences in ethnic backgrounds are also conspicuous in the drinking customs of the Upper-Lower class—Irish, Jewish and Italian immigrants, for instance, retain customs that still have a "home color" when they settle in this country. . . .

In the Lower-Lower class, drinking is socially unrestrained. There is the Saturday-night-to-Monday-morning binge, without much social control. Both men and women drink, although usually not in mixed groups. In the Lower-Lower class there is overt aggression; people are arrested for drunkenness, breaking the peace. There is much chronic drunkenness in this class.[44]

There can be no doubt that the use of alcoholic beverages in our culture is encompassed by powerful status implications. A study by Gregory Stone gave partial support to Dollard's analysis.[45] He substantiated the fact that the lower-middle class tends to deprecate drinking, for example. A study by Joseph L. Lawrence and Milton A. Maxwell in the state of Washington indicated that the heavy and unrestrained drinking at the bottom of the social scale, which Dollard had postulated, did not seem to be the pattern of the majority of this group, particularly the women.[46] They suggest that this view may be a part of the stereotype of the lower class. It is evident that additional sociological research is needed to give a more comprehensive scientific picture of the role of social class in the causation of alcoholism. Two volumes which report the findings of a wide spectrum of sociological and anthropological studies of drinking are Society, Culture, and Drinking Patterns, edited by Pittman and Snyder (see above, Chapter 1, n. 23) and Alcoholism and Society by Morris E. Chafetz and Harold W. Demone, Jr.[47]

Significant empirical evidence concerning the amount of drinking and of problem drinking among various social class groups was made available in 1963 when Harold A. Mulford reported on a scientific survey of a cross section of the noninstitutionalized adult population in the United States. Certain of his findings which are relevant to the subject under consideration are presented in the table below. The figures in column one represent the percentage of a given group who use beverage alcohol. Column two gives the percentage of the drinkers who could be classified as "heavy drinkers" [48] (i.e. they drink medium or large quantities more than once a month). Column three gives the percentage of drinkers who had experienced serious trouble as a result of drinking.[49] Income, occupation, and education are three "status characteristics" which are used in determining an individual's social class. The occupations given are illustrative of occupational categories with gradually increasing status from bottom to top.

Several generalizations may be drawn from these data. First, the percentage of those who drink tends to rise with income, education, occupational status, and size of community of residence. Although the trend is less clear, the percentage of heavy drinkers among the total drinkers seems to increase as these four factors rise. The percentage of those who have serious troubles as a result of drinking rises with the size of the community. In matters of education and occupational status, the percentage of problem drinking seems to be greater at each end of the continuum. Percentage of drinkers declines with age.

It is noteworthy that 7 percent of the Jewish drinkers, in this study, reported serious troubles from their drinking. This may mean that the traditional controls which tended to keep Jews from developing alcoholism are weakening as Jews become increasingly integrated into the mainstream of American life, including its drinking patterns.

### Certain Measures of Drinking Behavior, U.S.A. 1963 [50]

| | | ENTIRE SAMPLE | DRINKERS ONLY |
| | Percentage Who Drink | Percentage of Heavy Drinkers | Percentage of Troubles from Drinking |
|---|---|---|---|
| **Income** | | | |
| $10,000 and over | 87 | 14 | 9 |
| $7,000-9,999 | 85 | 12 | 10 |
| $5,000-6,999 | 68 | 11 | 9 |
| $3,000-4,999 | 64 | 5 | 12 |
| Under $3,000 | 54 | 8 | 7 |

| | Percentage Who Drink | Percentage of Heavy Drinkers | Percentage of Troubles from Drinking |
|---|---|---|---|
| **Occupation** | | | |
| Physicians; lawyers; dentists | 100* | 0* | 20* |
| College professors; engineers | 87 | 24 | 17 |
| Veterinarians; dept. store heads | 80 | 11 | 5 |
| Insurance agents; draftsmen | 84 | 15 | 6 |
| Bookkeepers; musicians | 76 | 12 | 7 |
| Electricians; construction foremen | 83 | 13 | 9 |
| Machinists; small business proprietors | 73 | 11 | 12 |
| Mechanics; shipping clerks | 76 | 19 | 19 |
| Farmers; carpenters | 67 | 11 | 15 |
| Laborers; janitors | 69 | 10 | 16 |
| **Education** (years) | | | |
| More than 16 | 79 | 21 | 13 |
| 16 | 89 | 15 | 4 |
| 13-15 | 76 | 6 | 9 |
| 12 | 79 | 10 | 9 |
| 9-11 | 70 | 13 | 11 |
| 8 | 60 | 10 | 11 |
| 0-7 | 46 | 7 | 16 |
| **Residence Community Size** | | | |
| 500,000 and over | 76 | 13 | 13 |
| 75,000-499,999 | 71 | 10 | 13 |
| 10,000-74,999 | 76 | 11 | 8 |
| 2,500-9,999 | 69 | 12 | 8 |
| Under 2,500 | 60 | 5 | 6 |
| **Sex** | | | |
| Males | 79 | 16 | 16 |
| Females | 63 | 4 | 2 |
| **Age** (years) | | | |
| 60 and over | 56 | 9 | 8 |
| 40-59 | 70 | 12 | 10 |
| 21-39 | 79 | 10 | 10 |

* It should be noted that there were only five persons in this category out of the total sample of 1509 persons.

| | Percentage Who Drink | Percentage of Heavy Drinkers | Percentage of Troubles from Drinking |
|---|---|---|---|
| Religion | | | |
| Jewish | 90 | 7 | 7 |
| Roman Catholic | 89 | 12 | 10 |
| Lutheran | 85 | 13 | 5 |
| Presbyterian, Episcopalians, and Congregationalists | 81 | 12 | 6 |
| Methodists | 61 | 5 | 8 |
| Baptists | 48 | 9 | 16 |

The melting-pot aspect of American life adds further to the conflict of attitudes and values concerning alcohol. A certain minister tells of overhearing an informal but heated discussion on the subject among three pre-adolescent boys. One of the boys was from an Italian, the second from a Jewish, and the third from a New England Protestant background. Each was a part of a tradition which had led him to feel deeply that it was "normal" to use alcohol in certain ways or not to use it. Their attitudes had been absorbed as they grew up in one of three very different groups. These attitudes were deeply ingrained in them, and it was disturbing to them to encounter other patterns in their playmates. The variety of their attitudes, projected on a larger screen with many other subcultural points of view added, is the picture of America's crazy-quilt philosophy for understanding and dealing with the problems of alcohol. Straus and Bacon give a succinct description of the situation: "At the present time American drinking practices and attitudes—and the philosophies and programs for meeting the problems associated with drinking—can still be summed up in one word: confusion." [51] It is within this baffling environment that young people must attempt to arrive at their own set of values and practices.

Several writers have mentioned the absence of unified cultural controls on drunkenness (comparable to those in the Jewish culture). The mere fact that an intoxicated man, at a certain stage of inebriation, has considerable entertainment value shows that our culture has sometimes made drunkenness socially rewarding. To the extent that it makes it either acceptable or rewarding behavior, it has indeed encouraged the "choice" of alcoholism as a symptom.

The discrepancy between the male and female rates of alcoholism is a vivid demonstration of this truth. The ratio is approximately four and one-half males to one female. This is due in part to the fact that 79 percent of the male population drink, as against 63 percent of the female. More important is the fact that in most groups a man who frequently becomes intoxicated loses much less social standing than a woman who is known to drink to excess. As someone has put it, if a group of college boys become intoxicated and create a commotion, most people will shrug their shoulders and say, "Well, boys will be boys." But if a group of college girls did the same thing, there would be a vocal response of moral indignation and decisive action on the part of the dean. It is noteworthy that the Mulford study figures, cited above, showed that heavy drinkers were four times as prevalent among male as among female drinkers. Even more striking is the fact that serious troubles from drinking were found to occur eight times as frequently among male drinkers as among female drinkers.

The high rate of alcoholism among Americans of Irish descent is thought to be due to the pressures in this subculture which encourage the use of alcohol as a means of interpersonal adjustment. This is what was behind the observation of one interviewee that "you don't have to be Irish to be an alcoholic, but it helps."

To summarize, the most important factors in the selection of the alcoholic symptom seem to be the availability and attractiveness of alcohol in a particular cultural group. If a person with a strong need for anxiety reduction lives in a setting which imposes heavy social penalties (loss of social standing) on drunkenness, he will probably turn to nonalcoholic escapes. If, on the other hand, a person who, in spite of his inner conflicts, can manage his interpersonal relations with fair adequacy without alcohol is placed in a group which encourages habits of excess, he may come to employ alcohol addictively.

### Level Three: Factors Which Perpetuate the Addiction

Why is it that once a person crosses a certain line in his drinking he is caught in a vicious cycle from which he usually cannot extricate himself unaided? And why is it that the addiction must grind on to such lengths before the person "hits bottom" and is open to help? Obviously these are key questions so far as both prevention and therapy are concerned.

It seems probable that the metabolic and endocrine changes observed in the later stages of alcoholism may play an important part in the perpetuation of the addiction. It is noteworthy that for some unknown reason an alcoholic can apparently never again drink in moderation.* There are examples in the literature of alcoholics who have had long and successful psychoanalytic therapy to remove their major inner conflicts. In spite of this therapy, they were still unable to drink moderately. It is possible that some irreversible

* See the discussion of this issue under "Goals of Counseling" in Chapter 8.

change in biochemistry gives the alcoholic a sensitivity or "allergy" (as AA has long claimed) to alcohol, so that one drink sets off a chain reaction leading inevitably to a drunk.

The "rat experiment" at Yale is a useful story to remember for counseling purposes, and it emphasizes the need for an open mind in this area. A group of experimental rats were found to prefer straight water to water spiked with alcohol. The enzyme system of their livers was then disturbed by surgery. They then favored the alcohol-water solution, rapidly developing an addiction to it. For ninety days all alcohol was removed. When reintroduced to the experimental situation, even after restoration of their enzyme balance, they went on with their addiction where they had left off.[52]

The phenomenon of craving which helps perpetuate a binge may be caused by one or more of several X factors of a physiological nature—depletion of chlorides in the blood, faulty elimination of certain waste products produced in the metabolism of alcohol, lack of vitamins in the brain, or some upsetting of the enzyme balance.

On the psychological side it is helpful to remember that the alcoholic's drinking is compulsive. When he crosses the line into his addiction, he becomes the puppet of his subconscious drives and conflicts. Because of the nature of a compulsion—most people including alcoholics think of their pet compulsions as normal—it is difficult for the alcoholic to recognize that his behavior is abnormal.

It is necessary now to return to the concept of alcohol as a "solution" for the alcoholic. Remember that by the time he reaches the stage of addiction, he has come to regard alcohol as a solution rather than a problem. So complete is his dependence on this solution that it is very difficult for him even to visualize any other solution for himself. He has organized his personality around alcohol. Becoming abstinent is not simply a matter of giving up a pleasant satisfaction. It is, in effect, giving up the core around which he has organized his life. This factor makes the alcoholic hold on to alcohol long after the solution has brought its own destruction.

So far as the individual bender is concerned, there seems to be a profound psychological factor involved in the dynamics of the problem. We have said that alcohol allows the person to regress to a comfortable level in his psychosocial development. For many alcoholics this may be the "oral" stage of infancy. The person finds inner unity by going back to the level at which he last experienced it. Once he has found this unity, he is unable to return to adult life. So the binge continues. The craving for this infantile comfort may be an important factor in the "craving phenomenon" and therefore in the perpetuation of addiction.

Our culture's attitudes toward alcoholism help to drive the person deeper and deeper into the addiction in which he is trapped. A substantial percentage of the American people still see alcoholism in moralistic, willpower terms, rather than as a genuine sickness which requires treatment. Thirty-five percent of respondents in a nationwide survey by Elmo Roper and Associates considered the alcoholic as "morally weak"; 58 percent accepted the alcoholic as "sick"; and 7 percent expressed no opinion.[53] There is evidence that much of the acceptance of the sickness conception is relatively superficial. Jellinek put his finger on this problem when he declared: "Generally, it may be said not only of the public at large but of the medical profession, industry and labor and all the other sections of public opinion, that their feeling is that the idea that 'alcoholism' is an illness 'is true, but not really true.' " [54] An Iowa survey supported Jellinek's view. Only 24 percent of the sample accepted the sickness view without reservations; 34 percent described the alcoholic as "weak" ("weak willed" or "morally weak"), without mentioning sickness; and 41 percent described him as both "weak" and "sick." Five out of eight who endorsed the illness concept also retain the moral weakness view.[55]

Public attitudes such as these militate against early detection and treatment of alcoholism. An individual is in his culture as a fish is in water. The person who is beginning to have trouble with alcohol naturally reflects the attitudes of his culture and erroneously regards his difficulty as a matter of willpower. As the tentacles of his compulsion close tighter around him, he struggles all the harder to "use a little more willpower" and to solve the problem himself. To admit that he cannot is tantamount to admitting he is mentally unbalanced or a moral jellyfish. Thus the culture drives him away from, rather than toward, the help he desperately needs. On the one hand his assumption that his problem is essentially one of willpower, and on the other hand, the fact that he is caught by a compulsion, make it increasingly necessary for his defensive rationalization system to work overtime. He must convince himself that he can stop when he really wants to and that it is not his drinking but external circumstances that are to blame for his troubles. All these factors tend to perpetuate his addiction and to make it necessary for him to reach a point of tragic spiritual, mental, and moral bankruptcy before he can accept help. There are important implications in all that we have been considering so far as the prevention and early treatment of alcoholism are concerned.

We have discussed the three levels on which the causes of alcoholism can be seen to operate. Now we turn to a causative factor which plays a role on each of the three levels, but which we treat separately for the sake of emphasis, because of its distinctive importance for our purposes. The religious philosophical factor should be seen as the fourth factor in the etiology of alcoholism, the other three being the physiological, the psychological, and the cultural.

70

## Level Four: Philosophical and Religious Factors in the Etiology of Alcoholism

An understanding of the distinctive contribution of a religious approach to alcoholism is dependent on insight into what might be called the vertical dimension of the alcoholic's problem. For in addition to disturbances in the interpersonal plane, the horizontal dimension, the alcoholic also suffers from disturbances in his relationship to the Ultimate.

There are three kinds of anxiety involved in the etiology of alcoholism: *neurotic, historical,* and *existential.* These three are involved in all neurotic problems. Anxiety—of whatever variety—rises from a threat to the essential security of a person and is therefore an experience of the total personality. The psychiatrist Harry Stack Sullivan called it a "cosmic" experience, a shaking of the individual's world and his perception of it. In contrast, "fear" is a reaction to a specific danger. Anxiety is an unspecific feeling of uncertainty and helplessness. The alcoholic's burden is not simply fear, but also free-floating anxiety.

As we have seen, much of the alcoholic's anxiety is pathological or neurotic, the result of inner conflict and repression which threaten his sense of worth. The individual who has repressed all his anger in order to feel acceptable to himself, having grown up in an environment where anger was taboo, feels anxiety whenever hostile feelings threaten to enter his awareness. Neurotic anxiety is thus a mechanism for keeping unacceptable feelings and drives out of awareness. It is the burden of neurotic anxiety which the psychotherapist often is able to reduce. This is the kind of anxiety we have already discussed in considering the psychological factors in the soil of addiction.

Neurotic anxiety is intermixed and increased by *historical* anxiety, that arising from the crisis of our time. Modern man has had many of his philosophical props knocked from under him. Traditional and comfortable certainties about God, man, and the universe have been threatened or destroyed for many by the impact of two world wars and the scientific revolutions wrought by Copernicus, Darwin, and Freud. Many who have never integrated the meaning of these major scientific discoveries into their philosophies of life find their hold on traditional certainties weakened by the indirect but profound influence of our scientifically minded culture. Man feels himself to be the accidental denizen of an insignificant grain of cosmic dust lost in the mechanical emptiness of an exploding universe which will ultimately snuff out his feeble life. He feels his impotence in the face of mass social forces over which he has no control. So, meaninglessness is a constant threat to his philosophical existence.

One of the two alcoholics interviewed who classed themselves as atheists described the problem when he spoke of what he called "my cockeyed philosophy of life": "A fellow sleeps to get strong, so he can work to get money to eat and have a place to sleep, so that he can get strong and be able to work to get money, and so on."

The collapse of a man's Weltanschauung leaves him at the mercy of the third type of anxiety—his *existential* anxiety. Existential anxiety—the anxiety arising from man's nature, the very facts of his existence as man—would seem to be an important factor in everyone's life, including alcoholics and those who would help them. In his book entitled *Shaking of the Foundations*, the late Paul Tillich put it clearly: "Man's essential loneliness and seclusion, his insecurity and feeling of strangeness, his temporality and melancholy are qualities which are felt even apart from their transformation by guilt. They are his heritage of finitude." [56] Existential anxiety is the threat to his essential self which inheres in man's "heritage of finitude." Man is the animal who knows he will die. He is a part of nature, subject to its powers, to sickness, pain, and death. Yet he can transcend nature and view his own end. In *Thus Spake Zarathustra*, Nietzsche put it thus, "Man is a rope connecting animal and superman." [57] From the awareness of his own contingency arises man's existential anxiety. In German philosophical literature this anxiety is called *Urangst*, or ultimate anxiety. Tillich, in his Terry Lectures at Yale,[58] has given us the most incisive treatment of nonpathological anxiety from the theological standpoint. Psychoanalysts such as Rollo May, Karen Horney, and Erich Fromm have dealt with it from the psychological point of view.

Existential anxiety arises also from man's rational capacities. Fromm observes:

Self-awareness, reason and imagination have disrupted the "harmony" which characterizes animal existence. Their emergence has made man into an anomaly, into the freak of the universe. He is a part of nature, subject to her physical laws and unable to change them, yet he transcends the rest of nature. . . . He is homeless, yet chained to the home he shares with all creatures. . . . Being aware of himself, he realizes his powerlessness and the limitations of his existence. He visualizes his own end: death. Never is he free from the dichotomy of his existence. . . . Reason, man's blessing, is also his curse.[59]

Man's capacity for feeling "I ought" is a blessing but also a burden, a source of existential anxiety. The creation myth in Genesis states this symbolically—the expulsion from Eden was the result of eating the fruit of a tree which made men "as gods, knowing good and evil" (Gen. 3:5). Thoreau witnessed to the eternal restlessness of man's spirit when he said that human beings are always "searching for some lost Eden." [60] Fromm says, "Having lost paradise, the unity with nature, he has become the eternal wanderer (Odysseus, Oedipus, Abraham, Faust)." [61] And it was Mark Twain who once quipped, "Man is the only animal that blushes or needs to."

Existential anxiety also arises from what Toynbee calls the "Promethean elan," [62] man's drive to assert himself. Viewing man's evolution during his 650,000 or so years on this planet, one realizes that he is involved in a perennial struggle to achieve autonomy, to rise above primitive dependence on the herd. He is a separate self with distinctive needs and potentialities; yet he needs the herd. When he gets too far from the herd, he becomes anxious. As Tillich has put it, modern man "is the autonomous man who has become insecure in his autonomy." [63]

Existential anxiety is unneurotic, yet it is the basis or ground of all neurotic anxiety. It is normal—the experience of all men. It becomes unbearable when a load of neurotic anxiety is added to it. A man is oppressed by its weight on his back only when his back also bears a heavy burden of neurotic anxiety. Because of this, existential anxiety is an important consideration for the understanding of alcoholism.

Both historical and existential anxiety contribute to all three levels of the causation of alcoholism. Since they complicate the alcoholic's neurotic anxiety, they contribute to the soil of addiction by helping to render him vulnerable. On the level of symptom choice—the second level—they operate by creating religious and philosophical needs for which alcohol provides pseudosatisfactions. On the third level these forms of anxiety contribute to the perpetuation of the addiction in the sense that they become more and more pronounced as the alcoholic continues to try to satisfy his religious needs by means of alcohol. That is, the more he drinks, the more hopeless and meaningless life seems to him.

The thesis stated above, that alcohol provides a pseudosatisfaction for the alcoholic's religious needs, is so fundamental to an understanding of both alcoholism and any religious approach to it, that it will be discussed at some length in Chapter 6. Suffice it to say here that alcohol seems to have the capacity to allay temporarily the alcoholic's existential anxiety. It gives him feelings of transcending his finitude, of participating in the larger life. The fact that alcohol is related dynamically in its effects to mystical elation was pointed out by William James in his Gifford Lectures.[64] The alcoholic thus seeks to satisfy his religious needs by nonreligious means. The tragedy of this is that by so doing he only magnifies his religious needs in the long run.

### Summary

In this chapter we have been reviewing the causative factors involved in alcoholism as they operate on three levels: (1) We have seen that there may be biochemical factors and that there most certainly are psychological factors in the soil of addiction which renders certain persons vulnerable to alcoholism. (2) We have seen that the availability of alcohol and its attractiveness as a symptom, as determined by social attitudes toward drinking and drunkenness, have a great deal to do with the matter of symptom selection. (3) We have observed that physiological changes as well as cultural attitudes toward alcoholism (which regard it as a question of willpower rather than a sickness) probably contribute to the perpetuation of the addiction once it is established.[65] We have traced the way in which alcohol serves as a neurotic "solution" to the alcoholic's inner problems. We have described the philosophical and religious factors which influence all three levels of causation and have indicated the manner in which alcohol serves as a pseudosolution to historical and existential anxiety. In Chapter 1 we saw the way in which the solution carried the seeds of its own destruction. It is when his alcoholic solution collapses that the alcoholic turns to *religious* solutions.

## REFERENCES

1. Carney Landis and M. M. Bolles, *Textbook of Abnormal Psychology* (New York: The Macmillan Company, 1964), p. 194.
2. *Religion in Illness and Health* (New York: Harper & Brothers, 1942), p. 37.
3. Lupica Benedict, "A New Dawn for Alcoholics," *Healthways*, IV (May, 1950), 39.
4. Harold A. Mulford, "Drinking and Deviant Drinking, U.S.A., 1963," *QJSA*, XXV, 637.
5. "Culture and Jewish Sobriety: the Ingroup-Outgroup Factor" in *Society, Culture, and Drinking Patterns*, p. 188. Many studies have confirmed the low rates of alcoholism about Jews. For example: Rates of rejection in the Armed Forces for chronic alcoholism in World War I (60,000 cases): Irish—3.0%; Negro—2.2%; Italian—1.2%; Jewish—0.2%; Chinese—0.0%. (Cited by Donald Glad, "Attitudes and Experiences of American-Jewish and American-Irish Male Youths as Related to Differences in Adult Rates of Inebriety," *QJSA*, VIII [December, 1947], 408.) Or, consider this example: First-admission rates for alcoholic psychosis (to mental hospitals in New York State) of those born in foreign countries (figures are per 100,000 of the same nationality in New York state hospitals, 1929-31): Irish—25.6%; Scandinavian—7.8%; Italian—4.8%; English—4.3%; German—3.8%; Jews (all nationalities)—0.5%. (Cited by Landis and Bolles, *Textbook of Abnormal Psychology*, p. 236.)
6. E. M. Jellinek, Lecture at the Yale Summer School of Alcohol Studies, July, 1949.
7. *Religion in Illness and Health*, p. 37.
8. Henry D. Thoreau, *Walden: or, Life in the Woods* (New York: Dodd, Mead & Company, 1946), p. 9.
9. "The Addictive Drinker," *QJSA*, X (December, 1949), 412.
10. *The Disease Concept of Alcoholism*, p. 87.
11. *Ibid.*, p. 108.
12. *Ibid.*
13. James J. Smith, "A Medical Approach to Problem Drinking," *QJSA*, X (September, 1949), 251.
14. "Meeting of the Medical Society of the State of New York," *New York Times*, May 10, 1950.
15. "A Critique of Physiopathological Theories of the Etiology of Alcoholism," *QJSA*, XI (March, 1950), 113-14.

16. (Austin: University of Texas Press, 1959).
17. Anne Roe, "Children of Alcoholic Parents Raised in Foster Homes," *Alcohol, Science and Society* (New Haven: Journal of Studies on Alcohol, 1945) pp. 115-28.
18. (New York: McGraw-Hill Book Company, 1949).
19. Two interviews were incomplete at this point, and two were with brothers.
20. C. Bühler and D. W. Lefever, "A Rorschach Study on the Psychological Characteristics of Alcoholics" (New Haven: Hillhouse Press, 1948), p. 61.
21. "Part II, Psychological Test Results" in *Studies of Compulsive Drinkers*, ed. J. F. Cushman and C. Landis (New Haven: Hillhouse Press, 1946), p. 84.
22. "A Rorschach Study," p. 37.
23. H. W. Main (pseud.), *If a Man Be Mad* (Garden City: Doubleday & Company, 1945), p. 152.
24. "The Sexual Adjustment of Alcoholics. A Clinical Study of a Selected Sample," *QJSA*, XVI (December, 1955), 675-80.
25. (Stanford, Calif.: Stanford University Press, 1960).
26. *Ibid.*, p. 152.
27. *Ibid.*, p. viii.
28. *Studies of Compulsive Drinkers*, p. 83.
29. *QJSA*, IV (December, 1943), 368-86.
30. *The Disease Concept of Alcoholism*, p. 107.
31. "An Analysis of the Influence of Alcohol on Experimental Neuroses in Cats," *Psychosomatic Medicine*, VI (1946),36-52.
32. "The Function of Alcohol in Primitive Societies: A Cross-Cultural Study," *QJSA*, IV (September, 1943), No. 2, 233.
33. "Personality Traits and the Alcoholic, A Critique of Existing Studies," *QJSA*, XI (December, 1950).
34. "Recent Trends in Alcoholism and in Alcohol Consumption" (New Haven: Hillhouse Press, 1947), p. 20.
35. "Alcohol: A Study of Social Ambivalence," *QJSA*, I (June, 1940), No. 1, 17.
36. "Cultural Differences in Rates of Alcoholism," *QJSA*, VI (March, 1946), No. 4, 497.
37. "Culture and Jewish Sobriety: The Ingroup-Outgroup Factor" in *Society, Culture, and Drinking Patterns*, pp. 188-89.
38. Ruth H. Landman, "Drinking Patterns of Children and Adolescents Attending Religious Schools," *QJSA*, XIII (March, 1952), 91.
39. "Cultural Differences in Rates of Alcoholism," p. 491.
40. "Alcohol: A Study of Social Ambivalence," p. 17.
41. It is significant that the Jewish controls on excessive drinking seem to be weakening as American Jews become less intensely identified with their ingroup and with the Orthodox religious position. Charles R. Snyder reports: "As religious affiliation shifts from Orthodox to Conservative to Reform and to Secular, signs of drinking pathologies show marked and systematic increase. Moreover, these changes cannot be attributed to the direct influence of social class or generational factors." ("Culture and Jewish Sobriety: The Ingroup-Outgroup Factor," p. 190.)
42. "Cultural Differences in Rates of Alcoholism," p. 482.
43. *Drinking in College* (New Haven: Yale University Press, 1953), p. 14.
44. From *Alcohol, Science and Society*, pp. 99-100. Dollard used the six-social-class framework suggested by W. Lloyd Warner. Class status is defined by such matters as occupation, the length of a family's residence in a community, income and property, the quality and place of residence, the mores and values which guide them, and education.
45. Gregory P. Stone, "Drinking Styles and Status Arrangements" in *Society, Culture, and Drinking Patterns*, pp. 121-40.
46. "Drinking and Socio-Economic Status" in *Society, Culture, and Drinking Patterns*, pp. 141-45.
47. (New York: Oxford University Press, 1962); see especially chapter 4.
48. See "Drinking and Deviant Drinking U.S.A., 1963." Mulford set up five categories

in terms of quantity and frequency of drinking. Those whom I have designated "heavy drinkers" were in the fifth category.

49. Troubles from drinking included the following: being left or being threatened to be left by one's spouse; losing a job or being threatened with firing; being warned by a doctor that drinking is injurious to the subject's health; being arrested on some charge involving alcohol; being accused by a family member of overspending on alcohol.

50. The complete table, including numbers in each category and data on geographical regions, is given on pp. 640-41 of the Mulford article. The table is entitled "Distribution of the Adult Population and of Selected Social Segments by Certain Measures of Drinking Behavior, U.S.A., 1963."

51. *Drinking in College*, p. 34.

52. E. M. Jellinek, Lecture at the Yale Summer School of Alcohol Studies, July, 1949.

53. From a survey in 1958, reported in Jellinek's *Disease Concept of Alcoholism*, p. 183.

54. *Ibid.*, p. 185.

55. H. A. Mulford and D. E. Miller, "Measuring Public Acceptance of the Alcoholic as a Sick Person," *QJSA*, XXV (1964), 314-23.

56. (New York: Charles Scribner's Sons, 1948), p. 170.

57. *The Works of Friedrich Nietzsche* (New York: The Tudor Publishing Company, 1931).

58. *The Courage to Be* (New Haven: Yale University Press, 1952).

59. *Psychoanalysis and Religion* (New Haven: Yale University Press, 1950), p. 22.

60. *Walden: or, Life in the Woods*, p. 54.

61. *Psychoanalysis and Religion*, p. 23.

62. A. J. Toynbee, *A Study of History* (Somervell's abridgment; New York: Oxford University Press, 1947), p. 276.

63. *The Protestant Era* (Chicago: University of Chicago Press, 1948), p. 192.

64. *The Varieties of Religious Experience, A Study in Human Nature* (New York: Longmans, Green and Company, 1902).

65. This tentative model for understanding the causes of problem drinking is offered in the report of the Cooperative Commission on the Study of Alcoholism: "An individual who (1) responds to beverage alcohol in a certain way, perhaps physiologically determined, by experiencing intense relief and relaxation, and who (2) has certain personality characteristics, such as difficulty in dealing with and overcoming depression, frustration, and anxiety, and who (3) is a member of a culture in which there is both pressure to drink and culturally induced guilt and confusion regarding what kinds of drinking behavior are appropriate, is more likely to develop trouble than will most other people." See Thomas F. A. Plaut, *Alcohol Problems, A Report to the Nation* (New York: Oxford University Press, 1967), p. 49.

# PART II

# SOME RELIGIOUS APPROACHES to ALCOHOLISM

# 3

# How Religion Has Been Used
# to Help Homeless Alcoholics

It is possible to learn a great deal about helping alcoholics by studying and evaluating the major religious approaches to the problem. One can profit by both the successes and the failures of those religious groups whose primary concern has been helping alcoholics. This is the purpose of the chapters immediately ahead. Three different religious orientations will be studied and compared: (1) the *evangelistic-authoritarian* approaches of the rescue mission and the Salvation Army; (2) a *psychologically oriented* approach, the Emmanuel Movement; and (3) a *permissive, self-help* approach, Alcoholics Anonymous. We will begin in this chapter with the evangelistic-authoritarian approach which has been used chiefly with low-bottom, homeless alcoholics.

Before proceeding, it might be helpful to the reader to indicate more directly the relevance of the next three chapters to the work of the pastor and others who are concerned with helping alcoholics. This present chapter will obviously be of greatest interest to those who work in downtown, urban churches where such alcoholics most frequently are encountered. The broader significance of the chapter lies in whatever light it throws on the psychological understanding of authoritarian religion in general. Chapter 4, dealing with the Emmanuel Movement, is of special interest to those who are concerned, as many clergymen are, with helping to develop a closer relationship between religion and psychotherapy, both in general and in the treatment of alcoholism. Chapter 5, the AA chapter, will have the most direct relevance to the work of the average pastor, since AA is his most vauable and effective referral resource. The more extensive coverage of this chapter is justified by the fact that a pastor needs to have as full an understanding as possible of this movement.

## Understanding the Homeless Alcoholic

A Skid Row can be found in almost any American city. In Chicago it is West Madison Street; in Los Angeles, Fifth Street off South Main. San Francisco has its Howard Street. In New York it's the Bowery. These and dozens of smaller counterparts are the "streets of forgotten men," stagnant catch-basins which collect the dregs of our social system. In such blighted areas one finds a high concentration of low-bottom alcoholics, men who are "on the bum."

A visit to the Bowery on New York's lower East Side reveals a run-down street, no longer canopied by the metallic arms of the Third Avenue El but still lined with noisy dives, cheap flophouses, pawnshops, used clothing stores, and rescue missions. In the warehouse doorways ragged, vermin-infested men lie in alcoholic oblivion. A huddle of disheveled, unshaven individuals talk raucously as they pass about a bottle of "Sneaky Pete"—cheap wine fortified with rubbing alcohol. Human derelicts wander aimlessly up and down the street, milling together like swarming insects. Two, in the belligerent stage of drunkenness, shout curses and exchange blows. A crowd gathers to watch. Every few feet "plingies" (Bowery slang for panhandlers) ply their trade, begging from all likely prospects who pass. Up "Dead Man's Alley" a "squeeze" is in progress—Sterno is being warmed over a fire of newspapers preparatory to squeezing it through a sock to make a drink called "Pink Lady." As one watches the scene, the words of a young alcoholic come to mind. Out of his own tragic experience he described the Bowery as "this dirty, dead trail of a thousand broken dreams in a thousand broken minds and bodies." [1]

Who are these men, and how do they manage to stay alive under such conditions? Sociologically they are classified as homeless. Fortunately, several extensive studies of homeless men have been made by the social scientists.[2] One of the most useful is the study made by sociologist Robert Straus.[3] By means of interviews, Straus studied the cases of 203 homeless men who came to the Salvation Army social service center in New Haven, Connecticut, in 1946. Let us review some of his findings.

The typical homeless man left his parental home at an early age, often following the death of a parent or serious conflict in the home. Early emotional instability and deficient socialization are characteristic. He stopped his education between the seventh and eighth grades. He has usually either never married or is widowed or divorced. He is constantly on the move, going from one Skid Row to another and rarely staying in one place more than a few weeks or months. Religiously he is either Catholic or Protestant, almost never Jewish. Concerning attitudes toward religion, Straus reports: "Nearly all of the men spoke of their religion in the past tense. They felt that they had lost touch with their faith, expressed little interest in church attendance." [4]

Many of them are unemployable. Others work at various unskilled or semi-skilled jobs for part of the year and are on the bum the rest.

Are these men homeless because they are alcoholics, or are they alcoholics because they are homeless? Straus found that heavy drinking preceded and seemed to be a contributing cause of homelessness in two thirds of the men. In the other third, heavy drinking *followed* and seemed to result from the condition of homelessness. He concludes: "Drinking seemed to be one of the several causes or one of the several results of homelessness."

It is important to remember that homelessness is in itself a pathosocial condition, that homelessness and alcoholism often arise from the same causative factors, and that each condition tends to enhance the other. For the person whose ability to relate meaningfully to others has been impaired by early emotional deprivation, alcohol and homelessness are two ways of escaping the pressures of adult interpersonal demands. It is when living closely with others becomes unbearably painful that one retreats into home-lessness, a life that demands almost nothing of the person. But homelessness removes not only the responsibilities but also the satisfactions of normal living. A homeless man—drifting and rootless—has almost no motivation for abstaining. The more he becomes divorced from normal life, the more he must resort to the pseudosatisfactions of alcohol. Thus a vicious spiral of homelessness and alcoholism is established.

In 1958 sociologists David J. Pittman and C. W. Gordon reported on a study of 187 "chronic police case inebriates." [5] These are low-bottom alcoholics who are constantly in and out of jail as a result of repeated drunkenness-related arrests. They constitute a sizable portion of the Skid Row population. Pittman and Gordon summarize their findings concerning this type of alcoholic.

Our study has shown him to be the product of a limited social environment and a man who never attained more than a minimum of integration in society. He is and has always been at the bottom of the social and economic ladder: he is isolated, uprooted, unattached, disorganized, demoralized and homeless, and it is in this context that he drinks to excess . . . he is the least respected member of the community. . . . He never attained, or has lost, the necessary respect and sense of human dignity on which any successful program of treatment and habilitation must be based. He is captive in a sequence of lack or loss of self-esteem, producing behavior which causes him to be further disesteemed. Unless this cycle is partially reversed, we doubt that any positive results can be attained.[6]

It is pathetically significant that over 90 percent of the men in the study had had no systematic treatment.

The Skid Row existence provides a kind of solution or adjustment for those who live there. Alcohol is the major ingredient of this solution.

81

Heavy drinking is regarded as normal, and the occasional abstainer is viewed with suspicion. Many of Straus's interviewees said that alcohol provided them with congenial companions and, in their present situation, let them forget their lack of possessions and status. Alcohol also serves as an alibi. When they are confronted by criticism or remorse, they point to the fact that they are afflicted by the unfortunate drink habit. When one sees the variety of ways in which alcohol is a form of adjustment for homeless men, it is possible to understand why a majority of those interviewed said they had no desire to stop drinking.

This does not mean that all Skid Row inhabitants are satisfied with their lot. Dressed in old clothes, the author spent an evening mixing with the men on the Bowery. Again and again they indicated their dissatisfaction. One inebriate advised: "Listen, Slim, don't hit this street like I did." A seaman said, "I'm just waiting until I can get off this binge and back on a ship." Even though many are not satisfied with their solution, it is the only one of which they see open to them. Their dissatisfaction is outweighed by the temporary rewards of alcohol and homelessness.

The fellowship of the Bowery—a fellowship made possible by alcohol—is another ingredient of this solution. This is a special kind of fellowship; one can participate or withdraw at any time. The Bowery has its unwritten code, its slang, and its newspaper—*The Bowery News, The Voice of Society's Basement.* Little groups of men band themselves together for the purpose of obtaining a constant supply of alcohol. Their common need is the bond that unites them.

There are other elements in the Bowery solution. The flophouse, known colloquially as the "scratch house," makes the Bowery the cheapest place in the city to rent shelter. However, if a choice between a flop and a bottle is necessary, the flop rates a poor second. Sleeping indoors is a luxury—alcohol a necessity. The ambulance from Bellevue Hospital is an element in the Bowery solution. The city hospital is to the homeless alcoholic what the sanitarium is to the solvent alcoholic. When injured by a "jackroller"—one who makes his living robbing them when they are drunk—or suffering from alcoholic delirium, the Bowery alcoholic is taken to Bellevue, the city hospital. When released, his first stop is usually the nearest gin mill. The "dead wagon" from the city morgue makes regular visits to the Bowery. After a cold night it goes about its grim business of collecting the newspaper-covered remains of those who were too drunk or too unlucky to find shelter.

Many of the men on the Bowery have gone far beyond the "bottom" described in Chapter 1. The spiral of progressive alcoholism has swirled downward through years of deterioration. Many of them have one of the diseases of chronic alcoholism—polyneuropathy, pellagra, cirrhosis of the liver, or others. However, many of the men on Skid Row are not in such a condition.

A study made in Seattle [7] showed that many Skid Row alcoholics are not in the final stages of their drinking careers. Some have just arrived. Others are there only temporarily and will leave when they are arrested or meet some other crisis. It is obvious that the possibility of helping this type is much greater than in the case of the deteriorated alcoholic.

The heterogeneity of the Skid Row population is an important consideration which has a bearing on both prognosis and treatment methods. Thomas B. Richards, an experienced worker with homeless alcoholics, states that for some the possibility of rehabilitation is minimal or nonexistent because of advanced alcoholic deterioration. For these, what is desperately needed is humane custodial care. According to Richards, the largest group of Skid Row alcoholics consists of those for whom rehabilitation is a realistic possibility. Many of these are in the younger age group. They are employable though largely unskilled occupationally and irresponsible in their life-styles. Thus, they are not beyond the possibility of restoration to a socially constructive life.[8]

The Pittman and Gordon study identified several different types among chronic police case inebriates: the *mentally disturbed* characterized by a general pattern of criminal behavior; the *older offender*, with no criminal involvement (except for a few arrests for public intoxication), whose main problem is his physical decline which makes him much less employable; and the *Negro inebriate*, often a recent migrant from a southern rural environment to the cities of the North and West, a person with no training and very unfavorable employment opportunities.[9]

It is with the various kinds of homeless men that the two hundred rescue missions on Skid Rows over the country do their work. The missions, too, are a part of the Bowery solution. At the very least they offer a bowl of soup, opportunity for delousing, and a warm place to sleep in winter. Beyond this, they hold out promise of release, salvation, and a blissful hereafter.

## The Rescue Mission Approach to Alcoholism

A raw wind is whipping up the street as we pause in front of the mission. Here is a five-story, stone building on which a large neon sign blazes forth the name of the mission. Smaller signs read: "A Friend to the Friendless"; "Free Facilities in the Basement, Clothing, Washing, Mending, Shaving, Shower Bath, Fumigation"; "Gospel Meeting Every Night, 7:30." As one enters the chapel, one immediately notices the characteristic atmosphere of blended body odor and alcohol. The organ plays old hymns. The chapel is nearly full. Here and there a man scratches vigorously; others doze in alcoholic slumber. Behind the back pew is an array of paper sacks and bundles tied in dirty newspaper. The worshipers have deposited their worldly possessions for the duration of the service. Over the pulpit at the front is a dark blue

83

banner on which bright yellow and red letters proclaim, "Jesus Saves." One looks at the faces of broken and defeated men. Eyes stare in cold, bloodshot cynicism.

The organist has stopped playing, and the evangelist begins to pray, asking God to reveal the proper hymn with which to begin the service. The prayer ended, the hymn "Nearer the Cross" is announced. Singing by the congregation is spotty. Another gospel song follows. Then a young lady evangelist testifies in song with the selection "It Is Well with My Soul." After a heartfelt rendition of the solo she asks rhetorically, "How about your soul, friend? Is it well with your soul?"

The leader of the service steps to the pulpit and says, "The important thing is to stop trying to do things in your own strength and let Christ take full possession of your life. Christ—he's the best friend we have." The congregation then sings, "What a Friend We Have in Jesus." The leader tells how he was saved from a life of gambling, alcohol, and sin. Several recent converts then testify. The leader then invites testimonies from anyone who wishes to tell what Christ has done for him. A sprinkling of short testimonies comes from the audience. One grateful man stands near the back and says, "I thank God that I can say through the blessed blood of our Lord Jesus that I'm sure I'll meet my dear mother in heaven."

After the testimonies the leader begins his message which includes the following:

I feel led to discuss the two highways—the broad road that leads to hell and destruction and the narrow highway that leads to heaven and eternal life. We get on the highway of righteousness only by the Lord Jesus, the way of the cross—he is our guide who takes us by the hand. Christ bridged the great gulf separating the two highways and therefore can snatch you from the highway of destruction over to the highway leading to heaven. Come to Jesus and say, "Lord, I'm a sinner," and he'll get you across the great chasm. I beg you, heed the word of God. Some of you are waiting to die, but it's not over then! The way of destruction goes *directly* into hell! (A tremor appears in the speaker's voice.) Put your sins under his blood. I have no fear when I die—my loving Savior will meet me and take care of me. Can you say, if the Lord calls you today, "Goodbye, world; I'm glad to leave the world and go to be with Jesus"? Can you say that and know that you will?

The message is followed by the invitation period. The congregation is led in prayer. While heads are bowed, those who wish intercessory prayer on their behalf are asked to "slip up their hands." The leader encourages response by recognizing the hands that go up—"There's one in the back." "I see your hand over on the side, brother." Then a hymn, "Almost Persuaded," is sung. Between each stanza the invitation to come forward and be saved is repeated. The wonderful blessings of "answering God's invitation" are presented with increasing emphasis, as are the awful consequences of refusing. The leader tells a story about a former crony on the Bowery who postponed coming to the altar one night too many, was hit by a truck, and "went to a Christless grave!" Pointing at his audience, the leader asks, "Are you ready for heaven?" When "Almost Persuaded" is exhausted, "Jesus Is Calling," another invitation hymn, is announced. Old emotions are stirred as the leader describes the death of his mother. While this is going on, former converts canvass the audience, "fishing" for converts—those "almost persuaded."

Those who respond to the invitation and go forward have a worker who kneels beside them to help "pray them through." The worker tells them how Christ saved and cleansed him, and helps the penitent to say a prayer, however short or faltering. If the procedure is successful, the penitent experiences a powerful emotional experience of forgiveness, release, and exaltation. The altar call, or invitation, usually lasts about fiften minutes, but it may go on longer if a substantial number have not been converted.

The essence of the rescue mission approach to alcoholism is contained in one word—salvation. Salvation, in mission thinking, consists of the kind of religious experience described above. To produce this experience is the goal of all mission activities. These activities may be divided into two categories: (1) the religious services including the gospel meeting such as was described, and smaller prayer meetings; (2) the work of physical and social rehabilitation.

The gospel meeting is the heart of the mission program. In order to receive food or shelter, a man usually must attend the religious meeting first. After the meeting the congregation files silently downstairs for supper consisting of soup and bread. After supper those who can be accommodated are given cots on which to sleep. Next morning they may shave and shower. After breakfast the converts of the previous evening are interviewed briefly by a mission worker, himself an ex-alcoholic. The worker asks a few questions about the convert's employment record and intentions. If a convert seems to offer possibility of permanent recovery, he is assigned to a bed and locker in one of the dormitories. Before he sleeps there he must be fumigated. He may be invited to stay at the mission until he can get back on his feet, but he is free to leave if he wishes. He may receive used clothing and, if he needs it, medical attention from the part-time clinic maintained at the mission.

If the convert decides to stay at the mission, it becomes his "home" for a while. He may be assigned work to do around the mission and, when he is recovered enough to be able, sent out on small jobs obtained by the mission's employment service. He is expected to attend Bible study, prayer, and gospel meetings. After a few days he will be asked to testify at a meeting. Members of the mission staff are available for counsel. Thus his conversion experience

85

is solidified and strengthened. After several weeks of testing the convert may be transferred from the mission itself to the "Home Uptown," a house where about twenty converts who seem to be making the grade are allowed to go. Here he will have a room of his own and a closet for his clothes. More important, he now has an address that has no stigma attached. He is off the Bowery. From here he seeks employment, often helped by the mission. In some cases the mission staff will help effect a reconciliation between the convert and his family. The goal of mission therapy is to eradicate homelessness as well as alcoholism. This is based on the realistic recognition that as long as a man stays on the Bowery his chances of recovery from alcoholism are very small.

Some rescue missions maintain fellowship groups for ex-alcoholics. Alcoholics Victorious, which was founded at the Chicago Christian Industrial League, is one of these. This fellowship now has chapters in rescue missions in various cities. The groups hold weekly meetings at which the men give testimonies, discuss personal problems, and help each other. Only alcoholics can belong. The creed of Alcoholics Victorious is somewhat comparable to the Twelve Steps of the AA program, except that it has a fundamentalistic Christian language and orientation.

## The Psychodynamics of Mission Therapy

How does the mission approach operate psychologically? The gospel meeting and rehabilitation can be analyzed in terms of four stages: *preparation, crisis, surrender-acceptance,* and *consolidation.*

It is necessary to prepare the individual for the emotional crisis experience which produces sobriety in some cases. There are several reasons for this. The mission clientele is composed largely of men who have little desire to stop drinking. Crises or "bottoms" during which the nonhomeless alcoholic is relatively accessible to help are, for many of these men, experiences of the past. They have, so to speak, used up their "bottoms" without finding help. We are dealing with the psychology of the realm beyond remorse and despair. It is necessary to revive these stuporous emotions if a crisis is to be induced. Preparation is also necessary because of the fact that, as Straus discovered in his study, most of them look with contempt on the very missions from which they receive food, clothing, and shelter. Religious services are something to be endured in order to get a much needed flop or a bowl of soup. Unless this negative attitude can be changed, it is unlikely that the alcoholic will respond in the way desired by the mission.

Group singing is of first importance in preparing the alcoholic for conversion. Studies in the psychology of music have shown that rapid, loud, rhythmic group singing of songs that stress the repetition of a few simple ideas tends to produce lowered inhibition, enhances suggestibility, a sense of group-ness, emotionality, and a tendency toward impulsive action.[10] Under the influence of a rapidly moving revival atmosphere, punctuated by the singing of the simple, primitive music of the gospel chorus, the defensive shell of the alcoholic is gradually softened. He begins to feel more a part of what is going on. Then, too, the singing of old salvation hymns may awaken long-forgotten emotional associations from the early life of the individual. A convert recalled: "I didn't think much of the service at first. But when they sang 'Jesus, Savior, pilot me over life's tempestuous sea,' it struck a spark somewhere. We used to sing that at home around the piano." [11]

Personal testimonies are a powerful form of preparation. The testifiers describe themselves as having lived on Skid Row and tell of their sins and degradation. This helps the derelict to identify with them and to listen to what they say. There is a strong element of positive suggestion in the participation of testifiers scattered throughout the audience. This participation helps mold the aggregate of individuals who enter the chapel into a unified pliable group. What is more, the testimonies may awaken a glimmer of hope— "Maybe there's a chance I can do it too."

The man in the mission pew is assailed by a barrage of emotionally charged illustrations and ideas which serve to reactivate his slumbering fear and guilt. Frequent mention of home and mother serves to awaken memories of life prior to the homeless state. Lurid threats of eternal punishment are sprinkled through mission sermons and interviews. One mission superintendent quoted the counsel he had given to an unconverted man: "I told him, 'Unless you accept the Lord, you're on your way to hell! You'll burn! You're still a little green, but you'll burn—not just smolder. Jesus said you must be born again —not may but must!'"

What might be called the "moralistic assumption"—that the alcoholic is completely responsible for his despicable condition—underlies all mission thinking and speaking. Alcoholism is a sinful habit acquired by the sin of using alcohol. This conception has stood unshaken from the days of Jerry McAuley, the "father of rescue mission." [12] A revealing encounter with AA ideology was described to the author by a mission employee: "A fellow from AA came in claiming that alcoholism isn't a sin but a sickness. I opened God's Word to I Corinthians 6:10 and Galatians 5:21 and proved to him that it was listed by God as a sin along with murder and stealing." Alcohol is the cause of both alcoholism and homelessness, according to mission thought.

By pressing the moralistic assumption the mission evangelist makes a head-on attack on the alcoholics' defenses. By stimulating his guilts and fears under the influence of group emotion, the evangelist is able in some cases to crack his defensive alibi system. When this happens, the individual is exposed to his real feelings of self-disgust. He is made to feel as miserable, hopeless, and helpless as possible. While his body is wracking from the physical effects of prolonged inebriety, the Bowery technique has created a "bottom," an emotional crisis, in which the alcoholic is open to help.

Into the emotional chaos and gloom a shining hope is projected. There is a way out! The sinner can do nothing for himself, but there is a Savior who cares. All the person must do is to accept this wonderful Savior and salvation will be his. Here is the pressure of opposites—eternal punishment or supreme beatitude.

Straus has pointed out that effective therapy for homeless alcoholics "must offer substitute reward values for abstinence which will be at least equivalent to the reward value of excessive drinking and which will not require greater effort than is required by drinking." [13] "Salvation" measures up on both scores. It requires only a decision. God does the rest. It is quick and effortless. It carries the rewards of acceptance and dependency. The alcoholic has but to surrender to God and he will be taken care of. For the lonely, emotionally starved alcoholic this kind of dependency carries great appeal.

The religious experience itself is another reward. If the person has been caught up in the proceedings—the rhythmic singing, the testimonies, the fervent prayers, the appeals to fear, to guilt, to memory, to hope, to dependency —in short, if he has felt the thrill of a pulsating religious group, he has found a substitute value for alcohol. Religious ecstasy provides another path to the feelings of expansiveness and larger life formerly achieved by alcohol.

The altar call is a masterpiece of positive suggestion. The various psychological pressures of the evening are recapitulated. Then follows the opportunity for a series of positive responses, in which the person moves from a small to a larger and larger "yes." The first is merely raising the hand when heads are bowed to request prayer. This intercessory prayer in itself has a powerful influence in that it focuses the feeling of divine attention on the individual. Then the leader may ask for those who want to be saved to raise their hands. As hands go up, he repeats the "nest egg" stimulus of "Thank you. Yes, brother. Three more back there." The third positive response is that of actually going forward. A hymn suggesting this response is sung (e.g., "Just as I am . . . I come, I come"), and all stand. The fact that everyone is standing makes it easier to get started to the front. The resistance of those who are wavering on the line is worn down by repetition and by personal invitations from those who are "fishing" for converts.

When a person does go forward (and does so sincerely), he has already taken a tremendous step. For this action means that he is motivated strongly enough to defy the opinion of his cronies who look with scorn on those who "take a dive for Jesus," and that he has relaxed his own defenses for the moment and is asking for help. The individual attention of the worker who helps "pray him through" plus the act of actually asking help from God often bring the man to a conversion experience.

It is impossible to describe fully the powerful religious experience which takes place in the convert. Those who attempt to put it into words tell of sudden release from guilt, of inner cleanness, of wonderful elation. They tell of feeling "back home" after years of spiritual wandering. Some tell of sudden release from the craving for alcohol. After his conversion Jerry McAuley told of feeling that "life was all new."

It would seem probable that it is the emotional intensity of such an experience which melts the alcoholic's shell of defenses and opens him to help. It is apparently the combination of the fear-guilt crisis with the offer of supernatural help which produces the surrender. The conversion experience would seem psychologically analogous to the following: A child who has been rebelling against parental authority finds the estrangement unbearable; he rushes back into the parent's arms. The parent accepts him, and the child feels a wonderful euphoria. He is accepted by the authority upon whom he is dependent. The parent will take care of him, and he will obey the parent. The alcoholic who experiences salvation is no longer fighting authority. He feels accepted.

The mission structure provides an environment in which the conversion experience may be consolidated. The dependence on an Almighty Power is buttressed and symbolized by concrete dependence on the mission workers and on the physical surroundings. His food and shelter are tangible evidences of the mission's parental care. For the shaky new convert the mission organization provides a closely knit "ingroup" where he is both accepted and needed. It is through his experiences in the religious group that his religious experience is consolidated. He learns the mission vocabulary. He is a member of an exclusive fellowship, the "saved" as distinguished from the great unwashed. Continued membership depends on compliance with its moral demands. One of the demands is abstinence, a by-product of salvation. The "born-again" Christian turns from worldly vices. Abstinence is rewarded—by God and by God's group. Social controls are reestablished. As one of the saved the convert is uniquely empowered to save others. We know that most alcoholics resent dependency. The shift from "helped" to "helper" is therefore essential to the consolidation and continuance of the religious experience. In addition, the new role provides an outlet for unresolved hostilities and aggression, turning these energies toward sin and sinners. The convert now has a group-approved channel for his negative feelings.

## How Effective Is This Approach?

It is the assumption throughout this book that no analysis of a religious phenomenon can be complete which omits the creative power of God. All healing depends on this power. This power is equally available to all religious approaches to alcoholism. Yet some are more effective than others. The question then is this: Why is one religious approach more or less adequate than another as a channel for the healing forces which are available in the universe? More specifically, how effective is a given approach in utilizing religious resources to produce and maintain sobriety?

The available evidence suggests that the mission approach is often effective in producing initial sobriety by arresting the "runaway symptom" aspect of alcoholism. For the year ending August 31, 1951, the mission described reported 5,824 "professed conversions." [14] Implied in the word "professed" is the recognition that not all conversions are sincere. One alcoholic interviewed told of drawing match sticks to see who was going to be saved so that the meeting would end and the food be served. Then there is the "mission stiff," a man who lives for years by exploiting one mission after another, becoming very skillful in going through the motions of a conversion. Even if one makes generous deductions for these phony conversions, there is still a sizable group which responds sincerely to mission therapy. This supposition is supported by those who have had extensive firsthand experience with missions. For example, a member of AA whose attitude toward missions was sharply critical admitted, "A hell of a lot are sobered up at such places."

When one considers the total number who attend mission meetings, the percentage of conversions is probably very low. Obviously many homeless alcoholics do not respond to mission therapy. The use of food and shelter as "bait" to get the alcoholic into the service enhances his negativism and resentment of religious institutions, making it more difficult to reach him with religious help. Further, the moralism of the mission in many cases stimulates the alcoholic's hostility and defensiveness rather than his sense of responsibility. Instead of cracking his defenses, the direct attack on him merely makes him more rigid. The attitude of general resentment toward missions, which exists on the Bowery, is in part a reaction to the battering of his ego-defenses to which the alcoholic must expose himself at the missions.

The mission conceptions of alcoholism and homelessness are grossly inadequate, overlooking nearly all that the social sciences have to tell about these two phenomena. The naïve moralism in this area can be maintained only by ignoring the facts that inebriety is as much a symptom as a cause of the disturbed interpersonal life of the alcoholic, that alcoholism is a complex disease involving physical, cultural, and sociopsychological as well as moral factors, and that homelessness is in itself a complex phenomenon, not the simple product of excessive drinking. The mission conception of the human situation—the nature of sin, free will, and responsibility—as it relates to alcoholism is philosophically and psychologically inadequate. If depth psychology has demonstrated anything, it has shown that human behavior, and especially neurotic behavior, is never simply a matter of freewill choosing between alternatives. Every act is conditioned by early life experiences which shaped the personality, by environmental factors in the present, and by historical contingencies. Untrammeled free will, in the sense that it is used in mission thought, does not exist. The concept is especially inapplicable to alcoholics. The more neurotic a person is, the more his actions are controlled by inner compulsions and the less freedom of choice he has.

It is the author's belief that many alcoholics sense, however vaguely, that their problem is not simply a matter of moral failure. The mission's treatment of their problems as moral derelictions must drive many alcoholics away from help by conveying a complete lack of understanding.

The mission's exclusivistic attitude toward its own approach lowers its level of initial effectiveness. Believing as it does that there is only one valid approach to alcoholism, it ignores the therapeutic resources available in psychotherapy, AA, and medicine. In a problem as complex as alcoholism this myopic view is particularly unfortunate.

What percentage of the alcoholics who receive initial sobriety are able to achieve long-term sobriety through this approach? It is impossible to cite reliable statistical evidence, for, as a mission staff member put it, "God keeps the records." Any mission can produce a group of cases of individuals who are known to have remained abstinent over a period of many years. But no one knows what percentage of the daily converts remain abstinent for a week, a month, a year, or for five years. Indications are that the percentage of long-term abstinence is low.

The fundamental reason why mission-induced sobriety is often impermanent is that homeless alcoholics are very difficult to help by any means. Beyond this, however, it is undoubtedly true that, in many cases, this approach does not deal with basic causes. Symptoms are shuffled—compulsive religion replacing compulsive drinking. Alcoholic converts often give one the impression that their solution is decidedly brittle—that they must keep very busy saving others or their own solution is likely to collapse. Too much fear and repression of negative feelings are employed. Too little self-understanding results from the experience. In many cases, the individual's basic problem, surface changes to the contrary notwithstanding, remains unaltered.

The emotionalism of the approach, through its basic means of operating, carries an inherent weakness. The clue to the weakness involved came to the writer from an alcoholic's autobiography in which he speaks of "sprees of salvation." [15] For some the mission experience is an emotional binge. Unless follow-up procedures are successful in maintaining the thrill, a spiritual hangover is apt to result. Out from under the influence of the leader and the surge of group emotion, the individual cools sufficiently to rue his actions and resent the manner in which he was swayed. Further, the primary emphasis on a sudden, dramatic experience leads to an underemphasis on the less dramatic process of growth following the conversion.

Another barrier to permanent sobriety lies in what might be called the "diminishing returns of authoritarianism." Recall that a pivotal conflict in many alcoholics is between their *need for* and *resentment of* dependency. Straus found that most of the men he interviewed both valued the security of the Skid Row institution and felt hostile toward it. This is the inner struggle. As the initial euphoria of the conversion experience and acceptance by authority dims, the old conflict begins to exert pressure. The essence of mission therapy is dependence—on God and on the mission. As the need to defy authority grows, the alcoholic reverts to his habitual defiance device—drinking. The authoritarianism of the mission approach was symbolized by one mission superintendent who paid his workers only fifty cents a week for their work because, as he put it, "that is all they can handle." Such benevolent authoritarianism is galling to the alcoholic who is hypersensitive to domination.

The fact that evangelistic aggressiveness is in some cases a product of disguised hostility is undoubtedly conveyed to the recent or prospective convert, to the detriment of permanent sobriety. Bowery resentment against mission evangelists is in part due to the feeling that they view men and are interested in them only as opportunities to save more souls.[16]

It would seem to be a safe assumption that a high percentage of converts are never assimilated into normal social living. Some of these remain "institutionalized," living at the mission and doing its work. They have capitulated to the dependent relationship. The fundamental tenet of benevolent authoritarianism—"Do what I say and I'll take care of you"—tends to make weaning from immature dependency difficult. Others slip back into the maelstrom of Skid Row. If the individual succeeds in leaving the Bowery and making the difficult break from homelessness, the mission has no structure for continuing the group support which he will continue to need.

On the positive side it is well to remember that the mission approach does help some alcoholics to long-term sobriety and reassimilation into society. The healing power of God *is* mediated through this approach to some degree. Even if a conversion involves the substitution of compulsive religion for compulsive drinking, there is a real gain for society. Further, the missions help ameliorate the grim lot of many Boweryites by their provision of physical essentials. The mission philosophy recognizes correctly that therapy for the low-bottom alcoholic must aim at returning him to society, must minister to his physical as well as his spiritual needs, and must involve some personality reorientation. Whether it achieves these goals in many cases or not, its goals are valid. The "halfway house" and fellowship groups for alcoholics are sound ideas that increase the likelihood that a given convert will make the grade.

It seems probable that the conversion experience may effect at least a partial reorganization of the personality in some cases. The director of research at Boston Hospital, Abraham Myerson, has written as follows: "Undoubtedly a Billy Sunday meets the deep needs of many alcoholics." [17] Back around 1930 L. Cody Marsh conducted an interesting experiment in group therapy with psychotics at Kings Park Mental Hospital on Long Island. His aim was to provide the "psychological equivalent of the revival on a secular level." He conducted "therapeutic classes" in which there was spirited group singing, rituals, inspirational lectures, and testimonials by patients who were making outstanding progress. After considerable experimentation, Marsh came to the conclusion that such group experiences had many positive results. Patients were motivated toward recovery, and there was a genuine release of emotion. There is undoubtedly an element of this kind of group therapy involved in the mission experience of some alcoholics. It is also well to remember that various missions differ somewhat in their approaches. Some are much more constructive than others.

An experiment at the Yale Plan Clinic for alcoholics has shown that homeless alcoholics are almost inaccessible to the usual out-patient clinic procedures. Many have passed the age when psychiatric therapies have marked effectiveness in reorienting character structure. Even if they were likely prospects for more basic therapies, the resources are not generally available at present. In the light of these circumstances, it is appropriate to be thankful for the degree to which the missions are successful in ameliorating the tragedy of Skid Row.

### The Salvation Army Approach to Alcoholism

The history of the Salvation Army is characterized by persistent concern with the practical application of religious ideals to the individual victims of social chaos. This practical orientation led the Army from its inception into the field of alcoholism. Firsthand experiences in the squalor of the London slums made the founder, William Booth, and his fellow Salvationists keenly sensitive to the problem. Booth agonized over the tragic plight of England's half-million drunkards, and their "effective deliverance" was the keystone of his earliest program of social reform, as outlined in his magnum opus, *In Darkest England and the Way Out*.[18] Through the years this movement has tried various strategies for helping alcoholics. In the early days "Drunkards' Rescue Brigades" were formed which went into the streets to help alcoholics.

For a while special "Inebriates' Homes" were established. At least two "Inebriates' Colonies" still exist, one on a Swedish island and the other on an island near New Zealand. A unique experiment in mass therapy for alcoholics was tried in New York just before the First World War. On a designated "Boozers' Day" as many as twelve hundred alcoholics were rounded up in Skid Row areas and transported on double-decker buses to a great hall where they were exposed to a gospel meeting on a grand scale. In 1914 the converts of these meetings banded themselves into a fraternal organization devoted to the reclamation of other drunkards. It was known by the intriguing title of "United Order of Ex-Boozers."

On the corner of Bowery and East Third Street is an attractive three-story $400,000 building housing the Bowery Corps of the Salvation Army. This is one of fourteen Skid Row corps maintained by the Salvation Army. It is a vital link in the Army's frontline attack on alcoholism. The importance which it attaches to this phase of its work is indicated by the excellent facilities provided.

The program, clientele, philosophy, and dynamics of the Bowery Corps are almost identical with those of the rescue mission. The program centers on the salvation meeting, which is almost indistinguishable from the gospel meeting described earlier. The program of physical aid and rehabilitation is quite similar. The dynamics of the conversion experience seem to be identical. One minor difference is that the regular salvation meeting is preceded by a "street meeting" in front of the headquarters. This is an abbreviated meeting designed to reach those who would not come to the indoor meeting and, if possible, attract them indoors.

A distinctive feature of the Bowery Corps program is Alcoholic Night, which is held once a week. This is a salvation meeting especially beamed at the problem drinker. Its existence shows a recognition of the fact that alcoholism is a problem which demands special attention. Originally, AA speakers were often included on Alcoholic Night. Under the present Corps leaders, AA speakers have been barred. One of the officers explained this restriction: "Some of the AA speakers would swear from our platform and say things not in line with our teaching. . . . Most of our institutions have AA groups. Here you're either saved or you're not."

It is significant that the Bowery Corps has recognized the need of new converts for a fellowship group. The Converts Club is such a group. Club members assist the officers in conducting meetings. One night a week there is a "fellowship meeting" open only to members of the Converts Club plus soldiers (regular members of the Salvation Army) and officers. This is the equivalent of the AA "closed meeting." Since most of the converts are alcoholics, the subject occupies the forefront of conversation at these meetings. Primarily because of the Converts Clubs, many converts continue to regard the Corps where they were "saved" as their spiritual home, even after they have become reestablished in society. At the Harbor Light Corps in Chicago, the Converts Club has grown to fiften hundred members. During one year they contributed over $10,000 toward Corps expenses.

In addition to the Skid Row corps, the Salvation Army has its Men's Social Service Centers which are spearheads in its approach to alcoholism. These are industrial homes which provide shelter, food, and employment for destitute men. During a recent year 21,265 men passed through the 111 such centers in this country. The Army is careful not to designate these as homes for inebriates, having discovered that they obtain better results with the more general label. The shops in the centers engage in repairing for resale huge quantities of used clothing and furniture. Major Peter Hofman, the head of one such center in Cleveland, reports, "We find our work program of immeasurable therapeutic value."

The centers conduct regular religious services which follow the familiar pattern. In addition, some of the centers have AA groups meeting on their premises. A man living at such a center may attend a gospel meeting one evening and an AA meeting the next. His rehabilitation may be due to a combination of influences, as in the case of Bob B.:

Bob B., 55, had been a machinist and stationary engineer. He had been drinking excessively for nearly twenty-five years and had spent eight years in various institutions taking cures. He came to Cleveland and placed himself under the care of the Salvation Army Social Service Center. The officers at the center tried various methods of approach, but still Bob B. could not stop drinking. They offered to introduce him to members of AA, but he refused flatly. Finally after a severe crisis and a terrific spree, he returned to the center completely licked. "For God's sake get me an AA man," he said. Within an hour he was in an AA hospital. After four days he was returned to the center. When he was able, the officers contacted an industrial plant and arranged for him to start work. Bob has been sober now for over two years, is active in an AA group in the plant where he works, and attends a Cleveland church. He returns to the center at least once a month to do personal work with the men there.[19]

Unlike the rescue mission which is usually an isolated entity, the Skid Row corps and the Social Service Center of the "Sally" (as the organization is known on Skid Row) are a part of a network of installations and services, the therapeutic resources of which are all available for helping alcoholics. The Family Service Departments, for instance, are staffed by officers who are trained social workers. These agencies do a great deal to help the families of alcoholics, seeking to "add to the casework technique the spiritual values that have played a major part in the development of the Army." [20] The officer in charge of a standard Skid Row corps may refer a converted alcoholic to Family Services, which may provide psychiatric therapy or otherwise aid in the reconciliation of the family.

## How Effective Is This Approach?

It is difficult to give an evaluation of an organization as large and as varied as the Salvation Army. In spite of its military, hierarchical structure, there are striking differences of approach from corps to corps, depending on the personality of the officer in charge. It would seem fair to say, however, that in general the Salvation Army represents evangelistic therapy at its best. There is good evidence that at least some of the corps have remarkable success in getting and keeping their clients sober.

Take the case of the late "Cap'n Tom" Crocker. As a young man Crocker was doing well as clerk in a Detroit court, that is, until his drinking got the best of him and he began to "borrow" funds entrusted to him by the court. Fired in disgrace, he was soon on Michigan Avenue, Detroit's Skid Row. Here he spent eight horrible years until finally, in the desperation of alcoholic delirium, he stumbled into a Salvation Army Rescue Corps and was soundly converted. He then joined the Army and went to work in that corps. Here his talent for helping alcoholics soon became apparent.

After a time the same judge who had fired him invited him to help as a court consultant for alcoholics. In 1948 Crocker was moved to the Army's Harbor Light Corps on West Madison Street in Chicago. The judge of a municipal court, having heard of his work in Detroit, invited him to help. This is how the plan worked. Each morning at court the alcoholics who seemed to have the best chance of making a comeback were culled out and turned over to Captain Crocker. (In six months he took 3,048.) They were taken to the Corps, where he talked to them in the following vein:

Remember you don't have to stay here. If you want to live like bums, I'm not going to stop you. Another thing, nobody has to do any phony praying to get help. I was on the street myself once, so I know a phony when I see one. But if you really want to lick Skid Row, I have the answer. We'll help you get a job and teach you how to use a fighting faith in God. But you'll have to supply the guts. [21]

The men who chose to do so were allowed to stay at the Harbor Light where they are exposed to conversion therapy and rehabilitation. The Chicago judge said of Crocker's work: "Right from the start he did a wonderful job." Of the 3,048 alcoholics mentioned above, 789 experienced conversion. Considering the type of low-bottom alcoholic involved, this proportion is strikingly high. Even more significant is the fact that 331 of the 789 converts returned to their homes.

Crocker was probably a uniquely successful worker with alcoholics, but there is evidence that other centers also enjoy considerable success. For instance the officer in charge of a rehabilitation center for homeless men in New York State writes, "We consider about 25 percent rehabilitated." What factors are responsible for the greater effectiveness of the Salvation Army, as compared to the rescue mission approach?

One factor of special importance is the greater degree of insight on the part of some Army leaders into the alcoholic's needs and behavior. Conceptions of alcoholism within the Army range from the moralism of the mission type to an attitude of enlightenment which regards alcoholism as a sickness. This enlightened wing is well represented among the higher officers of the organization and this, of course, is the basis of a realistic hope for more widespread effectiveness in the future. An interesting aside is the fact that William Booth himself regarded alcoholism as a disease, at least in some cases. He wrote: "After a time the longing for drink becomes a mania. Life seems insupportable without alcohol as without food. It is a disease often inherited, always developed by indulgence, but as clearly a disease as ophthalmia or stone." [22]

Booth was aware that there is a physical component in the disease and wrote of "treating the passion as a disease, as we should any other physical affection, bringing to bear upon it every agency, hygienic and otherwise, calculated to effect a cure." [23] Alcoholism has always been regarded by the Army as involving sin, but not in the naïve sense of being simply the personal failure of the individual alcoholic. Booth, in fact, spoke of gin as "the only Lethe of the miserable" and regarded the saloon as "a natural outgrowth of our social conditions." Society, he pointed out, "greased the slope down which these poor creatures slide to perdition." Society should therefore take responsibility for helping them.

Although some in the present-day Army do not share Booth's remarkable early insights, there seems to be a strong "back to Booth" movement in this regard. One hopeful indication of this is the fact that a number of key officers have attended the Yale (and Rutgers) School of Alcohol Studies. Another is the existence of a National Commission on Alcoholism. The commission, charged with the task of reviewing and improving the Army's approach to alcoholism, has come forward with a number of very progressive recommendations. For example:

The Commission recommends that the program of each Men's Social Service Center should be so arranged as to adequately meet the need of the alcoholic, and that it should include counseling services, medical and psychiatric services and a comprehensive recreational program under a trained recreational director. [24]

Because of his enlightenment regarding alcoholism, the Salvationist is often better able to convey genuine personal concern to the alcoholic. William James commented on this concern in his *Varieties:* "General Booth . . . considers that the first vital step in saving outcasts consists in making them feel that some decent human being cares enough for them to take an interest in the question whether they are to rise or sink." [25]

Another factor in the success of this approach is its well-developed system for consolidating the conversion experience. One aspect of this is the military structure of its organization. In World War II some men who had trouble with alcohol *before* and *after* had little trouble during their period of service because they found a security in the authoritarian army structure. The Salvation Army structure seems to serve the same function for some converts. They become a part of a worldwide military organization engaged in an all-out "war" against sin. They are made to feel uniquely useful (for saving others) and given a great mission. As soldiers or officers they must be absolutely obedient to their superiors. The organization provides for all their physical needs. There is a security in such a system that appeals to a dependent person. Further, wherever a Salvationist goes, he is a part of an in-group which requires absolute abstinence from alcohol from all its members.

Unlike the haphazard follow-up procedure of the mission, the Salvation Army has put its *modus operandi* into a systematic series of steps, similar to the "Twelve Steps" of AA:

1. The alcoholic must realize that he is unable to control his addiction and that his life is completely disorganized.

2. He must acknowledge that only God, his Creator, can re-create him as a decent man.

3. He must let God through Jesus Christ rule his life and resolve to live according to His will.

4. He must realize that alcohol addiction is only a symptom of basic defects in his thinking and living, and that the proper use of every talent he possesses is impaired by his enslavement.

5. He should make public confession to God and man of past wrongdoing and be willing to ask God for guidance in the future.

6. He should make restitution to all whom he has wilfully and knowingly wronged.

7. He should realize that he is human and subject to error, and that no advance is made by covering up a mistake; he should admit failure and profit by experience.

8. Since, through prayer and forgiveness, he has found God, he must continue prayerful contact with God and seek constantly to know His will.

9. Because The Salvation Army believes that the personal touch and example are the most vital forces in applying the principles of Christianity, he should be

made to work continuously not only for his own salvation but to help effect the salvation of others like himself.[26]

Although there is a real question as to how widespread the use of these steps is in actual practice, their existence indicates the greater concern of the Army with an orderly therapeutic process.

Another factor in the greater success of this approach is the eclectic spirit (as distinguished from the exclusivistic spirit of the mission) in which the resources of social work, psychiatry, medicine, and AA have been integrated with their basic evangelism. A remarkable exception to this was the case of Captain Tom Crocker who rejected the offer of a full clinical setup, complete with social workers and psychiatrist, in favor of the straight-evangelistic approach. His success probably indicates the crucial importance of the personality of the individual therapist, whatever his method. The bulk of Army leadership seems to believe that an effective approach to alcoholism must be a "team job." In keeping with its broader spirit, this leadership in general recognizes abstinence as a worthy goal of therapy. This is in contrast with mission thought which considered only complete salvation as a goal. One mission leader said, in fact, that it might be better for a man to stay drunk if he is going to hell anyway.

There are several weaknesses in Salvation Army thought and therapy which prevent it from being more effective with alcoholics. Some alcoholics, judging by the author's interviewees, deeply resent the authoritarian structure of the Army and the theologically disguised power-drives of certain officers. One of the author's interviewees, a convert of the Salvation Army, was sharply critical, comparing it to Roman Catholic authoritarianism. There is still a considerable amount of moralism concerning alcoholism among the rank and file Salvationists. There will probably always be a degree of "sin-sickness" in the Salvation Army conception of alcoholism. Although the benevolent authoritarian solution (in terms of organization and philosophy) may be the best available to many low-bottom alcoholics at the present, it is doubtful whether it contributes to the eventual spiritual growth and freedom of mankind. At the time when William Booth came forth with *In Darkest England* and his dictum that "society needs mothering," T. H. Huxley wrote a series of protest letters to the *London Times*, in which he pointed to the dangers of "blind and unhesitating obedience to unlimited authority" and showed that "mothering" adults does not contribute to their maturity and growth. One need only recall Erich Fromm's *Escape from Freedom* to be reminded that an authoritarian religious or political system may be attractive to neurotic people and yet not be psychologically constructive. This does *not* apply, of course, to the Salvation Army in general, but apparently there are some segments of its leadership which unwittingly use the Army system to encourage dependence, not independence, conformity to the system, not individual self-realization. We can agree with Huxley to the extent of recognizing that "mothering" adults is hardly the road to emotional and spiritual maturity.

In spite of these criticisms of the Salvation Army approach to alcoholism, it is still true that, compared with the rescue mission approach, the Army's is progressive and relatively more effective. In an area like Skid Row where so little is being done, it is not wise to be perfectionistic in one's judgments. Whatever the inadequacies of its approach, the "Sally" has been helping alcoholics for a long time. For nearly five decades it devoted itself to alcoholics when almost everyone else considered them hopeless. Concerning their work, Selden Bacon, of Rutgers, has said: "It has been criticized justifiably but nobody else is doing the job on Skid Row or has been doing it for the past fifty years." It is noteworthy that when the Yale Plan Clinic for alcoholics was first organized, it found it necessary to provide beds for some of its patients. After a vain search through the usual social agencies, the clinic leaders found one group that would help—the Salvation Army.

At its best, the Salvation Army approach can show highly significant results. Two Men's Social Service Centers in California received federal grants which permitted augmentation of their professional staffs and expansion of their rehabilitation programs. A follow-up study of 293 homeless alcoholics treated at the centers was done six months after they had left the centers. The approximately one hundred of these who were located showed the following improvement in their drinking patterns: 23 percent—great improvement; 25 percent—moderate improvement; and 53 percent—no improvement. In the area of vocational functioning, improvement was smaller: 18 percent —great improvement; 22 percent—moderate improvement; and 61 percent— no improvement. It must be pointed out that the educational level and past occupational attainment of this group were higher than typical samples of homeless alcoholics, improving their chances of recovery. However, the fact that nearly half of an above-average homeless group showed improvement in their drinking patterns and 40 percent showed improvement in their employment records is impressive indeed. Participation in some form of vocational counseling while in the programs was the factor most strongly correlated with later success.[27]

One must respect the Army for its devotion to low-bottom alcoholics, its willingness, in the words of its founder, to "net the sewers" for Christ. Without a doubt, a great host of reformed alcoholics must give thanks that in the Salvation Army's book there are no incurables. "A man may be down but he's never out" because "the word 'hopeless' isn't in God's dictionary!" This is the Army's dauntless faith.

## What We Can Learn from These Approaches

By way of summary, a listing of the practical implications which may be derived from these approaches will now be made. The degrees to which both do succeed indicate:

1. Low-bottom, homeless alcoholics can be helped by religious means.

2. Evangelistically oriented approaches which can induce a powerful emotional experience are able to help some alcoholics who perhaps could not be helped by more rational approaches. If a religious approach to alcoholism is to be effective, it must convey to the alcoholic the fundamental feeling of acceptance. For his sense of rejection by life, it must substitute an inner conviction that he has been accepted by life. (This is the experience of "salvation by grace through faith" which is so central in vital Protestantism.) Apparently the evangelistic approaches are able to be channels for his experience in some cases. Because of its general enlightenment, the Salvation Army is more successful than the rescue mission in this regard.

3. The "whole-man" type of therapy is essential with low-bottom alcoholics. This suggests referral of low-bottom alcoholics to those institutions especially equipped to help them physically as well as spiritually, and to provide residential facilities during treatment.

4. The importance of continuing support of converts by some type of fellowship group (such as Alcoholics Victorious or the Converts Club).

5. The necessity of substitute religious and group satisfactions to replace the satisfactions of alcohol.

6. The importance to their continued sobriety of putting converts to work helping others with like affliction.

7. Alcoholics have an advantage in helping other alcoholics. This is implicit in the fact that many of the most effective mission and Salvation workers are themselves ex-alcoholics. The Salvation Army explicitly recommends that, so far as possible, ex-alcoholics be used in such work, but it is also recognized that many nonalcoholic officers do commendable work with alcoholics.

8. Homelessness as well as alcoholism must be treated.

The relatively greater effectiveness of the Salvation Army approach suggests:

1. That referral of homeless alcoholics to a Salvation Army Corps is usually preferable to a rescue mission. There are great variations in the enlightenment and effectiveness of different missions and different Army corps. Some missions are more desirable than some Army installations, depending mainly on the leadership. However, one is more likely to find a more enlightened and effective approach in the Salvation Army than in the typical rescue mission.

2. That an adequate conception and understanding of alcoholism is a necessity in fashioning an effective therapy.

3. That the flexible, eclectic approach which utilizes the resources of all available agencies and therapies has a much better chance of succeeding than the exclusivistic evangelistic approach.

The failures and weaknesses of both approaches suggest:

1. The low-bottom alcoholics are an exceedingly difficult group to help because of their general disintegration and their exile from normal living.

2. The importance and difficulty of handling the dependency problem in a constructive fashion with alcoholics. Both these approaches resort to an authoritarian structure and philosophy as a means of helping alcoholics. Granting that this may be the best available solution for some alcoholics, one must still face the problem of the alcoholic's rebelliousness toward authority. The converts who become permanently attached to the authority-dependency system are the other side of the same problem.

3. The percentage of failures by both groups suggests the need for trying other than evangelistic approaches with homeless alcoholics. For the record it should be noted that there are other approaches which are being tried, including an experiment in the use of temporary institutionalization, Antabuse, and group psychotherapy with such alcoholics. (See Chapter 10 for a description of these approaches.) Further, AA has helped many low-bottom alcoholics. There are AA meetings in some municipal lodging houses, rehabilitation centers, and halfway houses focusing on "low-bottom" alcoholics. In several communities there are "Twelve Step Houses," and halfway houses have been organized and directed by the members of a certain AA group or groups. Although these are not affiliated with AA (the AA traditions do not permit official affiliation with any institution), their treatment is AA-oriented, and there is a close working relationship. In a sense, when such facilities reach members of the homeless alcoholic population, they constitute a kind of AA equivalent to the rescue mission. Recently, the use of the name "Twelve Step House" has been discouraged by AA, since it gives the erroneous impression that they are AA facilities.

## REFERENCES

1. Jerry Gray (pseud.), *The Third Strike* (New York and Nashville: Abingdon Press, 1949), p. 11.
2. Nels Anderson, *The Hobo* (Chicago: University of Chicago Press, 1923); E. H. Sutherland and H. J. Locke, *Twenty Thousand Homeless Men* (Philadelphia: J. B. Lippincott Company, 1936).
3. "Alcohol and the Homeless Man," *QJSA*, VII (December, 1946).
4. *Ibid.*, p. 385.
5. D. J. Pittman and C. W. Gordon, *Revolving Door, A Study of the Chronic Police Case Inebriate* (New Haven: Yale Center of Alcohol Studies, Publication Division, 1958).
6. *Ibid.*, p. 145.

7. Joan Jackson and Ralph Connor, "The Skid Road Alcoholic," *QJSA*, XIV (September, 1953), 468-86.

8. From an address by Thomas B. Richards, Executive Director, Men's Service Center and Halfway House, Rochester, N.Y., entitled "A.A. Oriented Halfway House and the Service Center," at the June, 1966, conference of the Association of Halfway House Alcoholism Programs of North America.

9. *Revolving Door, A Study of the Chronic Police Case Inebriate*, pp. 143-44.

10. C. M. Diserens and Harry Fine, *A Psychology of Music, The Influence of Music on Behavior* (Privately published, 1939).

11. "He Needs Your Helping Hand," A Bowery Mission brochure, 1949.

12. Jerry McAuley, *History of a River Thief* (New York: privately published, 1875).

13. "Alcohol and the Homeless Man," p. 399.

14. "What Does It Cost to Save a Man?" A Bowery Mission brochure, 1951.

15. Harold Maine (pseud.), *If a Man Be Mad*, p. 181.

16. This was the strong impression I got from talking to men on the Bowery and from the interviewees who had lived on the Bowery.

17. "The Treatment of Alcohol Addiction in Relation to the Prevention of Inebriety," *QJSA*, V (September, 1944), 197.

18. (London: International Headquarters of the Salvation Army, 1890.)

19. From a report presented by Major Peter Hofman at a symposium conducted by the Research Council on Problems of Alcohol (undated).

20. *Service, An Exposition of the Salvation Army in the U.S.*, p. 49.

21. Paul Robb, "Cap'n Tom—The Other Side of Skid Row," *Guideposts*, April, 1951.

22. *In Darkest England*, p. 48.

23. *Ibid.*, p. 186.

24. From the minutes of the Commission, May 16, 1946.

25. *The Varieties of Religious Experience*, p. 200, n. 1.

26. Presented at the Yale Summer School, 1943, by Envoy J. Stanley Sheppard and quoted in "The Salvation Army and the Alcoholic."

27. Lawrence Katz, "The Salvation Army Men's Social Service Center: I. Program," *QJSA*, XXV (1964), 324-32; "II. Results," *QJSA*, XXVII (1966), 636-47.

4

# The Emmanuel Movement—
# Religion Plus Psychotherapy

Whatever plan it followed, it would seem to be a calamity which the church need not add to her many other lost opportunities, to allow the cure and care of the drunkard to fall entirely into the hands of science, which admittedly needs all the help that faith in God can give in dealing with an ill so largely spiritual as the excessive use of alcohol.—Lyman P. Powell (1909)[1]

The Emmanuel Movement is of salient importance to one who would help alcoholics. Though it is no longer in existence as a movement, it is anything but a mere ecclesiastical museum piece. Its goals, working philosophy, understanding of man, conception of alcoholism, and even some of its methods are well worth emulating today. Here was perhaps the earliest experiment in a church-sponsored psychoreligious clinic. Here was the first pioneering attempt to treat alcoholism with a combination of individual and group therapy, the first attempt to combine the resources of depth psychology and religion in a systematic therapeutic endeavor. During its course the movement attracted many alcoholics and became well known for its success in treating them.

The movement came into being on a stormy evening in November, 1906, at the Emmanuel Episcopal Church in Boston, when the first "class" for those with functional illnesses was held. The guiding genius of the movement was a brilliant Episcopal clergyman named Elwood Worcester. His associate throughout most of its course was the Rev. Samuel McComb. Both men had had extensive graduate study in psychology and philosophy. Worcester had a Ph.D. from Leipzig where he studied under Wilhelm Wundt, founder of the first psychological laboratory, and physicist-psychologist-philosopher Gustav Fechner.

For a long time before 1906, Worcester had had a growing conviction that the church had an important mission to the sick, and that the physician and clergyman should work together in the treatment of functional ills. As a preliminary step he consulted several leading neurologists to ascertain whether such a project as he had in mind, undertaken with proper safeguards, would have their approval and cooperation. A favorable response was received, and the plan was launched.

The Emmanuel program of therapy consisted of three elements: group therapy administered through its classes, individual therapy administered by the ministers and staff at the daily clinic, and a system of social work and personal attention carried on by "friendly visitors." The growth of the movement was phenomenal. Three years after its inception, a California disciple could write:

The work, begun as a parish movement, has grown so that the local demands have overtaxed a large corps of workers while importunate calls from many cities in this and other lands for knowledge of the work, and pitiful calls for help from sick ones everywhere have to be put aside. . . . Meanwhile, in two years the work has been taken up by ministers of many faiths who see in the new movement a return to the faith and practice of the Apostolic Church. These . . . are finding new power in their work.[2]

This disciple also described the manner in which plans were being put into operation for training ministers who wanted to use the Emmanuel technique in their parishes, and for setting up the movement in large centers. By 1909 the movement had spread abroad and was represented in Great Britain by a committee under the title "Church and Medical Union." The Emmanuel clinic in Boston was deluged by patients. During one six-month period nearly five thousand applications were received by mail alone. Of these only 125 could be accepted. Hundreds of clergymen and many physicians were visiting Boston to study the methods. Influential physicians like Richard C. Cabot gave their support to the movement.

The first definitive book on the movement was *Religion and Medicine, The Moral Control of Nervous Disorders*,[3] which appeared in 1908. Demand for this book was so great that it went through nine printings in the year of publication. For twenty-three years Worcester continued as rector at Emmanuel. The movement continued to flourish there and in other parts of the country. The need for help was so great that often a line of patients cued outside the church. In 1929 Worcester resigned from his parish in order to give full time to the movement. A considerable sum of money had been received to carry on the work, so the movement was incorporated as the Craigie Foundation. In addition to the patients which he saw at his home, Worcester accepted many invitations to conduct week-long clinics and lecture series in prominent eastern churches. In 1931 Worcester and McComb produced *Body, Mind and Spirit*,[4] a book which showed clearly the development of their thought following the earlier books of the movement. For all practical purposes the Emmanuel Movement as such came to a close with Worcester's death in 1940.

It is noteworthy that three outstanding lay therapists for alcoholics in this country, Courtenay Baylor (who carried on the work at the Emmanuel Church for a time after Worcester's death), Richard Peabody, and Samuel Crocker, were products of the movement. A lay therapist is a nonmedical practitioner who specializes in helping alcoholics professionally. For a description of the method of treatment used by Courtenay Baylor, see Dwight Anderson's "The Place of the Lay Therapist in the Treatment of Alcoholics," *QJSA*, September, 1944.

### The Method of Treating Alcoholics

The Emmanuel classes were held once a week. In this group experience, alcoholics were lumped together with patients suffering from other functional illnesses treated by the clinic. A disciple of the movement, Lyman P. Powell, who had tried the technique in his own church, describes the procedure:

Any Wednesday evening from October until May you will find, if you drop in at Emmanuel Church, one of the most beautiful church interiors in the land filled with worshipers. . . . A restful prelude on the organ allures the soul to worship. Without the aid of any choir several familiar hymns are sung by everyone who can sing and many who cannot. A Bible lesson is read. The Apostles' Creed is said in unison. Requests for prayers in special cases are gathered up into one prayerful effort made without the help of any book. One Wednesday evening Dr. Worcester gives the address, another Dr. McComb, still another some expert in neurology or psychology. The theme is usually one of practical significance, like hurry, worry, fear, or grief, and the healing Christ is made real in consequence to many an unhappy heart.[5]

Other subjects discussed at the classes included: habit, anger, suggestion, insomnia, nervousness, what the will can do, and what prayer can do. The class was always followed by a social hour in the parish house. Reporting on the results of these group experiences, Powell says: "Though the mass effect of the service . . . is prophylactic, it is not at all uncommon for insomnia, neuralgia and kindred ills to disappear in the self-forgetfulness of such evenings."

The heart of the Emmanuel therapy was the clinic. Before a patient was accepted for treatment, he was required to have a careful diagnostic examination by a physician and, in some cases, a psychiatrist. If psychosis or organic pathology was disclosed, the individual was not accepted. If the disease appeared to be simply functional, the applicant was registered for treatment and directed to the rector's study. In the case of alcoholics, it was felt by Worcester that they should be seen every day, especially in early phases of their treatment. The new, nonalcoholic habits which the "psychotherapy" was implanting were to be treated as tender shoots until they took firm root. The patient was felt to need the daily support of the therapist until these new habits were firmly rooted, after which the therapist met the patient once or twice a week. Just how long the average alcoholic treatment took is not clear from the literature. No cases of alcoholism were listed among the quick cures—i.e., those effected in one or two sessions. A treatment period of at least several months seemed to have been involved in most of the cases cited.

The treatment itself included "full self-revelation" in which the patient poured out all the facts—physical, mental, social, moral, and spiritual—which might have any bearing on the sickness. This catharsis was felt to have a curative effect in itself often serving to "unlock the hidden wholesomeness" of the patient's inner life. The second phase of the treatment consisted of "prayer and godly counsel." This apparently was aimed chiefly at teaching the patient the techniques of prayer and helping him strengthen his spiritual life, rather than praying for the individual. The third phase was the use of relaxation and "therapeutic suggestion," the latter administered in some cases while the patient was under mild or deep hypnosis. It is noteworthy that although Worcester began by using hypnosis in many different types of difficulties, he eventually limited it to use with some alcoholics. Apparently he felt that the alcoholic needed the more powerful effect of hypnotic suggestion.

The patient is next invited to be seated in a reclining chair, taught to relax all his muscles, calmed by soothing words, and in a state of physical relaxation and mental quiet the unwholesome thoughts and untoward symptoms are dislodged from his consciousness, and in their place are sown the seeds of more health-giving thoughts and better habits.[6]

During the course of the movement there occurred a highly significant transition in the thought and methodology used. The change consisted of the gradual incorporation of psychoanalytic techniques, as Worcester began to learn of the dynamic psychology of Freud. This was accompanied by diminishing dependence on suggestion, the therapeutic device in vogue in the early days of the movement due to the influence of Worcester's European training with the physiological psychologists. Worcester stoutly defended the method of psychoanalysis. In 1932 he wrote: "I cannot agree with Stekel who advises that analysis be attempted in alcoholic cases only after other means have failed. I have found it helpful to begin my treatment with an analysis of childhood and youth." [7] Worcester used standard psychoanalytic techniques such as dream analysis and the probing of early memories as a part of his therapy.

107

Like others who have attempted to use such techniques with alcoholics, Worcester had encountered the problem of breaking the addictive cycle long enough to allow the therapy to have some effect. He developed his own unique solution which he felt was responsible for his success in keeping the patient sober while therapy got a foothold. The solution consisted of two parts: (a) making the analysis relatively brief; (b) combining analysis with his earlier method, therapeutic suggestion.

From insight gained through analyses of alcoholics, Worcester arrived at a profound understanding of alcoholism:

The analysis, as a rule, brings to light certain experiences, conflicts, a sense of inferiority, maladjustment to life, and psychic tension, which are frequently the predisposing causes of excessive drinking. Without these few men become habitual drunkards. In reality drunkenness is a result of failure to integrate personality in a majority of cases. Patients, however darkly, appear to divine this of themselves, and I have heard perhaps fifty men make this remark independently: "I see now that drinking was only a detail. The real trouble with me was that my whole life and my thought were wrong. This is why I drank."

He went on to say:

It is this consciousness of crippling dissociation of powers, of inhibition and repression which predisposes men to drink. In alcoholism in its early stages they find release of their faculties, the dissociation of their fears and inhibitions, as so many have said, "A short cut to the ideal." [8]

The aim of Emmanuel therapy was the reconstruction of the inner life so that the alcoholic could remain abstinent—Worcester had no illusions about alcoholics becoming social drinkers. There was a conviction that this reconstruction of personality must utilize the resources inherent in the person. Psychoanalysis was an important technique for releasing these resources.

While Worcester came to regard analysis as essential, he also observed that "few drunkards have been cured by analysis alone." He recognized that there are two levels to the alcoholic's problem—the underlying psychic conflicts and what he called the "habit itself," the effect on the nervous system of continued inebriety and the craving resulting therefrom. Analysis, he had found, had little effect on the latter, whereas suggestion often "supplied immediate help and permanent immunity from the return of the habit." His working hypothesis was that analysis relieved the psychic problems, "reducing the problem presented by the drunkard largely to a physical habit." Suggestion effected a strengthening of the will and a distaste for liquor so that the physical habit could be controlled.

Fortunately Worcester gives a sample of how he administered therapeutic suggestion to alcoholics:

Most alcoholic patients are highly suggestible and I have found few who failed to respond to the technique intended to induce mental repose and abstraction and physical relaxation. When the patient had attained this condition, I should address him in low monotones and offer him repeated suggestions, positive and negative, somewhat as follows: "You have determined to break this habit, and you have already gone _____ days without a drink. The desire is fading out of your mind, the habit is losing its power over you. You need not be afraid that you will suffer, for you will not suffer at all. In a short time liquor in any form will have no attraction for you. It will be associated in your mind with weakness and sorrow and sickness and failure. These thoughts are very disagreeable to you and you turn away from them. You wish to be free, you desire to lead a useful, happy life. Liquor is your enemy, but you are overpowering it and in a short time it will have no power over you at all." Then, as persons accustomed to depend on alcohol for sleep, when deprived of it, are apt to suffer from insomnia, I should add suggestions as to sleep and rest.[9]

In addition to the suggestion given by the therapist, the patients were taught autosuggestion so that their treatment could continue between sessions.

The third phase of the Emmanuel program consisted of the "friendly visitors," whose purpose was "to give to the environment of the patients care similar to that provided for their bodies by the physicians, and for their minds by the clergymen." [10]

Very often patients . . . need more than anything else a friend to show personal sympathy and interest, to encourage them, and to make sure they are following the prescribed directions. Victims of alcohol especially need this assistance to prevent relapse after the conclusion of treatment before they have acquired full self-reliance.[11]

Worcester and McComb reported that the system was very successful. They pointed out that alcoholics profited from becoming friendly visitors to other alcoholics who were beginning their treatment and that they made very effective visitors. One thinks immediately of the AA system of sponsorship and the principle of Twelfth Step work in this connection.

Our patients . . . need occupation to keep them from being self-centered. Clerical work has been found useful, but the best *results have come from sending them as friendly visitors to others* less fortunate. Not only does this have a good effect on the visitor, but new converts are proverbially enthusiastic, and *the alcoholic who finds himself released from his bondage is a most valuable assistant in encouraging and keeping up to the mark patients who have just begun.*[12]

The friendly visitor system was administered by a committee which included several trained social workers. Through this system the alcoholic was aided in finding employment and, if necessary, given a financial loan for a limited time while he readjusted his life. The friendly visitors often helped the patient readjust in the area of his family life.

Philosophically the Emmanuel Movement stands in contrast to the approaches studied previously. All of Worcester's writings reflect the conception that all life is permeated by the divine spirit, a belief which had its roots in the panpsychism of his teacher, Fechner. In discussing "Man's Life in God," Worcester wrote:

The secret of all spiritual religion is the union of the human soul with the divine soul, the belief that man's spirit and God's spirit are in their essence one. Without this belief man's relations with God become formal and external. The world, robbed of the haunting presence of the indwelling deity, becomes irreligious and profane.[13]

Because he held that the spirits of God and man are in their essence one, Worcester did not think of man as depraved or lost in sin. Man's spirit is a part of God; his realization and healing consist not in surrender to an external Power, but in the redirecting, releasing, and reeducating of the inherent powers—the hidden wholesomeness—of the spirit within. This positive conception of man contrasts vividly with mission and Salvation Army doctrines of the impotent, sinful man who can be saved only by surrender to an external Power. Rather than seeing man's beatitude in the abnegation of self, Worcester felt that the purpose of therapy was to help the person "find freedom and to discover a better way of life for himself." Prayer was considered an important means of releasing the divine energies within the soul trapped by one's neurosis.

Worcester felt that many religious workers in the field of healing had made the mistake of supposing that God can cure in only one way. God cures by many means. An act of healing, whatever the means used, is religious, since the divine spirit permeates all of life. The healing of bodies and spirits by medicine, rest, kindness, and self-understanding is just as much an act of God as healing which depends on prayer and suggestion. Further, healing of mind and spirit is not some sort of divine magic but is the divine spirit working through the orderly forces of nature. This general orientation provided the basis for a thoroughly cooperative relationship between the various healing disciplines involved in Emmanuel therapy.

In his view of man Worcester (in contrast to the previous approaches) held to a thoroughly unrepressive attitude toward man's desires and feelings. He recognized that the tendency, especially among Christian thinkers of the past, has been to deny these factors in human life. Concerning the conflict between reason and conscience on the one hand, and emotion and desire on the other, he writes:

The first step toward a possible solution of this fundamental problem of human life . . . is to recognize the legitimacy of both these elements of our being. In our disposition to do this lies whatever superiority we possess over former generations and our chief hope for the future.[14]

This handling of the problem reflects Worcester's psychoanalytic orientation.

The problem of responsibility, a key problem whenever religion and psychology meet, was handled in a realistic manner by this approach. Worcester could not have fallen into freewill moralism concerning alcoholism. For one thing, from the beginning of the movement, he recognized alcoholism as an illness. Further, his training in psychology had acquainted him with the role played by the subconscious mind in all behavior, including alcoholism. In 1908, long before the idea had become generally accepted, Worcester wrote:

We believe that there is a subconscious element in the mind and that this element enters into every mental process. Our daily life is influenced far more than the shrewdest of us suspect by the subconscious activity which is at work, exercising a selective power even in apparently accidental choices. Hence the real causes of our acts are often hidden from us.[15]

Worcester was convinced that "it is the subconscious that rules in the mental and moral region where habit has the seat of its strength." Further, he believed that therapeutic suggestion was able to influence and guide the subconscious mind into paths of health. As the influence of Freud grew in his thinking, the importance of subconscious factors was further enhanced.

There was another reason why Worcester avoided a moralistic conception of alcoholism and human ills in general. As early as 1908 he had recognized that the first six years of a child's life are the most important and determinative of his life. It was therefore relatively easy for him to accept the findings of the psychoanalysts in this area. In his last book he wrote: "The great psychological thinkers and workers, Freud, Jung, Adler, and others, were quick to perceive the significance of childhood as the chief determinant of life." [16]

### An Evaluation of This Approach

How effective was the Emmanuel therapy in breaking the addictive cycle and providing initial sobriety? And how successful was it in providing long-term sobriety? It is impossible to answer these questions with certainty, since the movement no longer exists and apparently there are no quantitative records. For several reasons, however, it seems probable that the Emmanuel movement enjoyed a relatively high degree of success in providing at least temporary sobriety. We know that the Emmanuel workers accepted for treatment only those who wanted to stop drinking and who came on their own volition. AA experience has shown that these mental attitudes on the part of the alcoholic are essential prerequisites for successful therapy. These Emmanuel requirements meant that only patients who were "at bottom" and who would accept responsibility in asking for help would be treated. Second, we know that the Emmanuel therapists had the advantage over "straight-religious" approaches of having medical assistance—a valuable aid in effecting initial sobriety. Third, we know that suggestion administered as in this therapy by a person with status, exercises a powerful control over behavior. This is especially true in the case of insecure and dependent people, such as alcoholics frequently are. Fourth, we know from various reports that suggestive therapy has produced impressive results with alcoholics. Prior to the Emmanuel movement, Charcot treated 600 cases over a twenty-year period and reported 400 "cures." Tokarsky of Moscow reported that 80 percent of the 700 alcoholics he had treated were cured, and Wiamsky of Saratow claimed about the same percentage of cures out of the 319 cases he treated. Unfortunately, no definition of "cure" was given in these reports.[17]

It seems probable that many of those who gained temporary sobriety through Emmanuel therapy stayed sober for an extended period. The fact that Worcester and McComb over the years acquired a reputation for success in treating alcoholics indicates that many of their patients must have stayed abstinent. In 1932 they were able to report: "It is well known that we have obtained as good and as permanent results in these fields as any other workers." If most of their cures had been short-lived, they would not have enjoyed this reputation.

Several cases are presented in Emmanuel literature which show that sobriety extended over long periods. Worcester tells, for instance, of treating a very difficult alcoholic with homicidal tendencies who had been given up as hopeless by the doctors. At the time of writing, the man had enjoyed seven years of sobriety. Worcester reported having little success in treating "dypso-maniacs"—apparently the equivalent of periodic alcoholics—as contrasted with "ordinary alcoholics" (steadies). In spite of this, he tells of successfully treating a woman "dypsomaniac," who had been judged hopeless by two psychiatrists. Worcester writes: "As I have kept in contact with this woman, I can say that she was cured in the sense that for twenty-two years there has been no return of the fatal cycle, nor has a drop of liquor passed her lips." [18] That a good deal of success was enjoyed by the movement, even in cases where relapses occurred, is shown by Samuel McComb's statement: "There are other cases of alcoholism where a relapse has occurred, but it has only been temporary; and fathers and sons have been restored to their families with what a joy only those who have felt the curse of intemperance can realize." [19]

Writing in 1931, the Emmanuel leaders could report, "On the whole our successes have been far more frequent than our failures." [20] This statement was made with the perspective of twenty-five years of experience in the movement.

There are many points at which the Emmanuel approach was superior in theory and practice to the evangelistic approaches. While recognizing the importance of group experience, the Emmanuel approach also supplied individual psychotherapy. This combination of individual and group therapy represents an obvious advance over the mass evangelistic approaches. As the Emmanuel approach came to incorporate psychoanalytic procedure in its therapy, it dealt to some degree with the underlying causes of inebriety, rather than simply relieving or changing symptoms. Worcester's observation that alcoholics respond best to relatively brief therapy concurs with modern findings.

The Emmanuel approach achieved an integration of the healing resources of medicine, psychology, social work, and religion. In the Salvation Army we saw a certain eclecticism in which the resources of other professions were drawn on as supplements to the basic religious approach. In contrast, the Emmanuel workers saw medicine, psychology, and social work as *integral parts* of a total "religious" approach to healing. The medical and psychiatric screening of patients not only protected the church clinic but also improved the possibility of favorable outcome.

The goal of Emmanuel therapy—to promote the freedom and growth of the individual by releasing inner resources, in contrast to authority-centered approaches,—is in keeping with the healthy needs of the alcoholic. We have seen that alcoholics often have neurotic needs which encourage the formation of immature dependency relationships. Their healthy needs are for increased self-esteem and constructive autonomy. In contrast to previously studied approaches, which encouraged dependency and surrender to authority, Emmanuel thought encouraged independence and growth in responsibility. Worcester shunned the use of exhortation and persuasion as being "wholly out of place in treatment." They may provoke opposition on the patient's part, or "they may even be dangerous, because they impose the teacher's personality and philosophy on the patient instead of allowing him to find freedom and to discover a better way of life for himself." [21]

Instead of depending on religious thrill and a sudden, dramatic conversion, Emmanuel therapy relied on the gradual type of religious change. We have discussed the limitations of religious thrill as a means of helping alcoholics. It seems clear that Emmanuel's psychotherapy offered greater possibility of lasting personality change than was true in the evangelistic approaches. The Emmanuel workers recognized that evangelistic approaches have value for some alcoholics; they also saw that many alcoholics cannot be reached by those approaches. Powell, an Emmanuelite, wrote: "While men like Jerry McAuley and the Salvation Army leaders have done something, the emotional motive which they use does not avail in every case." [22]

The Emmanuel approach recognized fully that the alcoholic needs individual and group support during his recovery. The "friendly visitor" system combined the principle of AA sponsorship with the resources of a social caseworker. Undoubtedly this friendly, individual attention and help were major factors in the success of the approach.

The approach was well equipped to help the alcoholic find real self-acceptance and release from guilt. Its superiority lay in its splendid conception of alcoholism and its understanding of the psychodynamics of human behavior. Twenty-seven years before AA began, this approach was regarding alcoholism as a disease to be treated like other functional diseases. In this early period there was a degree of moralism connected with the conception of all functional illnesses. The influence of psychoanalytic concepts gradually removed this moralism, revealing the manner in which behavior is conditioned by early experiences and by unconscious forces which are not subject to the will.

The therapy sought to reduce the alcoholics' guilt rather than to enhance it as in the previous approaches. It achieved this by its disease conception of alcoholism and its positive conception of man, allowing the therapist to establish a nonjudgmental relationship with the patient. By means of his acceptance of the patient, the therapist was able to help the patient achieve self-acceptance. Self-acceptance, it is well to remember, implies a sense of being accepted by life. This the Emmanuel therapist was well equipped to convey because of the positive, life-affirming philosophy and theology of the movement. There is a sense, of course, in which the experience of "accepting oneself as being accepted," to use Paul Tillich's description of salvation, results from any psychotherapy which is successful. Emmanuel therapy apparently was frequently able to convey this experience. When guilt is reduced, the energies previously employed in the guilt and self-punishment process are freed and made available for therapeutic ends.

Forgiveness was achieved in Emmanuel therapy not by petitioning an authoritarian Deity, but by modifying the unmerciful superego of the patient. McComb wrote as follows concerning what he called the "New England or Quaker conscience": "The great need here is for a new conception of God. The mind must be taught to rest in his fatherly love, in his tenderness and grace. . . . By the constant presentation to the mind of these ideas the conscience is gradually lightened of its morbidity and the will is set free to act." [23]

Rather than concerning itself with specific "sins," the Emmanuel approach focused attention on the underlying causes of these symptoms—namely, the sick personality. This also aided in reducing the alcoholic's guilt load. In addition, the psychoanalytic concept that alcoholic behavior is determined in large measure by subconscious factors (beyond the realm of willpower) had a tremendous guilt-reducing effect. The positive conception of man and the recognition that his drives and feelings are not inherently evil both contribute to healthy self-acceptance on the part of the patient. Likewise the conception of the healing process as resulting from the release of inner resources (as contrasted with external divine intervention) tends to enhance self-esteem by enabling the patient to feel a sense of achievement in his improved condition. It also serves to keep the responsibility for healing with the patient. The alcoholic's inferiority is reduced not by identifying with a powerful authority-figure, but by becoming aware of his "higher and diviner self" which is his most real self.

The Emmanuel workers recognized clearly that religious symbols can be employed in ways that promote guilt and neurosis as well as in ways that promote maturity and health. They threw their influence behind the latter. As a result we do not find the emphasis on fear and guilt which was present in the previous approaches.

With only minor changes, the mature Emmanuel concept of alcoholism would be acceptable in the most enlightened circles today. In one way it was superior even to the AA conception. Because of its orientation in depth psychology, it recognized that the selfishness and egocentricity of the alcoholic are actually symptoms of deeper problems and conflicts. This is in contrast to the AA position which does not seem to recognize the symptomatic nature of selfishness. (It should be added that many individual AA's, particularly those who have had psychotherapy, do recognize the nature of selfishness.) Because of deeper understanding of personality, the Emmanuel therapy was beamed more accurately at the roots of alcoholism than is the AA therapy. Its use of psychoanalytic techniques in its therapy provided it with the practical means of getting at these underlying causes. Such techniques are not present to any great degree in AA. The Emmanuel approach was superior to AA in that it made individual as well as group therapy available to the alcoholic. Further, because of its psychoanalytic grounding, it was less repressive than AA in its attitude toward the self.

In spite of its areas of theoretical superiority, it seems probable that from a practical standpoint, Emmanuel was less effective than AA. Its therapy was less adequate than AA in that it lacked an all-alcoholic support group. Further, it did not capitalize fully on the recognition that helping other alcoholics helps the alcoholic patient to stay sober himself. Nor did it capitalize on its recognition that one alcoholic has a natural entree to another. Even though

115

its goal was nonauthoritarian, its therapy was dispensed by an authority figure. It lacked the advantage of AA's self-help orientation, particularly the feeling on the part of the AA members—"We're licking this thing ourselves" and "This is our fellowship." Since the Emmanuel approach was dependent on professionals, the number of alcoholics who could be helped was quite limited as compared to AA.

The central weakness of the Emmanuel approach to alcoholism would seem to be the use of suggestion. Although Worcester's therapeutic aim—increasing the freedom of the patient—was psychologically sound, his method actually defeated his aim. The thing that was not recognized was that suggestion is an essentially authoritarian tool, that it substitutes the authority of the "suggester" for the autonomy of the individual, thus establishing an unconstructive dependence on the therapist. The Emmanuel workers did not realize that the "strengthening of the will" which they observed in alcoholic patients was actually the result of the projection of their authority on the patient. Carl R. Rogers includes suggestion under "Methods in Disrepute" in his discussion of counseling. He writes:

The client is told in a variety of ways, "You're getting better," "You're doing well," "You're improving," all in the hope that it will strengthen his motivation in these directions. Shaffer has well pointed out that such suggestion is essentially repressive. It denies the problem which exists, and it denies the feeling which the individual has about the problem.[24]

It should be noted that suggestion was generally accepted as a therapeutic device during the early period of the Emmanuel movement. In fact, medical schools were teaching the technique as a healing tool. As we have seen, the Emmanuel workers put decreasing emphasis on suggestion as their knowledge of psychoanalysis increased. Though their methodology became relatively less repressive, it would seem probable that the effectiveness of their psychoanalytic procedures must have been vitiated in part by the continued use of suggestion.

Worcester was insightfully accurate in recognizing the two levels of alcoholism and in his belief that something had to be done to hold the addiction in check while psychotherapy sought to deal with underlying causes. Unfortunately, the device he employed (suggestion) impeded the effectiveness of the psychotherapy.

Why did this movement not survive? First, it was centered around two strong and unusual personalities. There were few clergymen with the kind of training and general qualifications possessed by Worcester and McComb. Apparently the movement was not successful in training younger men to carry on the tradition. Second, the fundamental methodological weakness of the movement may have contributed to its demise. The continued use of a repressive device like suggestion over a long period of time may have resulted in diminishing enthusiasm and decreasing therapeutic return. Of course there is a sense in which the movement continues in its influence on the clergymen whose interest in psychotherapy and healing was stimulated by their contacts with the movement, its literature, or others who had felt its influence.

## What We Can Learn from the Emmanuel Approach

The Emmanuel Movement was the first organized attempt to apply the joint resources of psychology and religion to the problem of alcoholism. Its degree of success suggests the possibilities that lie in this direction. It was the first approach to understand and seek to treat the underlying causes of alcoholism. In spite of its methodological error, its general orientation was positive and life-affirming, so much so that its critics labeled it "hedonistic." The practical values as well as the psychological validity of this outlook have been discussed in our evaluation.

This approach provides an impressive demonstration of the importance in dealing with alcoholics of one's conception of alcoholism and the human situation in general. In its understanding of the psychodynamics of alcoholism and its incorporation of psychoanalytic insights and methods, this approach was decades ahead of its time. In these regards, as in its handling of the problem of guilt and responsibility, the Emmanuel Movement has a great deal to teach many religious leaders today. Among other things it provides an example of the way in which a psychoanalytic orientation can mediate the acceptance of God, thus enhancing self-acceptance. As we have seen, it did this, not by encouraging surrender to an external diety, but by resolving inner conflict, thus releasing God-given resources within the personality. The resolving of inner conflict was achieved through psychoanalytic techniques which were based on a recognition of the dynamic significance of the unconscious and by an actual accepting relationship with one of God's children, the therapist.

The Emmanuel Movement pioneered in the field of church-sponsored psychotherapeutic clinics. Its story should cause organized religion to reflect on its general role in a society plagued by widespread neurosis and inadequate facilities for treatment. Startled by the overwhelming influx of patients, the Emmanuel leaders wrote:

The mere fact that disinterested clergymen and physicians were willing to be consulted . . . has brought persons to us in such numbers that, although we have a good-sized staff, it is impossible for us to see one person in five for a single conversation. This one fact should cause the Church to reflect. Why should there not be adequate assistance for men and women who desire and need personal, moral and spiritual help? [25]

117

Although this was written many years ago, the question is still relevant and pressing in our day. A partial answer is emerging in the pastoral counseling movement and the two hundred or so church-related counseling services which have been established in recent years.[26]

## REFERENCES

1. *The Emmanuel Movement in a New England Town* (New York: G. P. Putnam's Sons, 1909), p. 126.

2. Thomas P. Boyd, *The How and the Why of the Emmanuel Movement, A Handbook on Psycho-Therapeutics* (San Francisco: The Emmanuel Institute of Health, 1909), p. xiv.

3. (New York: Moffat, Yard and Co., 1908.)

4. (Boston: Marshall Jones Company, 1931.)

5. *The Emmanuel Movement in a New England Town*, pp. 10-11.

6. *Ibid.*, pp. 12-14.

7. *Body, Mind and Spirit*, p. 229. Used by permission of Gordon S. Worcester.

8. *Ibid.*, p. 232.

9. *Ibid.*, pp. 234-35.

10. Elwood Worcester and Samuel McComb, *The Christian Religion as a Healing Power* (New York: Moffat, Yard and Co., 1909), p. 125.

11. *Ibid.*, pp. 128-29.

12. *Ibid.*, p. 128. [Italics supplied.]

13. *The Living Word* (New York: Moffat, Yard and Co., 1908), p. 105-6.

14. *Body, Mind and Spirit*, p. 203.

15. *Religion and Medicine*, pp. 97-98.

16. *Making Life Better* (New York: Charles Scribner's Sons, 1933), p. 197.

17. *The Emmanuel Movement in a New England Town*, pp. 113-14.

18. *Body, Mind and Spirit*, p. 229.

19. "The Healing Ministry of the Church," *Religion and Medicine Publications*, No. 1 (New York: Moffat, Yard and Co., 1908), p. 25.

20. Quoted by Francis W. McPeek in "The Role of Religious Bodies in the Treatment of Inebriety in the United States," *Alcohol, Science and Society*, p. 416.

21. *Body, Mind and Spirit*, p. 118.

22. *The Emmanuel Movement in a New England Town*, p. 113.

23. McComb, "The Healing Ministry of the Church," pp. 16-17.

24. *Counseling and Psychotherapy* (Boston: Houghton Mifflin Co., 1942), p. 21.

25. *The Christian Religion as a Healing Power*, p. 10.

26. The American Association of Pastoral Counselors is the professional organization which establishes standards of training for pastoral counseling specialists and for the operation of pastoral counseling centers.

# 5

# Alcoholics Anonymous—
# Our Greatest Resource

If I were asked to give my strongest impression resulting from the study which underlies this book, it would be this: *In all the dark history of the handling of the problem of alcoholism, the brightest ray of hope and help is Alcoholics Anonymous!* There are two corollaries to this: (1) AA is the most effective referral resource available today. (2) It behooves everyone concerned with helping alcoholics to be thoroughly familiar with AA.

The fact is that, because of AA, some 375,000 alcoholics,[1] a high proportion of whom had been labeled "hopeless" by their families, friends, doctors, and clergymen, are today living constructive, happy lives without alcohol. The existence of 375,000 success stories is evidence enough that here is something of momentous significance. AA is not the complete answer to the problem of alcoholism. Nor does it claim to be. Like any approach to any human problem, it has its inadequacies. Everything considered however, AA offers the best referral resource for these reasons: (1) It is available in almost every community in our country. (2) It is free. (3) It has a higher percentage of success in achieving sobriety than any other approach, religious or nonreligious.

### How AA Began and Grew

A minister of my acquaintance calls AA "a modern chapter in the book of the Acts." He has been as close to AA as almost any clergyman in the country and, therefore, has a wide experience on which to base his judgment. Whether or not one accepts his description as entirely accurate, it is impossible to gainsay that AA—past and present—provides a thrilling spiritual story. It is the story of how a group of men and women who had been consigned by society to its scrap heap, banded themselves together and conquered the "unconquerable" craving, becoming an inspiration to their fellow men. Two names dominate the early chapters of this story—Bill W. and Dr. Bob—

119

founder and co-founder of AA. Bill W. is a lanky, homespun Vermonter. He was born in East Dorset, Vermont, in 1895. His father was owner-operator of a marble quarry.[2] When Bill was ten, his parents were divorced, and he went to live with his grandparents in the same town. His schooling, which had started in "a one-room schoolhouse with a chunk stove" was continued at a boarding school in Manchester and then at Burr and Burton Seminary and Military College in Norwich. The First World War interrupted his college career in the third year. He was married just before he went overseas.

While in the army Bill began to drink. In mentioning the reason for his previous abstinence he says, "I had been warned . . . too many people had died of it." Coming out of the army, he faced a difficult adjustment. As he puts it, "I had been an officer and thought I was pretty good. I came out and all I could get was a clerk's job with the New York Central. I was such a damn poor clerk that I got fired at the end of a year." After a while he got a job as an investigator for a security company on Wall Street. He completed a night-school course at Brooklyn Law College but never received the diploma because he was intoxicated and did not attend the graduation. In retrospect he comments whimsically, "Wasn't that just like a drunk?"

By the late twenties Bill and Lois, his wife, had saved some money. Bill began to dabble in stocks with considerable success. Meanwhile his drinking was mounting steadily. When the crash came in '29, Bill found himself $60,000 in debt. He drank himself out of an opportunity for a comeback. By 1932 Bill was in bad shape physically, and his wife had to go to work to support them. From 1932 to 1934 he went downhill at an "awful rate." At the end of a series of hospitalizations, a medical specialist in alcoholism, William Silkworth, confided to Lois that her husband was "hopeless." He explained that Bill's attempt to adjust his neurosis by means of alcohol had lead to an obsession which condemned him to go on drinking and, further, he had a physical sensitivity—an "allergy"—to alcohol which guaranteed that he would go insane or die, perhaps within a year. Bill points out that this concept of the fatal power of the disease, provided by Silkworth, became in AA a powerful deflationary tool, shattering the ego at depth and laying the subject open for conversion.

Meanwhile an alcoholic named Roland H., the director of a large chemical company, had been seeking help from the famous Swiss psychoanalyst, Carl Gustav Jung. Jung had told him that nothing but a religious conversion could help his alcoholism. Seeking desperately for this he returned to America, came under the influence of the Oxford Group Movement,[3] and was "changed." Roland and another Oxford Grouper went to see an alcoholic named Ebby T., to whom they were able to pass on the Oxford philosophy and experience.

Bill W., having received what amounted to a death sentence from the doctor, maintained three months of fear-inspired sobriety. As is true of almost all such sobriety, it was limited in duration. One day as Bill sat half-drunk in the kitchen of his Brooklyn home, Ebby T., whom he had known for a long time, paid him a visit. Ten years later Bill could say, "It was perhaps right there on that very day that the Alcoholics Anonymous commenced to take shape." [4]

Bill noticed immediately that there was something different about his friend, so he asked, "Ebby, what's got into you?" Ebby replied, "Well, I've got religion." This came as a shock to Bill since he had thought Ebby, like himself, to be a confirmed agnostic. Knowing Bill's prejudices, Ebby went on to say, "Well, Bill, I don't know that I'd call it religion exactly, but call it what you may, it works." This aroused Bill's curiosity. He insisted that Ebby explain. So Ebby told of his encounter with the Oxford Groupers:

Some people came and got hold of me. They said, "Ebby, you've tried medicine, you've tried religion, you've tried change of environment . . . and none of these things has been able to cure you of your liquor. Now here is an idea for you. . . . Why don't you make a thorough appraisal of yourself? Stop finding fault with other people. . . . When have you been selfish, dishonest . . . intolerant? Perhaps those are the things that underlie this alcoholism. And after you have made such an appraisal of yourself, why don't you sit down and talk it out with someone in full and quit this accursed business of living alone? . . . Why don't you take stock of all the people . . . you have hurt—all of the people who annoy you, who disturb you. Why don't you go to them and make amends; set things right and talk things out, and get down these strains that exist between you and them? . . . Why don't you try the kind of giving that demands no reward? . . . Seek out someone in need and forget your own troubles by becoming interested in his." [5]

Then Ebby told Bill how he asked the Groupers where religion came into the picture; they had replied: "Ebby, it is our experience that no one can carry out such a program . . . on pure self-sufficiency. One must have help. Now we are willing to help you . . . but we think you ought to call upon a power greater than yourself, for your dilemma is well-nigh insurmountable. So, call on God as you understand God." [6] Those who are acquainted with AA will see many of the principles which later became central in that group inherent in the Oxford Groupers' approach to Ebby.

Ebby was careful not to force any of his views on Bill. He merely said that he was leaving the ideas that had helped him with the hope that they might help his friend. In spite of Ebby's permissive approach, Bill was irritated by this blow to his pet philosophy of self-sufficiency. So he continued to drink. But he couldn't help turning Ebby's words over in his mind. At last, in his desperation, the question hit him: "Well, how much better off am I than a cancer patient? But a small percentage of those people recover and the same is true of alcoholics." So Bill W. became willing to do anything that might help him get rid of the obsession that had condemned him to death. He was at his "bottom"—open to help.

In order to get the alcohol out of his system so that he could think the whole thing through, Bill had himself admitted to Towne Hospital in New York City. When Ebby came to visit him, Bill's first thought was, "I guess this is the day he is going to try to save me. Look out." (Incidentally, this is the way many alcoholics feel when approached by those with religious ideas.) But Ebby skillfully evaded Bill's defenses, talking only in general terms until Bill himself asked him to review his story.

After Ebby left the hospital that day, there occurred what is known semi-facetiously in AA as Bill's "hot flash." Here is his description of what occurred:

When he was gone, I fell into a black depression. This crushed the last of my obstinacy. I resolved to try my friend's formula, for I saw that the dying could be openminded. Immediately on this decision, I was hit by a psychic event of great magnitude. I suppose theologians would call it a conversion experience. First came an ecstasy, then a deep peace of mind, and then an indescribable sense of freedom and release. My problem had been taken from me. The sense of a Power greater than myself at work was overwhelming, and I was instantly consumed with a desire to bring a like release to other alcoholics. It had all seemed so simple—and yet so deeply mysterious. The spark that was to become Alcoholics Anonymous had been struck.[7]

Bill called William Silkworth to his bed and tried to tell him what had happened. The doctor said he had heard of such experiences but had never seen one. Bill asked, "Have I gone crazy?" to which he responded, "No, boy, you're not crazy. Whatever it is, you'd better hold on to it. It's much better than what you had just a few hours ago."

When Bill came out of the hospital, he felt very grateful to the Oxford Group. So he attended Group meetings and worked with alcoholics at the Calvary Mission, telling about his religious experiences and trying to induce it in them. The Calvary Mission, a result of the Oxford Group impetus in the Calvary Episcopal Church of New York, was a rescue mission. It represents a significant exception to the dominant Oxford Group interest in the upper classes. Bill and his wife worked tirelessly, day and night. Often their Brooklyn home was filled with alcoholics in various stages of sobriety.[8] Silkworth continued to encourage Bill in his efforts and to provide him with numerous opportunities to work with alcoholics. In spite of everything, at the end of six months, Bill had sobered only one person—himself. But a key AA principle was growing from his failures, for he had learned, as he put it, "that working with other alcoholics was a powerful factor in sustaining my own recovery." [9]

Six months after his conversion Bill accepted a job opportunity in Akron.

Just when the venture seemed certain to succeed, the whole thing collapsed. Overwhelmed by the failure, Bill had one "comforting" thought: "With a fifth of gin, I could be a millionnaire—at least for a while." [10] He wondered how God could be so mean to him, after all the good he had done for Him. Suddenly he realized that he might get drunk again, unless he found another alcoholic to talk to.

From the church directory in the hotel lobby, Bill chose the name of a clergyman at random. Over the phone he told him of his urgent need to work with another alcoholic. The clergyman gave him a list of ten Oxford Groupers and suggested that surely one of them would know an alcoholic. The first nine calls proved to be of no avail, but on the tenth he was greeted by a warm southern voice, a nonalcoholic Oxford Grouper who insisted that she understood how he felt and that he should come to her home at once. This lady, Henrietta S., arranged for Bill to meet Dr. Bob S. at her home the next day. The next day—the day after Mother's Day in 1935—the fellowship of AA was born.

Dr. Bob had had a long series of terrifying bouts with alcohol. He had been hospitalized repeatedly and was losing his medical practice. In 1933 he had begun attending Oxford Group meetings, seeking help. He sought the counsel of two prominent ministers who were active in the movement. For two years he did everything they and the other Groupers suggested. He read the Bible daily, prayed intensely, and attended church regularly. In spite of everything, his drinking increased.

The meeting of Bill and Dr. Bob illustrates another cardinal principle of AA—the fact that an alcoholic has a natural advantage in establishing rapport with another alcoholic. When Dr. Bob appeared at Henrietta's door, she discreetly whisked him and Bill off to the library. Bob's first words were, "Mighty glad to meet you, Bill. But it happens I can't stay long; five or ten minutes at the outside." Bill laughed and observed, "Guess you're pretty thirsty, aren't you?" Bob replied, "Well, maybe you do understand this drinking business after all." Their first talk lasted for hours.

Out of Bill's desperation the AA principle of enlightened self-interest was taking shape. He explained to Dr. Bob how much he needed him if he was to stay sober. Bill showed Dr. Bob the missing ingredient in his solution—that "faith without works is dead." And so the two men sought another alcoholic to help. The first case, supplied by a neighboring minister, was unsuccessful. (Fifteen years later this "unsuccessful" prospect appeared at the funeral of Dr. Bob, a successful member of AA.) Then they tried a prominent Akron lawyer who had lost nearly everything through alcoholism. They found him in a city hospital, chained to a bed. They explained the medical nature of his sickness, and of their own drinking and recoveries. The man on the bed shook his head, "Guess you've been through the mills, boys, but you

123

never were half as bad off as I am. For me it's too late. I don't dare to go out of here. Alcohol has me, it's no use." This feeling of being worse than anyone else is common among alcoholics. Bill and Dr. Bob made no attempt to argue away the man's hopelessness.

They returned to the hospital the next day. When they entered the man's room, he cried to his wife who was visiting him:

> Here they are. They understand. After they left yesterday I couldn't get what they told me out of my mind. I laid awake all night. Then hope came. If they could find release, so might I. I became willing to get honest with myself, to square my wrongdoings, to help other alcoholics. The minute I did this I began to feel different. I knew I was going to get well.[11]

This man rose from his bed never to drink again. He became AA number three. And so AA began to grow.

After a few months of working with Dr. Bob in Akron, Bill returned to New York and began to apply the principles there. There followed the years of trial and error from which AA proper emerged. For a time the, as yet, nameless movement was connected with its parent, the Oxford Group. Gradually in both New York and Akron, it became an independent entity. AA had learned much from the Oxford Group Movement. Most important had been a demonstration of the power of a nonprofessional, religiously oriented group to help people with their problems. AA had also learned some things about what not to do in trying to help alcoholics. The aggressive evangelism and clamor for public figures characteristic of the Oxford groups had to be eliminated from any program which would work with alcoholics. The modifications and changes of the Oxford technique were made on a trial-and-error basis by the early members of what came to be called AA. The modifications probably became more important, so far as the success of AA is concerned, than the original Oxford techniques and ideas with which they started. These modifications allowed AA to be adapted to the special psychological needs of alcoholics.

In the fall of 1937 Bill visited Dr. Bob, and the two began counting noses. They were amazed to be able to count forty alcoholics who had been dry for a significant time. Suddenly the awareness dawned on them that something new, perhaps something great, had been started. They saw that, as someone has put it, "God had lighted a torch and shown alcoholics how to pass it from one to another." From that moment plans for spreading the good news to the thousands of alcoholics who could be helped began to take shape.

The growth of the movement was slow at first. By the end of the fourth year there were one hundred members. Progress was the most rapid in Ohio. The first amoeba-like branching-off from the original Akron group took place in May, 1939, when enough men were coming to that group from Cleveland to make it advisable to start a separate group there. Disagreement among members of this new Cleveland group resulted in two other groups there in 1939. During the winter of 1938 a modest gift from John D. Rockefeller kept the work from floundering. In the spring it was decided to publish a book which would record the collective experiences of the early members to help other alcoholics. The completion of the Big Book—as it is affectionately known in AA—in April, 1939, marked a milestone in the growth of the movement. "The Way Out," which was the first choice for a title, turned out to be the title of twelve other books; so they decided to call their new book *Alcoholics Anonymous*. Thus the little fellowship of about one hundred recovered alcoholics acquired a name.

Sales were so slow at first that a deputy sheriff appeared one day at the Newark office of AA to dispossess them because they could not pay the printing debt. A grateful member saved the situation by mortgaging his business to raise the needed money. The group's fortunes improved rapidly in the fall of 1939 when *Liberty* magazine and the *Cleveland Plain Dealer* each published an article about AA. Inquiries poured in from distant places. The movement was spreading like a chain letter. During 1940 it reached such places as Chicago, Detroit, Little Rock, Houston, Los Angeles, and San Francisco, via the book and by members moving to new homes. In 1941 an article by Jack Alexander appeared in the *Saturday Evening Post*, entitled "Alcoholics Anonymous, Freed Slaves of Drink, Now They Free Others." The "handful of drunks" watched with mingled joy and amazement as thousands flocked in seeking help. Since then AA has grown by geometric progression. In April, 1954, the *AA Directory* gave the active membership as 128,196. By January, 1967, the estimated worldwide membership stood between 350,000 and 400,000. AA's General Service Office in New York was in direct communication with an expanding network of some 12,000 groups, including 7,821 in the U.S., 1,241 in Canada, and 2,136 groups outside the U.S. and Canada. In addition there were some 700 prison groups and 600 hospital and rehabilitation center groups.[12] The growing international impact of AA was reflected in these 1965 membership estimates: 13,803 members in Mexico, Central and South America; 3,966 in the United Kingdom; 7,313 in Europe; 2,816 in Africa; 3,228 in Australia; 749 in Asia; 1,543 in New Zealand; and 61 in Oceania. Many of the groups abroad were established by AA seamen and traveling businessmen. The jet age has accelerated this growth, producing what might become an international "sobriety explosion." In one Asian country, AA's development was cultivated mainly by a U.S. Army sergeant and a native clergyman. AA literature is now available in a dozen languages. In many countries there are AA groups meeting in hospitals and prisons, as well as in the usual community settings. (In the U.S., the 400 hospital groups have over 11,000 members and the 500 prison groups have some 25,000 members.) [13] How effective AA will be in non-Western cultures (with different attitudes toward guilt, pleasure, and the goals of life, for example) and what modifications will eventually occur in the AA program in such cultures has yet to be determined.

A significant milestone in AA history was the First International Conference held in Cleveland in July, 1950, the fifteenth anniversary year of its founding. Seven thousand AA delegates met in an atmosphere of gratitude and victory and, with humility, rededicated themselves "to the single purpose of carrying the good news of AA to those millions who still don't know." [14] A Twentieth Anniversary International Convention was held in St. Louis in July, 1955. More than 10,000 AA members and spouses attended the Thirtieth Anniversary International Convention in Toronto, Canada, in July, 1965. AA's from numerous countries spoke with deep gratitude for what the fellowship and recovery program had meant in their homelands. Amid general rejoicing for AA's startling effectiveness with "lost cause" alcoholics, there was a persistent note of determination that this success would not lead to complacency. When Bill W. and his wife Lois were introduced at the mass meetings, there was thunderous applause and repeated standing ovations. In one talk, Bill reminded the convention: "When we remember that in the thirty years of AA's existence we have reached less than 10 percent of those who might have been willing to approach us, we begin to get an idea of the immensity of our task and the responsibilities with which we will always be confronted." [15] He also stressed the need for cooperation with all who work on the alcoholism problem, including the more than one hundred agencies (in the U.S. and Canada) now engaged in rehabilitation, research, and alcohol education.

Administratively each local AA group is autonomous. In 1938 an Alcoholic Foundation, composed of five nonalcoholics and four alcoholics, was formed to handle the publishing of the book. In 1942 the Foundation was incorporated— to assure continuity. It was made the custodian of AA "tradition and policy," as well as repository of funds, collected from literature sales and a strictly voluntary contribution of one dollar per member by local groups. The Foundation maintains a General Service Office in New York City, which acts as a clearinghouse for all AA groups. It distributes literature, answers letters of inquiry from all over the world, and advises members about group problems. In 1950, The AA Grapevine, the official periodical of AA, published a proposal by Bill and Dr. Bob that a General Service Conference of AA be formed. This proposal, which was subsequently adopted and is now in operation, provided for a small body of state and provincial delegates meeting yearly to assume direct responsibility for the General Service Headquarters. The plan aims at providing a representative group to "take the place of Dr. Bob and Bill," to keep the Foundation (renamed the General Service Board) firmly anchored to the movement it serves, and to insure the continuity of the services of AA. A significant event in the growth of AA occurred in 1955 with the publication of a new edition of the Big Book. It has 612 pages, as compared with 400 in the original edition, and contains 29 new "stories" of recoveries, representing a wider geographical and vocational range; included were more stories by younger alcoholics and "higher-bottom" cases.

On November 19, 1950, Dr. Bob died after a prolonged illness. Bill W. is now devoting most of his time to writing material which will be helpful to members of AA. His major literary productions are *Twelve Steps and Twelve Traditions* and *The AA Way of Life, A Reader by Bill,*[16] These have become companion volumes to the Big Book in AA circles. Bill is now having what he calls "a season of reflection," during which he is trying to get some light on the question: What does it all mean? [17] Meanwhile the movement which Bill W. and Dr. Bob started continues to grow and flourish. One reason for this is the robust sense of responsibility on the part of many AA's for reaching the unreached alcoholics. This was reflected in the "responsibility" theme of the Thirtieth Anniversary Convention; at that inspiring meeting, AA members were invited to rededicate themselves to the unfinished task, in these words: "I am responsible. When anyone, anywhere, reaches out for help, I want the hand of AA always to be there. And for that: I am responsible." [18] It was evident that this sense of responsibility is globe-encircling, including all of the world's twenty-five million still-suffering alcoholics.[19]

## How and Why AA Works

The seventy-seven interviews which I had with AA members gave me convincing proof that there is no such thing as a blanket answer to the question of how and why AA works. For AA is a permissive organization, and each person who comes to it works out his own program. The best that one can hope to do is to describe certain common principles and experiences drawn from the interviews which are typical of many in AA. We shall do so by describing a hypothetical alcoholic whom we shall call "Joe." Joe is actually a composite of the experience of many different alcoholics.

Joe might have come in contact with AA in one of many ways. For example, a friend or business associate with the same problem might have suggested he try AA, or his doctor or minister might have recommended it to him. But let us say that his wife is the person who made the initial contact. She has had about all she can take of Joe's drinking. For several years it has been making life almost unbearable. Now he is in the middle of another bender. All his promises and good intentions have come to naught. In her desperation she remembers a magazine article about AA. She looks in the telephone directory to see if it is listed. She dials the number, and an AA group secretary answers.

127

The harassed wife asks if they will "try to do something with Joe?" The secretary, herself an alcoholic, inquires whether Joe is interested in stopping, or at least in talking to someone who might be able to help him. If the reply is, "No, but the Lord knows he needs it!" the secretary will explain that the AA approach works only in cases where the alcoholic has some desire for help, and that to talk to Joe now would probably only antagonize him. The secretary may suggest a chat with his wife instead. In such a talk the secretary will try to help her understand the true nature of Joe's problem and perhaps suggest certain things which she can do as his wife in helping him get to AA eventually.

If Joe is willing to talk to someone, the secretary will suggest that he come to the office or AA clubhouse from which she is talking. Here—in the emphasis on Joe's willingness for help and to come to the AA headquarters—is evident one of the primary reasons for AA's effectiveness, viz., the initiative is kept with the alcoholic. This principle is followed in all AA procedures. When one recalls the hypersensitivity of the alcoholic to authority, the importance of this principle is self-evident.

If Joe is too sick to navigate, however, the secretary sends a pair of AA volunteers—"Twelfth-steppers"—to his home. They find Joe retching and shaking in bed. They introduce themselves, and one of them mentions that he had the "shakes" himself less than a year ago. If Joe needs a drink desperately, one of them may go out to buy a bottle. The other begins to talk, not about Joe—which would raise Joe's defenses—but about himself. He tells about his own grim experiences with alcohol. The first AA returns with the whiskey which soon quiets Joe's pounding nerves. Then this AA tells about his drinking—the jobs he lost, the trouble he caused, the desperation, hopelessness, and loneliness he felt.

Joe senses that these fellows know what they're talking about. The bridge of communication which one alcoholic is able to establish with another is being constructed. Herein lies another key to AA's effectiveness. The candid accounts of their drinking experiences by the AA's may cause Joe to open up a bit. He is still suspicious, but he advances a cautious question about "the program" which they have mentioned. "How much does it cost?" "Do I have to sign a pledge?" The men explain that there are no dues or fees and that most of the work is done by volunteers like themselves who do it to keep sober. "Sobriety insurance" they call it. This sounds slightly insane to Joe, but as he gradually grasps what they are saying, he realizes that he is helping them by allowing them to help him. Thus he does not feel the extreme burden, which would eventually become unbearable to his alcoholic ego, of being entirely the recipient in the helper-helped relation. This is another reason for AA's effectiveness. From the beginning it allows him to feel useful and not entirely dependent.

128

The men go on to explain that there are no pledges and no "musts" in the AA program and that even long-time members only agree with themselves to stay sober a day at a time. This, they explain, is the "Twenty-four Hour Plan." In plain English this means, "Tomorrow I may go on the damnedest bender you ever heard of but I'm not going to have a drink *today*." [20] They explain that anybody can stay sober for twenty-four hours if that person really wants to. The twenty-four hour plan is one of several tools which AA will provide Joe to help him over the first hard days and weeks. These tools help in breaking the addictive cycle—drinking to anesthetize the effects of previous drinking—and are another reason for AA's remarkable effectiveness.

As to joining, the AA's assure Joe that anyone who admits that alcohol has him licked and wants help is a member. They go on to tell how they discovered, after years of trying to handle alcohol, that alcohol was handling them. Their lives had become unmanageable because their bodies didn't react to alcohol like the body of a normal drinker. Because they had a physical allergy to alcohol, their schemes to "drink like a gentleman" were foredoomed to failure. Further, it was the first drink that set them off on a binge. By presenting alcoholism to Joe as a problem which is at least in part a *physical sickness* for which there is no known cure, they achieve several things which contribute to AA's effectiveness. They help reduce Joe's staggering guilt-fear load which has paralyzed his psychic energies. They reduce his guilt by showing him that since it is a sickness, his alcoholism is not primarily a matter of willpower. They reduce his fear that he is insane by providing him with the first rational explanation for his bizarre behavior. The psychic energies thus released are made available for therapeutic use. By pointing out that his sickness is in large measure physical, they avoid the moralism and guilt that still tend to cling to mental or emotional illnesses in our culture. By emphasizing the fact that there is no cure for the illness, they stress its seriousness. But they also point out that the AA program has allowed them to live happily with their illness—like insulin does with the diabetic.

The presence of two well-dressed men who "talk his language" and seem to understand the horror of his alcoholic world begins to penetrate Joe's isolation and to awaken in him this spark of hope: "If they did it, perhaps I can too." Because they are there to help themselves by helping him, and because they do not lecture or try to sell him anything, Joe relaxes his defenses. Since they have been through the same dark valley, the AA's can anticipate his fears and suspicions, his alibis and defenses. Joe senses that here are two men he cannot fool. He begins to feel a little less alone.

Throughout all their contacts with Joe, the AA's are careful not to say to Joe that *he* is an alcoholic. They know that there is only one person whose decision about that can make the slightest difference—Joe himself. By telling him what they think about him they might prevent him from coming to his own admission that alcohol has him licked. But, if Joe shows even the mildest interest, the men will invite him to an AA meeting. If he has reacted negatively or shows that he obviously has not "had enough" in his struggle with alcohol, the men will leave with the hope that they have planted some seed which will stimulate his desire for help at some later date. (In the cases of those interviewed by the writer, there was often a time gap ranging from one month to five years between the first contact with AA and the beginning of real participation.) In any case the Twelfth-steppers will leave their names and phone numbers with the suggestion that Joe call them any time he feels like taking a drink. In preinflation days this was known as "nickel therapy." This is another of the tools which AA provides Joe in order to help him over the periods of temptation. But Joe must use the tools himself if they are to be effective. Thus the initiative is kept with him. If he eventually succeeds in the AA program, he will know that it is his success. Before the AA's go, they may leave a copy of the AA book or other AA literature.

If Joe is obviously in serious physical condition, the AA's may suggest that he be hospitalized so that he can receive detoxification treatment, vitamin therapy, and a sound diet. AA itself does not own any therapeutic facility, nor is it affiliated with any; but it glady cooperates with hospitals and treatment centers in many places. This is done through the Institutional Committees, composed of AA's who commit themselves to regular availability for Twelfth Step work in institutions, including general hospitals, mental hospitals, and correctional facilities. Two patterns of alcoholic hospitalization have emerged. Some hospitals have separate alcoholic wards; more assign alcoholics to general medical wards and rooms just as they would any other sick person. Research has shown that, with modern tranquilizers and detoxification methods, alcoholics cause no greater disturbance than any other group of seriously ill patients. In both patterns, the volunteer services of AA members are invaluable parts of the treatment program. With the doctor's encouragement and the patient's agreement, the AA's make frequent visits, surrounding the hospitalized alcoholic with acceptance and offering him the AA recovery program. Equally important, they continue to offer him fellowship and help during the shaky days after he leaves the hospital. Several of the interviewees attributed their successful beginnings in AA to the fact that they had had such hospitalization. The advantage of the all-alcoholic ward is that the entire atmosphere can become saturated with AA's spirit of hope, particularly if the nurses and attendants are AA members. In a number of hospitals (mainly mental hospitals), recovered alcoholics are working very effectively as lay therapists.

The term "sponsor" came into use as a result of certain hospital programs which admitted alcoholics only if they were sponsored by an AA member.

It was soon discovered that the principle of having a person designated to guide a new man during his early days in AA had great merit. So the idea was applied to new members in general. Let us say that one of the men—we'll call him "Harry"—who called on Joe has "hit it off" with him and has become his sponsor. Harry calls on Joe almost every evening. He may phone him each morning, just to say hello. Often he brings other AA friends along to meet Joe.

As soon as Joe is feeling a little better, Harry takes him and his wife to an open meeting of the local AA group. Closed meetings are for alcoholics only; open meetings welcome nonalcoholic relatives, friends, and anyone else who is interested, as well as the alcoholics themselves. Here is something of what takes place. Before proceeding, it is important to make several points clear. This description is based on an actual meeting that took place in the New York City area—with the exception of the third talk which happens to have been given in a Chicago AA meeting. Names and places have been altered to protect anonymity. In spite of this basis, it is impossible to convey the real feeling of an AA meeting on paper. Neither the talks—of which portions are given—nor the meeting should be taken as being typical, for there is no such thing as a typical meeting or talk. Each talk is a unique entity, reflecting the experiences and personality of the speaker. Then too, meeting practices vary greatly from one section of the country to another.

The meeting is held in the parish house of a church, rented by the AA group at a nominal rate. Camaraderie pervades the hall. There is spirited conversation and laughter as those present mix informally. It is obvious that these people enjoy being together. Harry enters with Joe and his wife. They are soon surrounded by AA's, some of whom have already been to see Joe. Joe is still somewhat foggy, but he is impressed with their interest in him and by their general appearance. These people look successful and happy. Joe wonders, "Can these folks be alcoholics? Maybe they'll bring the drunks in later." He feels relieved that none of his new friends seem to notice that his hand still trembles when he reaches out to shake theirs or that he can't carry on much of a conversation. The folks he meets seem to represent a cross section of occupations—a plumber, a dentist, a stevedore, an artist, a corporation lawyer. As has been said, "AA's membership is as diverse and exclusive as a classified telephone directory." [21]

A little after 8:30 P.M. the chairman of the group raps a gavel, calling the meeting to order. Conversation gradually subsides as the members move to take seats. Joe looks around. There are about 125 present, one third of whom are women. Ages range from the white-haired grandfatherly man to several young people in their late twenties. On the walls of the room are several placards: "Easy Does It," "First Things First," "Live and Let Live," and

"But for the Grace of God." Joe, who feels down on life in general, including God, winces internally at the last one.

The chairman begins to speak:

This is the regular Friday night open meeting of the East Brooklyn group of Alcoholics Anonymous. I would like to welcome all of you, especially the newcomers. Our AA magazine says on its masthead: "Alcoholics Anonymous is a fellowship of men and women who share their experience, strength, and hope with each other that they may solve their common problem and help others to recover from alcoholism. The only requirement for membership is an honest desire to stop drinking. AA has no dues or fees. It is not allied with any sect, denomination, politics, organization, or institution; does not wish to engage in any controversy, neither endorses nor opposes any cause. Our primary purpose is to stay sober and help other alcoholics achieve sobriety." That pretty well says it for my money. We're fortunate in having a group of speakers from the Uptown Group No. 2 with us. It's a pleasure to welcome them and to present Bob Green, who will lead tonight's meeting. (Applause as the leader comes forward from the audience.)

Bob Green takes the speaker's stand:

My name is Bob Green, and I'm an alcoholic. It's good to be here tonight. As the chairman said, this is a fellowship. We're all here because this is the best way we know of helping ourselves stay sober.

The leader for the evening continues for a few minutes, telling a little about AA and about his own experiences with alcohol. He concludes his opening remarks in this way:

I want to say a word to the newcomers. Only as we strive to help you, can AA continue or any of us stay sober. The only thing we ask is that you keep an open mind. We're going to hear from three speakers tonight. If you don't hear something tonight that rings a bell with your experience, keep coming to meetings. And I must add that anything that I or any speaker says represents our own opinions, and is not necessarily the opinion of AA in general. With this I'll give you my first speaker, Jake White. (Applause.)

Jake says:

My name is Jake White, and I am an alcoholic. After twenty-two years of drinking, I actually quit. I got so bad I had to sneak liquor into my house. My wife kept calling my drinking to my attention, so I had to get the liquor in without her knowledge. I would put a couple of bottles in my coat and stalk past her—when you're half loaded nobody sees anything—(laughter) and hide them in the hamper. Usually when I tried to get the bottles out of the hamper quietly, I got the bottles but the hamper came with them. (Laughter.) One time after a

132

particularly bad bout, my wife said to me, "Why don't you make me the happiest woman alive?" I said, "How?" She replied, "Drop dead!" (Laughter.) Finally my wife kicked me out. I had said to her, "This house is half mine, let's divide it." We did. She took the inside and I took the outside. (Laughter.)

So I took a furnished room and got a job in a hospital—admissions desk on the maternity ward. (Laughter.) I soon discovered that in a Jewish hospital the fathers of new baby boys throw a party when the kid is a week old. So I could freeload quite regularly. Finally it got bad, so I quit just before they fired me.

My family had given me up long before. I was getting so bad I was scared of myself. Lying in a cheap furnished room, drinking, dreading the time when the liquor would give out, or I wouldn't be able to keep it on my stomach. I finally called up the only brother who would still speak to me and asked him to come down. He protested but finally came and got me in the county hospital for eleven days. While I was there a social service worker asked me if I'd heard about AA. I said, "What's that?" He gave me an AA pamphlet to read. On Sunday the boys came to visit me, and I saw the light for the first time. I went to AA; it was the thing I had been looking for. At that time there were only about twenty-five members in Brooklyn. I listened to their stories—they had been on the Bowery, been in all sorts of places I had never been. I began to feel I was not as bad as them—forgetting to take the inventory and check my own record. After four months I said to myself, "Maybe with all my knowledge of AA, I could take a couple of beers."

The first night I had six, but woke up the next morning feeling fine. I was scared to death of what would happen if I got drunk. The third night of my experiment I got drunk, papa threw me the hell out, and I was back in the furnished room. (Laughter.) For the next five years I was on the bum. I would sit in a cheap gin-mill telling drunks they should go to AA—just the thing for them. (Laughter.) I lost job after job. One year it took two envelopes to send in my income tax slips, I had so many of them. (Laughter.)

I lost all hope and resigned myself to an alcoholic death. Then two men came to see me. I knew before they spoke that they were from AA. I was never so glad to see anyone in my life. That was May 23, 1948. No drinks since then. I poured the liquor I had tied to the bed springs down the drain when those men left. I was really through.

AA doesn't fail—we fail it. It works, if we will work it. To the newcomer I want to say two things. First, the most important thing in AA is to get active in the work and get to know people in AA. The more people you know, the better time you'll have and the easier to stay sober. Second, it's easier to stay sober than to get sober. I owe everything to AA. If it wasn't for AA, I'd probably be dead by this time. Instead, I've got my home together again and I'm holding down a job and enjoying life—without booze. When I talk to the "Man upstairs," I say "thank you" for AA. (Applause.)

Following Jake's speech, the leader interjects some of his own experiences, confirming something Jake has said. After mentioning that alcoholism is no respecter of age, color, or sex, he introduces his second speaker, an attractive woman of about forty. She begins by telling about how she helped her brother get into AA but resisted it herself, even after she was in serious trouble, because she couldn't imagine that anything could help her. She relates: "I got so bad I couldn't comb my hair. . . . I drank by myself behind closed doors. I never could tell where sleep ended and blackouts began." Finally, as a last resort before suicide, she decided to try AA. With the exception of one brief slip at three months, she had been sober for two years and ten months. The speaker then turns to a discussion of the fourth step, describing at some length how it helped her. Finally, she concludes her talk with these words:

To the newcomers I'd like to say, don't be discouraged if you don't get it right away. You can do it, if you put a little of the effort into the program which you formerly put into getting and hiding liquor. I have a lot to be thankful for—to AA, my sponsor, and the Higher Power. One is the fact that before AA when I woke up, I used to say, "Good God, morning!" Now I can say, "Good morning, God." (Applause.)

After the second speaker, the leader from the visiting group turns the rostrum over to the secretary of the local group who makes announcements concerning future meetings and says: "There are no dues or fees in AA, but we do have expenses, so we'll now pass the hat." During the collection there is a buzz of conversation. Some stand and stretch. Since most AA's smoke, by now the air in the room is a blue haze.

After a few minutes the leader introduces the third speaker who is one of the old timers of the visiting group. He mentions his own drinking experiences only briefly and spends most of his time telling how the various steps have helped him.

We are like a man who has bought a farm with the sole thought of raising wheat. And raise wheat the farm does—the finest of wheat. But as the farmer goes about the task of raising wheat, he finds the most beautiful of flowers springing up in odd corners; he notices for the first time a grove of stately trees. And as time goes on, he strikes oil in this acre and gold in that; here he finds coal, and there he finds silver, and now he comes upon a curative spring. And the end is not yet. Each day he comes upon new comforts, new beauty, new riches; each day he rises to new adventures; each day's discovery sets him atingle for the next.

Does my allegory sound far-fetched—just some words strung together to make a speech? Let's take inventory—an old AA custom. Everything in AA stems from the twelve steps of the Recovery Program. . . . Let's look at the twelve steps, not to discuss them and what they mean, but solely to see what they give us over and above sobriety.

In the first step, we admitted that alcohol had made our lives unmanageable. With that admission comes the first peace we have known in years. Why? Because for years a battle had been raging inside us—our mind and our conscience on one side, this strange and savage appetite on the other. And now the battle is over.

In the second and third steps we came to believe that a Higher Power could help us and we placed our will and our lives in his hands. And what do we get? A resurgence of faith and of hope. A great gift, indeed, to us who have lived in despair. The fourth and fifth steps led us to take inventory of our lives and to tell the exact nature of our wrongs. The devil of remorse that had long plagued us has gone. The burden of evil that bent our shoulders and weighted our limbs has gone.

And so we break with the past. So we become new men. That's not a figure of speech. The seven remaining steps make that just as real as the platform I stand upon. In the sixth and seventh steps, we make restitution to ourselves by casting off the shoddy, sodden garments of the drunkard; by clothing ourselves in tolerance, in humility, in honesty and charity. In the eighth and ninth steps, we made restitution to others. Those four steps help us get rid of those alcoholic lenses that were before our eyes—the ones that caused us to see not the decent, kindly folk about us but grotesque and distorted figures—demons in a land of nightmare.

Perhaps the greatest gift of all the steps, next only to sobriety, is contained in the next two—the steps of the daily inventory, the daily seeking of closer union with God. And so to the twelfth step. It told us that we'd have a spiritual experience. Some of us were a little doubtful about that. We realize now that it's impossible to make a real effort to fulfill the other steps without having a spiritual experience. The twelfth step told us, too, to carry this message to other alcoholics. No man in this audience, I don't care what his life has been, has ever savored a satisfaction so complete, so unalloyed, as that which comes to one who is the instrument by which an alcoholic enters into and is redeemed by AA.

Yes, there are reasons—a hundred times the number of those I have cited—for joining AA, over and above and beyond achieving just plain sobriety.[22]

When the third speaker finishes, the leader thanks the local group for the privilege of "carrying the message," and says, "Now let's stand and close the meeting in the usual way." The group then repeats the Lord's Prayer in staccato phrases. This comes as a jolt to Joe who has been pleasantly surprised up to this point by the lack of "religious" practices in the meeting. The smoking, the laughter, the occasional "damn" during the talks had made him feel comfortable and somewhat relaxed.

Feeling socially awkward, Joe starts to make an excuse to leave, but before he can get it out, he is ushered by several AA's to a table where coffee and doughnuts are waiting. Harry makes sure that his "baby" gets comfortably acquainted with some group stalwarts who drift over to the table. Among others, Joe meets a fellow who works at his trade. They begin to "talk shop" and before long have exchanged telephone numbers. Joe's AA circle is beginning to grow. Conversation, mostly about AA activities and alcoholism, fills

135

the room in waves. Twelfth Step work is going on over coffee cups. After about a half hour members begin to leave. Many stay for as long as an hour.

Let us pause for a moment and analyze what has happened to Joe. He has begun to become a part of an emotionally meaningful group which can provide him with a supportive web of relationships within which he can apply the principles of AA. It is an attractive group. The alcoholic has always associated "cures" with the unpleasant. In contrast, here is a group which is enjoying sobriety. It gives Joe's ego a lift by making him as a newcomer feel important. He is no longer an outcast. Someone actually wants him in his group! During the course of Joe's drinking he has become generally desocialized. Here is a group that can reverse the process and serve as a doorway to the land of the living. It can do this because it is, sociologically speaking, an ingroup whose close ties of fellowship provide the environment for resocialization. The intensity of the fellowship has been compared by one AA speaker to that shared by those who have been through a battlefield experience together. This attractive ingroup is open *only to alcoholics*. Joe's reluctance to admit that alcohol has him licked is counterbalanced by the fact that this admission is his ticket of entrance to the group. His chief liability has thus become an asset. Equally important is the fact that here is a group of people who speak with complete candor and lack of guilt about their common "sickness." Joe feels a great relief. He thinks, "Since they don't blame themselves for their alcoholism, they won't blame me for mine." It is by reversing the usual moralistic, punitive attitude toward alcoholism in our culture that AA is able to provide a solution to the problem.

Already Joe's isolation is beginning to break down. He realizes that he is not alone and is not uniquely cursed. He has seen a room full of examples of those who do not even regard it as a curse. He has seen a hundred examples of the fact that the AA program works. Joe has begun to identify with some of the speakers as they described their experiences.

The AA group can help Joe because it is anonymous and nonexploitative. Anonymity quiets his early fears that someone will find out he's an alcoholic. (Actually everyone who knows Joe has long been acquainted with the fact.) Anonymity also casts an atmosphere of clandestineness around the movement which gives it a certain added appeal, especially for those alcoholics who are in the "gang" stage of psychosocial development. The fact that AA is free and is based on the principle of alcoholics helping other alcoholics in order to help themselves means that Joe need not fear either financial or emotional exploitation. All this helps him identify with the group. As he begins to feel a sense of belonging, i.e., to derive emotional satisfactions from the group, the group is able to influence his attitude and behavior along group-approved lines. This is an unconscious process by which normal social controls, which have had little meaning to Joe in the advanced stages of his alcoholism, are reestablished. The AA group provides an interpersonal environment where successful abstinence is rewarded by group approval and acceptance. This is very important in keeping Joe sober during the early months in AA.

When they reach Joe's house after the AA meeting, Harry is invited in for another cup of coffee. While his wife fixes it, Joe queries Harry about the signs at the front of the meeting hall. Harry explains:

Those are the AA mottoes, Joe. They're more of the tools that AA gives us to use, if we want to, in staying sober. Take "Easy Does It," for example. It means different things to different AA's, but it's good advice for most of us. For most it means taking life in our stride rather than letting everything upset us. Before AA when we'd get mad or hurt, we'd go get drunk. The motto helps remind us of the cost of getting upset and, when we do, the cost of getting drunk. For a newcomer, "Easy Does It" suggests that our problems have been piling up over the years and we can't expect them to be solved magically overnight. This is where "First Things First" comes in. When we come into AA, we have all kinds of problems. We discover that it pays not to forget that staying sober is always our first problem; other problems can be solved gradually, but only if we maintain our sobriety. "Live and Let Live" reminds us to keep our damn noses out of other people's business. If they want to get drunk, that's their business. If they want to believe an elephant is their higher power, that's up to them too. We alkies are short on tolerance before we hit AA. We get mixed up in other people's business, get hurt and mad, and then drunk. This motto helps keep us from judging the other guy. "But for the Grace of God" simply reminds us that we're not different or better than the next drunk—just luckier. It helps in Twelfth Step work to remember this and to remember that you're just one drink from a drunk yourself.

Joe points out to Harry that he's afraid he can't go for the "God business." Harry reassures him, "That's O.K. A lot of us felt that way when we came in. Take what you can use from the AA program and forget the rest for the time being. Your 'higher power' can be whatever suits you—nature, science, the AA group—why I have one friend in AA whose first higher power was a Fifth Avenue bus that almost knocked him down. He stayed sober, and gradually his ideas began to change." By its general permissiveness concerning theology, AA is able to help countless alcoholics whose prejudices against overt religion would keep them from identifying with a more orthodox approach.

Joe's wife brings in the coffee, and the conversation continues. The question of the "Twelve Steps" comes up. Harry takes the worn copy of the Big Book he has loaned to Joe and opens it to page 59, where the steps are listed and their workings explained. He points out that the "we" refers to the early members who pooled their experience and wrote the steps. Joe takes the book and glances over the steps:

137

Here are the steps we took, which are suggested as a Program of Recovery:

1. We admitted we were powerless over alcohol—that our lives had become unmanageable.

2. Came to believe that a Power greater than ourselves could restore us to sanity.

3. Made a decision to turn our will and our lives over to the care of God *as we understood him*.

4. Made a searching and fearless moral inventory of ourselves.

5. Admitted to God, to ourselves, and to another human being the exact nature of our wrongs.

6. Were entirely ready to have God remove all these defects of character.

7. Humbly asked Him to remove our shortcomings.

8. Made a list of all persons we had harmed, and became willing to make amends to them all.

9. Made direct amends to such people wherever possible, except when to do so would injure them or others.

10. Continued to take personal inventory and when we were wrong promptly admitted it.

11. Sought through prayer and meditation to improve our conscious contact with God *as we understood him*, praying only for knowledge of his will for us and the power to carry that out.

12. Having had a spiritual awakening as the result of these steps we tried to carry this message to alcoholics, and practice these principles in all our affairs.

Joe gulps and says, "It's a big order for a guy like me." Harry responds, "Yes, it's a big order for all of us, and nobody is ever able to follow the Program fully. Just remember that the steps are only suggested. Take them cafeteria style. Use what you can. Don't worry about the others. When you have taken the first step and admitted your problem, you are a part of AA." Thus Harry again demonstrates the permissive atmosphere of AA. In subsequent conversations and AA experiences Joe will gradually absorb the AA philosophy implied in the steps.

Before Harry says goodnight, he learns that Joe and his wife used to play bridge before Joe's drinking interfered with their social life. So he invites them to play with a group of AA's who meet once a week in various homes. Here is another expression of the AA fellowship. Harry also arranges to take Joe to the "beginner's meeting," at which a member with several years' sobriety will lead a study of the Twelve Steps, as well as discuss problems raised by the newcomers. In addition, he makes a date with Joe to attend the closed meeting of the local group two nights later. Harry knows that he must keep Joe immersed in AA if he is to maintain his sobriety during the first difficult days and weeks.

There are no passwords, esoteric practices, or secret cures involved in a closed meeting. The fact that one is there means that the person admits he has an alcoholic problem. The closed meeting is usually smaller in size than the open. It almost always involves extensive opportunity for what might be called "audience participation." There may be a panel consisting of AA's who answer questions from the floor; or there may simply be an individual chairman who steers a general discussion concerning one of the steps or of problems raised by anyone present. Here are some of the questions raised at one closed meeting:

> Will someone give me some help on the eighth and ninth steps?
> How can I achieve tolerance?
> Is it necessary for a person living in a suburb to attend meetings in his own home town?
> Is it possible to achieve the power of sobriety without the spiritual side of AA?
> Can a person have such an aversion to alcohol that he will not be tolerant in Twelfth Step work?
> How can I expect AA to help me when other groups have failed?

Each of these questions is discussed roundly by those present. Near the close of the meeting a man asks for and receives help on a specific Twelfth Step case which is giving him trouble.

Attending a closed meeting has the following values so far as newcomer Joe is concerned. Because it is all-alcoholic, he feels more protected than in open meetings. It gives him a chance to talk in a smaller group where everyone has the same problem. He feels much freer to talk because he knows he is "among those who understand." The closed meeting provides opportunity to make new friends within the AA circle. It gives him a feeling of being a part of something from which the world in general is excluded. This gives his very battered ego a boost.

There are other expressions of the AA fellowship in which Joe can participate. For example, there are the AA clubs. There are at least two kinds. Those like the "24-Hour Club" in New York City are devoted purely to AA sociability. Unlike AA proper, there are membership dues. One must be an AA to join. The other type of club serves both as an "open house" for AA sociability and as a center for Twelfth Step work. Every year about 5,000 "flying squadrons" of Twelfth-steppers go out from one such club in New York. There are no dues, support being derived from voluntary contributions. All AA's are welcome. Until Joe finds a job, he will probably spend a substantial share of each day at such a club, drinking coffee and chatting with AA friends who drop in. This, like AA fellowship in general, serves as a substitute for the fellowship of the tavern and is an important factor in keeping Joe sober. Although established by AA members, the clubs are not a part of AA proper.

For Joe's wife there is the "Al-Anon Family Group." Here she will find understanding and help in a group of wives who are attempting to deal with their own personality problems by applying AA principles.

During the first few weeks, Joe is "as conscious of alcohol as a toothache." He thinks about it all the time. But he holds on desperately to his newborn sobriety. Sometimes he wonders if it is worth it; then he remembers the horror of the last binge. He breaks the twenty-four hour plan into sixty-minute periods, saying, "I'll not take a drink for this hour!" This and the desire not to let Harry down are all that keep him from the first drink. Gradually the craving subsides.

After Joe has had a few weeks of sobriety, Harry invites him to go along on a Twelfth Step call. To please Harry he agrees, in spite of butterflies in his stomach. To his surprise Joe discovers that telling his story to the alcoholic gives him a real lift. He feels useful and important. He begins to realize that his alcoholism has prepared him in a unique way to help other alcoholics. As Harry put it before they arrived at the prospect's house, "Your story will probably do this guy more good than the advice of a fancy psychiatrist at twenty bucks an hour." Joe also discovers that seeing someone else in the throes of a hangover refreshes his memory of his own recent condition. All this helps Joe keep sober.

Joe is in the "honeymoon" or "pink cloud" stage. The first long hours have lengthened into days, the days into weeks. He is beginning to recuperate physically, and he revels in his newfound sobriety and friendships. His higher power is the AA group. He hasn't paid much attention to the Twelve Steps. Everything looks rosy to Joe.

After about three months of sobriety, the elation may begin to diminish. He may begin to think of good reasons why he can't attend meetings so often. Then one day, when he steps into a bar "to make a phone call," the idea hits him that surely one drink wouldn't hurt him. So he tries an "experiment." Sure enough, nothing happens—at first. He continues to "nibble," avoiding meetings and AA friends. After a few days the compulsion hits him, and he "goes off the deep end." Joe's binge lasts for several days during which he experiences worse remorse than he has ever known before. He feels that he has betrayed his AA friends.

For a while after his slip Joe continues to avoid Harry. Finally he screws up his courage and goes to a meeting, expecting the worst. To his surprise nobody looks askance at him or treats him with condescension. When he tells Harry about his slip, his sponsor smiles and dismisses it with, "Could have happened to anybody, and often does, Joe." The attitude of the group toward Joe is simply, "Glad to see you back."

Joe's slip causes him to take stock. With the aid of Harry's counsel, he sees that prior to the slip he had *admitted* intellectually but not *accepted* emotionally the fact that he, Joe Blank, is an alcoholic. The slip has been a great persuader in his case, enabling him to accept the truth about himself. He has now really taken the first step. In so doing he has surrendered some of his alcoholic grandiosity about himself. He is less defensive because he is less vulnerable. His ego-image has been a burden. The burden is now reduced, and Joe is really open to help from the AA program. It should not be inferred from this description that an alcoholic must have a slip in order to "get" the AA program. Thirty-seven percent of the interviewees had not had any slips.

Joe realizes that up to now he has almost ignored the Twelve Steps. So he begins to read the AA book and work on the "fearless and searching moral inventory" described in steps four through ten. These steps, Harry tells him, are really a unit and are important "to keep you sober, not to get you that way." They do this by getting at the roots of the alcoholic's problem. The theory is as follows. Because of the alcoholic's "allergy" to alcohol, one drink sets off a physiological chain reaction, leading eventually to intoxication. Since this allergy is incurable, the problem is to help the alcoholic keep from taking the first drink. This is the central purpose of the AA program. It accomplishes this in a variety of ways, many of which have already been discussed. It indoctrinates him with the idea behind the AA slogan "It's the First Drink That Does It" until it becomes almost a conditioned reflex. This helps counteract the rationalization process which leads to the first drink. AA helps the person call on the help of some higher Power (God, as the individual understands him) to help withstand temptation. It teaches him to keep busy helping other alcoholics. And, very important, it helps him to reduce the interpersonal friction that drives the alcoholic to take the first drink. This is the purpose of steps four through ten. The word "moral" is a stumbling-block for him at first until Harry explains that it simply means those feelings and actions, past and present, which tend to make an alcoholic drink.

And so Joe makes a list of the various people he has hurt by his drinking. He talks the whole picture over with his trusted friend, Harry, discussing feelings and events he hasn't dared verbalize before. This of course brings catharsis to his spirit, and he feels as though a load has been lifted. This gives him courage to make some direct amends where they are obviously in order. When this process is completed, he feels that he can really look the world in the eye. By straightening out some of his past messes, he reduces both his guilt about the past and anxiety about the future. All this helps him maintain happy sobriety. Harry reminds him that the personal inventory habit is a continuing part of the AA program.

Here we see the AA handling of the problem of responsibility. It has reduced the alcoholic's guilt by recognizing the physical element in the problem. Yet, it prevents him from using this as an alibi by adding that the factor which keeps the disease from being controlled is "alcoholic thinking"—selfishness, fear, resentment, lack of humility—matters for which the alcoholic is responsible. Thus, though Joe is not responsible for having an alcoholic bio-chemistry, he is responsible for doing something about his personality.

When Joe has achieved a full three months of sobriety without a slip, he is asked to speak at an AA meeting. He finds that telling his story has a remark-able effect. He is pleased when the audience laughs at some of his drinking escapades. He finishes on a note of gratitude to his sponsor and his other AA friends who have "saved my life." After the meeting, members of the group gather round to congratulate him. Somehow he feels that he now really be-longs to this fellowship. He has declared publicly that he is an alcoholic. He has told his story before a hundred people—the story he could not even admit to himself a few months before. There is a sense of release in this, as there is a sense of satisfaction in the thought that his talk may have helped some new-comer, perhaps several, to find the AA solution.

As a result of his moral inventory and his other experiences in AA, Joe's attitude toward the "spiritual angle" gradually changes. Like the majority of AA's his "spiritual awakening" is of the type which William James called the "educational variety," rather than the "hot flash" type such as was experienced by Bill W. He begins to join with the others in saying the Lord's Prayer in closing the meetings. He observes that "the folks who seem to get the most out of the program are those who develop the spiritual angle." Then one day he suddenly realizes that he is sober and enjoying it! This impresses him as being nothing short of miraculous. There must be some higher Power to effect such a miracle. He finds that he has been getting an increasing "kick" out of Twelfth Step work. That he has become less self-centered also seems a miracle to Joe. So he begins to do some praying on his own. Although he still doesn't use the word "God," Joe begins to mention the "Man upstairs" in his talks and conversations. Gradually he begins to feel a "conscious contact" with his higher Power and to gain help therefrom.

What has happened to Joe? As he has cleaned up the debris of his past and has become accepted in vital fellowship, he gradually relinquishes his bitter-ness and hostility toward life in general. This naturally affects his religious life. Then too, he has come to depend on the AA group for many of his inter-personal satisfactions, and will therefore be influenced by group values. The man who has achieved success in the "spiritual angle" is likely to have prestige in the group. In spite of the theological permissiveness of AA (which is real and important) there is, implied in the literature, a rather orthodox theology—viz., a personal God, with whom one can communicate, who is interested in individuals and will help those who are obedient to his will. This point of view exerts an ideological gravitation on those who remain a part of the group. Another way to put this is that religious growth tends to take place within a group dedicated to certain religious ideals.

In terms of the psychology of alcoholism, this development is most significant. Joe has made three important "acceptances," (or "surrenders")—each is a step away from grandiose isolation of alcoholism. Each represents the relaxing of the perfectionistic ego-image or self-concept which is the alcoholic's defense and his curse. First, he accepted the fact that he is an alcoholic. Second, he accepted the help of the group, and the group was his higher Power for a time. Now he has accepted a higher Power who is in but *beyond* the group. This may mean dynamically that he has outgrown the utter dependency on the group which characterized his early days in AA. It most certainly means that he has stopped fighting authority and authority symbols as such. Corroborating this is the fact that there is apparently a definite correlation between length of sobriety and relative orthodoxy of the theology among AA's. For example, the author divided his interviewees in terms of their God-concepts, ranging from atheist-agnostic to orthodox. Those in the atheist-agnostic category, though several had been associated with AA for considerable periods of time, had—with one exception—relatively unstable and brief periods of sobriety. As one AA said in commenting on this fact, "They're still fighting."

It would seem clear that a more mature and satisfying relationship with the higher Power serves several very important functions with regard to staying happily sober. For one thing it gives one a sense of "at homeness" in the universe which helps satisfy the "longing to belong" that is a deep human need. For another, it puts the power and resources of faith at the disposal of the individual for use in meeting the problems of living. What is more, such a relationship helps allay the ultimate anxiety which is an important part of every problem, and is especially prominent in alcoholism.

As Joe's sobriety becomes more stable, some of his AA behavior patterns will gradually change. Chances are that he will no longer feel the necessity of attending so many meetings and engaging in so much Twelfth Step work as in the first year or two. He will attend a meeting or two a week because he enjoys the fellowship. After a year or so he will begin to venture outside the social circle of AA. This is an indication of his increased self-esteem and the consequent diminishing of his need for the psychological protection of an all-alcoholic group. The majority of his friends will still be in AA, however. He may join in church activities—the Big Book encourages this. His participation indicates both his expanding interpersonal circle and his growing interest in spiritual values. If he does join the church, he will very likely be a great asset to it. After the first year or two Joe will begin to put greater emphasis on the psychological and spiritual aspects of the AA program and less on his drinking history. It may be that, as his alcohol-caused problems decrease, his underlying personality problems will reassert themselves and he will seek psychotherapeutic help. In any case his personality problems are no longer complicated by alcohol, and he is better able to cope with them, with or without professional assistance.

Let us leave our friend Joe now, with the reminder that there is no such individual as a "typical AA." Just as each person's alcoholism develops differently, so each person's AA experience is a unique entity. In conclusion, it might be well to mention that a long-time member of AA who read this chapter expressed the feeling that "Joe" is perhaps a somewhat more advanced case than is the average newcomer to AA today.

### How Effective Is AA?

Just how effective is the AA approach? The answer will be divided into three categories: (1) AA's effectiveness in breaking the addictive cycle and producing initial sobriety; (2) its effectiveness in producing long-term sobriety; (3) the extent to which the approach is successful in changing underlying personality-structure, rather than simply controlling symptoms. (In fairness to AA, it should be pointed out that AA itself does not aim at changing personality-structure. Sobriety alone is its basic goal.)

The fact that AA has grown from one person to over 375,000 in thirty years would seem to be *ipso facto* evidence that it is very effective in producing initial as well as long-term sobriety. Based on his observation of the first fifteen years of AA's existence, Bill W. gives some estimates:

Of those alcoholics who wish to get well and are emotionally capable of trying our method, 50 percent recover immediately, 25 percent after a few backslides. The remainder are improved if they continue active in AA. Of the total who approach us, it is probable that only 25 percent become AA members on the first contact. Carrying a certain amount of indoctrination, the remainder depart for the time being. Eventually two out of three will return to make good. . . . A list of 75 of our early failures today discloses that 70 returned to AA after one to ten years. We did not bring them back. They came of their own accord.[23]

These estimates reflect the situation in the early years of AA when mainly "last gasp," highly motivated alcoholics were seeking help. Since that time many younger alcoholics and those in earlier stages of the illness have approached AA, often tentatively and halfheartedly. Consequently, the proportion of estimated recoveries has tended to decline. No one really knows how much it has declined or what percentage of all those who now make some gesture toward AA eventually become affiliated with the fellowship and recover.

But even if one makes generous deductions for possible inaccuracies in membership estimates, a possibility that is readily admitted by AA leaders, the overall picture is one of remarkable effectiveness in helping thousands achieve both initial and long-term sobriety. If AA is currently effective with

50 percent (or even 40 percent) of those who make a determined effort to "work the program," it is still two or three times as successful as any other widely available treatment. It may be that AA's success rate is still above 50 percent for such persons.

There is no gainsaying the fact that AA sobriety is often of long duration. One study of an AA Group in a mental hospital showed that slightly over 50 percent achieved stable sobriety, the majority with no slips.[24] I personally know several AA's who have been without a drink for more than twenty years. The combined uninterrupted sobriety of 75 of my interviewees was 205 years, or an average of 2.7 years. Even more significant, from the standpoint of human values, than the record of uninterrupted sobriety is the fact that even those who had had frequent slips during their AA experience had been sober the bulk of the time. This would not have been true without AA, an organization to which they return quickly for help after a slip.

AA has demonstrated such amazing effectiveness, first on the level of producing initial sobriety because:

1. It waits until the individual is at least somewhat receptive to help. This means that the alcoholic has suffered enough through his drinking so that the pain outweighs the pleasure (or anesthetic satisfaction) of alcoholism. AA rightly recognizes that an alcoholic's own desire for sobriety is an indispensable ingredient in any plan of help. AA is successful because it relies on attraction as its means of bringing new members. The fact that it is an attractive fellowship enhances its effectiveness. The essential ingredients in this attractiveness are AA's lack of moralism, lack of unction, and its group acceptance.

2. AA immediately relieves the stresses of the advanced stages of alcoholism. A psychotherapist may seek to go directly to the underlying causes of the addiction; the evangelistic approach is immediately concerned about the general condition of the soul; AA on the other hand concentrates on the secondary level of the problem—helping the alcoholic to stop drinking by helping to diminish the pain and problems resulting from the excessive drinking itself.

3. It does this by providing the alcoholic with certain tools such as the twenty-four hour plan which it teaches him to use to control the craving. This is in contrast with the evangelistic approaches which sought to produce initial sobriety by means of a torrid religious experience. Because many alcoholics have strong prejudices against anything religious, the AA method appeals to many who cannot respond to the other.

4. AA immediately reduces many of the stresses of guilt and fear by allowing the alcoholic a new way of thinking about his problem. The AA conception of alcoholism—recognizing a physical factor in the sickness—renders the alcoholic's behavior intelligible to himself and greatly reduces the fear and guilt which were supplying him with added desire for the "blessed oblivion" of alcohol.

145

5. AA immediately surrounds him with an accepting fellowship of individuals who have been through his experience and can therefore establish rapport when professional counselors have failed. It is this supportive fellowship which carries him through the first trying days of recovery. The fact that the fellowship is frequently focused through an individual sponsor who can become a parent-figure for the new AA "baby" is important. (Of course, many AA's have no sponsor.) The dependent relationship in AA allows the course of social regression which the alcoholic has followed to be reversed. The AA ingroup can serve as a substitute family. Again, AA uses supportive group therapy rather than religious therapy to promote initial sobriety.

6. AA's fine relationship with hospitals, doctors, and alcoholic clinics allows the newcomer to have the medical adjuncts to therapy which are often so important in establishing initial sobriety. This is in contrast with what might be called the "all religious" approach.

Beyond this success in inducing initial sobriety, AA is most effective in helping alcoholics achieve prolonged sobriety because:

1. In contrast with the rescue mission and Salvation Army, AA deals with a smaller proportion of those whose alcoholism is complicated by the added problem of homelessness.

2. The fact that AA depends neither on religious thrill (as evidenced, for example, by the lack of group singing), nor on a "hot flash" type of religious experience, makes for a more stable sobriety. Religious ecstasy is apt to produce an emotional hangover, which is destructive to sobriety. In AA, religious resources are made available on a more temperate basis and are utilized more for maintaining than producing sobriety. Because of its permissive attitude toward theological ideas, it accepts the alcoholic at the point he has reached in his religious life and allows his religious formulations to grow as his experiences change. Because the "spiritual angle" of the AA program is so subtle, it can "slip up on a fellow," as one AA put it.

3. AA provides substitute satisfactions to replace those of alcohol. Enjoyable and continuing fellowship in a group overcomes loneliness, a great enemy of prolonged sobriety. In addition there is an abundance of oral satisfactions—smoking, talking, and oceans of coffee—to replace the orality of alcoholism.

4. It sustains sobriety by keeping the alcoholic busy helping "those who do not know." It gives him a sense of mission and of unique usefulness. Becoming a sponsor imposes a responsibility on a person to set a good example for his "baby." This motivates the sponsor in the direction of continued sobriety. It also helps him feel important, boosting his self-esteem.

5. By providing a suggested series of steps, AA provides a continuing program of spiritual growth which is important, especially after the first enthusiasm of belonging has dimmed. It is significant that half of these steps are

146

devoted to altering the attitudes and interpersonal frictions which, in alcoholics, tend to produce a binge.

6. AA is successful in sustaining sobriety because it brings the pressure of responsibility to bear on the alcoholic when he is able to handle it. In the early phases the person finds help in the "allergy" conception. As he acquires more stable sobriety, he is confronted by the necessity of taking responsibility for the changing of those attitudes which lead him to drink. Then he is motivated to use the Twelve Steps.

7. AA is more successful in maintaining sobriety because it is successful in strengthening the person's *real* self-esteem, as distinguished from his grandiosity. It does this by keeping the initiative with him throughout the process, by making him feel accepted in a group, by respecting his rights as an adult to think and do what he himself wants to (including getting drunk), and by giving him a sense of unique usefulness in helping other alcoholics. As AA increases his self-acceptance, it diminishes his need for defensive grandiosity, which, like medieval armor, was a terrible weight as well as a protection.

8. AA tends to produce long-term sobriety because it is nonauthoritarian in organization and constituency. Each group is autonomous in all matters which affect only that group. Central agencies are considered as coordinating and service groups for AA as a whole. This decentralized democracy distributes the sense of responsibility to each member and reduces the inherent frustrations of authoritarian or hierarchical organizations. This makes for healthy group life and thus enhances the prospects for individual sobriety. The fact that AA is a self-help program in which there are no outside "authorities" is very significant in the light of the alcoholic's tendency to be rebellious toward authority.

9. The fact that AA can provide continuing group support makes for long-term sobriety. AA is so well distributed that wherever a member goes he is likely to find a group.

Closely related is the question as to whether AA will continue to exist, or will meet the fate of movements such as the Washingtonians, the first organized attempt by alcoholics to help alcoholics on a large scale. This movement began in the 1840's in Baltimore. At the beginning the Washingtonians focused attention on helping alcoholics. By means of mass meetings, testimonials, pledges, and material help, they succeeded in aiding hundreds. Unfortunately they did not follow the AA practice of admitting only alcoholics. The movement rose meteorically, spreading to city after city. Soon it was inextricably mixed with the temperance movement, attracting thousands of nonalcoholics. This sealed its doom. It was thoroughly absorbed into the temperance movement and, having lost its distinctive task of helping alcoholics, declined and died within a few years. It is the author's opinion that AA has an excellent chance of survival and continued growth because it has avoided the mistakes of the Washingtonian movement and has protected itself against the perils of institutionalism and the dangers of becoming side-tracked into other causes. It has done this by the formulation of "traditions" based on the trial-and-error experience of many groups. These traditions are officially recognized within the movement and are generally observed—so much so that AA, for example, has refused to accept several sizable bequests left by grateful members. The complete statement of the traditions, along with a discussion of them, is found in the book by Bill W., *Twelve Steps and Twelve Traditions*.[25] They are given here in the brief form printed in *The Grapevine* each month:

## THE TWELVE TRADITIONS

1. Our common welfare should come first; personal recovery depends upon AA unity.
2. For our Group purpose there is but one ultimate authority . . . a loving God as he may express himself in our Group Conscience. Our leaders are but trusted servants . . . they do not govern.
3. The only requirement for AA membership is a desire to stop drinking.
4. Each Group should be autonomous, except in matters affecting other groups or AA as a whole.
5. Each Group has but one primary purpose . . . to carry its message to the alcoholic who still suffers.
6. An AA Group ought never endorse, finance or lend the AA name to any related facility or outside enterprise lest problems of money, property and prestige divert us from our primary spiritual aim.
7. Every AA Group ought to be fully self-supporting, declining outside contributions.
8. Alcoholics Anonymous should remain forever non-professional, but our service centers may employ special workers.
9. AA, as such, ought never be organized; but we may create service boards or committees directly responsible to those they serve.
10. Alcoholics Anonymous has no opinion on outside issues; hence the AA name ought never be drawn into public controversy.
11. Our public relations policy is based on attraction rather than promotion; we need always maintain personal anonymity at the level of press, radio and films.
12. Anonymity is the spiritual foundation of all our Traditions, ever reminding us to place principles above personalities.

There is still the third criterion of AA's effectiveness. To what extent does the AA approach alter underlying personality structure rather than simply controlling symptoms? Is AA's effectiveness in producing long-term sobriety the result of the resolving of psychological conflicts which lie at the roots of alcoholism, or is it the result of an effective means of keeping the conflicts repressed or under control? As far as AA itself is concerned, this question is of little interest. The sole object of AA is sobriety. But the student of human personality and religion must ask the question. To him the "how" of the production of sobriety goes to the heart of an understanding of the dynamics of AA. Is the sober member of AA really a new person, or has he achieved a more effective way of controlling his unresolved inner conflicts?

Data from the author's interview files suggest that sweeping generalizations in answer to this question are not possible. In some cases, the alcoholic's AA solutions seemed rigid and repressive, as if the persons involved were having to hold themselves very hard to keep from slipping. On the other hand, some of the alcoholics seemed relatively relaxed and uncompulsive about their AA solutions. For instance when the interviewees were asked how they now handle their hostile feelings, twenty-nine gave answers showing repressive handling, such as: "I feel all bound up—all under control. I want to say, 'to hell with it all' "; or "Anger is something I must *absolutely* avoid." On the other hand, there were fifteen cases in which anger was being handled quite constructively. For example, "I don't keep resentment inside me. I go talk it over with the person"; or "Before, if my wife and I had a fight, I'd go out and slam the door and get drunk. Now I just go out and slam the door." The manner in which a religious approach to problems deals with the so-called "negative feelings" such as anger constitutes a reliable barometer for measuring the degree of repressiveness involved.

One reason why AA has certain repressive tendencies is its inadequate conception of human personality. The AA point of view, as set forth in the recognized literature of the movement, does not take full cognizance of the fact that personality factors such as selfishness, resentment, and hostility, which are controlled through the AA program, are actually *symptoms* of deeper problems of inadequacy, insecurity, and inner conflict. For example, anger, as AA says, does produce slips in alcoholics. It does so, however, not because anger in itself is a destructive feeling, but because it is considered "bad" by the person's conscience. This is why angry feelings have a destructive effect. Because of early conditioning, anger is unacceptable to the self-concept and therefore threatening to the person, producing anxiety. It is this anxiety that causes the alcoholic to drink. Since it does not recognize this, AA therapy tends to control symptoms rather than influence underlying causes in some cases. As we have said, many individual AA's do recognize the symptomatic nature of selfishness and negative feelings. Nevertheless, these individuals tend to feel that AA cannot and should not emphasize such a recognition in its general approach, for to do so would be to make it seem too much like psychiatry. This psychologizing, they feel, would frighten away many alcoholics who can come and accept it in its present form.

149

However, in those cases in which AA results in a basically repressive solution —"sitting on the lid harder"—sobriety is always precarious. Even if such a person stays sober, other symptoms are likely to appear. In most cases these symptoms are relatively harmless and considerably less objectionable than active alcoholism. The substitute compulsions seen in AA are examples of this—frantic Twelfth Step work and endless oral activity. In some cases the substitute symptoms are not so harmless—e.g., "nervous breakdowns" following long periods of sobriety in AA. The common assumption regarding wives of AA's is that they have unmixed joy over their husband's affiliation. Although this is true, by and large, the writer has known of cases in which the alcoholics have become so irritable and unpleasant that the wives almost wished they were drinking again. While the "almost" should be emphasized, this unpleasantness is still indicative of unsolved inner conflicts.

There are several things that must be said on the other side of the picture. If one compares AA with a psychoanalytically oriented therapy, it is probably valid to label it "repressive inspirational," as one writer on the subject has done.[26] But if one compares it to the evangelistic approach to alcoholism, it is relatively unrepressive. Then too, AA is accurate in regarding sobriety as a value in itself. As long as an alcoholic is drinking, his "motor" is racing, but his personality resources are out of gear. Keeping the individual sober is a prerequisite to the solution of any personality problem. By keeping him sober and by its social therapy the AA approach does actually "solve" many of his personality problems. This is especially true of those alcoholics whose underlying psychopathology is relatively minor. When they stop drinking and become accepted in the AA group, they often make very adequate adjustments.

All therapies contain positive and negative controls on behavior. Compared to most religious approaches to alcoholism, AA has less negative and more positive controls. Being nonauthoritarian, AA does not use irrational fear as a motivation. Fear of losing status in the group by having a slip and fear of what alcohol can actually do are both realistic fears. Major motivations are positive—e.g., the desire to achieve the psychological rewards of full participation in the group. It is because AA satisfies so many of the alcoholic's needs that it is able to control his attitudes and behavior in the direction of sobriety.

AA recognizes that there must be a reorientation of the personality if the person is to stay sober. Personality change and sobriety are mutually interdependent. As one interviewee put the matter: "I don't know if I'm sober because I'm happy or happy because I'm sober."

AA emphasizes the importance of self-understanding (steps four and ten). Several interviewees showed that they had gained considerable dynamic insight through this phase of AA. Within the supportive relationship of AA, these individuals had been able to do in a limited way what one is able to do in a psychotherapeutic relationship—viz., feel secure enough to relax one's usual defenses and take an honest look at painful aspects of the self.

It is my conviction that individual psychotherapy is sometimes needed in addition to AA in order to produce permanent, noncompulsive sobriety. This is not to suggest that most AA's need psychiatric treatment. Rather it is to indicate that in those cases where underlying psychopathology is severe, psychotherapy is a necessary supplement to AA therapy. This is fully in accord with much AA thinking. Bill W. suggested to me, for example, that the fourth or inventory step provides a natural bridge for the AA who needs it to receive psychiatric help.[27]

Alcoholism is like a building of several stories. AA is admirably equipped to take care of the upper levels—the runaway symptom levels. It can halt the addictive cycle and repair the personality damage resulting from the addiction. Once a person has been sober for a considerable time, the underlying psychopathology may need to be treated. This is where psychotherapy can be a valuable supplement to the AA program. The two can actually be complementary—the social therapy of AA giving indispensable group support and resocialization during the psychotherapy, and the psychotherapy aiding the person in forming more satisfying relationships in AA and beyond by resolving some of his inner conflicts. In order for this to happen the psychotherapist must have some appreciation and understanding of AA in particular and of religious dynamics in general.

If AA could combine its amazing program of social therapy with psychotherapeutic insights and techniques, particularly group therapy, an approach to alcoholism with maximum effectiveness might be produced. AA might then bring new life to many who cannot find fully satisfying sobriety in the present program. What is more, if such a development should take place, AA might set a pattern for a more fundamental cooperation between religion and psychology in dealing with human problems in general.

It should be reemphasized that AA, by itself and in its present form, is a tremendously hopeful and helpful program. One of those interviewed expressed a sentiment that is echoed by thousands of alcoholics today: "AA was for me the birth of hope!" The fundamental reason why it has been so is that AA has developed a means of conveying the *experience of acceptance* to the alcoholic. Through its *accepting fellowship* it has been more successful than any previous approach in helping the alcoholic to feel accepted by life and, therefore, to accept himself. As we have said before, this is what has been described in religious terms as "salvation by grace through faith." Thus AA has found an answer to the alcoholic's deep feeling of isolation, loneliness, and rejection. In this sense, AA is a religious therapy par excellence for alcoholism.

There are many aspects of AA's program and philosophy which can be applied to other problems of living. It is a tribute to AA that this has actually been tried by several groups, e.g., "Narcotics Anonymous" and "Divorcées Anonymous." The church, too, can learn much from AA, both about alcoholism and the healing power of creative religion. One of the incidental rewards that most people who become interested in AA derive from their contact is a little gem known as the "AA Prayer." After having been attributed to nearly every saint and seer in history, it finally was traced to Reinhold Niebuhr.[28] It is good philosophy not only for alcoholics but for those who wish to help them:

> God grant me the serenity
> To accept the things I cannot change,
> Courage to change the things I can
> And wisdom to know the difference.

Ruth Fox, a New York psychiatrist, has said that if her patients acquire the ability, through several years of psychotherapy, to live by the principles of this brief prayer, she would regard their therapy as successful.

## REFERENCES

1. Estimated world AA membership, January, 1967: between 350,000 and 400,000 (Communication from AA's General Service Office).

2. Biographical data on Bill's early life are from personal interviews.

3. The Oxford Group Movement, or Buchmanism, was a movement inspired by a Lutheran minister, Frank Buchman. It first flourished on college campuses (including Oxford) and then spread to other areas. It was an attempt to bring vital Christianity into the lives of people, changing them to live by certain ethical absolutes and motivating them to change others. It stressed the importance of groups in this change and appealed mainly to the "up and outers."

4. W. W. (Bill W.), "The Fellowship of Alcoholics Anonymous," Alcohol, Science and Society, p. 462. A comprehensive history of AA by a co-founder is contained in Alcoholics Anonymous Comes of Age (New York: Harper & Bros., 1957).

5. Ibid., p. 463.

6. Ibid.

7. W. G. W., "Alcoholics Anonymous" (panel discussion, "Chronic Alcoholism as a Medical Problem"), New York State Journal of Medicine, L (July 15, 1950), 1709.

8. Lois W., The AA Grapevine, February, 1950, p. 12.

9. W. G. W., "Alcoholics Anonymous" (panel discussion).

10. Oscar W. Ritchie, "A Sociohistorical Survey of AA," QJSA, IX (June, 1948), 122.

11. The AA Grapevine, January, 1951, p. 7.

12. Communication with AA's General Service Office, January 20, 1967.

13. Figures from AA 30 (AA World Services 1965), p. 19.

14. "We Come of Age," The AA Grapevine, September, 1950, p. 3.

15. The AA Grapevine, October, 1965, p. 21. It was the author's privilege to participate in the Toronto Convention.

16. The first of these was published by Harper & Brothers, 1953; the second by Alcoholics Anonymous World Services, 1967.

17. Interview, February 10, 1953. Additional biographical data on Bill W. are to be found in the Big Book, pp. 10-26.

18. *AA 30*, p. 45.

19. This is the AA estimate; see *AA 30*, p. 19.

20. The Editors of *Fortune*, in collaboration with Russell W. Davenport, *U.S.A., The Permanent Revolution* (New York: Prentice-Hall, 1951).

21. *Ibid.*, p. 149.

22. This AA talk is condensed from one given by a member of the Chicago Group on the fifth anniversary of his sobriety, May 22, 1945.

23. W. G. W., "Alcoholics Anonymous" (panel discussion), p. 1708.

24. P. L. Smith, "Alcoholics Anonymous," *Psychiatric Quarterly*, XV (1941), 554-62. The fact that half of a group of alcoholics who were in a mental hospital recovered is significant.

25. Used by permission of AA General Service Headquarters.

26. Thomas W. Giles, "Group Psychotherapy," *Psychosomatic Medicine*, April, 1943.

27. Personal interview.

28. Niebuhr says: "Of course it may have been spooking around for years, even centuries, but I don't think so. I honestly believe that I wrote it myself." (*The AA Grapevine*, January, 1950, p. 6.)

# 6

# The Psychodynamics of a Religious Approach to Alcoholism

To be realistic and adequate, it is essential that a religious approach to alcoholism include an awareness of the distinctive contributions which a religious as compared with a nonreligious approach can make. Any attempt to throw more than superficial light on this matter carries one into a consideration of the dynamic relationship between alcohol and religion, a relationship to which sufficient psychological attention has not been given.

## The Dynamic Meaning of Alcoholism

*An understanding of any religious approach to alcoholism must include the recognition that, for the alcoholic, religion and alcohol often are functionally interchangeable.* Just before committing suicide, a seemingly "hopeless" alcoholic was asked by a psychiatrist, "Who can help you?" To this the alcoholic replied: "No person or institution. Only what I do not now possess—a belief, a faith in something outside myself, something stronger, more overwhelming than my weakness—some form of *spiritual substitute* that yet evades me." [1]

If a religious approach is to be successful, it must supply what this alcoholic called a "spiritual substitute" for alcohol. The ability to provide such a substitute is a most important advantage which a religious approach has over a nonreligious approach. It accounts in part for the fact that religious approaches have proved to be relatively effective in this area.

There are two ways in which religion and alcohol are deeply related in terms of their dynamic function. Because of the intensity of their negative feeling concerning alcohol, many religious leaders have overlooked the fact that alcohol has answers, however unfortunate in the final analysis, in two problem-areas of life in which religion also gives answers. In the first place both give answers to the problems of weariness, boredom, drudgery, rejection, and loneliness in our dog-eat-dog society. Thomas Wolfe, whose books contain

154

many insightful references to alcoholism, asks the question, in *Of Time and the River*, to which alcohol has been the answer for many:

Where shall the weary rest? When shall the lonely heart come home? What doors are open to the wanderer? And which of us shall find his father, know his face, and in what time, and in what land? Where? Where the weary heart can abide forever, where the weary of wandering can find peace, where the tumult, the fever and the fret shall be forever stilled.[2]

Alcoholism is a tragic response to areas of tragedy in our culture. The insecurity and emotional malnutrition bred by an anxious, puritanical, competitive society has resulted in many damaged orphans of the spirit. These are people who, because of their fears and inner conflicts, are cut off from trustful, fulfilling fellowship with other human beings. Alcohol has always had something to offer these, the weary, the anxious, the lonely, the spiritual wanderers. It offers the illusion of unity with one's fellows, temporary deadening of anxiety, and the quieting of inner conflict. Its relief is temporary and illusory, but available to many who have found no other. A fluid which for a time can banish disappointment, frustration, and feelings of inadequacy, which can give feelings of self-confidence and the illusion of strength has tremendous appeal, an appeal which those who seek a better way must take into account.

In the mood of a psalmist Thomas Wolfe speaks through one of his characters, expressing the feelings of those who satisfy their religious needs by means of alcohol:

Immortal drunkenness! What tribute can we ever pay, what song can we ever sing, what swelling praise can be sufficient to express the joy, the gratefulness and the love which we, who have known youth and hunger in America, have owed to alcohol? We are so lost, so lonely, so forsaken in America: immense and savage skies bend over us, and we have no door.[3]

Through the use of wine, man has anesthetized the sufferings caused by social chaos. This was what William Booth had in mind when he wrote, "Gin is the only Lethe of the miserable." The author of Proverbs 31 offers this prescription for the alleviation of social suffering: "Let him drink and forget his poverty, and remember his misery no more." As the social burdens of civilization and industrialization increased, the desire for the escape of alcohol grew. Many centuries ago the psalmist (104:15) thanked God for the wine "that maketh glad the heart of man." Some men, as Jellinek once put it, began to use wine not to gladden the heart but to put to sleep the soul.[4] The tragic inadequacy of the use of alcohol as an opiate for social chaos becomes apparent when the cure is recognized as a cause of further chaos.

Religion, too, has always had something to say to the weary, the anxious, the lonely, the spiritual wanderer. In our discussion of the religious approaches to alcoholism we have seen how religion can give real fellowship, abiding comfort, and strength. Like alcohol, religion has offered solace and a haven from the burdens of society. At times it has, like alcohol, become an opiate, blinding men to social injustice. But at its best it has shown men principles by which they could work for justice and has inspired them to live by these principles. In this sense, it is totally unlike alcohol as a solution to social chaos.

But man's burdens are not limited to those imposed by social disequilibrium and chaos. There is another dimension to his problem. His very finitude, his earth-boundedness, his impotence in the face of the forces of nature and death—these facts are inherent in his nature as a creature, and all of them impose a burden on his soul. This is what we have discussed as "ultimate anxiety." Man is the animal who knows that he will die; he is the animal who wants to transcend his animality—to become something larger, more powerful, to feel infinite. Alcohol can give him an illusion of transcendence. In *Look Homeward Angel, A Story of Buried Life*, Thomas Wolfe describes this power of alcohol to give feelings of grandiosity. His character Eugene is intoxicated for the first time. Here are his musings: "In all the earth there was no other like him, no other fitted to be so sublimely and magnificently drunken. . . . Why, when it was possible to buy a God in a bottle, and drink him off, and become a God oneself, were men not forever drunken?" [5] In discussing religious mysticism during his Gifford lectures, William James recognized this similarity of function between alcohol and religion:

The sway of alcohol over mankind is unquestionably due to its power to stimulate the mystical faculties of human nature, usually crushed to earth by the cold facts and dry criticisms of the sober hour. Sobriety diminishes, discriminates, and says no; drunkenness expands, unites and says yes. It is in fact the great exciter of the Yes function in man. It brings its votary from the chill periphery of things to the radiant core. It makes him for the moment one with the truth. Not through mere perversity do men run after it. . . . The drunken consciousness is one bit of the mystical consciousness.[6]

Because alcohol has the power to give temporary feelings of adequacy, expansiveness, and ecstasy, it has been regarded in many cultures as something magical, even divine. In Greek mythology, for example, Dionysus, the god of wine, was also the divine representative of the future or larger life. In the Greek, Roman, and Jewish traditions we find wine used as a frequent symbol of abundant life and of the "fluid of life." The figures of drunken men were sometimes carved on ancient gravestones as symbols of the life beyond death. The use of wine in the Christian tradition—viz., in the Catholic mass and the sacrament of the Lord's Supper in certain Protestant churches—is another example of the manner in which alcohol has symbolized the ecstatic element in religion.

When one sees the way in which the vital, the ecstatic element in life has often been crushed by the mundane and the puritanical in our culture, the "charm of the Dionysian," as Nietzsche called it, is apparent. Alcohol has the ability to give temporary feelings of mutual acceptance and unity among men, and between man and the rest of creation. In a world of barriers and separation, the desire for such unity is very strong. Nietzsche describes the way in which alcohol satisfies this desire:

Under the charm of the Dionysian not only is the union between man and man reaffirmed, but Nature which has become estranged, hostile, or subjugated, celebrates once more her reconciliation with her prodigal son, man. . . . Now all the stubborn, hostile barriers which necessity, caprice or "shameless fashion" have erected between man and man, are broken down. . . . He feels that the veil of Maya has been torn aside and were now merely fluttering in tatters before the mysterious Primordial Unity.[7]

Alcohol gives the individual the temporary ability to accept himself. Tillich has written concerning man's inner schism, "The depth of our separation lies in just the fact that we are not capable of a great and merciful divine love toward ourselves." [8] To the person who is not able to accept and love himself, alcohol gives the temporary illusion of self-acceptance. It stills the inner conflict and makes him feel unified and at peace with himself. Alcohol also gives a brief "taste" of being accepted by (and acceptable to) others. We have discussed man's isolation from his fellow men in our culture. Etiologically speaking, the parent who does not feel accepted, by himself and others, is unable to give his child the warm, vital experience of being accepted. Having never felt accepted, the child grows up unable to accept himself and, therefore, unable to accept others or feel accepted by them. Thus, the experience of rejection, and the anxiety which results from it, is passed on through the generations. Alcohol gives a person suffering from rejection the temporary experience of interpersonal unity. The problem has its broader dimension— the feeling of being rejected by and isolated from life or God, to use the religious term. This feeling becomes intermingled with a man's ultimate anxiety. As a part of its pseudo-answer to life's problems, alcohol apparently can give some people a feeling of mystical unity with Life.

The saddest part of all this is that so many people are able to find the experience of acceptance only via alcohol. That so many must find their spiritual satisfactions in this way is a profound tragedy. The situation was aptly described by William James when he wrote: "It is part of the deeper mystery and tragedy of life that whiffs and gleams of something that we immediately recognize as excellent should be vouchsafed to so many of us only in the fleeting earlier phases of what in its totality is so degrading a poison." [9]

There was pathos in the experience of the alcoholic interviewee who recalled: "When I reached a certain point in a drunk, I felt as though I were on the edge of a beautiful land. I kept drinking to try to find it." Bill W., co-founder of AA, once said, "Before AA we were trying to find God in a bottle." It is, at least in part, because men have not found God elsewhere that they seek him in a bottle.

## The Dynamic Significance of the Religious Experience

It is apparent that personal religion and the religious fellowship can be paths to the experience of being accepted. The genius of Protestantism has been its emphasis on what is described in biblical language as "salvation by grace through faith." This is essentially the experience of acceptance. Through a religious experience the person feels accepted by God. He does not earn this acceptance. It is his because he is a child of God. When he comes to the place in his own experience, often through suffering, at which he can accept the fact that he is not God, he is able to establish a relationship of creative trust, i.e., "faith," in God. Someone has described this step in spiritual maturation as "resigning as General Manager of the universe." This creative trust opens the door of one's heart to the grace or acceptance of God. It is when one feels accepted by God that one can "accept himself as being accepted," to use again Tillich's phrase. When one has accepted himself, one is able to accept and feel accepted by others. It is through this feeling of divine acceptance that one's ultimate anxieties are allayed.

Thus, religion has genuine answers to the spiritual problems to which alcohol gives pseudo-answers. Sound religion gives one a feeling of unity, of self-forgiveness, of acceptance, and of the larger life. When religion has not had its spiritual vitality squeezed out, it can satisfy man's need for Dionysian experience. In a lasting and genuine way it can help men accept or overcome their anxiety about their own finitude. Religious faith, in fact, provides the only satisfying answer to ultimate anxiety.

When a person uses alcohol as a persistent substitute for all that a religious orientation can give him, his alcoholic solution, sooner or later, is bound to crumble in a heap around his head. It is then that religious resources, mediated through a religious group, can often bring healing. They accomplish this by being a channel for the experience of being accepted, thus providing a substitute for his unsuccessful alcoholic way of life. To the extent that a religious group can mediate this experience of being accepted it is an effective approach to the problem of alcoholism.

As we have seen in Part II, religious groups provide spiritual substitutes for alcohol in a variety of ways. The chart on pages 160-61 gives a synoptic view of the ways in which the four religious groups studied sought to provide constructive answers to the problems of the alcoholic in place of the destructive answers of alcohol. Column I, entitled "The Alcoholic Feels," describes the major emotional problems of the alcoholic at the stage of his sickness at which he usually has arrived when he comes to a religious group. Column II, "Alcohol's Solution," describes the unsatisfactory answers which alcohol gives to these problems. Since the dynamics of the rescue mission and the Salvation Army are quite similar, the solutions which these approaches give are lumped together in Column III. The solutions of the Emmanuel Movement and AA are presented in Columns IV and V. In the case of each movement, the solution is that achieved by the operation of that approach *at its best*.

## Summary

If, as has been presented in this chapter, alcoholism is to be understood as in part a tragic attempt to satisfy certain spiritual needs, it is obvious that an effective religious approach to the problem has certain inherent advantages over a nonreligious approach. Let us summarize the most important of these advantages:

1. A religious solution can provide the individual with a *sense of super-human help*, not only in meeting the specific problem of alcoholism, but in bearing the general frustrations, disappointments, drudgery, and interpersonal friction which contribute to the etiology of alcoholism. The help of a "higher Power" is reliable and available even when the help of individuals or of the group is not. In AA this help is often thought of as supplementing the therapeutic help of the group. Because of the alcoholic's grandiosity and his ambivalence toward authority, the opportunity provided by a religious approach for him to come to terms with a "Power greater than himself" can be a real growth experience. It may mean that he surrenders some of his infantile grandiosity by coming to accept his need for help from above himself. In a healthy sense, it may mean an acceptance of his creature-hood and finitude, his human dependence on the Creator, and his need for relatedness to the rest of creation. In some cases, the sense of superhuman help may result in an immature dependency relation—a childish relationship to Deity. In such cases religious regression has replaced alcoholic regression, which, though not ideal from a standpoint of mature religion, is a relatively constructive substitution.

2. A religious approach can provide the alcoholic with a *feeling of being accepted by life*. As we have seen, in AA an individual first experiences acceptance by the group and, on the basis of this experience, gradually is enabled to accept himself. When his higher Power changes from "the group"

| I<br>THE ALCOHOLIC FEELS | II<br>ALCOHOL'S SOLUTION | III<br>RESCUE MISSION AND SALVATION ARMY SOLUTIONS | IV<br>EMMANUEL'S SOLUTION | V<br>AA'S SOLUTION |
|---|---|---|---|---|
| 1. Trapped in the vortex of an addictive spiral. | Anesthetizes pain of this feeling but accelerates velocity of the spiral. | Breaks spiral by powerful emotional experience of "salvation" induced by fear and guilt plus promise of new life. | Uses suggestion and auto-suggestion to break the spiral; medication recommended where necessary. Supportive group experiences. | Provides practical tools (e.g. 24-hour plan), for maintaining sobriety, plus example and support of sober group. Medication recommended where necessary. |
| 2. Depressed. | Gives feeling of elation, followed by worse depression. | Gives feeling of thrill or religious ecstasy. | Encouragement of the therapist, plus the reduction of guilt through analysis. | Group uplift, plus the reduction of the guilt at the root of depression. |
| 3. Isolated, rejected, unacceptable, in a "shell," desocialized. | Gives temporary feeling of nearness to people. | Melts shell by powerful emotional experience, plus acceptance by the ingroup of the "saved." | Provides relationship to an accepting person—the therapist—plus some group acceptance, providing the experience of acceptance. | Gives an accepting group in which resocialization and growth in responsibility can take place. |
| 4. Guilt and self-rejection. | Depresses self-critique; allows atonement via self-punishment. | Salvation experience gives sense of forgiveness by supreme Authority plus devices of atonement. | "Sickness" conception of alcoholism, plus acceptance by therapist, plus reduction of guilt via insight into one's own psychic life. | "Sickness" conception reduces guilt and releases energies for therapeutic ends. Nonjudgmental group sharing common problem. |
| 5. Nameless fears, awful pain, jitters. | Anesthetizes pain and fears; quiets jitters; eventual oblivion. May increase fears by releasing repressions. | Fears reduced when alcohol leaves body. Sense of protection by God. | Dependence on an authority figure plus analysis of the roots of fears. Medication for jitters. | Medication for jitters. Safety in group. Understanding of strange alcoholic behavior. |
| 6. Oppressed by a sense of futility, tragedy (in the philosophical sense), and finitude. Ultimate anxiety. | Gives temporary panacea; anesthetizes all anxiety; gives sense of larger life. | Gives a religious experience of larger life, meaningful relationship to the Ultimate here and hereafter, experience of acceptance. | Offers a new sense of relatedness to the whole of creation and awareness of divine potentialities within. | Gradual, growing sense of meaning and relatedness to people. Growing faith and assurance about life, strong experience of acceptance. |

| | | | | |
|---|---|---|---|---|
| adult interpersonal demands. | regression. | the wonderful Power, and on authoritarian group. | followed (in theory) by independence through insight. | group in which one may grow in interpersonal adequacy. |
| 8. Inadequate, weak, inferior. | Gives an illusion of adequacy, superiority by depressing self-critique. | Gives feeling of strength through identification with the saved and with the Supreme Power. | Inferiority feelings reduced as he understands real causes of addiction. Becomes more adequate in interpersonal realm. Identification with therapist; strengthening of self-esteem. | Strength from group identification. His weakness (alcoholism) now seen as sickness and becomes basis of unique usefulness and acceptance by the group. Strengthens self-esteem. |
| 9. Defensively grandiose, magically powerful. | Gives feeling of expansiveness and magically powerful condition. | Gives opportunity to become instruments of divine power. Reduction of guilt reduces need for grandiosity. Partial surrender of grandiosity in salvation experience. | Strengthening of self-esteem plus psychological maturity removes need for grandiosity. | Reduces need for defensive grandiosity. Rewards "humility." Surrender of grandiosity possible in accepting group. |
| 10. Useless. | Makes him feel he is world's benefactor, or not care that he isn't. | Gives a sense of mission to help save others. | Insight allows one to achieve a more constructive role in relation to others. | Gives sense of unique usefulness in helping alcoholics. |
| 11. Tension of repressed aggression and rage. | Melts frozen rage, giving partial release of repressed aggression while defenses are lowered. | Allows release of aggression in group-approved channels—i.e., toward unsaved. More effective repression, strengthened by group and religious sanctions. | Reduction of the inner pressures through therapeutic release; repression of some by suggestive therapy. | Through moral inventory removes many of the precipitants and occasions of anger and frustration. Release by aggressive activity in helping others. |
| 12. Egocentric, "selfish," lack of group controls. | Increases egocentricity. | Other-directed activities and interests rewarded by group. Group controls possible because of group satisfactions. | Psychoanalytic reduction of inner conflicts removes a degree of need to be "selfish." Patients could become friendly visitors, etc., thus acquiring other-directed interests and activities. | A planned program of other-directed activities (Twelfth Step) designed to keep the individual from egocentric isolation. Enlightened self-interest recognized as legitimate. |
| 13. Pressure from inner conflicts, guilt of unlived life. | Gives the illusion of inner unity, freedom, self-direction. | Pressure continues but somewhat offset by unifying religious devotion. | Character change through self-understanding resulting from psychoanalysis. | Some character change through group therapy, social participation, self-analysis. |

to God, it is often an indication of psychological growth in the sense that he now feels accepted by life itself (instead of just the ingroup of fellow alcoholics). To put it another way, the alcoholic has reestablished contact with larger areas of experience. He has become less defensive because he has experienced acceptance. He is no longer a rebelling child. Nor does he feel that he needs to earn acceptance from God. He is accepted as a child of God; he can therefore accept himself. We have seen that success worship on the part of parents is often a factor in the psychological roots of alcoholism. The child feels he must achieve impossible goals in order to be acceptable. In this context, the significance of the religious experience of self-acceptance on the basis of being accepted by God is evident.

3. A religious approach can provide the alcoholic with a means of handling his *ultimate anxiety*.[10] If it is true that philosophical anxiety—anxiety about death, meaninglessness, and finitude—is a factor in the etiology of alcoholism, then a religious solution makes a unique contribution toward eliminating the causes of alcoholism. It does this by providing the individual with a sense of relatedness to and participation in the larger life. It helps to satisfy his need for experiences in which he transcends his finitude and receives mystical life. It gives him a faith in the trustworthiness of the Ultimate and the triumph over death and the fear of death. It provides him with a concept of Providence and the feeling that he is not alone in the crises of life. All this helps him to handle his ultimate anxiety in a constructive fashion.

4. An effective religious approach can help the individual to discover a purpose in living by establishing his personality on the foundation of a *meaningful philosophy of life*. A religious approach is the time-tested way of satisfying what Erich Fromm has called the universal human need for a "system of thought and action shared by a group which gives the individual a frame of orientation and an object of devotion." [11] By satisfying such a need a religious approach gives order, meaning, and other-directedness to living. All of these are of prime importance in providing a secure foundation for happy sobriety. By giving the alcoholic a purpose in living, a sense that he is an important part of a God-given plan to help others, one provides a positive reason for not drinking. What we are discussing here is quite different from simply rationally satisfying answers concerning basic philosophical problems. It is the zest and emotional involvement which comes from feeling oneself a part of something that really matters.

5. A religious orientation can provide a *group approach* to alcoholism with a *unifying commitment to a group-transcending value*. It is of great significance that the religious group always has an object of reference beyond itself. It thinks of itself as a channel through which a Power greater than itself can operate. This tends to give the group a stronger sense of purpose and a greater cohesiveness. There have been some speculations about the feasibility

of, and at least one unsuccessful attempt to have, an AA group without the "spiritual angle." The predominant view in AA is that any such attempts are foredoomed to failure. The spiritual angle and the group therapy are not distinct entities but are interrelated. It seems to be true that for alcoholics it is important to feel themselves a part of something that is bigger and more important than the individual AA group and that this "something" is more than simply a creation of human ingenuity. This sense of what might be called the "vertical dimension" of the religiously oriented group can be a powerful factor in satisfying not only the longing to belong but the need to belong to something that has fundamental and abiding significance.

## REFERENCES

1. Jerry Gray (pseud.), *The Third Strike*, p. 32. [Italics supplied.]
2. (New York: Charles Scribner's Sons, 1935), p. 2.
3. *Ibid.*, p. 281.
4. Summary lecture at the Yale Summer School of Alcohol Studies, 1949.
5. (New York: Charles Scribner's Sons, 1947), p. 525.
6. *The Varieties of Religious Experience*, pp. 377-78.
7. *The Works of Nietzsche*, pp. 172-73.
8. *Shaking of the Foundations*, p. 158.
9. *The Varieties of Religious Experience*, p. 378.
10. For a more comprehensive discussion of the role of ultimate or existential anxiety in alcoholism, see Howard J. Clinebell, Jr., "Philosophical-Religious Factors in the Etiology and Treatment of Alcoholism," *QJSA*, September, 1963.
11. *Psychoanalysis and Religion*, p. 21.

PART III

# THE MINISTER'S
## APPROACH to
# ALCOHOLISM

# 7

# The Ethical Problem in Alcoholism

Inebriety has been a simple moral problem to the layman for so long that the underlying problems are only now receiving attention from physicians. A Minneapolis newspaper recently printed a story about "John Bones" who was sentenced to the workhouse for the 107th time. The tone of the article was one of whimsical despair at the unalterable depravity of "Mr. Bones" who has wilfully spent some 18 of the past 20 years as a guest of the city.

—Charles C. Hewitt [1]

One question concerning alcoholism in which most religious leaders are keenly interested is this: What is the ethical problem in alcoholism? It is obvious to them that alcoholism is not a simple moral problem, and yet they are aware of the fact that there must be ethical implications involved. It seems probable that failure on the part of many ministers to find adequate answers to this question is one important reason why organized religion has not made a larger contribution to the solution of the problem.

One of the leading Roman Catholic authorities in the field of alcoholism is John C. Ford, professor of moral and pastoral theology, Weston College, Weston, Massachusetts.[2] At the annual meeting of the National Council on Alcoholism on March 18, 1955, Father Ford made a statement that should be an axiom in the clergyman's approach to alcoholics. He said, "One must never approach an alcoholic on the basis of what is usually called 'morality.' " Anyone who has dealt in an insightful manner with even one alcoholic can vouch for the validity of this statement. From a practical standpoint, to moralize with an alcoholic is the ultimate in counseling futility.

However, it is essential that a minister be clear in his own mind as to what the ethical problems are in alcoholism. This is not simply an exercise in the theory of ethics, but has definite practical implications. For whether an individual is aware of it or not, his relationship with alcoholics will be influenced by what he believes in his heart concerning this basic question.

To the person concerned with the ethical dimension of living it is not

167

satisfying simply to say that alcoholism is a sickness, implying that the ethical issue has thereby been eliminated. To him every personal and social problem is also an ethical problem. From the 146 questionnaires returned by the ministers who attended the first seven years of the Yale Summer School of Alcohol Studies,[3] it is apparent that there exists not only a considerable variety of opinion but also some confusion regarding the nature of the ethical problems in alcoholism. This is not surprising in the light of the fact that the answer involves one's entire orientation concerning morality and human behavior in general.

## Sin and Alcoholism

Does alcoholism involve sin and, if so, in what sense or senses? In what way is the sin involved related to the sickness involved? These are difficult questions to which there are no facile or complete answers. It is important to recognize at the outset that the word "sin" has been used in a variety of ways in the literature on ethics. Most of these uses or definitions have been applied to alcoholism. Here is an evaluative summary of some of the more frequent conceptions:

1. *Alcoholism is a sin and not a sickness from start to finish.* Only a very small minority of the Yale ministers (about 5 percent) held to this position. This was the view which we encountered previously in the study of the rescue mission. According to this conception, alcoholism begins as the sin of drinking and ends as a sinful habit. It is entirely a matter of immoral behavior. At no point can it be called a genuine sickness, except perhaps a "sin-sickness."

The inadequacy of this view will be obvious to anyone who is acquainted with the scientific evidence concerning alcoholism. Whatever the disagreement among different scientific schools of thought regarding the causes of the problem, there is wide agreement that in its advanced stages alcoholism is both a psychological and a physiological disease. The "all-sin" view errs in oversimplifying the causation of alcoholism, ignoring the psychological, social, cultural, philosophical, and perhaps physiological factors which play significant roles in its etiology.

2. *Alcoholism begins as a personal sin and ends as a sickness.* This would seem from the questionnaires to be one of the most common views held by clergymen. Earlier we saw it as the predominant view of the Salvation Army approach. Briefly put, this is the view: Drinking alcohol is, per se, a sin for a variety of reasons. One who drinks exposes himself to the danger of becoming an alcoholic. Once the drinking has passed a certain point and is out of volitional control, it becomes a sickness. Although the person is no longer responsible for drinking—since he now drinks compulsively, i.e., beyond the control of his will—he is responsible for having caught the compulsion or illness.

168

This view is more adequate than the first. It is more apt to result in effective therapy since it recognizes that in its advanced stages alcoholism is a sickness. This view, like the first, has the limitation of oversimplifying the causation of alcoholism, ignoring or de-emphasizing the complex array of factors discussed in the early chapters of this book. It is not within the scope of this book to attempt to adjudicate the disagreement among sincere Christians as to whether drinking per se is a sin. However, if one chooses to regard it as a sin, it is well to remember that even the early drinking of the alcoholic is part of a total behavioral pattern which is strongly influenced by his damaged personality as well as by cultural pressures. He is not a completely free agent. The alcoholic is a compulsive person even before he becomes a compulsive drinker. If personal sin implies personal freedom of choice, then the sin involved in the early stages of alcoholism is limited to the degree that the person's freedom is limited. Here we are in the middle of the key problem of ethics—responsibility—which we shall discuss subsequently.

3. *Alcoholism is a sickness which involves the sin of abuse.* This view holds that it is the abuse and not the use of alcohol which constitutes the sin in alcoholism. This is the Roman Catholic point of view. The sin is the sin of excess involved in becoming and remaining an alcoholic. The Catholic Church recognizes that a neurotic compulsion is involved in at least some alcoholics' behavior and holds that "culpability is reduced according to the strength" of their neuroses.[4]

This position, together with position 2, has the practical difficulty of making it necessary to establish a degree of responsibility or to find a line of demarcation beyond which a person is not responsible. In a concrete case this is utterly impossible.

4. *Alcoholism is a sickness which is caused by a combination of factors involving both sin and sickness.* This is a fair statement of the view of those ministers who regard drinking as wrong but who also recognize the existence of various etiological factors which are beyond the control of the individual. From an entirely different standpoint, it also expresses the view of AA. As has been said, AA, although it takes no sides in the matter, does not regard drinking as morally wrong. It emphasizes its conviction that the alcoholic has an "allergy" to alcohol. It goes on, however, to express its belief that one is driven to drink by selfishness—the word "sin" is not used—and its symptoms. One *is* responsible for these factors which produce the "mental obsession" to drink, even though one *is not* responsible for having an atypical physical response to alcohol. We will evaluate this AA conception of responsibility subsequently in this chapter.

5. *Alcoholism involves sin in the sense that it has destructive consequences.* This is the first of three nonjudgmental conceptions of sin as applied to alcoholism. One of the Yale ministers wrote: "Alcoholism is a sin in that it

169

hinders the person from abundant living and true happiness. It is not a sin insofar as morals are concerned." Another wrote: "It is a sin in the sense that it detracts from his relationship with God, his family, and his community." These are descriptions of the consequences of alcoholism rather than judgments as to the responsibility involved. If sin is defined as anything which harms personality, then alcoholism is most certainly a sin. If one accepts this definition of sin as a legitimate one, there can be no quarrel with the application.

6. *Alcoholism is a social sin.* One of the Yale ministers stated this point of view very well when he said: "Alcoholism is a sin only in the sense that it is a sin attributed to society, especially a Christian society—that we have been unable to bring about a world free from the tensions and conflicts of the present day. I do not consider it a personal sin."

Another put it this way: "It may be a sin, but it is more a symptom or an evidence of a sinful condition in some parts of our society—more sinful for Christian and civilized people to not only allow but promote the conditions that cause it."

Whatever one's view of the personal responsibility involved on the part of the alcoholic, one can certainly accept the fact that "society greases the slope down which he slides." The chaos and psychological insecurity of our world, the confusion and conflict of values regarding drinking and drunkenness, the traumatic circumstances to which many children are subjected—these are a part of the sickness of our society of which the sickness of alcoholism is one manifestation. In discussing the ethical aspects of alcoholism E. M. Jellinek said in effect at the Yale Summer School of 1949: "Alcoholism certainly is a moral problem. If six out of every hundred persons who went swimming at a certain beach contracted a disease that had all sorts of destructive effects, it would certainly be regarded as a question of public morals and safety." Society is involved in the causation of alcoholism; it therefore has a responsibility for its treatment and prevention.

7. *Alcoholism involves original sin.* In presenting this point of view I am not discussing the untenable position of biblical literalism which holds that man's nature is corrupted by the sin of a generic ancestor, Adam. Instead I am attempting to describe the dynamic meaning which is implied in the conception of "original sin" (a meaning which has been reaffirmed by the findings of modern depth psychology), the only sense in which the conception is intelligible.

It is a fact of experience that, as someone has said, "Every man is born with a pack on his back." This is to say that each person must take into account the "given" in his own particular situation—the hereditary and environmental factors, the historical situation into which he happens to have been born, the elements of powerful childhood conditioning which occurred before he was in a position to exercise power of choice, and the inherent limitations of his finitude which are involved in his existential or ultimate anxiety. Further, a realistic analysis of human experience leads one to the conclusion that all evil cannot be explained as the result of ignorance, as the Socratic tradition has claimed. There seems to be a certain recalcitrance at the very center of man's nature which inhibits him in doing that which he knows to be good. This has been referred to, in traditional language, as the "bondage of the will." [5] Even in his best acts, man seems to have an inescapable self-centered-ness—a condition which causes him to deify his institutions, the things he has made, and even himself. The alienation from God which results from this idolatry is at the very root of man's aloneness and anxiety. By making himself the center of the universe, man cuts himself off from his own fulfillment—a fulfillment which can take place only as he establishes a genuine relatedness to the rest of creation and to the Creator.

This tendency toward self-deification, which is close to the heart of the concept "original sin" as the term is used by many contemporary theologians, is quite evident in the alcoholic. The selfishness of the alcoholic is, as we have seen, to a large extent a symptom of inner conflict and insecurity; but his selfishness is also to some degree an expression of the egocentric nature of man. As we have seen in the discussion of the etiological factors in the introductory chapters, the alcoholic is an illuminating example of the influence of the "given" on human behavior. Whether or not one uses the term "original sin"—and its usefulness has certainly been limited by the manner in which it has been employed by the literalists—the facts of experience which men were trying to verbalize when they coined the term must be taken into account in understanding the alcoholic and his situation.

In deciding where one stands in the matter of the ethical problems involved in alcoholism, one may well combine several of the conceptions mentioned. An adequate view must certainly include recognition of the factors mentioned under sections 5, 6, and 7. The conception expressed in section 4 will undoubtedly prove satisfying to many ministers, though the difficulties involved should certainly be faced. At this point, the truth of the statement made earlier in this chapter—that there is no facile or complete answer to the question—should be apparent. The following discussion should make it more so.

## The Problem of Responsibility

A more systematic examination of the problem of responsibility in the light of depth psychology as it is related to alcoholism is now in order. Before pushing ahead it is well to heed the reminder of David E. Roberts, who wrote in *Psychotherapy and a Christian View of Man*:

171

The concept of responsibility has been a source of endless difficulties in psychology, philosophy and theology. Any one who has pondered the problems of freedom and determinism will probably sympathize with the sentiment which prompted Milton to assign discussion of this topic to some little devils in Satan's legions who liked to bandy it about during moments of relaxation—without getting anywhere.[6]

Depth psychology has demonstrated that much of man's behavior which had formerly been attributed to free will, inherent badness, or chance, is actually caused by unconscious forces over which one has no control. It does not follow that the personality is a sort of robot whose behavior is completely determined by external or internal forces. What is implied is that *all behavior is caused*—that it does not simply happen by chance—that the realm of the psyche is orderly and law-abiding. All behavior is caused and, equally important, *the self is one of the causes*, to a greater or lesser degree. The goal of spiritual or psychological health is the enhancement of self-determinism—the growth in the capacity of a self to achieve responsibility for itself. To the extent that a person is driven by inner compulsions, he is not self-determining and therefore not able to be responsible. The relatively self-determining self is able to handle the factors in the "given" and mold them in a creative fashion. The compulsive person is the victim of the "given." He is driven and determined by it. In other words, there are many factors—heredity, environment, historical circumstances, childhood conditioning, unconscious drives—which impinge on the person as he makes a decision. The manner in which the self relates or arranges these factors is the creative element. The more compulsive a person is, the less creative he can be about the use of these factors and the more machinelike are his reactions.

There must be some degree of self-determination in any person who is not completely detached from reality, but in many persons it is greatly limited. The evidence we have concerning the early life and adjustment of alcoholics points, in many cases, to a serious limitation of their capacity for self-determination. Everything we know points to the appropriateness of a nonjudgmental attitude toward the alcoholic.

Christian theology has held that all men are sinners in the sense that they tend to abuse the degree of freedom which they possess. Alcoholics, of course, share in this attribute of humanity. The important thing to remember is this: The factors that separate alcoholic-sinners from other sinners (that is, the factors which make alcoholics alcoholics) are factors over which there is little self-determination. Real understanding of the alcoholic and the etiology of his sickness leads one directly to the feeling expressed by the familiar words used as a motto in AA, "There, but for the Grace of God, go I." This is not sentimentalism, but the essence of psychological insight and the basis for real

Christian charity. When one reaches this point in his feeling toward alcoholics—a point which involves considerable self-understanding—he is no longer interested in trying to pin sin on the alcoholic. His only interest is in helping him grow in his capacity for self-determinism. He can now approach the alcoholic without condescension and is therefore in a position to help him.

## Objections to the "Sickness" Conception of Alcoholism

One objection to the sickness conception of alcoholism is that it provides an excuse for the alcoholic and thus keeps him from feeling responsible for his sorry condition. This objection has its counterpart in the traditional Augustinian-Pelagian controversy. David E. Roberts wrote: "Pelagius was an earnest, practically minded moralist who was convinced that men could promote good ends if they tried hard enough; therefore, he sought to close off the 'excuse' that they are compelled to do evil by sinful predispositions." [7]

Instead of attempting to settle the matter on theoretical grounds, I would like to turn directly to the practical question: *How does growth in the capacity for self-determination and responsibility occur?* Psychotherapy and AA have given us our clearest answers. Psychotherapy has shown that one does not cure irresponsibility or egocentricity by a direct attack upon them, nor does one produce real self-determination by increasing the individual's guilt-load. The assumption of traditional moralism is that by emphasizing the individual's personal culpability one would make him more responsible and more moral. Psychotherapy has demonstrated the basic fallacy of this assumption. By increasing the guilt-load one makes the individual more driven by compulsion, less self-determining, and therefore less responsible. Direct attacks on irresponsibility and egocentricity only increase defensiveness and inaccessibility to help. The moralistic approach may change surface behavior through psychological pressures, so that it *seems* that the individual is behaving more "morally" because he may be more compliant to the ethical code of a particular subculture. But, if a real morality involves self-determination, the individual is actually behaving less morally rather than more so. His concern will be compliance to a code and not basic human values.

Psychotherapy has shown that growth in the capacity for self-determination comes as the person feels less guilty and more able to accept himself. When the individual begins to realize that many of the things about his life for which he has been blaming himself, consciously or subconsciously, are actually the result of early experiences over which he had no control, he becomes better able to accept responsibility for making constructive changes. By proceeding on the assumption that people are what they are to a large degree because of their basic character structure, a structure which was formed in the very early years of life, psychotherapy has been able to release many from the vicious

173

cycle of guilt and compulsion which has made self-determination impossible. It is well to remember that this can happen in psychotherapy because the individual feels accepted by the therapist and can therefore lower his defenses and face the truth. Equally important the therapist can accept the person because he has resolved his own conflicts to a large degree and can accept himself. Here is a basic problem of all counseling, including the counseling of alcoholics.

AA teaches the same lesson with one important modification. Almost every alcoholic has a terrific guilt-load. The counselor whose orientation is moralistic overlooks this because the fact does not fit the moralistic formula that guilt is the means of producing moral responsibility. He overlooks it, too, because the alcoholic usually hides his real feelings behind a wall of indifference. This wall is his defense. A direct attack only increases his need to defend himself. AA, in contrast, immediately reduces the alcoholic's guilt-load by providing him with two things: group acceptance and the sickness conception of alcoholism. It says, in effect, "You are not responsible for the fact that you have an allergy to alcohol." Then, within the web of meaningful interpersonal relations, AA proceeds to utilize the alcoholic's growing capacity for self-acceptance and responsibility by saying in effect, "But you can become responsible for changing your personality pattern so that you won't be driven to drink." Note that AA waits until the person is sober and feels accepted in the group before encouraging him to face up to the necessity of personality change. The timing is crucial.

We have seen that the Emmanuel approach, in contrast to AA, recognized that selfishness in adults is a symptom of childhood emotional deprivation and inner conflict, and saw the importance of unconscious motivation and childhood conditioning. Theoretically the Emmanuel approach was closer to depth psychology and superior to AA in its handling of responsibility. From a practical standpoint, however, AA has two advantages. First, in our culture with its tradition of voluntaristic moralism it is difficult for people to accept the idea that an individual is not personally responsible for having a neurosis and yet is responsible to society for getting help, i.e., for becoming more responsible. Second, in our present cultural setting the AA emphasis on a physical component in alcoholism is probably more effective than the concept of psychological causation in reducing the guilt-fear load and facilitating therapeutic change.

Another thing demonstrated by AA is the importance of waiting until the alcoholic is able to accept at least minimal responsibility for himself before attempting to help him. It also shows the importance of utilizing this minimal capacity for self-determination when it emerges. AA insists that the individual must be willing to be helped before AA can help him. An alcoholic is often literally unable to accept help until he reaches a certain point psychologically, his "bottom." He is incapable until then of accepting responsibility for accepting help. Any counselor will save himself a lot of frustration if he remembers this, rather than assuming that the alcoholic could accept help if he really wanted to. Once the minimal capacity for self-determination has emerged, it is crucial that it be utilized in the counseling process. Only as this capacity is respected and employed, will it grow. All this is not to suggest that one must simply sit and wait passively until the alcoholic goes through the agonizing process—to all concerned—of reaching bottom. In Chapter 9 we will discuss the matter of "elevating the bottom."

If it were true that emphasizing the sickness conception of alcoholism tends to deter the alcoholic from getting help because he now has an excuse for his trouble, a case could be made against the use of the conception. Actually, the opposite usually is true. So long as an alcoholic thinks of his trouble as primarily a matter of willpower and of morality, he will tend to go on struggling futilely to reform himself. This is what cultural patterns of thought have taught him to do. On the other hand, if he thinks of his trouble as primarily a sickness, he will tend to seek the help he must have if he is to recover. There are strong pressures in our society for sick people to get treatment.

Marty Mann has an answer to the objection that the sickness conception will provide an excuse to drink.

Some people have raised the question as to whether teaching an alcoholic that his drinking is an illness will not give him a heavy weapon to use against those who are trying to persuade him to stop that drinking; saying that he might then be able to shrug the whole thing off with some statement like "How can I help it—it's a disease, isn't it?" or "You must let me do as I please—I'm a sick man and I can't help being like this." Actually, there are no known examples of this result of such teaching. Those who raise the question have forgotten that alcoholics, almost if not entirely without exception, spend their time trying to drink, "like other people," not to drink alcoholicly. They rarely want to drink the way they inevitably end up drinking.[8]

Another reason why it is difficult for some to accept the disease conception of alcoholism is because, unlike the physiological diseases to which it is often likened, alcoholism involves the search for pleasure. In some cases, the minister's orientation causes him to feel, "I can accept the sickness conception of alcoholism only if I am convinced that the alcoholic, being a sick person, really experiences unmixed suffering." Giorgio Lolli, formerly medical director of the Yale Plan Clinic, discusses this problem incisively in his article entitled "On 'Therapeutic' Success in Alcoholism." [9] He points out that a psychotherapist who has this orientation is certain to have difficulty in working with alcoholics. Sooner or later he will be confronted by the disturbing realization that alcoholics experience pleasures during some phases of their drinking episode and that the search for pleasure is deeply involved in their addiction. To say this is not to deny the terrible psychological pain that is also involved. Lolli writes: "An even dim awareness of the pleasurable connotations of some phases of the drinking episode cannot fail to stir up anxieties in those therapists whose conscious and even more whose unconscious life is governed by the principle: 'I shall help the sufferer and punish the celebrant.'" [10] Although Lolli does not apply this principle specifically to the minister, it is obvious that it often does apply to him, perhaps to a greater degree than to those in other professions. The ministry often attracts persons who have had an above average dose of the pleasure-anxiety which is one of the dubious products of the tradition of puritanism in our culture. Pleasure-anxiety in the individual is that which makes him feel guilty and anxious when he is experiencing pleasure, especially physical pleasure. It is the feeling that pleasure for its own sake is self-indulgence and, therefore, wrong.

Lolli goes on to say:

The therapist who is unable to accept the pleasurable connotations of alcoholism will seldom be able to affect favorably those whom he should help. Lack of acceptance of this pleasurable connotation often leads the therapist to rejection of the alcoholic. This rejection is rationalized in a variety of ways, the most common of which is expressed in the statement, "The case is hopeless." [11]

Lolli points out that a physician who would be eager to help a tuberculous patient after his twentieth relapse often labels an alcoholic as hopeless after two or three minor relapses. He says that the label is more apt to be applied to those alcoholics in whose drinking the pleasurable aspect is least concealed, the so-called psychopaths, as compared with the manic-depressive alcoholics whose hangovers are characterized by overwhelming dejection and self-recrimination. The rejection implied in the label "hopeless" reactivates the alcoholic's hostilities and anxieties, thus contributing to the continuation of his drinking.

This problem has more general connotations. As Freud pointed out, the pain-pleasure principle operates in all neuroses. In the case of difficulties such as alcoholism it is simply more obvious. If the presence of elements of self-gratification prevents a malady from being considered a true sickness, then all neuroses must be eliminated from the category of sickness. All neurotic "solutions" involve some satisfaction, however warped. Lolli writes: "A realistic understanding of the pleasurable connotations of addiction to alcohol will help the therapist to alleviate his own emotional problems relating to 'pleasurable' experiences in other human beings and thus make his work with the alcoholic more effective." [12] One can carry this a step further and say that if a minister resolves his own conflicts regarding pleasure, he will relate himself more constructively not only to alcoholics but to people in general. In a sense, constructive confrontation of the pleasurable aspect of the sickness of alcoholism can be a growth experience for the minister as a counselor. What is more, it may lead to a constructive revision of his thinking concerning man's ethical problem as it comes to focus on the general relationship of sin and sickness.

It is interesting that most of the objections one hears to the sickness conception of alcoholism have been given very convincing answers by persons of moral conviction in the past. Around the middle of the nineteenth century a young physician named J. Edward Turner decided to devote his life to the treatment of inebriety. For sixteen years he worked indefatigably for the establishment of what came to be called the New York State Inebriate Asylum. Turner made over 70,000 calls on potential subscribers to the work and met with all the stock objections to the treatment of alcoholism as a disease. One farmer declared: "I cannot believe the disease theory of drunkenness. My Bible teaches that the drunkard is a criminal in the sight of God, and he is forever debarred from heaven." [13] A college professor refused his support on the grounds that: "The enterprise of building asylums for the drunkard would encourage drinking. The moderate drinker would imagine that if he became a drunkard he would go to an asylum and be cured, and hence the fear of becoming such would be entirely removed."

Henry Bellows, of Union Theological Seminary in New York City, along with many other clergymen, worked actively with Turner. At the laying of the cornerstone for the institution on September 24, 1858, Bellows made a statement upon which those who object to the treatment of alcoholism as a sickness could well ponder today, over one hundred years later:

I remark that it can never weaken the sense of moral responsibility, anywhere, privately or publicly, to acknowledge anything that is true; and that there is not the least reason to fear, that to make provision for the rescue of the miserable victims of an hereditary or abnormal appetite for drink will diminish in the least, in those conscious of the power and obligations of self-control, the disposition of the conscience to exercise them.

We might as well expect public schools for the indigent to weaken the standard of private education among the wealthy; or asylums for the deaf and blind, to make possessors of perfect eyes and ears careless of their safety and indifferent to their preservation; or humanity towards the aged and the suffering to promote idleness and improvidence among the young and healthy . . . as to imagine that asylums for inebriates will promote and increase drunkenness.

As we have seen, the ethical problem in alcoholism is complex and difficult to define. Each person will have to arrive at his own working hypothesis, based on his thinking and feeling about the fundamental problem of freedom, determinism, and personal responsibility. It is hoped that by pursuing certain lines of thought such as those suggested in this chapter, some readers will come to see some new dimensions of the truth of the classic statement by William James quoted earlier concerning alcohol: "Not through mere perversity do men run after it."

Lolli, in an article entitled "The Addictive Drinker," gives a cogent statement of the problem as it appears at present to a scientist.

More is unknown than is known about the addictive drinker. What is already known breeds a more tolerant attitude toward him and favors a shift of attention from his objectionable deeds to those unfortunate experiences that determined them. The moral issue is not denied but reinterpreted in the light of medical, psychiatric and sociological facts. This reinterpretation helps considerably in efforts to free the addict from his ties of alcohol.[14]

Such a statement could well be taken as a guide in one's reinterpretation of the ethical problem in alcoholism.

## REFERENCES

1. "A Personality Study of Alcohol Addiction," *QJSA*, IV (December, 1943), 383.

2. Father Ford's books on the subject include: *Depth Psychology, Morality and Alcoholism* (Weston, Mass.: West College Press, 1951) and *What About Your Drinking?* (New York: Paulist Press, 1961).

3. For a description of this study, see page 180.

4. For a discussion of the Catholic view of the moral responsibility involved in alcoholism see James H. Vanderveldt and R. P. Odenwald, *Psychiatry and Catholicism* (New York: McGraw-Hill Book Co., 1952), pp. 356-57.

5. A most illuminating discussion of the remarkable parallelism between the Pauline-Augustinian conception of original sin and the psychoanalytic conception of neurosis is found in Chapter VII of David Roberts' *Psychotherapy and a Christian View of Man* (New York: Charles Scribner's Sons, 1953), pp. 104-17, entitled "Bondage to Sin."

6. *Ibid.*, p. 94.

7. *Ibid.*, p. 95.

8. *New Primer on Alcoholism*, pp. 202-3. With respect to the statement that there are "no known examples" of the use of the sickness as a rationalization for one's drinking, it is my experience that some alcoholics with *character disorders* (as contrasted with psychoneuroses) do use it this way.

9. *QJSA*, XIV (June, 1953), 238-46.

10. *Ibid.*, p. 241.

11. *Ibid.*

12. *Ibid.*, p. 242.

13. These quotations, including the statement by Bellows at the cornerstone laying, are from a description of the work of Turner in an article by Francis W. McPeek, "The Role of Religious Bodies in the Treatment of Inebriety in the United States," *Alcohol, Science and Society*, pp. 413-14.

14. *QJSA*, X (December, 1949), Nos. 3 and 4, 414.

# 8

# Laying the Groundwork for Counseling Alcoholics

How to understand the alcoholic and what can be done for him rank first and second in the list of problems which prove most puzzling [to religious leaders]. While religious influence in the deepest sense seems almost indispensable to the real cure of an addict, few seem to find this through conventional religious channels. Not all the reasons for this are clear; but the fact deserves further attention and study. Unless more light is thrown on this question, "therapeutic religion," or the religion which heals, may be developed quite outside the church.[1]

This paragraph was written in 1942 by Seward Hiltner, at that time head of the department of pastoral services of the Federal Council of Churches of Christ in America. Although well over two decades have passed since it was written, it describes the need and challenge of the present situation, to a considerable degree.

## The Minister's Attitude Toward His Opportunity

In this day in which teams of scientists are devoting their skill to the problem of helping alcoholics and AA has achieved such impressive success in leading thousands to sobriety, the pastor examines his own meager success in the field and wonders whether he should leave such work to the scientists and to AA. Is there a real need any longer for him to be active and informed concerning alcoholism? Can he expect to be reasonably effective if he is? We will attempt to throw some light on these questions in the six chapters that lie ahead. For one of the greatest needs of the minister is a definition of his role in the problem of alcoholism—a clear picture of where he is needed and in what areas he can function most effectively.

One important element in this definition of his role is the recognition that dealing with alcoholics in a constructive manner is a major opportunity as well as a major problem for the parish minister. Ministers who have had

179

experience in a parish do not need to be told that they will have opportunities to help alcoholics. Such opportunities—a rather euphemistic term for some of the encounters a minister has with alcoholics—are thrust upon him, whether or not he wants them or is prepared for them. The question is not whether he will deal with alcoholics; the question is whether he will deal with them in a more or less constructive manner. But for the young man just beginning his ministry and for the older minister who has just not had many opportunities in this area, it is important to cite evidence that many ministers are active and relatively successful in helping alcoholics.

A survey conducted by Yale University in cooperation with the National Council of Churches revealed that fifty to fifty-five thousand alcoholics a year are seen by ministers in the United States.[2] More significant than the mere number is the fact that the minister, so the survey showed, is often the first person seen for help, outside the family of the alcoholic. Other studies confirm the fact that the average minister sees several alcoholics in the course of a given year. For example, a study made by the New York Academy of Medicine and reported in "A Survey of Facilities for the Care and Treatment of Alcoholism in New York City"[3] showed a high number of referrals to clergymen. Another example is from a report of the New Hampshire Board for the Treatment of Inebriates which mailed a questionnaire to various professional persons within the state.[4] The 91 clergymen who returned questionnaires reported having counseled with a total of 353 alcoholics during that year. Interestingly enough, this was nearly double the number of cases reported by a group of 119 New Hampshire clergymen two years before. During the same two-year period, AA grew from 3 groups to 14 in the state. This suggests, although the samples are too small to be conclusive, that an increase in the work of AA actually *increases* pastoral opportunities with alcoholics. If this is true, it is a most convincing answer to those who feared, as well as those who hoped, that AA would render the church's ministry to alcoholics unnecessary.

With the financial help of Columbia University's interdepartmental seminar on religion and health, this writer conducted a survey of the 324 clergymen who had attended the Yale Summer School of Alcohol Studies during the first seven years of its existence (1943-1949). Questionnaires designed to ascertain their thinking and action concerning alcoholism were mailed to them; -146 were completed and returned. Eighteen denominations, including all the major Protestant groups, were represented. Geographically, the respondents represented 37 states and Canada. The work and thought of these 146 ministers are being cited as vivid and concrete examples of what a group of clergymen who are trained in the field are thinking and doing. On the point under consideration, it is significant that the 75 ministers who gave definite information in this area had seen an average of 4.9 alcoholics per year

180

since attending the Summer School. This average includes sixteen men who had counseled with no alcoholics during this period. Thus, the evidence from the various sources mentioned indicates that the pastor should expect to have a number of opportunities each year to help alcoholics. He has a job to do, and he must be prepared to do it well!

Can a minister hope to be effective in dealing with alcoholics? The feeling expressed by some AA members that "only an alcoholic can help an alcoholic" has influenced the thinking of many ministers to the detriment of their confidence in their own ability to really help the alcoholics who come to them. Again, the experience of the 146 Yale ministers can be helpful. How effective were they in dealing with the alcoholics who came to them? The picture is encouraging. In general, those who had had considerable opportunity to work with alcoholics showed a great deal of understanding and realism concerning the psychology and methods of such work. It is probably true that those who had considerable insight and success in working with alcoholics tended to develop a reputation for success in this area and therefore attracted more alcoholics to them. Several of the ministers either mentioned or implied that they had acquired such a reputation and that physicians, court officials, or other clergymen had referred alcoholics to them for help. In other words, the very fact that such a large proportion of the Yale ministers had worked with a substantial number of alcoholics is *ipso facto* evidence that they were doing an effective job with them.

The ministers were asked to give an evaluation of their success in dealing with alcoholics. Feeling toward the value of their work ranged from that of one minister who reported: "I have never found a drunk who wasn't worth my time and attention and it meant a lot to them," to the man who wrote, "As far as my experience goes, it is a discouraging piece of work trying to help people who do not want it." The general feeling was between these extremes, the majority closer to the first—viz., work with alcoholics involves many discouragements, but it is exceedingly important and worthwhile. As one minister put it, "Some cases have responded beautifully. In others, I have been able to do exactly nothing." Two thirds of the ministers reported 50 percent or better success in dealing with alcoholics. Most of the ministers reported working closely with AA, and the majority of them had a positive attitude toward the use of psychiatric referral with alcoholics when needed. The overall impression derived from the questionnaires was one that shows the fallacy of the conception that only an alcoholic can help an alcoholic. The impression was this—here is a group of individuals making a significant and continuing contribution to the work of helping individual alcoholics to sobriety. It is likely that many of these men would have been making a significant, though perhaps not as great, contribution even if they had not attended the Yale Summer School. Their effectiveness is but a sample of the work with alcoholics that thousands of ministers over the country are actually doing. There is no valid basis for the feeling of any minister that he cannot make a significant contribution to helping alcoholics because he *is* a minister or *isn't* an alcoholic!

However, realism demands that a minister face both his advantages and limitations in dealing with alcoholics. The 146 Yale ministers were asked to list what they felt were a minister's chief advantages and limitations. The general feeling was that the minister has more advantages than limitations. The limitations most often mentioned could be divided into two categories: the alcoholic's attitude toward the minister and the minister's attitude toward the alcoholic. In the first category were the alcoholic's fear that the minister will censure him, the alcoholic's suspicion of the minister as a professional "do-gooder," the alcoholic's resentment of religion, and the difficulty of establishing rapport because the alcoholic may feel that the minister (not being an alcoholic) never quite understands him. One respondent wrote, "Most folks figure the minister has a set attitude toward alcoholics and will therefore not give him much opportunity except in 'hopeless' cases." In the second category of limitations were mentioned such matters as the minister's tendency to moralize and to "preach at" rather than to "counsel with." Included in the advantages mentioned were the natural entree to the family, confidentiality of relationship, the fact that there are no fees involved, that many people naturally take their problems to their pastor, and, most important, that the minister has the dynamic of the Christian faith and fellowship available for helping the alcoholic. One respondent summarized the feeling which several expressed: "The only important limitation a minister has is the initial hesitancy of the alcoholic to approach a minister. Beyond that, it is an advantage to be a minister, provided you have the right attitude and understanding."

## Discovering Opportunities to Help

One of the striking discoveries from the Yale ministers' responses was a wide range in the number of helping opportunities which the individual ministers had. Sixteen had had no opportunities. On the other hand, twenty-one men had been very active, sixteen of these having seen an average of ten or more per year. Obviously, for the minister who is interested in rendering maximum service in this area, it is important to ascertain the factors which influence the number of opportunities a man has.

The type of parish one serves is an important factor in this matter. For instance, a pastor in a downtown church is more likely to have a considerable number of transient alcoholics come to him than is a minister of a suburban church. Another factor is the minister's relationship with AA. A large proportion of those respondents having much higher than average yearly figures were those having AA groups meeting in their church halls, or otherwise having a close relationship with AA. Another factor is the denomination to which one belongs. Although the picture is not clear from the questionnaires, it seems probable that some alcoholics tend to shy away from ministers who belong to denominations associated in the public mind with the militant temperance movement. Apparently some alcoholics do so without bothering to discover whether or not the individual minister actually represents his denomination's position. However, in this regard, there is little doubt that the personality and approach to people of the individual minister are much more important factors than is his denomination.

A minister's general attitude toward alcohol, alcoholics, and alcoholism seems to have a direct relationship to the number of alcoholics who come to him for help. The Yale ministers were asked what position they advocated regarding prohibition and the use of alcohol. Those who advocated total abstinence and the return of prohibition had seen an average of 3.6 alcoholics per year. Those who advocated total abstinence but did not favor prohibition had seen an average of 3.9 alcoholics per year. Those who advocated moderation and opposed prohibition, in contrast to the first two groups, had seen an average of 6.5 alcoholics per year. Those who advocated no position but left the decision to the individual had seen an average of 11.9 alcoholics per year. Significantly, all but one of the sixteen ministers who had had no counseling opportunities were included in the first two positions.

The Yale ministers were asked to indicate whether they considered alcoholism a sin or a sickness (or both) and what they considered the chief causes. For purposes of comparison, two extreme groups within the total group of respondents were studied. It was found that those who considered alcoholism primarily or entirely a matter of sickness had seen a yearly average of 9.3 alcoholics, whereas those ministers who considered alcoholism primarily or entirely a matter of sin had seen a yearly average of only 2.3 alcoholics. In other words, those ministers who accept the sickness conception of alcoholism had had over three times the average yearly opportunities available to those who did not accept it.

On the question of the causes of alcoholism, the Yale ministers were again divided into categories. At the two extremes were (a) those who considered alcohol and drinking to be the primary causes of alcoholism and (b) those who considered the sociopsychological and physical factors to be the primary causes. Those in the first group, that is, those who fail to take cognizance of the modern scientific findings concerning alcoholism, had seen an average of only 1.9 alcoholics per year, while the other group had seen an average of 6.8 per year.

From these figures it is apparent that a minister's general attitudes toward alcohol and alcoholism have a great deal to do with whether or not he discovers the alcoholics who are potentially available to be helped by him. If a minister is known as a militant advocate of prohibition and temperance, and if he treats alcoholism in a moralistic fashion in his public pronouncements, it is likely that some alcoholics who might otherwise seek his help will give him a wide margin. The alcoholic does not come to him because he fears, with good reason in some cases, that he will meet censure rather than understanding. The decisive factor in this matter does not seem to be the minister's personal convictions regarding the use of alcohol, but the way in which he chooses to present his convictions. Alcoholics are often hypersensitive to those they consider "bluenose" or "reformers"—i.e., those who condemn all drinking. Therefore, a minister who holds to the temperance view would seem to be in a position of having to choose whether he will make this a major emphasis or whether he wishes to counsel alcoholics. It may be that there is no actual decision involved in most cases since the man who has the inclination to do the one would probably not be adept at the other. However, the personality of the minister, as we have said, is of primary importance in this whole question. This explains why there are some pastors who are outspoken temperance advocates and yet carry on effective counseling ministries with alcoholics.

Let us look more closely at this personality factor, in the light of the problem of discovering opportunities to help alcoholics. It is probable that a majority of all alcoholics are of the "hidden" variety—individuals who are having serious problems with alcohol but whose behavior is still enough within the bounds of social conformity to allow their alcoholism to be kept secret within the family. The interpersonal suffering and chaos caused by their social malignancy is assiduously kept from the outside world. The pastor wants to discover these situations within his parish, not only because the alcoholic and his family need help which he may be able to give, but because help rendered at this stage of the illness may save them from years of suffering.

The hiddenness of so much alcoholism constitutes the most baffling aspect of the problem from the standpoint of treatment. It is ironic that in spite of the new helping resources that are now available, the majority of alcoholics and their families continue to suffer the ravages of the illness. The major reason for this is simply that a hidden illness cannot be treated. One student of the problem estimates that not over one million of the five million plus alcoholics in his country are now or have been in treatment of any kind. It is essential that more effective ways be found of bringing the hidden alcoholics out of hiding to be helped. The minister has a significant role to perform in helping to solve this problem.

How does one encourage people in this sort of trouble to come to him and entrust their painful problems to his confidence? We have seen how the minister's attitudes toward alcohol and alcoholism influence his opportunities to help. Equally important, and somewhat related, is what the late Otis R. Rice, pioneer in pastoral work with alcoholics, called "remote preparation for counseling of alcoholics." [5] By this he meant the pastor's general relationship with his people in his varied contacts with them. This is determined by the pastor's personality structure. Has he made his people feel that he is really interested in them as persons and not just as means of running a church machine? Has he established a relationship with his people that has made them feel that they can be sure he will keep their confidence and that he will not be made uneasy by their recital of the grim facts of their situation? Is he relatively shockproof? Can he be counted on to really listen to them rather than to talk because what they are saying makes him anxious? Will he be *with* them in feeling, or will he be sitting in judgment as they pour out their hearts? Are his general attitudes moralistic, or do his sermons and talks reveal a deeper understanding of human behavior? If a pastor's remote preparation is good, then people with painful problems, including alcoholics, *will* come to him seeking help.

The clergyman is in a strategic position to attract the hidden alcoholic out of his dark closet of fear and despair. There are at least three specific means of accomplishing this:

*1. Educational seed planting.* A productive way of creating greater openness to help is to deal with alcoholism in a sermon or talk, and to do so in an understanding and accepting manner. If the minister reveals a nonmoralistic, enlightened grasp of the problem, the alcoholic or, more often, his spouse, may feel motivated to seek the pastor's help. An appreciative mention of AA and other treatment methods may awaken the person's hope that perhaps something *can* be done about his problem. Mentioning alcoholism or AA in a sermon almost invariably results in at least one counseling opportunity. In most congregations there is at least one individual who has a personal but hidden interest in the problem. If that person senses that the minister has both insight and a nonjudgmental attitude toward his problem, it is likely that he will muster his courage and ask for a personal conference. In some cases, being introduced to the illness conception and early symptoms of alcoholism will help to open the person's eyes to the nature of his problem and his need for help. This is especially true of the spouse or other relative of the alcoholic who has not recognized the illness.

By his own public statements and also through his role of helping to develop an alcoholism education emphasis for the youth and adults in his church school, the minister helps to plant the *seeds of understanding* of the nature and treatment of alcoholism. (The contents and methodology of alcoholism education will be discussed in Chapters 12 and 13.) Some of these seeds will have a preventive effect. Others will flower subsequently in counseling and pastoral care opportunities.

*2. Pre-counseling and pastoral care.* In his normal pastoral functions, the clergyman has regular contact with a network of families. Furthermore, unlike most other professionals, he is expected to call in the homes of his people without a special invitation. These two facets of his professional role definition give the minister a potential advantage over those in the other helping professions, so far as the early recognition of distressed persons is concerned. If his emotional radar is tuned to the wavelength of persons, the minister often will sense that a particular family is troubled (perhaps by hidden alcoholism), long before the crisis becomes full-blown and the family is forced by its pain to seek outside help. If a pastor suspects that a particular person or family may be showing the surface stress of a hidden problem, he should make himself easily available to them psychologically, by frequent pastoral care contacts. The process of building relationship bridges over which burdened people can bring their hidden problems to the minister for help is a part of the process which Seward Hiltner calls "pre-counseling." Clergymen in those traditions in which hearing confessions is a regular function have an opportunity to identify hidden alcoholics. Whether or not the opportunity is used depends on the minister's sensitivity to the problems which lurk behind surface disturbances and his ability to help his parishioner move from the confessional to the counseling relationship.

Some of the distress signals which may indicate the presence of hidden alcoholism and/or other problems are these: disturbed children, veiled antagonism between spouses, chronic financial problems, repeated job losses for no apparent or convincing reason, drinking at inappropriate times, guilty avoidance of the clergyman or embarrassment when he calls, a radical change in behavior such as an unexplained withdrawal from church participation. Some of these symptoms may be coded cries for help by individuals or families who cannot bring themselves to ask for help openly.

Here is an illustration of the bridge-building function of pastoral care in creating counseling opportunities in cases of suspected alcoholism:

A pastor had reason to suspect, because he had observed several of the above signs of disturbance, that one of his parishioners, Mr. L., was having serious trouble with alcohol. Yet neither Mr. L. nor his family had contacted him concerning the problem. So, he made it his business to devote more than average attention to L. and his family. He called in their home for various reasons which were actually incidental to his main purpose. After a number of pastoral contacts of this type, he received a phone call from Mrs. L. saying that she would like to talk with him about a problem connected with the women's group in the church. When she came to the pastor's study, Mrs. L. began by discussing this problem. Later in the interview she opened up concerning her husband's drinking. Through their discussion, the pastor discovered that L. himself was apparently not ready to admit that alcohol was giving him trouble, and that he was not willing to talk with the pastor about his problems. So, the minister concentrated on helping Mrs. L. who was open to counseling help. He encouraged her to pour out her painful, pent-up feelings, and thus gain some relief from their pressure. He discussed with her the nature of L.'s problem and the crucial importance of helping him move toward at least minimal openness to outside treatment. Furthermore, he offered Mrs. L. an ongoing supportive counseling relationship to assist her in coping constructively with her feelings and problems in her relationship with her husband and children.

This pastor utilized well his professional entrée to the L.s' home. When he called on them, he did not initiate a discussion of L.'s drinking. To have done so probably would have defeated his purpose by putting L. and perhaps L.'s wife on the defensive. Instead, he concentrated on strengthening a relationship of trust with the L.s. This eventually made it possible for Mrs. L. to confide in him.

Under what circumstances should the minister take the initiative in raising the issue of excessive drinking with a parishioner? This will vary, depending on the clergyman's style of relating and the circumstances in a particular case. In general, there are two guidelines which should be followed. First, *take the initiative when it is reasonably clear that the person has a drinking problem, when the pastor-parishioner relationship bridge is strong enough to survive the threat of such a confrontation and when the person does not open up on his own, in spite of frequent opportunities. Second, it may be essential to take the initiative, even if the relationship is not robust, when irreversible emotional or physical harm is being done to the children.* If the person is an alcoholic, he will usually experience even the best-intentioned pastoral concern about his drinking as an accusation and a threat. Thus, taking the initiative is a calculated risk which may do more harm than good in the sense of solidifying the alcoholic's resistance to accepting help. For this reason, one usually is not justified in taking the risk, except in emergencies or in cases in which the pastor has a sturdy relationship with the person. In some cases, the alcoholic may give subtle clues that he is on the verge of discussing his problem and would like to do so, but is having trouble "breaking the ice." A gentle observation or question by the pastor may help. Here are some examples of possible "openers":

I get the feeling that there's something that's worrying you, but it's not easy to talk about.

You seem to have a burden on your mind. Can you tell me about it?

Do I sense that you are wondering if your drinking might be moving toward becoming a problem?

You seem to be carrying a load of some kind. Can I help?

The important thing is to offer help and to raise if necessary the possibility of a drinking problem in such a way as to allow the person to reject the statement without rejecting the minister. If the person is highly defensive, this is easier said than done, and the minister will sometimes miscalculate the degree of initiative he can take and achieve constructive results.

3. *Counseling.* Many people spontaneously turn to a clergyman when they are going through "deep water" of any kind. Among those seeking pastoral help are some whose disturbance in living is associated with or caused by alcoholism which may be hidden from themselves, in that they do not recognize the compulsive quality of their drinking. Some who are dimly aware that their use of alcohol is out of control are afraid or ashamed to admit this fact to others. By being sensitive to the possible presence of hidden alcoholism behind marital and other problems, the pastor can help the person or the family identify the hidden problem and seek appropriate help. Another group of alcoholics encountered in pastoral counseling are those whose abnormal drinking is painfully obvious to the "significant others" in their lives, but not to themselves. Such persons often resist help tenaciously. The various methods which have proved useful in motivating the resistant alcoholic will be discussed in the next chapter.

## Goals in Counseling Alcoholics

What are the goals of counseling with alcoholics? A clear, realistic answer to this question is essential to effectiveness. Much of the lack of precision in counseling procedures is a result of the counselor's confusion about goals or his striving for unrealistic ones.

The master goal of all pastoral counseling, including that which involves alcoholism, is *to help the person grow toward his full potential for personhood, constructive relationships, and productive living.* When counseling with an alcoholic, another goal is implicit in this master goal—*helping the person to achieve ongoing abstinence from the use of beverage alcohol.* Stable abstinence is, for most alcoholics, a prerequisite for progress toward a happier, more constructive life.*

The inability of the addicted drinker ever to drink again in controlled fashion was accepted as axiomatic for many years by most lay and professional persons engaged in helping alcoholics. The axiom was summarized by a phrase often heard in AA—"Once an alcoholic, always an alcoholic!"—and

---

* In counseling with some chronic alcoholics, more limited goals prove to be the only ones that are realistic or achievable. For example, a reduction in the number of binges, hospitalizations, days lost from work, arrests for drunkenness per year represent significant improvement, even though the ideal goal of permanent abstinence is not achieved. In an illness like alcoholism, any degree of improvement is valuable, however short the ideal goal. See *Alcohol Problems, A Report to the Nation* by Thomas F. A. Plaut, p. 35.

by the statement frequently repeated by those doing therapy with alcoholics —"Alcoholism can be arrested and treated, but not cured." This basic therapeutic assumption has been challenged in recent years. Because so much is at stake in terms of counseling goals, it is necessary to review the new evidence.

The challenge was initiated by the publication in 1962 of a report by a British physician, D. L. Davies, entitled "Normal Drinking in Recovered Alcohol Addicts." [6] He told of seven men, out of a group of ninety-three treated for alcohol addiction, who subsequently had been able to drink normally for periods of seven to eleven years. The treatment consisted of Antabuse and individual discussion with the patients during brief hospitalization, plus social work services for their relatives. There was no systematic psychotherapy. On the advice of the hospital staff, four of the seven moved from vulnerable occupations (with high exposure to drinking situations) to nonvulnerable ones. Each of the seven, after periods of complete abstinence of up to a year, resumed drinking that remained within the limits regarded as normal by their groups. None of them had been drunk even once in the seven to eleven years. All kept their drinking at a relatively mild level. Two of the men, whose excessive drinking prior to their hospitalization was believed to be symptomatic of chronic anxiety states, continued to be about as anxious as before, but their abnormal drinking patterns disappeared! In speculating on the meaning of his findings, Davies suggested that in some alcoholism it may be that treatable occupational and social factors, rather than irreversible biochemical or personality changes, are what tip the scales toward addiction. After presenting his startling evidence, Davies stated: *"It is not denied that the majority of alcohol addicts are incapable of achieving 'normal drinking.' All patients should be told to aim at total abstinence."* [7] Earlier he had pointed out that the seven who became social drinkers had been advised by him to refrain from all drinking. They chose to ignore the advice. Sixteen physicians, all with wide experience in treating alcoholics, were invited by the editor of the journal which published the Davies report to comment on it.[8] These points stand out in their discussion. Several suggested that the Davies study and other evidence in the literature indicate the need to question and perhaps revise the widely held assumption that *no* alcoholic can ever drink again in controlled fashion. A number of long-experienced therapists challenged Davies' report. The possibility that his seven subjects were habitual heavy drinkers (Alpha alcoholics) but not "true addicts" was raised. Or perhaps they were "danglers" who sway around the demarcation line between alcoholic and nonalcoholic patterns. Under favorable conditions they were able to control their drinking; but under stress, a single drink might start a spree. Another respondent suggested that every alcoholic may have a critical blood alcohol level which reactivates his addiction. Davies' seven

189

had apparently kept their blood alcohol below this level. However, most alcoholics would prefer abstinence to drinking that the person cannot "feel." A number of commentors said that, in many years of practice, they had never known an alcoholic who was able to return to social drinking. Those therapists who had observed such cases agreed that the occurrence is exceedingly rare and that no one can predict which patients may have this capacity. Most important, there was general agreement that *the goal of total abstinence is the only realistic and humane one in counseling with alcoholics.* R. Gordon Bell, addiction specialist of Ontario, Canada, put it well:

For every alcohol addict who may succeed in reestablishing a pattern of controlled drinking, perhaps a dozen would kill themselves trying. At this stage of our knowledge and clinical orientation to the complex problems of alcohol addiction the only policy likely to prolong life consistently and improve human capacity to function in an intelligent manner is one of total abstinence. It is possible that we may eventually be in a position to pick out the small percentage of alcohol addicts who could begin a new moderate use of alcohol after a one or two year period of abstinence, provided that a satisfactory resolution of their personal and social problems had been achieved and the need for alcohol as a drug no longer exists. If this ever comes about, it will be the result of more comprehensive, prolonged clinical study than has been undertaken to date. Until we are in a position to predict who may be able to resume moderate controlled drinking, clinical studies of this kind should be carried on with a minimum of publicity. Otherwise the health and safety of a great many people could be seriously jeopardized.[9]

The possibility that in rare cases recovered alcoholics may reestablish the ability to drink in controlled fashion is largely an academic issue from the counselor's standpoint. Learning the secret of controlled drinking is the frantic desire of many drinking and partially recovered alcoholics. It is often their downfall! It would be utter folly, therefore, to suggest to an alcoholic that he might recover his ability to drink socially. Even to imply that a rare alcoholic does recover this ability is to foster a dangerous, unrealistic hope for the vast majority of alcoholic counselees, each of whom wants desperately to believe that he is that rare person who may recover control. The effect would be to strengthen the individual counselee's resistance to facing the hard reality that he must learn to live without alcohol if he is to live at all. If an alcoholic in counseling mentions the Davies study or the more extreme views of Arthur H. Cain,* the pastor should discover what meaning

* There is a wide gulf between the views of the scientific community, as reflected in the above discussion, and those of Arthur H. Cain in *The Cured Alcoholic* (New York: The John Day Company, 1964). He makes the extreme claim, based on a small number of cases, that it is possible for "any alcoholic, with the exception of alcoholic psychotics, to learn to drink normally" (p. 229). He asserts that 19 alcoholics he has treated have

190

these have for the person and then move decisively to help him face reality, including seeing the lethal dangers of building his hopes on either the Davies or Cain studies. If an alcoholic seems to be using the Davies report as a defense against facing reality, he should be confronted gently but firmly with what he is doing, and helped to face three facts: (1) Most experts in the field of alcoholism agree that if controlled drinking among genuine alcohol addicts actually occurs, its incidence is very rare; (2) in the Davies study, control was possible only *after* a period of complete abstinence; and (3) control was possible only if the person kept his consumption at a non-intoxication level. It is well established that many alcoholics have tried to drink socially, after a prolonged period of abstinence, and have been unable to do so.

The long-range goal of counseling with alcoholics, then, is permanent abstinence leading to the development of potentialities for constructive living. Subsumed under this goal are four operational objectives which may be seen as overlapping stages of treatment: *Helping the alcoholic (a) to accept the fact that his drinking is a problem with which he needs help; (b) to obtain medical treatment; (c) to interrupt the addictive cycle and keep it interrupted by learning to avoid the first drink; (d) to achieve a resynthesis of his life without alcohol.* The pastor's role and uses of community resources vary at each stage of the recovery process, and from one alcoholic to another. The process and methods of achieving these goals will be described in the next two chapters.

Alcoholism is a complex illness. The minister should view the achievement of the goals of treatment as a *team* effort involving, as a minimum, a physician, an AA member, the alcoholic, and himself. Ministers who have attempted to "go it alone" in counseling alcoholics have found their effectiveness to be doubled or even tripled when they learned to utilize all of their community's helping resources to the hilt. The pastor should think of himself as a team member with important functions with respect to all four operational goals. He should see himself as the *coordinator* of the team in providing help for those alcoholics who come to him, unless there is some other persons or agency which can fulfill this function more efficiently. The minister can maximize help to the alcoholic by adding to his own unique resources the specialized services of such resources as AA, Al-Anon, medicine, the alcoholic clinic or inpatient treatment facility, family services, etc. Most alcoholics seen by the minister require one or more of these forms of

---

recovered the ability to drink normally. Since most of them, however, choose to abstain, their use as examples of reestablished control is open to serious question. He does not state *how long* those who do drink have been able to do so in controlled fashion. This is a crucial consideration since many alcoholics can control their intake for limited periods. Cain's entire approach is highly questionable; its impact on drinking alcoholics could be tragic.

specialized help, in addition to pastoral counseling, in order to recover. Skill in relating the alcoholic to the particular helping resources he needs is an essential aspect of effectiveness in helping alcoholics.

Most clergymen are happy to refer alcoholics to those agencies and groups specifically designed to meet their problems. They recognize that AA, for instance, is tailor-made to meet the stresses and strains of alcoholism, and they accept the fact that alcoholism, as Harry Emerson Fosdick has put it, is like a stained-glass window in that it can best be seen and understood from the inside. They have accepted as their starting point a fact which has been well stated by Marty Mann:

> The pastor will also have discovered that he, himself, cannot do an AA job on the alcoholic. He will see with his own eyes at meetings and at interviews he may witness that the man or woman who has actually been through the appalling experience of alcoholism has an edge on him that no substitute knowledge can replace. For one thing, the sober AA member is the embodiment of hope. He is the living promise that it can be done. He makes faith in the possibility of recovery a thing that can be seen and touched and heard—himself. And, step by step, he can tell not how it can be done, but *how he did it*.[10]

Most pastors rejoice in the increasing availability of specialized agencies and groups to treat alcoholism. They say, in effect, "Thank God for AA." They realize that when they have made an effective referral of an alcoholic, they have actually made a great contribution to his eventual sobriety. Representative of the many alcoholics who have found their way to AA and happy sobriety through the help of their clergymen is Bob P., who has been sober in AA for several years. He recalls:

> I was at the end of my rope. I used to joke about not going to church, saying that the last time I went was when I got married and I've never forgiven the church for that. But in despair I went to church. After the service I got the minister aside and told him I wanted to stop and couldn't. He said, "I'll get in touch with a fellow who can help you." That's how I got in touch with AA.[11]

Some ministers tend to be too eager to refer the alcoholic. Out of the frustration of repeated failure, they are strongly motivated to shift responsibility to someone else. As any insightful minister knows, "referral" may be another way of saying, "Let George do it." The danger is that this attitude will be communicated to the alcoholic with whom it registers as rejection. Furthermore, by "passing the buck," the minister misses his opportunity to help the alcoholic in those unique ways of which he is capable. However, if the minister thinks of referral to a specialized agency, *not as a shifting but as a sharing of responsibility*, this tendency will be minimized.

192

Even if a minister were completely self-sufficient in his adequacy to help alcoholics, the prohibitive time element involved in counseling alcoholics is a practical limitation. An experienced pastoral counselor of alcoholics states: "Ordinarily one must see an alcoholic three or four times a week for the first few weeks, and then a couple of times a week for a month or two more, and then once a week for a considerable length of time." [12] Most ministers, though not as busy as they sometimes give the impression of being, work under heavy schedules. Intensive counseling with even a few alcoholics may involve time which the minister can find only by neglecting other important aspects of his work. Intensive counseling of alcoholics involves a considerable amount of frustration and emotional drain. A pastor has to be an unusually mature and secure person to take this in his stride.

For one or more of these reasons, most pastors are glad to make maximum use of community resources. This is true even of those who in the past have been effective working alone. One of the Yale ministers wrote: "Before 1949 I worked with alcoholics myself with a rather good degree of success. Since then I have found that it takes too much time and the clinic which has been established here is better. I either go with them to the clinic or feel certain they will go on their own."

### Preparation for Counseling Alcoholics

In order to counsel alcoholics with any degree of effectiveness, one must have a basic understanding of alcoholism and of AA. He should have assimilated the kind of information presented in Parts I and II of this book and in Marty Mann's New Primer on Alcoholism. He should understand the nature of the sickness so that he can interpret it to the alcoholic and his family. And, very important, he must have some insight concerning the psychological attributes of alcoholics. These attributes provide the starting point of his approach to alcoholics. (Ideally, such basic knowledge about alcoholism and counseling alcoholics should be acquired by every minister during his seminary education.) So far as AA is concerned, every pastor ought to read and digest the contents of Alcoholics Anonymous, the "Big Book" (Alcoholics Anonymous Publishing, 1955), which can be obtained through any local AA group. He ought also to be familiar with some of the basic AA pamphlets such as "Alcoholics Anonymous in Your Community," "Medicine Looks at Alcoholics Anonymous," "AA, 44 Questions and Answers About the Program of Recovery from Alcoholism," "Is AA for You?" "A Clergyman Asks About Alcoholics Anonymous," "This is AA," "AA for the Woman," and "Young People and AA." Two additional AA books will help to broaden and deepen the minister's understanding of this fellowship: Alcoholics Anonymous Comes of Age (New York: Harper & Bros., 1957)

and *The AA Way of Life, Selected Writings of AA's Co-Founder* (New
York: AA World Service, 1967). Both books reflect the insights of Bill W.

Second, preparation for counseling alcoholics should involve training in
the general principles and techniques of counseling. Training in pastoral
counseling should include not only intensive study of the literature and case
seminars, but also clinical training in a hospital under a trained supervisor.
(The Georgian Clinic in Atlanta has a clinical-training program for clergymen, which focuses on the treatment of alcoholism.) Equally valuable is a
"training analysis" or a period of intensive counseling in which the pastor
or pastor-to-be has an opportunity to resolve some of his own emotional
problems with the help of a trained psychotherapist. The reason why this can
be so valuable becomes apparent when one recognizes that many of the
mistakes and lack of effectiveness in counseling are due, not to a lack of
intellectual understanding of techniques, but to problems of interpersonal
relationship. These problems stem from the pastor's own emotional quirks
and blindspots.

An invaluable form of training which is available to almost any minister
who is motivated to sharpen his counseling tools is *supervision* of his
counseling relationships. What is required is the availability of a well-trained
counselor or psychotherapist (pastoral counselor, chaplain supervisor, social
worker, psychiatrist, clinical psychologist) who can be engaged to provide the
supervision. Arrangements should be made for weekly meetings with the
supervisor, continuing over at least a year and preferably two. The focus of
the sessions is on case material, tape recordings, or verbatim reports which
the minister brings from his counseling relationships. Groups of three to six
clergymen sometimes arrange to meet as a group with a supervisor to reduce
the cost to each participant. Ongoing supervision is one of the most effective
ways of enhancing a minister's counseling skills.

From a practical standpoint it is impossible for many pastors to have
either clinical training or a personal analysis. It is important, as well as
comforting, to recall that Giorgio Lolli has said that individuals who are
relatively free from basic anxieties can have a beneficial influence on alcoholics,
regardless of training.[13] Many pastors have done and are doing good counseling
with alcoholics without having the advantages of the specialized training now
available to some seminarians. This should not, however, cause us to forget
that counseling alcoholics is difficult counseling in which the better one's
preparation, the greater one's chances of effectiveness. Even those with
good training have many, many failures in this field. For this reason, supervision of one's counseling should be regarded as essential preparation for
counseling with alcoholics.

The third type of preparation for counseling alcoholics is an acquaintance
with the insights contained in the literature dealing specifically with this kind

of counseling. There is a growing amount of this literature. Almost any issue of the *Quarterly Journal of Studies on Alcohol* contains an article dealing with the subject written by a psychologist or psychiatrist. Fortunately for the minister, there are several helpful discussions of pastoral counseling with alcoholics available. Thomas J. Shipp, a Methodist minister with wide experience in helping alcoholics, has produced a practical book entitled *Helping the Alcoholic and His Family*.[14] Another useful volume is John E. Keller's *Ministering to Alcoholics*.[15] Keller, a Lutheran minister with long experience in counseling with alcoholics, has served on the faculty of the Rutgers Summer School of Alcohol Studies. Both Shipp and Keller have been profoundly influenced by the philosophy and approach of AA. *Alcoholism, A Source Book for Priests*[16] provides some understanding of the Roman Catholic approach to alcoholism. Clifford J. Earle's book, *How to Help an Alcoholic*[17] and Seward Hiltner's pamphlet, "Helping Alcoholics, A Guide for Pastors in Counseling Relationships with Alcoholics and Their Families,"[18] though somewhat older than the Shipp and Keller books, are still useful resources for the pastoral counselor. An excellent general discussion of helping alcoholics is found in Marty Mann's *New Primer on Alcoholism*,[19] entitled "What to Do About an Alcoholic." Two other useful books are: *Alcoholism, A Guide for the Clergy* by Joseph L. Kellermann (published by The National Council on Alcoholism, 1963) and *The Alcoholic* by Fred B. Ford (published by Andover Newton Theological School, 1958). There is considerable overlapping among these books with respect to methods of counseling alcoholics. Nevertheless, since each writer brings his own unique experience and personality to the helping encounter, there are insights in each book that can contribute to the minister's total preparation for counseling alcoholics.

Fourth, if a minister is especially interested in counseling alcoholics, he should attend one of the summer schools of alcohol studies. The majority last for a week, are held at state universities, and are cosponsored by the state alcoholism programs and the universities. The largest such school, held at the University of Utah, attracts over four hundred students from many of the western states. An international school, held at the University of North Dakota, involves the cooperation of several state and provincial (Canadian) alcoholism programs. The curricula of such schools is designed to be of particular usefulness to teachers, physicians, clergymen, social workers, law enforcement and probation officers, industrial leaders, directors of alcoholism programs, and other persons interested in alcoholism education, research, and rehabilitation. Advanced training is available at the Rutgers Summer School of Alcohol Studies, a three-weeks program of seminars and lectures. This was the first summer school of alcohol studies; some five thousand students from all over the world have attended since 1943 when it began at Yale.

This school is one part of the Rutgers Center of Alcohol Studies, an interdisciplinary project which engages in wide-ranging research, publishes the *Quarterly Journal of Studies on Alcohol* as well as a variety of books and articles, and maintains the "Classified Abstract Archives of the Alcohol Literature" with over 10,000 entries on punch cards for automatic retrieval by topic. Researchers can quickly obtain abstracts as well as a bibliography on any topic which has been discussed in the scientific alcohol literature of the world.[20]

A fifth type of preparation for counseling alcoholics consists of *becoming closely related to several AA members and to an AA group.* In many ways this is the most important single form of preparation. Fortunately, since AA groups are now established in almost every center of population in this country, this form of preparatory experience is easily available to most ministers. All that is required is for the minister to make the effort to attend "open" meetings of AA with some regularity and thus to establish close relationships with key AA members. Attending AA meetings and talking with experienced members can allow the clergyman to learn many of the things about alcoholism and alcoholics which he needs to know in order to counsel effectively with alcoholics. (Attending Al-Anon meetings can serve in the same way, with reference to counseling with the spouses of alcoholics.) Since the minister's relationship with AA is so crucial to his counseling effectiveness, it will be discussed in more detail in the section which follows.

### Getting Acquainted with the Available Resources

One of the most important aspects of preparation for pastoral counseling of alcoholics is that of determining what resources are available for referral in one's community, and of acquiring firsthand knowledge of these resources. Obviously it is desirable, though not always possible, to acquire this knowledge in advance of the need for it. A pastor may want to use a checklist such as the following:

### REFERRAL RESOURCES AVAILABLE IN MY COMMUNITY

_____ Alcoholics Anonymous.
_____ Al-Anon group.
_____ Alateen group.
_____ A physician who has an enlightened approach to the physiological side of alcoholism.
_____ Hospitalization facilities. Where and how available to alcoholics.
_____ A psychotherapist (psychiatrist or consulting psychologist) who understands alcoholism and is sympathetic toward AA.
_____ A Skid Row treatment center.
_____ An enlightened Salvation Army installation, or rescue mission.

_____ A Local Council on Alcoholism affiliated with the National Council on Alcoholism.

_____ An Alcoholic Information Center sponsored by the Local Council.

_____ An Outpatient Alcoholism Clinic sponsored by a public or private agency.

_____ An inpatient alcoholic rehabilitation center with a sound program of therapy, including AA and group therapy. (10 percent of state mental hospitals now have special alcoholism wards or programs.)

_____ A rest-farm or similar institution which accepts alcoholics and is run on sound principles.

_____ A half-way house for alcoholics.

Obviously, few ministers will have the time to do the research necessary to utilize such a checklist in full. It is presented here to suggest the range of possible resources. Actually, the local AA group or, where one exists, the local Alcoholic Information Center are the practical sources of reliable information concerning community resources. Seasoned members of AA will usually know such things as the practices of local hospitals, where to house homeless alcoholics satisfactorily, and which physicians or psychotherapists are effective in treating alcoholics.

How does one establish contact with the local AA group? It is usually listed in the telephone directory under "Alcoholics Anonymous." A phone call will put one in touch with the group secretary, the local AA clubhouse, or, in larger communities, the intergroup office. The person who answers can give information about meetings or make arrangements for the minister to come to the AA office for a discussion about AA in general or a particular alcoholic whom he is trying to help. AA groups welcome such professional inquiries. If AA is not listed in the telephone directory, one can get information concerning it from other clergymen or from local civic officials, especially the judge of the local court. If this fails, one can write the AA General Service Office, 305 East 45th Street, New York, New York 10017. This office will send the desired information, including the location of the nearest group. If there is no group nearby, he may wish to contact the office for assistance in helping to start a group. Twelve of the Yale ministers reported having been instrumental in helping to start one or more AA groups. A useful AA pamphlet is entitled "The AA Group, an Informal Handbook on How the Group Functions and How to Get One Started."

A practical discussion of how a pastor can work with AA and get help from it is found in an article by Marty Mann, executive director of the National Council on Alcoholism, entitled "The Pastors' Resources in Dealing with Alcoholics." As a part of this article she gives some suggestions for starting an AA group:

There may be some towns where AA has not yet started. The pastor who finds himself in such a situation need not give up hope. It takes two alcoholics trying to get well to make a group, but only one alcoholic trying to get well to start a group. If the pastor knows even one alcoholic who he thinks really wants to stop drinking, he can very well help him to start an AA group. But he must always remember that it is the alcoholic who is starting the group, and not himself. In other words, he should remain in the background, ready to offer advice and assistance but not taking a prominent part in the activities of the one, two or three alcoholics who are trying to get started. His greatest usefulness will always be in providing new prospects for the first ones to work on, in spreading the word among his colleagues, and even in actually bringing the AA and the new prospect together.[21]

It is essential that a clergyman stay in the background of a group he helps start because if a group were too closely associated with a professional in religion, agnostic alcoholics would stay away. Further, if it were associated with a leader of a certain faith, alcoholics of other faiths might be kept away.

Ministers have had a fairly prominent role in helping to start new groups. For instance, the extensive work of AA in the St. Louis area grew from the efforts of a clergyman who shepherded several alcoholics, whom he was trying to help, up to Chicago to get a firsthand view of AA in action. These alcoholics started the first group in St. Louis. It is worth recalling that a clergyman had a small part in the actual beginnings of AA itself. It was a minister who gave Bill W. the name of Harriett S. who arranged the meeting of Bill with Dr. Bob.

The pastor who moves to a new community will wish to establish a working relationship with the local AA group at his first opportunity. This means getting acquainted with one, or better, several AA members who can be called on for assistance. The group chairman or secretary is a good one to know since he or she is usually an alcoholic of stable sobriety and sufficient experience in AA to be quite helpful.

It is impossible to overemphasize the value of actually attending several "open" AA meetings. This will accomplish several things that are important. It will show the AA members that the minister is interested in their work. It will give him an opportunity to establish rapport with the members he will need to call on for help with alcoholics at a later time. The coffee-cup fellowship after the meeting is an ideal time for this. Further, it will give the minister a greater understanding of both AA and of alcoholism. A pastor will wish to read the basic AA books and pamphlets, which can be obtained from the local group, but no amount of reading is a substitute for the experience of observing AA in action. Attending an occasional AA meeting is an important opportunity for the pastor throughout his tenure in a pastorate.

An important benefit of attending AA meetings is the lift and spiritual refreshment it gives the clergyman. In order to acquaint theological students in pastoral counseling courses with AA and to help them feel more at ease with alcoholics, the author asks his students to attend an open meeting of AA. Here are some typical reactions from students to their first exposure to AA:

It was one of the most meaningful spiritual experiences I have had. God's love was truly present in this group of people.

There was a depth fellowship which I wouldn't mind being a part of.

One of the truly great spiritual moments in my life happened on Tuesday night at the local AA meeting!

To me both the honesty and the acceptance were overwhelming.

My desire was really to become a part of their fellowship which I can't because I'm not an alcoholic. Why can't the churches develop this kind of fellowship? Surely more people than alcoholics agonize over the waste of their lives. Some I am sure have descended into hell and have returned. What is this contentment with hollow forms, "a pile of broken images," to quote Eliot?

Once a working relationship is established, the pastor will discover that referral to AA is a two-way street. Alcoholics who learn to know and trust him will come to him with their problems. Especially fortunate in this regard are the pastors who have AA groups meeting in their churches. Marty Mann summarizes what she considers the ideal relationship between a pastor and AA: "In short, the pastor's relationship with his local AA group should be one of reciprocity, of a free exchange of information and ideas on the particular case for which he desires help." [22]

One of the more outspoken alcoholics I interviewed told of a young minister who apparently tried to use the AA group as a means of obtaining members for his church. She declared: "I gave him a piece of my mind. I guess it won't hurt him—he won't get drunk." Obviously, any pastor who gives AA members the feeling that he has ulterior motives has vitiated any effectiveness he might otherwise have had in working with them.

Since AA is the pastor's most valuable referral resource, it might be well to discuss certain reservations that some ministers feel regarding AA which inhibit their relationship with it. The Yale ministers were generally reluctant to mention what they regarded as faults. One wrote: "I can see what I believe to be some weak places in AA, but it is marvelous that it works. I think we had better just leave it alone and use it." Nearly all of the ministers were long on their praise of AA. Here are some sample comments which reflect a prevalent appreciation of AA among ministers: "The church could learn something about real fellowship from AA. The church should learn to be a warm, friendly place where alcoholics and others may find acceptance, strength, and self-confidence." "The church might learn to go after folks as AA's do, make allowance for their failures, and never give up." "The church needs to follow AA by turning from its enmity for the bottle to a friendship for the man." "The AA movement has captured the essence of evangelical Christianity's power." Another minister pointed out that the church could see in AA a demonstration of "the effectiveness of their practice of first-century Christianity."

Some of the Yale ministers did qualify their praise by mentioning what they regarded as imperfections in AA. Since these are representative of feelings held by many clergymen, it would seem important to discuss them, as a potential means of enhancing good relations between ministers and AA. The most common criticism of AA was that it has no concern for social drinking. Many ministers are baffled by the indifference on the part of AA's as to whether nonalcoholics do or do not drink. From the standpoint of AA, there are two reasons for this. First, most AA's are convinced that alcohol, per se, is not the basic cause of their problem. Rather, they feel that their unique response to alcohol is the cause. Second, it is official AA policy not to "endorse or oppose any cause" nor to be drawn into any public controversy. The wisdom of this policy has been amply demonstrated. The Washingtonians are a grim reminder to AA's of what might happen to their movement should they ever be diverted from their "one primary purpose . . . to carry its message to the alcoholic who still suffers." It is clear that AA can do its own work best by doing only its own work.

Several of the Yale ministers objected to the fact that AA does not emphasize Christ in its program. In this regard it should be remembered that AA's theological permissiveness is an important reason why it attracts many alcoholics who would shy away from orthodox religion. As one of the Yale ministers put it, "AA's great virtue is its ability to reach and help men and women who are outside the church's sphere of influence." If AA is to serve alcoholics of all and no religious backgrounds, it must avoid becoming identified with any one theological position. This has become increasingly important as AA has become more international and intercultural in scope. Though the word "Christ" is not used in the AA approach, it would be difficult to find more Christlike concern and service than is found in AA at its finest. Further, a moment's reflection will be enough to remind a minister that "God as we understand him" is an apt description of the average church member's actual (as distinguished from his creedal) faith. One might even apply the same to the faith of ministers.

The fact that AA's therapy sometimes results in the substitution of other compulsions such as gambling was mentioned by several of the Yale ministers. The implication of this criticism is that the therapy has not solved the under-

200

lying personality problem. In this regard, it should be remembered that no solution to any psychological problem is completely effective. All solutions— religious and otherwise—are successful only to a degree. To judge an approach adversely because it does not produce some radical realignment of personality is to forget the reality situation in our society in which radical solutions are simply not available to most people. As a practical consideration, it is true that in most cases where substitute compulsions appear, they are much to be preferred over alcoholism for both the alcoholic and for society.

Several ministers mentioned the clannishness, smugness, and lack of recognition of AA's limitations on the part of some AA's. These forms of behavior need to be seen as characteristics of relative newcomers in AA. As a member becomes more secure and less defensive, these characteristics which sometimes irritate outsiders tend to disappear. However, it is well to remember that the strong sense of belonging to an ingroup is an essential part of the therapy of AA. The assumption sometimes made by AA's that "only an alcoholic can help an alcoholic" is, of course, not true. But it is true that an alcoholic has a special entrée to another alcoholic. The boost to the AA's self-esteem that comes from recognizing this fact, though it may result in a certain amount of smugness, is invaluable to the AA's continued sobriety. The attitude of superiority to professionals—"AA did it when the doctors, ministers, and psychiatrists failed"—can be understood and accepted in this light. It reflects adversely on the professional's own self-esteem if he allows such attitudes to disturb him or his relationship to AA.

Some clergymen, particularly those steeped in the psychology of puritanism, are critical of the "bragging about past sins" and the swearing which AA's sometimes do in their talks. Although this reaction is essentially the clergyman's problem, it may be helpful to recognize the dynamics of this behavior. Verbalization of one's past escapades before a sympathetic audience is actually a part of the cathartic process of working through one's guilt feelings. The fact that a person can now tell in public of experiences which a few months before were too painful for him even to admit to himself is a sign of real progress. The fact that he can now see the ludicrous implications of behavior that was formerly only tragically serious helps to make it less likely that he will repeat it. Verbalization of alcoholic behavior is a means of identifying with the group. Dynamically, swearing is a symbol of something quite important —viz., that this is not a "churchy" or pious group but a real he-man approach. These forms of behavior tend to diminish as a person's sober tenure in AA lengthens. However, the entertainment value of past escapades tends to perpetuate the behavior after it has fulfilled its dynamic function.

Some of the Yale ministers mentioned AA's lack of a preventive program as an imperfection. There is little justification for this criticism when one remembers that AA has dedicated itself to the specific and tremendous under-

201

taking of helping alcoholics. This limited goal represents a legitimate and necessary division of labor. However, as we shall see in the chapter on prevention (Chapter 12), the indirect preventive effect of AA's influence is very powerful.

Several of the Yale ministers, as well as other clergymen whom I have known, have criticized AA because some of its members tend to make it a religious cult. It should be remembered that those who make AA their religion have found a measure of vital faith and service within its fellowship. As a recovered alcoholic, who is a devoted churchman, put the matter: "Many people find so much more acceptance in AA than in the church, they make AA their church." It is doubtful that those who make AA their religion would be in the church were AA not in existence. In many cases they would probably not even be alive. From the interview material of this writer, it is evident that AA is a bridge back to the church for 50 percent or more of its members. Official policy of AA encourages this. Thousands of ministers over the country could echo with enthusiasm the sentiments of one of the Yale ministers who wrote, "The churches should be grateful to God for the many fine, active members that AA has saved and sent into their fellowship."

We return now to our discussion of the referral resources which are available. If a minister is fortunate enough to live in one of the eighty-two communities (in thirty-two states) in which there is a local Council on Alcoholism, he should support its work as well as encourage his parishioners to do so. These councils, affiliates of the National Council on Alcoholism, operate Alcoholism Information Centers which disseminate knowledge about the problem to anyone who is interested, including schools, churches, industry, the news media, and individual information-seekers. The central functions of the local councils are education and prevention, but their Information Centers also advise with alcoholics, relatives, and others concerning finding treatment in their community. The location of the nearest Alcoholism Information Center can be ascertained by writing the National Council on Alcoholism (2 East 103rd Street, New York, New York 10029). If a local council does not exist in one's area, a pastor has an opportunity to do as several other clergymen have done and "spark" the formation of such a council. The National Council is glad to assist and advise a group of community leaders in such an undertaking. Five of the Yale ministers had been instrumental in helping to organize local councils.

The National Council on Alcoholism (NCA) and its local affiliates are valuable sources of information and guidance for the clergyman on any matters related to alcoholism. NCA is the national voluntary health agency in the alcoholism field. It "strives for the prevention and reduction of alcoholism through a program of education, community and industrial services and the promotion of research." [23]

202

Forty-four states and seven Canadian provinces have tax-supported alcoholism programs with three facets—education, research, and treatment. The minister should check to see what resources are available through such a program in his state. If none exists, he may decide to encourage his state officials to consider establishing a program. The North American Association of Alcoholism Programs, founded in 1949, is the organization through which the network of tax-supported programs cooperate. With headquarters in Washington, D.C. (323 DuPont Circle Building, Washington, D.C. 20036), it provides information about public and professional alcoholism programs, as well as serving and representing its member-agency's interests at the national and international levels. The goals of the Association are these:

To facilitate the exchange of information about education, research and treatment activities. To promote legislation and standards which will contribute to the care and control of alcoholism. To encourage professionals to deal with alcohol problems within their own disciplines, and to contribute new knowledge for better understanding and management of these problems. To encourage cooperation among all who are engaged in activities involving alcohol.[24]

The prospects for the rapid development of new education, research, and treatment resources throughout the country were brightened in 1966 by a rising tide of interest on the national level. In March, 1966, President Johnson became the first U.S. president in history to include a significant request regarding alcoholism in his Health and Education Message to Congress, stating:

The alcoholic suffers from a disease which will yield eventually to scientific research and adequate treatment. Even with the present limited state of our knowledge, much can be done to reduce the untold suffering and uncounted waste caused by this affliction. I have instructed the Secretary of Health, Education, and Welfare to: Appoint an advisory committee on alcoholism; establish in the Public Health Service a center for research on the cause, prevention, control, and treatment of alcoholism; develop an educational program in order to foster public understanding based on scientific fact; work with public and private agencies on the state and local level, to include this disease in a comprehensive health program.[25]

Later in 1966, the Secretary of Health, Education, and Welfare announced the Federal Alcoholism Program, including the establishment within the National Institute of Mental Health of a National Center for the Prevention and Control of Alcoholism. The program includes research, education, and professional training to combat alcoholism.[26]

In 1961, a substantial National Institute of Mental Health grant established the Cooperative Commission on the Study of Alcoholism. In October, 1967, the distinguished scientists who composed this group issued a significant volume, *Alcohol Problems, A Report to the Nation* (prepared by Thomas F. A. Plaut). This report presents a comprehensive approach to the solution of alcohol problems, including problem drinking, and makes specific recommendations for meeting the needs in the areas of treatment, research, prevention, and training personnel. It highlights the widespread neglect and crucial need for a nationwide policy and program of realistic action. The report provides the basis for a major breakthrough in the field of alcoholism.

A particularly encouraging development in treatment resources is the growth of industry-sponsored programs. Usually coordinated through the personnel and medical departments of a company, these programs have achieved remarkable recovery rates: from 50 to 80 percent of the alcoholic employees treated. From 1960 to 1965, the number of companies having alcoholism programs rose from 75 to 203. NCA maintains an Industrial Services Department to stimulate the growth of such enlightened programs. It is fortunate that humanitarian and economic considerations coincide in this area and that industrial leaders are increasingly recognizing that it is less expensive to provide treatment for alcoholic employees than to ignore the problem and to pay the costs of accidents, inefficiency, absenteeism, strained interemployee relationships, and eventual retraining of a replacement for the untreated alcoholic.

## Understanding the Medical and Psychotherapeutic Resources

In addition to possessing an overview of his community's resources for helping alcoholics, a minister needs an understanding of the *role* of medical and psychotherapeutic resources in this helping process. This understanding allows one to draw upon these resources effectively and to interpret them to alcoholics who need them. In fact, one of the first questions a pastor should ask himself, when he comes into contact with an alcoholic, is this: *Does this person need medical, psychiatric, or psychotherapeutic help, in addition to pastoral care and AA?* To answer this question accurately, the minister may need to refer the alcoholic to a physician or psychotherapist *who understands alcoholism* and who can evaluate the person's need for particular therapies.

It will be helpful to the minister to acquaint himself with a more comprehensive discussion of the medical and psychological therapies than is presented in this volume. Chapter 2 of the Cooperative Commission's report, mentioned above, includes an overview of treatment resources. Chapter 10 in Marty Mann's *New Primer on Alcoholism* offers a survey in nontechnical language. More detailed and technical descriptions of the various therapies are found in R. J. Catanzaro (ed.), *Alcoholism: The Total Treatment Approach* [27] and

Ruth Fox (ed.), *Alcoholism: Behavioral Research and Therapeutic Approaches.*[28] An excellent survey of therapies by Ruth Fox, medical director of the National Council on Alcoholism, is presented in a journal article: "A Multidisciplinary Approach to the Treatment of Alcoholism." [29] The discussion that follows draws on this article at a number of points.

For our purposes, the medical and psychiatric therapies may be divided into three categories according to their purpose: (1) those therapies that aid in the physical rehabilitation of the person suffering from the effects of an acute binge and/or prolonged excessive drinking over many years; (2) those that help to keep the addictive cycle broken and thus maintain sobriety for sufficient time to allow other therapies to take effect; (3) those that aim at lessening the alcoholic's personality problems—both those that contributed to the *causation* of his addiction and those *resulting from* the interpersonal chaos of progressive alcoholism.

Looking more closely at the first of these categories, it is well for the clergyman to remember that many alcoholics are in serious physical condition by the time they are ready to accept help. The medical problems are of at least two types—problems related to the *withdrawal of alcohol from the body* (ranging from severe hangovers to delirium tremens and alcoholic hallucinosis) and problems of severe *malnutrition* (cirrhosis of the liver, polyneuropathy, Korsakoff's psychosis, and general malnutrition). The therapies for problems of withdrawal are usually short-term, as compared with the extended therapies which often are required to deal with problems of malnutrition.

An alcoholic who is coming off a protracted binge may suffer excruciatingly when alcohol is no longer present in his bloodstream. His painful "withdrawal symptoms" may drive him back to the source of chemical comfort, alcohol, and/or drugs. In a small percentage of cases, withdrawal symptoms may be fatal, unless the person is given proper medical attention. Detoxification procedures are available in progressive hospitals. Having such medical assistance may lay the groundwork for other therapies as well as save lives. Ruth Fox states: "Detoxification is aided enormously by tranquilizing drugs, so that these patients can now be successfully treated even in the open wards of a general hospital without causing any disruption of the normal routine of the hospital." [30] Most physicians prefer tranquilizers to the older sedatives of the barbiturate group in treating alcoholics. For a time it was believed that the tranquilizers were the "wonder drug" answer to the addictive problems posed by barbiturates. But subsequent experience has shown that at least some of the tranquilizers are definitely addictive.[31] Some alcoholics do become "hooked" on tranquilizers, even though these seem to be less addictive than the barbiturates. It is clear that caution is indicated in the use of any mood-changing drug by alcoholics and other addiction-prone persons.

Whether or not the alcoholic is hospitalized during the detoxification period (usually requiring only a few days), the chances are that he will need massive doses of vitamins and minerals to overcome the devitaminosis and general malnutrition resulting from "drinking one's meals" over a long period. A high protein diet is also emphasized by some physicians to overcome the deficiencies of amino and fatty acids.[32] The process of physical rehabilitation includes treatment of any of the various diseases of malnutrition and general physical abuse which accompany prolonged alcoholic addiction. These diseases are by-products of alcoholism, and their treatment, which may be a long-term process, is an essential contribution of medical skill to full recovery.

Commenting on the use of brief hospitalization during the detoxification period, Fox states: "A plan of rehabilitation should be worked out before the patient leaves the hospital—a plan which can be carried out in a doctor's office, an aftercare clinic, or an outpatient department especially geared to the alcoholic." [33] Such a plan should include whatever combination of therapies is required to help a particular alcoholic achieve stable sobriety and productive living. In most cases, regular attendance at AA should be an integral part of the plan of rehabilitation.

Turning to the second category of therapies, it is important to be cognizant of the fact that some alcoholics cannot halt their compulsive drinking for long, even with the help of initial detoxification procedures and continuing affiliation with AA. When a minister encounters an alcoholic who cannot stop drinking long enough for any therapy to be effective, he should suggest one or more of those stopgap measures which aim at providing just such a period of sobriety. A typical case is of a middle-aged business executive who, on a conscious level, desires to stop drinking. After prolonged heavy drinking culminating in a binge, he is in wretched condition physically and emotionally. Each time this happens, he is hospitalized, "boiled out," and restored to some extent physically through the skills of medicine. After a few days or weeks of post-hospital sobriety, he begins to drink again, as a result of anxiety and unconscious pressure, as well as his ability to rationalize and convince himself that "this time it will be different." Thus the cycle continues to repeat itself. In this case, the use of Antabuse interrupted the cyclical pattern and permitted group psychotherapy and AA each to play significant roles in the man's achievement of sobriety.

Antabuse, an American trade name for tetraethylthiuram disulfide, is a drug which deters the alcoholic from drinking and thus blocks the addictive cycle. The drug is also referred to as "disulfiram" in the alcoholism literature. One of the physicians who pioneered in the use of this drug in the United States, Ruth Fox, describes its positive values:

206

This is a medication given orally which interferes with the metabolism of alcohol so that even one drink will cause a toxic reaction of a shock-like nature. When not on disulfiram the alcoholic fighting the urge to drink may have to say "no" to this impulse several hundred times a day. When on disulfiram he needs to make but one decision, and that is on the taking of the pill. The effect lasts four days, which of course abolishes all impulsive drinking. Since the pill is taken every day, the ability to drink safely is well in the future. It also abolishes the preoccupation with drinking, which frees the mind for other things. Then, too, it helps the distressed family to know that the patient is even temporarily safe from alcohol. Most patients get a great lift from feeling that they can live without alcohol.[34]

Antabuse must be prescribed by a physician and should be taken under his careful supervision. It is not a "cure" for alcoholism, but it does provide a biochemical fence which holds back the addiction while other therapies have an opportunity to help the person learn to live without alcohol.

A word of caution may be in order. Nobody knows how many easy fortunes have been made by those exploiters of human misery who peddle some pill or potion which they claim will cure some burdensome ailment. Those afflicted by alcoholism, and their families, have been among those so exploited in the past. Perhaps our society is more sophisticated now and therefore less in need of caution about this danger. But gullibility springs eternal, fed by desperation and the need for hope and help. Therefore, it is still appropriate to emphasize in one's educational work that there are no quick cures for alcoholism, no "pills for papa's coffee." [35] The goal of treatment, it should be pointed out, is not "cure" but arresting the progression of the illness by interrupting the drinking and helping the person to learn a new and more productive way of life sans alcohol. In the current scene, exploitation of alcoholics tends to occur in certain "drying out places" which offer little or no treatment of the addiction or opportunities for rehabilitative experiences. It is wise to view with some suspicion any institution or treatment program which is secretive about its methods of treatment of which makes what seems like exaggerated claims about the success of its treatment.

The aversion treatment, also called the conditioned reflex treatment, is another means of producing a period of abstinence. In contrast to Antabuse, the method is psychological rather than biochemical. In the United States this method is used relatively infrequently; whereas in England and Russia its use is widespread. An aversion to the smell, sight, and taste of alcohol is induced in the following manner. A drug (emetine or apomorphine) is administered, producing nausea and vomiting. Just before this occurs, the patient is given his favorite forms of beverage alcohol. After several such experiences, the person begins to associate alcohol and nausea. The conditioned reflex (à la Pavlov) thus established produces nausea whenever the person encounters alcohol. The duration of the aversion varies from person to person. In some cases it lasts for many years. Since conditioned reflexes tend to become weakened with the passage of time, periodic reinforcement of the aversion is required in most cases. Like the Antabuse treatment, this approach is adjunctive to other therapies; most programs using it couple it with group or individual psychotherapy. In some alcoholics, the craving for the anesthetic effects of alcohol is so powerful that they will continue to drink, in spite of the nausea, until the reflex is broken.

Another form of aversion treatment involves the use of posthypnotic suggestion to create the aversion to alcohol. Lincoln Williams, who uses hypnosis extensively with alcoholics, reports that the suggestion that the person will be indifferent to alcohol is sometimes successful, provided a deep trance can be achieved. He makes it clear, however, that hypnosis (including autohypnosis which he teaches his patients) is only an adjunct to psychotherapy.[36]

The third category of therapies consists of the various forms of pychotherapy. If it is true, as it seems to be, that one underlying cause of much alcoholism is intrapsychic conflict, then psychotherapy should be a useful approach. A small minority of sober alcoholics have found their sobriety via this path alone. (For example, Dwight Anderson gives an autobiographical description of such an experience in the second chapter of The Other Side of the Bottle.) But, by and large, psychotherapy alone has not been impressive in its degree of success with alcoholics. This is particularly true of psychoanalysis and psychoanalytically oriented psychotherapy. Such depth therapies are long and psychologically painful processes. The alcoholic, with his low frustration-tolerance, cannot tolerate the anxiety accompanying the therapy. When it becomes too painful, he retreats to his ever-accessible pain-killer, alcohol. (One of the interviewees told of having six martinis before each visit to his psychiatrist.) Heavy imbibing prior to therapy sessions negates the possibility of constructive therapeutic results. As if this were not enough, alcoholics defeat the therapy by missing appointments, arriving late, not paying their bills, and trying (often with self-defeating success) to deceive the therapist. The late E. M. Jellinek once said, in effect, that a therapist who had not tried to work with alcoholics usually recommends long and intensive psychotherapy when he encounters such a patient; but the therapist who has had some experiences in attempting to work with alcoholics will be more inclined to phone the nearest AA group. Too rapid transfer of responsibility to AA can constitute a problem in those cases in which the alcoholic needs both psychiatric help and AA.

If an addiction to alcohol is superimposed on severe mental illness—a psychosis of the schizophrenic, manic-depressive or chronic brain-damage types—it is essential to get the alcoholic to a psychiatrist. In such cases, inpatient treatment in a psychiatric hospital or in the psychiatric ward of a general hospital is usually indicated. In the vast majority of cases of alcoholism, however, severe mental illness is not involved, and psychiatric hospitalization is inappropriate. Most alcoholics do not need inpatient psychiatric treatment, and they are out of place with psychotic patients. (Inpatient facilities designed specifically for treating alcoholics serve a valuable function.)

Psychotherapy—of a supportive and relationship-oriented variety rather than a depth, uncovering type—has a crucial role in the treatment of some alcoholism. The time when it can be most effective, it should be emphasized, is *after the alcoholic is sober for a substantial period of time*. As indicated earlier, alcoholism is an illness of at least two levels—the underlying personality problems and the addiction itself (the "runaway symptom," to use Tiebout's phrase). Psychotherapy may be of help in dealing with personality and relationship problems; it is usually grossly ineffective in halting the addictive cycle. The runaway symptom of drinking to overcome the effects of previous drinking must be interrupted before psychotherapy has a real chance of being useful. One alcoholic recalls: "I went to see the psychiatrist when I couldn't stop drinking. I was shaking and in a hell of a shape. He started asking me questions about my childhood. I thought to myself, 'The damn fool!' I didn't go back."

In choosing a psychiatrist to whom to refer an alcoholic, it is important to pick one who understands alcoholism and is appreciative toward the AA approach. It is particularly important that he be aware of the fact that the addiction must be interrupted before psychotherapy can be effective. Speaking as a psychiatrist, Ruth Fox declares:

I believe psychiatrists are in error in considering that alcoholism is *merely* symptomatic of an underlying personality disturbance and that treatment of the latter will cause the excessive drinking to cease. Unless the addiction itself is recognized and help given to the patient to attain sobriety, there cannot be a successful outcome. After sobriety has been attained, the patient may then be responsive to the various techniques of psychotherapy.[37]

Particularly tragic is the alcoholic who has been assured by a psychotherapist that his drinking is "merely a symptom of an underlying anxiety" and whose addiction (and general deterioration) steadily increases while he undergoes therapy ad infinitum. Having been told that his drinking is "purely symptomatic," and this by a highly trained, respected professional, the person is practically paralyzed in his ability to face the all-important facts that he is an alcoholic and must find a way to interrupt the addictive cycle.

It is noteworthy that the degree of underlying personality pathology and the type of therapy that is needed to treat it cannot be ascertained, in many cases, until the alcoholic has achieved sobriety and the psychological effects of protracted excessive drinking, per se, have been removed. Persons who appear to be very sick psychologically while they are drinking may prove to be relatively capable of coping with the demands of living after a period of sobriety.

Significantly, seven of the alcoholics interviewed had sought psychiatric help after achieving sobriety in AA; several others were contemplating obtaining such help. The cause of Frederick N., from Chapter 2, comes to mind. At the time of the interview he had been in AA for four years, and during most of the time he had been plagued by slips. Finally, in desperation, he went to see a psychiatrist who was also favorable to AA. As a result of the help he received in resolving some of his inner conflicts, he has enjoyed his longest period of continuous sobriety. He now feels that through his psychotherapy he has "gotten the program in AA."

If an alcoholic is severely psychoneurotic, he may need extensive psychotherapy in addition to AA. The aim of this therapy is to reduce the flood of anxiety which makes his hold on sobriety precarious and his life somewhat miserable when he is without the anesthetic effects of alcohol. If a person feels worse rather than better, after a month or two of sobriety, he probably could benefit from psychotherapy to deal with some of the inner sources of anxiety, guilt, and tension. Alcoholics with schizoid type personalities often are unable to feel comfortable with the degree of human closeness which is present in an AA group. Such persons may receive more help from a one-to-one relationship with a psychotherapist or counselor who will allow them to keep whatever distance is necessary to allow them to feel relatively safe.

Short-term therapy (a few weeks or months) with a psychiatrist who is knowledgeable in the area of alcoholism can be valuable for many alcoholics who do not require longer-term psychiatric treatment. Such short-term therapy aims not at deep underlying problems, but at helping the person do things that will improve his chances of achieving productive sobriety—things such as accepting the fact that he is an alcoholic, learning how to face and handle his fears and resentments constructively, changing his ways of relating so that the guilt-isolation-anger spiral is not triggered so often. In short, the therapist helps the alcoholic begin to travel on the pathway which leads to a new way of life with dependence on relationships rather than alcohol. In the same direction, short-term marriage counseling can be useful in assisting the alcoholic and his wife to adjust to the demands of sobriety and to make their relationship more mutually satisfying and fulfilling.

Some of the most encouraging developments in the treatment of alcoholics are in the employment of group therapy methods. Ruth Fox states:

Group therapy is perhaps the most effective type of treatment for the alcoholic aside from AA. There is almost immediate identification and mutual support, which makes the alcoholic feel immediately accepted. The group represents a nonthreatening, socially rewarding yet challenging atmosphere in which their many problems can be discussed. Problems about drinking, their jobs, and their families come up first, but soon they begin to discuss and show their deeper feelings of anger, resentment, sensitivity, guilt, distrust, loneliness, depression, fear, sense of inferiority, and worthlessness. When met with the sympathetic warmth and understanding tolerance of the group, many of these painful feelings are drained off.

The various interactions between members of the group, both negative and positive, give a chance for analysis of typical modes of reaction in the outside world. . . . Typical maneuvers or defenses, such as denial, rationalization, and projection become evident and are discussed in nontheoretical terms. Many strong and lasting friendships grow up in the group.[38]

The highest recovery rates are achieved in programs in which a combination of therapies, tailored to the particular needs of the individual, is used.[39] It is obvious from this that the treatment of alcoholism is a team job. Fortunate is the pastor who lives in one of the 220 areas in the United States and Canada in which alcoholic clinics are available for referral. In such facilities the "clinical team" consists of various combinations of the following—an internist, a psychiatrist, a psychologist, a social worker, and, in a few clinics, a pastoral counselor and a recovered alcoholic who serves as a counselor. Each member of the team has special skills to bring to the common task of helping alcoholics recover. The internist is equipped to treat the physiological problems and administer Antabuse; the psychologist is trained to do testing through which the alcoholic's therapeutic needs can be evaluated, and he may be trained to do research and psychotherapy; the psychiatrist, being a medical doctor like the internist, can prescribe medication, but his unique skills are in the area of individual and group therapy and their relationship to drug therapies; the social worker may be trained to help the alcoholic work through his marital and vocational problems and do group as well as individual therapy; the social worker may also work with spouses; the pastoral counselor is specially equipped by training to help the alcoholic with his "spiritual" problems as these relate to his sobriety and his interpersonal relationships; he may also be trained to do group and marital counseling; [40] the recovered alcoholic on the team often can "reach" the less-motivated alcoholics and serve as a bridge-person to help them relate to AA. Few, if any, clinics have all these members on their team, but the principle of interprofessional teamwork is the heart of the working philosophy of these clinics. The cycle, when successfully implemented, accounts for much of their success.

## REFERENCES

1. "Alcohol Addiction—A Problem for the Church," *Information Service*, Federal Council of Churches. Vol. XXI (April 25, 1942), No. 17.

2. Survey reported by E. M. Jellinek to the Yale Summer School of Alcohol Studies, July, 1949.

3. Report of a study undertaken by the Committee on Public Health Relations of the New York Academy of Medicine under a grant from the Research Council on Problems of Alcohol, 1947.

4. "Alcoholism in New Hampshire," report for the biennium ending December 31, 1948, p. 40.

5. "Pastoral Counseling of Inebriates," Alcohol, Science and Society, p. 439.

6. QJSA, March, 1962, pp. 94-104.

7. Ibid., p. 103.

8. See QJSA, issues of March, June, and December, 1963. The Davies report and the comments by the sixteen experts were later published in booklet form by the Rutgers Center on Alcohol Studies.

9. "Normal Drinking in Recovered Alcohol Addicts, Comment on the Article by D. L. Davies," QJSA, June, 1963, p. 322.

10. "The Pastors' Resources in Dealing with Alcoholics." Reprinted by permission from the April, 1951, issue of Pastoral Psychology. Copyright 1951 by Pulpit Digest Publishing Company, Great Neck, N. Y.

11. Talk at an AA meeting in the New York City area.

12. Otis R. Rice, "Pastoral Counseling of Inebriates," p. 438.

13. Lecture at Yale Summer School, 1949.

14. (Englewood Cliffs, N. J.: Prentice-Hall, 1963).

15. (Minneapolis: Augsburg Publishing House, 1966).

16. (Indianapolis: National Clergy Conference on Alcoholism, 1960).

17. (Philadelphia: The Westminster Press, 1952).

18. Distributed by the Division of Social Education and Action, United Presbyterian Church, Philadelphia.

19. Chapter 13, pp. 196-224.

20. For information about the Rutgers' program write: Rutgers Center of Alcohol Studies, Smithers Hall, Rutgers, The State University, New Brunswick, New Jersey 08903.

21. Pastoral Psychology, April, 1951, pp. 18-19.

22. Ibid., p. 15.

23. NCA Annual Report, 1965.

24. Flyer describing NAAAP, January, 1964.

25. Memorandum from NAAAP, March 1, 1966.

26. NCA Newsletter, Fall, 1966, pp. 1, 6.

27. (Springfield, Illinois: Charles C. Thomas, 1967).

28. (New York: Springer Publishing Co., 1967).

29. Reprinted from American Journal of Psychiatry, CXXIII (January, 1967), 769-78.

30. Ibid., p. 770.

31. Among the tranquilizers named as addictive by the AMA and the U.S. Public Health Service's Addiction Research Center are such familiar ones as Miltown, Equanil, Librium, Valium, and Doriden. (See Time, July 2, 1965, pp. 36-37.)

32. Fox, "A Multidisciplinary Approach," p. 772.

33. Ibid., p. 770.

34. Ibid., p. 773.

35. This phrase is the title of a chapter in Dwight Anderson's book The Other Side of the Bottle (New York: A. A. Wyn, 1950).

36. Fox, "A Multidisciplinary Approach," p. 775.

37. Ibid., p. 773.

38. Ibid., p. 773; see Ruth Fox, "Modified Group Psychotherapy for Alcoholics," Postgraduate Medicine, XXXIX (March, 1966), A-134 to A-140.

39. In one two-year follow-up study of 178 alcoholics, it was found that 24 percent of those who had received conditioned reflex therapy plus group therapy had improved; 26 percent of those who had had individual therapy plus group therapy had improved;

36 percent of those receiving hypnotherapy plus group therapy and 53 percent of those who had been given Antabuse plus group therapy showed improvement. (See Robert S. Wallerstein, *Hospital Treatment of Alcoholism*, Menninger Clinic Monograph Series, No. 11 [New York: Basic Books, 1957]).

40. At the Georgian Clinic much of the group therapy is done by well-trained pastoral counselors. A significant pilot project in training clergymen in the skills of helping alcoholics was launched in 1964, funded by a grant from the National Institute of Mental Health. For a description of the clinic see: "The Georgian Clinic, a Therapeutic Community for Alcoholics," *QJSA*, XXI (March, 1960), No. 1, 113-24.

9

# The Process of Counseling with Alcoholics: Relationship and Motivation

Learn your theories as well as you can, but put them aside when you touch the miracle of the living soul. Not theories but your own creative individuality alone must decide.                                                —Carl G. Jung[1]

Before describing the principles and methods of counseling with alcoholics, it should be emphasized that *the heart of any effective counseling process is a relationship characterized by warmth, genuineness, acceptance, caring, and trust.* This quality of relatedness is described in psychological language as "therapeutic" and in religious language as "redemptive." Such a relationship is the basic channel of the helping process. If it does not exist, no amount of finesse in "counseling techniques" is of value. If a therapeutic quality of relationship does exist, constructive changes can occur in spite of weaknesses in a counselor's methodology. Within such a relationship, skill in counseling techniques is a potent factor in enhancing the healing-growth process.

Each counseling relationship is a new creation. Each is unique, developing as it does from the interaction of two unique individuals, a counselor and a counselee. Because of this, all counseling is, to some extent, "by ear." This is the meaning of Jung's words (quoted above), addressed originally to psychotherapists but applicable to all types of counseling relationships. The uniqueness of each relationship makes counseling both an art and a science. A counselor's effectiveness depends on his discovery of his own creative style which will allow him to *connect with others* and *to use himself* (in his uniqueness) as a growth facilitator in relationships.

One danger of any description of counseling approaches is that the artistic essence of the helping process may become obscured by a concern with technique. To reduce this danger, it should be made clear that what follows is a description of general guidelines, principles, and methods which have proved useful in counseling with many alcoholics. They should be seen as suggestive

214

rather than definitive; rough guideposts rather than precise directions. To be most useful to the reader, they should be employed experimentally, evaluated critically, and adapted to his own particular mode of relating. It is salutary to remember that different counselors, using a variety of methods, obtain positive and roughly comparable results with alcoholics. It should be clear from this that there is no one "right" way of counseling with alcoholics. The point is not that counseling techniques are unimportant but that each counselor must develop his own approach which will release his unique personality resources in the counseling relationship.

Counseling is a disciplined art in that it is based on generic principles which transcend the infinite differences in both counselors and counselees. In learning to play the piano, there are principles of harmony, rhythm, and technique which must be mastered as a part of the discipline of the art. By mastering these, the person becomes free to use them as a foundation for developing his own unique musical expression. As he progresses in skill, the music he produces becomes more and more his own. It flows through and from him, expressing a musical individuality as much his own as his fingerprints. In an analogous way, the counselor aims at that mastery of the principles of his art which will free him to develop his own style of counseling—a style which releases his unique personhood in the human encounter called counseling. If the process of learning and adapting the principles in the laboratory of actual counseling experience with alcoholics can be supervised by someone skilled in counseling, one's growth will be greatly accelerated.

### Establishing a Counseling Relationship

Counseling with an alcoholic is fundamentally the same as counseling with anyone else in that the general principles of sound counseling apply in both cases. To discuss these principles in detail is beyond the scope of this book.[2] However, it is necessary to apply the general principles to the specific problem of counseling with alcoholics, and to do so with particular reference to some of the psychological characteristics which are typical of many alcoholics.

When the minister makes contact with an alcoholic, the first step in counseling is to begin to build a relationship-bridge with him. As in other counseling, this is done by listening in depth and relating with one's full being. Karl Menninger has observed that "listening is the most important technical tool possessed by the psychiatrist." [3] It is also the pastoral counselor's most important tool. Listening requires suppressing one's urge to interpret, reassure, or ask a series of informational questions. Listening in depth means listening with the "third ear" (as Theodor Reik put it), or being sensitive to the feelings that are behind the words and the subtle messages communicated in mood, posture, and facial expression. "Psychotherapeutic listening" [4] is different in basic ways from the superficial listening of most everyday relationships. It is a skill which the counselor must learn through disciplined practice.

Intensive listening allows the counselor to begin to sense how the alcoholic feels about himself, others, and his problem. Gradually the counselor begins to grasp precious fragments of understanding of his inner world of hopes, fears, and pain. He begins to see how life looks through his eyes. Listening and responding with warm understanding serves to establish the first strands of the interpersonal bridge called "rapport" over which the counseling process moves back and forth.

It is not easy for a nonalcoholic to understand the inner world of an alcoholic, but it is also not impossible. Heart-understanding can be acquired by really listening to recovering alcoholics and allowing them to become one's teachers. If an alcoholic counselee senses that the pastor really desires to understand, even though his initial efforts to do so are fumbling, this may open the door. The alcoholic's awareness that the counselor cares and is trying to understand allows the counselor to establish a beachhead from which he may move into the dark terrain of the alcoholic's world. As one becomes familiar with the typical experiences and feelings of many alcoholics, it is easier to pick up the feelings of a particular alcoholic more accurately and respond to them more precisely. Often one can sense what the person is feeling before he actually verbalizes it fully. As the counselor is able to stay on the alcoholic's emotional wavelength, the relationship is strengthened by the alcoholic's awareness—"This man really does understand and care!"

In Chapter 2 we noted that many alcoholics are plagued by low self-esteem and a sense of isolation (and differentness), as well as guilt and anxiety. These painful feelings make them defensive and increase the difficulty of establishing rapport with them. Because of this, the first interview may require more time than would be true in some other counseling. One must move slowly and work carefully in building the relationship. Because of his anxiety the alcoholic is hypersensitive to anxiety in others. If alcoholics make a minister anxious, this will be communicated to the alcoholic counselee, to the detriment of the relationship. Because the alcoholic feels so guilty (although he often hides it behind a façade), he often expects and even courts rejection. His emotional antennae are always up, and he is hypersensitive to condescension and rejection. The counselor should try to avoid saying anything that might be interpreted as criticism or passing judgment on him.

The emphasis on the importance of listening does not mean that the counselor should function passively or give the impression of detachment. Because of his low self-esteem, the alcoholic is easily threatened by feelings of being alone and under scrutiny. Not knowing what a silent counselor is thinking, he tends to project his own self-disparagement onto the counselor and thus feels judged by the latter's silence. To be effective, the counseling relationship must be a warm, human relationship. It should be more than this, but it must not be less. The "more" consists of the counselor's skills and understanding not present in noncounseling relationships. But the human quality is the indispensable foundation of whatever else is present.

The late Otis Rice once suggested that the counselor must "stay close to the alcoholic's ego." [5] Somehow the pastor must let the alcoholic know that he is with him emotionally—that he is reaching out to him as one human being to another. Conveying this is important because the alcoholic tends to see the clergyman as one who reaches down rather than out to him. Because the minister is perceived as a "superego figure" by many people—as one who represents the "oughts" of society—counselees may believe that he is sitting in judgment when he is not.

There are various ways of staying close to the alcoholic's ego. Not threatening him with a barrage of questions but rather responding to his painful feelings in an empathic, accepting way has an ego-supportive effect. Jellinek stressed the importance of not asking any save "tiny little questions" during the early phases of counseling, thus respecting the alcoholic's right to stay as hidden as he needs to stay.[6] In contrast, asking questions which seem impertinent or irrelevant may strike the alcoholic as prying into his private affairs.

The pastor should do whatever he can to let the alcoholic know he is "feeling with" him in his problem, as he sees it. The appropriate use of what Rice said one of his colleagues called "encouraging grunts" [7] lets the alcoholic feel that one hears. It may be helpful to paraphrase occasionally what he thinks the alcoholic is saying and feeling in order to communicate understanding or correct misunderstanding. How one responds or at what points are not crucial issues. What is crucial is that one's responses be an expression of a genuine fellow-feeling and growing understanding on the counselor's part.

Often an alcoholic comes to a minister because he wants desperately to unburden himself. The pastor is not only the most accessible professional person to many people, but he is also the one to whom many turn for help with guilt feelings. As the alcoholic pours out his painful feelings, three helpful things occur. First, emotional unburdening takes place. This has value in itself, lightening his guilt load enough to free some of his previously paralyzed energies for use in coping. Second, as the counselor listens and resonates, the bond of rapport grows stronger. Such a bond develops between any human beings who share an emotionally meaningful experience. Being listened to, in one's agony, by an accepting authority figure is a profoundly meaningful experience. Third, by avoiding getting in the way of the verbal-emotional flow, the minister usually acquires much of the relevant information which he

217

needs in order to understand the person's problem. What he does not obtain spontaneously, he can get by direct questions.

Here is an illustration of how one minister got in the way of the developing therapeutic relationship:

An alcoholic came to talk to his pastor and began to pour out all manner of self-condemnation and remorse. Feeling that the man's self-blame was exaggerated and distorted, the pastor sought to reassure him, pointing out that after all there were extenuating circumstances involved. Each time the acoholic tried to express his deep feelings of guilt and despair, the pastor pointed out that things weren't as bad as he seemed to think. Finally the alcoholic left and did not return for another interview.

The two facts that this minister had overlooked were that reassurances of this kind do not reassure, and that the man's negative feelings must be expressed and accepted before they could be replaced by more positive ones. By attempting to reassure, the pastor unintentionally convinced the man that his feelings were not recognized or understood. Thus, instead of helping the alcoholic experience forgiveness, the minister had blocked the path of confession by which one moves from guilt to forgiveness.

The use of the "we" approach is a method of staying close to the alcoholic's ego by avoiding putting him in an exposed position. Otis Rice, who suggested this approach, gave these illustrations of how it might be put: "Now what can we find in the situation?" or "What can we do with the problem you have brought?" The use of "we" lets the alcoholic feel the counselor's collaboration and support in the difficulties he is facing. It puts the counselor on his side as an ally. Jellinek once told of discussing an alcoholic's relationship with his wife and of doing so, not in terms of "your wife," but in terms of his relation with his own wife. The interjection of the counselor's personal relationships may seem to some to be anathema so far as principles of good counseling are concerned. In practice, this approach seems to be a sound way of keeping the alcoholic from feeling on the spot and from raising his defenses. Since he is uneasy about his dependency needs, it is supportive to know that the counselor has needs and problems too. The example, par excellence, of the use of the "we" principle is the manner in which AA's operate in their Twelfth Step work.

The AA member stays close to the alcoholic's sensitive ego by talking about his own drinking problem and AA experiences. Thus he communicates forcefully that he is not talking down to the other person or judging him. This is what Paul Tillich once described as the "principle of mutuality," a principle that is basic in all pastoral counseling. Tillich pointed out that the counselor must communicate to the counselee the message that he understands well on the basis of his own experience.[8] Marty Mann has this useful idea concerning the pastor's approach to the alcoholic:

> The pastor who feels it is his bounden duty to act as a spiritual mentor to an alcoholic who comes to him could perhaps succeed if he could recall out of his own experience some time of deep crisis or personal suffering in which he found comfort from his faith, and could tell that story simply and directly. In other words, if he could come down from his symbolic mountain above the battle and meet the tormented soul of the alcoholic on its own level of suffering; the soul could perhaps accept comfort from him and gain some of his faith.[9]

She recommends that if the minister can't draw on his own experiences in meeting personal crises, he should tell of someone he has known who has received help with the problem of alcoholism.

In the author's experience, reference to one's own problems or struggles is best made in a kind of "in passing" manner. This lets the alcoholic know that the minister *has* problems, is aware of his fallibility, and is speaking as one who shares the foibles and limitations of the rest of the human race. Alluding casually to one's problems lessens the risk that the alcoholic will resent a comparison of what seem to him to be the clergyman's relatively minor problems with his all-consuming and devastating *Problem*.

The fundamental way of staying close to the alcoholic's ego is by communicating acceptance in the relationship. In *Modern Man in Search of a Soul*, Carl Jung declared:

> If the doctor wants to offer guidance to another, or even to accompany him a step on the way, he must be in touch with the other person's psychic life. He is never in touch when he passes judgment. Whether he puts his judgments into words, or keeps them to himself, makes not the slightest difference.[10]

A basic factor which influences the acceptance-climate of the relationship is whether or not the pastor really accepts the sickness conception of alcoholism. Unless he accepts it at a *heart* as well as at a *head* level, he will convey a judgmental attitude in spite of his conscious intentions. By accepting the sickness conception with all of its ramifications, the counselor divorces from his mind the feeling that he is dealing with what is basically a moral deviation or perverse habit; he accepts alcoholism as one symptom of the common sickness of our culture, in which all of us share.

Protecting the alcoholic's ego so that he will not become defensive is not the same as protecting him from the consequences of his immature behavior. The former is therapeutically constructive; the latter is unconstructive. Accepting the alcoholic does not mean approving his destructive behavior which is harmful to himself and others. It is important that the alcoholic know that

219

the counselor, who accepts him as a person, does *not* approve of his irresponsible behavior. It is because the counselor accepts and cares about him and his family that he does not approve of behavior which hurts any of them. Only as the people around the alcoholic are able to be *both* accepting and firm will he be required to face the reality of the adult world and his irresponsible relation with it. Allowing him to avoid reality by protecting him is what John Ford calls "cruel kindness." A part of the counselor's firmness must be insistence that people who are sick have an obligation to society to obtain treatment.

## The Alcoholic's Motivation

During the first contact with an alcoholic, *it is essential to find out to what extent he is open to help and what kind of help, if any, he desires.* If the alcoholic's initial motivation is inadequate and this is overlooked by the counselor, the usual result is that nothing productive occurs even though there may be an extensive exercise of "going through the motions" of counseling. It is an axiom in counseling that people can be helped only with those problems which *they* regard as problems and with which they want the counselor's help, to some extent.

In order to discover the nature of the alcoholic's motivation, questions such as these should be in the counselor's mind as he listens and talks with the alcoholic during the first interview:

What does *he* see as his problem?
From his point of view, is his drinking a problem or a solution?
Does he see it as a cause of his other problems or simply a way of gaining relief from them?
Does he feel that he needs help from others? From me?
If so, what kind of help does he want? (Does he want someone to pacify his wife, intervene with his boss, help him learn to drink in moderation, or help him lick his drinking problem in whatever way is required?)
Why did he come for help *now?* (He has had the problem for several years.)
Was he threatened or dragged into coming by his spouse?
Is there some special crisis that puts him under acute pressure at the moment, but which will pass?
Is his primary motivation for coming external pressure or internal pressure?
Why did he come to a clergyman?
Does this throw light on the kind of help he expects?

If, as the first interview progresses, the counselor finds that he is not getting clear answers to questions of motivation such as these, it is appropriate to ask enough of them to gain a picture of the alcoholic's reason for coming and the help he expects.

Generally speaking, an alcoholic's motivation is inadequate, so far as successful treatment is concerned, if he mainly sees alcohol as a solution, wants help in changing those around him or avoiding the consequences of his immature behavior, and/or comes because he was pressured (either by a person or by crisis circumstances of which he feels himself the victim). Conversely, motivation adequate to successful treatment is usually present if he sees alcohol as one factor which contributes to his many troubles, has some desire to change himself or his way of behaving, and comes primarily because of inner pain which he sees as resulting from his use of alcohol, directly or indirectly.

In sizing up the alcoholic's motivation, the key question is this: *Is he able to admit that alcohol is giving him serious trouble and that he needs help in handling it?* In attempting to answer this, it is important to bear in mind that the alcoholic's motivation, like all human motivation, is mixed. Few, if any, alcoholics desire unambivalently and wholeheartedly to stop drinking. That is to say, they seldom completely want to stop drinking, nor do they want to stop drinking completely. They are pulled in opposite directions by inner forces. A part of their psyche wants to stop; another part drives them to continue drinking. Put another way, many alcoholics want to stop because they are afraid of the disastrous consequences of continuing, and yet they are also afraid to stop because alcohol has become the center of their psychological universe. To some extent, this conflict is present in most alcoholics.

Thus, to ask: Is this alcoholic ready to stop drinking? is not a precise or satisfactory way of ascertaining the adequacy of his motivation for recovery. *The useful question is whether his desire to stop is stronger than his desire to continue.* Put differently, one can ask whether the pain resulting from drinking outweighs the satisfactions derived therefrom. Often this is not easy to determine. It is helpful to think of the alcoholic's motivation as something like a teeter-totter which tips back and forth. At times the pain of drinking and the fear of the probable consequences of continuing outweigh the craving for alcohol's anesthetic effects and the fear of life without it. When this happens, the alcoholic "hits bottom"—becomes open to help. At other times his motivational teeter-totter tilts away from being receptive to help. A hangover period following a binge may present a "little bottom"—i.e., a state of emotional receptivity during which the alcoholic's defenses against recognizing his need for help are temporarily cracked by the physical and emotional pain of the experience. The counselor should encourage the alcoholic to get help immediately and not "to wait until he feels better." There is quaint wisdom (which is relevant to the "fall" which is alcoholism) in the old Christian hymn:

221

> Come, ye weary, heavy-laden,
> Lost and ruined by the fall;
> If you tarry till you're better,
> You will never come at all.[11]

In the light of the complexity of human motivation, the familiar statement, "You can't help an alcoholic until he is ready!" is, at best, a dangerous half-truth. The danger is that the counselor will use it to avoid his responsibility which is to discover, stimulate, and mobilize the alcoholic's latent motivation toward accepting help. Since few, if any, alcoholics are ever completely "ready," it is more productive for the counselor to ask: Does this person show a possible willingness to consider sobriety, providing he can be shown that there is a better way than the one which he has been following? This question recognizes that the person may not be able to admit his need for help (even to himself) until he has some ray of hope that help *for him* is a possibility. Beyond this question, it is crucial to ask: What can I as a counselor do to help this person become more open to help?

I recall a Twelfth Step call upon which I accompanied an experienced member of AA. The person upon whom we were calling mentioned that he wasn't sure whether he was an alcoholic or just a heavy drinker because he had never taken a morning drink. (Later he admitted that this was usually because he hadn't made sure the night before that he had a supply for the next day.) The response of the AA member suggests both a useful test of a person's motivation to stop and an excellent general approach to an alcoholic:

To discuss whether one is a heavy drinker or an alcoholic can easily become a matter of semantics. The important question is this: Are you satisfied with your life as it's been going for the past year, two years, five years? Take any period you want. If you are, there's no problem. If you aren't satisfied and feel that alcohol is the cause or at least part of the cause of the way your life has been going, then the thing to do is to make a decision that you're going to stop. Then the problem is to make the decision stick—that's where AA comes in.

The discussion turned in the direction of the individual's painful experience during the recent binge and his resolve not to let it happen again. The AA member said, in effect:

The problem is to make your present feeling stick—to keep it alive. You're very sincere now, we're assuming that, but how about in three months or six? AA is the way you keep the desire alive—keep on remembering that you have a problem with alcohol. After you've been away from alcohol for a while, you begin to question whether it's really a problem or not. AA helps keep your present desire from dying.

Toward the end of the visit, the AA member said: "You have to remember, John, that nobody really cares if you have a few drinks. It's up to you. If you want to stop drinking, then AA can help you. But it's your decision." The purpose of such a statement was apparently to make sure that the initiative was left with John and that he did not feel that he had been persuaded to stop drinking. Here is a demonstration of the recognition that the alcoholic himself must make the initial decision to accept help (however mixed his feelings about it), before any real counseling or therapy can begin.

The extent to which the alcoholic considers drinking a cause, as contrasted with an effect, of other circumstances and problems is often a significant indicator of his degree of motivation. I remember one alcoholic who was in wretched condition, but who could not admit that his drinking was a real problem. Again and again he would attribute his drinking to his poor sexual relationship with his wife. Undoubtedly his poor sexual relationship (and the inadequate interpersonal relationship which underlay it) was a contributing cause of his drinking. But the fact that he could not recognize that alcohol was a problem per se and one cause of his poor sexual adjustment showed that his motivational teeter-totter had not yet tipped toward openness to help with his alcoholism.

### The Resistant Alcoholic

Many alcoholics who come to ministers and other counselors are still resisting facing the truth about their addiction. They, therefore, resist any real commitment to help. About one third of the persons seeking treatment at outpatient alcohol clinics in one state did not return after the first interview.[12] Deficient motivation was undoubtedly a cause of many of these failures to continue treatment. Recall that Jellinek's chart (Chapter 1) showed that the mean age for "felt religious need" was 35.7; where as the mean age for "hit bottom" was 40.7. This helps explain why many alcoholics come to ministers before they are "ripe"—open to help. I would suspect that the majority of alcoholics, at the point of their first contact with clergymen, are still resisting to a considerable degree. It is very important, therefore, to learn the skills which frequently are effective in helping to motivate the resisting alcoholic.

A pastor was completely baffled by the behavior of a man in his early thirties who in the period after his binges would come to see him full of remorse and good resolutions. Each time the minister would attempt to help him relate to AA without avail. In spite of repeated defeats in his "battle with the bottle," he was still sure that he could "lick the thing" himself. To the minister it was apparent that the man was not yet "at bottom," and he pointed this fact out to the family. To this the family posed the obvious question in its most disturbing form: "Do you mean that we must sit and watch him go down and down and down, and do absolutely nothing?"

223

Few things in life are more heartrending or frustrating to a counselor or to the family than to watch helplessly while the alcoholic engages in what amounts to protracted suicide. But, as a matter of fact, it is *not* necessary simply to wait and do absolutely nothing. The discussion which follows delineates what the counselor can do to discover and stimulate the alcoholic's motivation to accept help. The family's role in this process will be explored in Chapter 11.

There are two general principles for work with recalcitrant alcoholics. First, *avoid if possible doing anything which may destroy the possibility of developing a helpful relationship at some later time.* Private sermons and pleadings should be avoided for this reason, as well as for the fact that they are utterly ineffectual. Second, *attempt to sow seeds of understanding—of the person and of alcoholism—which may take root and eventually flower in openness to help.* Implicit in this suggestion is the concept that motivation of a resisting alcoholic is a process which may extend over a considerable period of time.

In some cases, the need to help motivate an alcoholic is indicated by the circumstances under which the pastor is contacted.

A pastor received a phone call from a parishioner, Mrs. P., in which she asked in a tearful voice, "Will you please come over and talk to Henry? He's having his problem again." Because of his strong desire to be helpful, the pastor's automatic response was to accept her plea as a challenge to his ability to help. When he arrived at their home, he discovered that Henry was quite drunk and in no mood to talk to the pastor about anything, particularly not about his drinking. In fact, he was intoxicated enough to be unrestrained in his expression of resentment toward his wife for calling the minister and toward the minister for "sticking his nose in other people's business!"

By responding as he did, this pastor had allowed himself to be drawn into the power struggle between P. and his wife, on the side of the wife. This naturally incurred P.'s resentment which practically eliminated the possibility that the minister might have been of real help at some later time, when P. had become more receptive. Nevertheless, having gotten himself in this situation, the minister might have salvaged something for the future by saying to Mr. P. that he had come thinking he needed him, but since he was mistaken, he apologized. If he had done this and accepted the man's resentment, the door might have been left ajar for future help.

A more constructive approach would have been this. When Mrs. P. called, he might have first determined whether she and the children were in danger of physical harm from P. If so, he would have suggested some direct action to the wife such as going to stay with relatives for a few days or calling the police if P. became violent. Further, he should have found out more about P.'s condition and attitudes during his phone conversation with Mrs. P. An important question would have been: "How does your husband feel about talking with me, at this point?"; another would have been: "Does he feel that his drinking is a problem with which he wants help?" In view of the situation which these questions would have brought to light, the minister could then have said, "It would probably do more harm than good for me to try to talk with your husband if he does not want to talk with me. It would only antagonize him and perhaps give him added reason to go on drinking. However, as soon as he is sober, I suggest that you consider telling him that I will be glad to talk with him anytime, about whatever he wants to discuss with me. If he can come to my study, fine; or, if he wants to talk but doesn't feel up to coming here, I'll come to your home. In the meantime, why don't you keep in touch with me and let me know how things are going?" If P. does respond to the minister's invitation—either by coming to his study or indicating his willingness to talk with him at the P.s' home—he will have exercised some initiative in the matter, thus improving the possibility of a constructive outcome. Coming to the pastor's study may indicate stronger motivation on P.'s part, and it will give the minister an opportunity to talk with him without having Mrs. P. complicate the interview. If P. does not respond, it would be appropriate for the minister to make a pastoral call in a few days, to make himself available to be of assistance either to Mr. or Mrs. P., or both.

It should be emphasized that Mrs. P.'s phone call provides an opening for the minister to give pastoral care to her and the children, and perhaps to counsel with her, even if P. does not become accessible to help. In many cases, a person who calls requesting help for someone else is, in this indirect way, asking for help himself.

When a minister goes to see an alcoholic at his request, it is often advisable to obtain his permission to bring a member of AA along. If possible he should find a person in approximately the same age bracket and general socio-educational background in order to increase the chances of his establishing rapport with the alcoholic. In calling on a woman alcoholic, it is crucial for the minister to take a woman member of AA with him. In general, it is wise for a male minister not to call on female alcoholics who are drinking and alone, unless a stable female AA member is available to accompany him. Taking an AA member along is particularly helpful if the pastor's visit to an alcoholic is made during the period following a binge. The AA member may be able to utilize the alcoholic's openness to help during this time in a way that the nonalcoholic minister cannot.

When the minister talks with a resistant alcoholic, in whatever setting, it

225

is important to find out if he has been nagged or dragged to come to the minister (or let the minister come to him). If the alcoholic has come under third-party pressure, *the counselor's first job is to get rid of the third party.* Unless this occurs, there will usually be no real counseling relationship. If the spouse or relative is physically present, it may be advantageous to get a "feel" for the quality of the interaction between that person and the alcoholic. After this, however, it is imperative that the pastor talk with the alcoholic alone. A polite but firm request such as this usually suffices:

> *Pastor:* I appreciate having your perspective on the situation. Now I believe it would be helpful for me to have a chance to talk privately with your husband about the situation. You'll find a magazine in the next room.

Even if the "motivating party" is absent physically, he *is* present psychologically; he must be removed psychologically before a counseling relationship with the alcoholic can be established. This may be accomplished by an approach which begins like this:

> *Pastor:* I realize that your wife thinks that you have a problem with alcohol, or she wouldn't have pushed you to come to see me. But what I'm mainly interested in at this point is knowing how the situation looks from your point of view. I can imagine that things must look somewhat different from where you stand. What seems to be the trouble, as you see it?

Hopefully, as this approach is followed, the alcoholic will sense that the counselor is not siding with the wife in the struggle between them by accepting her view as the complete and accurate picture. Equally important, the alcoholic may begin to realize that the counselor is genuinely interested in understanding the situation, including his perception of it, and he is interested in being of whatever help he can be to them. When this happens, the alcoholic begins to lower his defenses and to risk some openness with and trust of the counselor.

In removing the pushing person from the alcoholic-counselor relationship, it is important not to criticize or side against that person. The pastor's responsibility is usually to be of all the help that he can both to the alcoholic and his spouse (or other relative). The spouse may need help as desperately as does the alcoholic. If the counselor's criticisms are quoted (or misquoted) to the spouse in a moment of angry attack, the possibility of being of help to that person is virtually destroyed. Further, by being critical of the spouse, the counselor may have contributed to the worsening of an already deteriorated relationship between the alcoholic and a "significant other" who has a concern for the alcoholic, however misguided it may seem.

The wife-motivated alcoholic is familiar to most pastors. Like many other things in counseling, shifting the initiative from the wife to the alcoholic is usually easier said than done. However, its importance cannot be over-emphasized. In a workshop on counseling alcoholics, at the Yale Summer School,[13] E. M. Jellinek told how he proceeded when an alcoholic had been "brought" or "sent" by a spouse. He described inviting the alcoholic into the counseling room, whereupon he would direct the conversation to some irrelevant subject. During the course of this light discussion, he might drop a few seed thoughts about the nature of alcoholism. For example, he might ask, "Have you heard about the experiment they tried at Yale?" He would then tell about the rat experiment (see Chapter 2) which he found useful in conveying to the person the reality of the physical component in alcoholism. After a while he would say, "Well, I guess you've been in here long enough to satisfy your wife. You may go now if you wish." This approach has a kind of shock value, and it tends to put the counselor on the "same side of the table" as the alcoholic. It prevents the alcoholic from keeping his hostile feelings toward his wife attached to the counselor by perceiving him as her ally. Further, it forces the person to make a choice—to leave or to stay on his own initiative. Respecting his ability and right to make this choice enhances his self-esteem and strengthens his relationship with the counselor. I would recommend the use of this technique in those situations in which the alcoholic remains resistant (actively or passively) during the interview in spite of the use of the other strategies described in this chapter.

It is important during the first interview to help the person verbalize his feelings toward being there. Whether the person comes under pressure or threat, on the one hand, or merely fighting his inner resistances to admitting he needs help, on the other, the counselor should assist him in getting his negative or conflicting feelings out into the open. As these feelings are being discussed, the counselor should let the person know, by his attitudes, that he respects his right to whatever feelings he may have.

*Pastor:*   I can imagine that it must annoy you to feel pushed into seeing me.

If the alcoholic's hidden resentment is overlooked by the counselor, he may stay as tightly defended as a clam for no apparent reason. Not recognizing and helping the person ventilate such feelings accounts for the failure of many potential counseling relationships to "get off the ground." The hidden feelings about being coerced or of weakness for having to ask for help may function like a logjam blocking the flow of interaction in counseling. The log-

227

jam tends to be dispersed as the alcoholic senses the counselor's acceptance of his feelings, including his reluctance to admit that he needs help.

In dealing with the resistant alcoholic, it is essential for the counselor *to accept the person's right not to accept help.* This is a right which he can exercise regardless of the counselor's preference in the matter. In some cases, the pastor's acceptance of the alcoholic's right and freedom not to accept help actually is a dynamic factor in enabling the alcoholic to accept help. Speaking symbolically, it is as though the counselor must respect a person's right to go to hell before he can be an instrument in helping him move toward heaven. Implicit in this is the principle of not attempting to push help toward a person who has no openness to his need for it. A person's "right to fail" should be respected.

In working with any counselee, but particularly the one who is resistant, it is important *to discover the point or points at which he is hurting.* It is at this point that the offer of help is most likely to be accepted. Often the *hurt-points* can be found by encouraging the alcoholic to talk about his problems *as he sees them.* About what is *he* worried, afraid, angered, frustrated, hopeless? What would *he* like to see changed? Which of his wants or needs are not being met, as *he* sees matters? The late Harry M. Tiebout once pointed out that even the most adamantly resisting alcoholic usually has an Achilles heel and that it is the counselor's job to find it in order to reach the person with help. A person's Achilles heel—the place where he is "motivatable"—is the place where he is hurting, worried, or aware of some need for help.

I am not suggesting that the alcoholic necessarily be given the kind of help for which he is asking the counselor. Frequently, what he wants would in the long run work against his recovery, for instance, a loan or gift of money, intervention with an authority to protect him from the consequences of his behavior, or bringing pressure to bear to change someone else in the alcoholic's interpersonal world. What I am recommending is that the counselor begin by *understanding* what the alcoholic wants and then, if necessary, attempt to modify gradually his expectations of what the counselor can do.

The counselor should encourage the resistant alcoholic *to talk about his drinking*—when he drinks, with whom, how he feels, what happens when he drinks? Does he see any relationship between his "hurt-points" and his drinking? Early in counseling, the alcoholic is usually defensive. He will therefore give an inaccurate or incomplete picture of both his drinking pattern and his feelings about drinking. He may be much more concerned about his drinking than he admits to the counselor at this point. But, if the counselor resists the temptation to put too much pressure on him, he may gradually reveal more of the truth as the relationship grows stronger.

Whether or not the alcoholic gives an accurate picture of his drinking, his discussion of it gives the counselor an opportunity to plant seeds of understanding (educative counseling) and seeds of creative anxiety. Several of the following questions can be asked as they fit into the flow of the conversation:

Have you ever pulled a blank (had a memory loss) while you were drinking?

Do you ever have a desire to drink alone, just to get loaded?

Do you sometimes find yourself drinking more than you intend?

Are your "must" times coming earlier in the day?

When you're at a party, do you ever find yourself sneaking a quick one on the side when no one is looking?

Do you ever take a drink in the morning to ease a painful hangover?

Have you ever found yourself taking a drink to get you through tough social situations?

Do you ever get a bit defensive when your wife questions you about whether you're drinking too much?

Does food lose its appeal when you're drinking?

Is your efficiency at work ever cut down by a hangover or by drinking at lunchtime?

Have you lost time from work because of drinking?

Do you feel that the problems in your marriage may be increased by your drinking?

Do you sometimes spend money you can't really afford on liquor?

Without seeming to "grill" the person, which would make him defensive, a few of these questions can be sprinkled into the discussion, followed by the observation that these are some of the typical early symptoms of problem drinking or alcoholism. It is well to make it clear that a person need not have all or any of these experiences to be headed for trouble with alcohol, but that they are frequently present in the early stages of what becomes a serious drinking problem.

The defensive alcoholic often will deny that he has had any of the experiences mentioned by the counselor. This does not mean that the effort has been wasted. If the person is in the process of losing control over alcohol, the odds are that he will have had several of the experiences mentioned. What the counselor may have done was to help him begin to recognize the symptoms of alcoholism in his drinking behavior. After he leaves the minister, he may ruminate: "I certainly pulled the wool over that stupid minister's eyes . . . but I wonder if there's anything to what he said about blackouts." Hopefully, the seeds of creative anxiety which the minister has sown will eventually flower in willingness to face the reality of his drinking problem and his need for help.

Two instruments which are "useful tools in diagnosing alcoholism" (and can be so described to the alcoholic counselee) are Seliger's list of twenty questions (see Chapter 1) and the "valley chart," p. 231. Here is an illustration of how the chart can be used with the mildly resistant alcoholic.

Pastor:  It might be helpful for us to use a kind of diagnostic approach to see if you might, by chance, be on the road to the illness. Here, as you go down the left-hand side of the chart, you'll find the typical symptoms which identify the various stages of this progressive illness. Let's take a look at these to see if any of them fit.

The medical model of diagnosis is useful at this point in helping the alcoholic take an objective look at his drinking pattern. By tracing the road down into advanced-stage alcoholism, the counselor gives the person a preview of where he may be headed if he continues drinking. The road up toward recovery, on the right-hand side of the valley chart, shows the typical stages of the recovery process after one hits bottom. There is value for the alcoholic in seeing these alongside the road down, since it tends to kindle hope that recovery is possible. The chart in larger form is available from the National Council on Alcoholism (2 East 103rd Street, New York, New York 10029). The counselor who does not have a printed chart can draw his own, during the counseling interview, discussing the alcoholic's reactions as they proceed. The essential thing in all this is for the counselor to be familiar with the warning signs of alcoholism so that he can help the person recognize them in himself, if they are present.

In attempting to motivate the resistant alcoholic and in the early phases of working with an alcoholic who is gradually becoming more open to help, it is advisable to emphasize the physical component in alcoholism. Drawing an analogy between this problem and allergic reactions or diabetes is an effective way of communicating to the alcoholic that his illness is a reality—that it's not "all in his mind"—and that obtaining treatment is therefore essential to recovery. Psychological explanations still carry overtones of moralism and free-will-ism in our culture, whereas medical analogies seem to escape these overtones to a large degree. Most people have an allergy of some kind or know someone who has; most are acquainted with someone who has diabetes. This serves as a bridge to accepting the physiological component in the illness of alcoholism. The parallelism between alcoholism and diabetes makes the latter a particularly useful communication device. Both the alcoholic and the diabetic have conditions which are incurable but treatable. Both must learn to live within the limitations imposed by the condition and, if they accomplish this, both can live productive lives. Both conditions involve some malfunction of the organism and, if untreated, become progressively more severe and inimical to healthy living.

Helping the counselee understand the basic facts about alcohol addiction is an essential part of all alcoholic counseling. This is true even in those cases

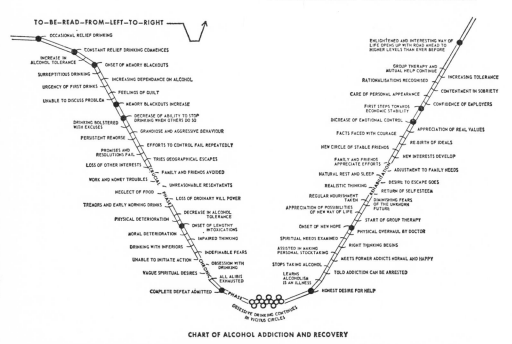

**CHART OF ALCOHOL ADDICTION AND RECOVERY**

Reprinted from M. M. Glatt, "Group Therapy in Alcoholism," *The British Journal of Addiction*, Vol. LIX, No. 2 (January, 1958). Used by permission of the author.

in which the person appears to be quite open to recognizing his illness and accepting help with it. As indicated earlier, all motivation is mixed. In every alcoholic, the counselor should assume the presence of some degree of resistance. Relative openness to help may lessen as the pain and the memory of the suffering resulting from excessive drinking subside. The person may begin to question whether he is really an alcoholic, since he feels so well and is obviously in competent control of his life. It is at this point that the person's knowledge of the nature of his illness, including the tendency to rationalize, can help him resist taking a course that will probably eventuate in a drinking bout. In the case of the alcoholic who has not achieved sobriety as yet, the appearance of openness to help may hide an underlying resistance; it may be a passive-aggressive way of defeating the counselor by seeming to agree and comply.

In counseling aimed at motivating a resistant alcoholic, it is sometimes helpful to point out that loss of control is gradual in most alcoholism and is, therefore, a matter of degree. The process is often so gradual as to be imperceptible to the person, particularly because of the universal human tendency to see one's own behavior as "normal" even when it is grossly abnormal. It is also important to discover and attempt to change the person's inner picture of an "alcoholic" if he is holding to a Skid-Row stereotype which naturally excludes him. Furthermore, it is helpful to point out that one need not be a psychiatric cripple in order to lose control of alcohol. All of these procedures are aimed at removing the misconceptions which make it difficult for the individual to see his own alcohol problem.

After some degree of trust exists between the alcoholic and the pastor, the use of *constructive confrontation* may be in order. If the alcoholic continues to avoid the truth by rationalizing his abnormal drinking, confrontation in one of its various forms may help. The counselor may describe for him how his alibi system functions [14] and why he feels he must defend his need to drink. By showing understanding of how difficult it is for the alcoholic to let go of his alibis, the counselor may help him to do so. He may begin to become aware of the fact that it is his alibi system which blinds him to the danger signals which are present in his drinking pattern. If the alcoholic is nearly "ripe" for treatment, this direct attempt to reduce the operation of his rationalization system may be effective. If not, he may become more defensive for the time being; but, the seeds of recovery may have been planted.

Here are some of the factors which cause the alcoholic to avoid facing his need for help: [15] his fear of the pain of abstinence (life without his pain-killer); his fear of not belonging to a drinking group which he enjoys; his feeling that alcohol is all that "works" for him; the blow to his self-esteem of admitting loss of control and, in the case of a male, of his inability to "drink like a man"; his fear of recognizing that he has a socially unacceptable condition; his fear of unsympathetic and punitive professional helping persons; his fear of what it might do to his job, family, church, or social relations to be identified as an "alcoholic." It is important that these inner barriers to admitting his need for help be discussed with understanding and empathy by the counselor. If the person can bring his fears into the open, the help of the counseling process becomes available for coping with them.

Constructive confrontation may include saying to the resisting alcoholic that he appears to have some of the warning signs of addiction. If the person is obviously defensive, it is wise to understate the case and thus avoid a head-on collision with his defenses which would only make them more rigid. The late Harry M. Tiebout once told of an alcoholic who came to see him in a defiant mood. He described his drinking pattern and then demanded of Tiebout, "Tell me, does that make me an alcoholic?" Rather than giving a direct answer that the man could easily have rejected, Tiebout responded, "I suppose that what really matters is your answer to that question. But frankly, I'm glad I'm not in your shoes." Several years later, the man introduced himself after an AA meeting at which Tiebout had been guest speaker.

He reported that he had been sober for some time in AA and that Tiebout's words had been a key factor in his decision to seek help.

Constructive confrontation means confronting the person with reality and helping him look at it squarely. In biblical terms, it is "speaking the truth in love" (Eph. 4:15). If the alcoholic feels the minister's concern, he may listen, and the words may have an impact even though the person has to deny verbally that they describe the way things really are. The alcoholic may resent the minister's picture of the truth about his drinking and its consequences; yet, in spite of this, constructive wheels may be set in motion in the alcoholic's thinking. It is important to *offer help and hope* at the same time one holds up reality, firmly and acceptingly. It is less difficult for the alcoholic to face the grim fact that his life is in shambles because of his drinking if he knows that there are effective ways of stopping and of rejoining the human race.

The various methods of attempting to motivate the resistant alcoholic, described in this section, are all ways of "elevating the alcoholic's bottom." This apt phrase was suggested by internist Daniel J. Feldman, formerly with the Consultation Clinic for Alcoholism, Bellevue Medical Center, New York University.[16] He pointed out that it is possible to save some alcoholics from years of suffering by hastening the point at which they become open to help— "hit bottom" psychologically. Feldman emphasized two factors in this process: "acceptance" and "bringing reality through." By acceptance he meant accepting the alcoholic as a sick person. If a counselor cannot do this, he should refer the alcoholic to someone who can. Obviously the alcoholic cannot be receptive to the help that is appropriate to a sickness until he accepts the fact that he has a sickness; a counselor's lack of acceptance of this fact will reinforce the alcoholic's resistance to accepting it. "Bringing reality through" is the same as constructive confrontation. Feldman advises counselors: "Keep holding the reality situation before him in a factual, nonjudgmental way. For example, 'I'm not saying that it's good or bad—that's for you to decide—but it's a fact that your employer is just about through with you.'" It is usually better to mention the ways in which the person is hurting himself and blocking himself from goals he desires, rather than to call his attention to the harm he is doing to his family. As long as he is drinking, he will be highly ambivalent toward them. On one level he feels overwhelming guilt feelings about his harming of them; on another level (often unconscious) his drinking may be a way of expressing hostility and resentment toward them. If the counselor is able to keep the reality situation before the alcoholic without the therapeutic bond of acceptance being broken, he may move him toward openness to help.

A key factor in elevating the "bottom" of the resisting alcoholic consists of working with the spouse to "release" him emotionally. This working concept, drawn from Al-Anon, will be explored in more depth in Chapter 11. Briefly, it consists of three actions: (a) letting go of the obsessive and futile efforts to "get my husband sober"; (b) letting go of her overprotective behavior by which she has unwittingly kept him from experiencing the painful consequences of his behavior which may have been precisely what he needed to become open to help; (c) letting go of the assumption that any improvement in the family situation is totally dependent on her husband's achieving sobriety. This third release enables the wife and children to develop their own lives and relationships, whether or not the alcoholic decides to accept help. When a spouse succeeds in releasing her husband in these three ways, a crisis is created in his psychic economy which may result in his becoming accessible to help sooner than he otherwise would.

The first two elements in release also apply to the counselor's attitudes and behavior in relationship to the alcoholic. The counselor must let go of any illusion that he can "get the alcoholic sober." Ultimately, motivation to recover can come from only one place—within the alcoholic. Second, the counselor can be alert to the danger of unwittingly becoming an overprotector of the alcoholic.

Almost without exception, alcoholics attach themselves to those upon whom they can lean and upon whom they can depend for protection from the consequences of their drinking. It is possible for a counselor to allow himself to be used in this way. One of the Yale ministers told of working closely with an alcoholic, saying, "He recovered, but only after I too had withdrawn my support, and he was forced to return to a hospital for treatment."

An alcoholic's strong dependency needs, coupled with the role of parent-image into which the minister is cast by the emotionally immature, make it easy for unconstructive dependency relationships to develop. One minister tells of the hours and hours he spent trying to get and keep an alcoholic parishioner sober. The experience ended in failure and convinced the minister that he had made the mistake of "babying" the alcoholic—doing things for him which he should have been doing for himself. This conclusion fits with the recognition in AA that it is not helpful to pamper or "hold the hands" of a still-drinking alcoholic.

It is essential *to keep the responsibility for recovering with the alcoholic.* In his efforts to "get and keep" the alcoholic sober, the minister had taken over this responsibility. This is bound to fail since no one can get or keep another person sober. The alcoholic's dependent side tends to draw the counselor into the trap of assuming responsibility for his sobriety. Some alcoholics will expect the minister to be a wonder-worker who can, by some magic religious formula, cure him of his alcoholism. This is where it is wise to let the alcoholic know, gently but firmly, that no one, including God, can cause him to recover from his alcoholism unless he takes the initiative and is willing to work at recovery. He must use his own God-given resources, with the help of the counselor, AA, and other resources, to work out his own sobriety. No one can do it for him or to him.

The alcoholic's ambivalence toward authority is a psychological characteristic which must be taken into account in counseling. The alcoholic may be relatively mature in many ways, but he is often like an adolescent in his relationship to authority, alternately craving and resenting dependence. He tries to make the counselor into an authority figure, upon whom he can be dependent and *against whom he can then rebel.* If the counselor falls into this trap, the counseling relationship will be seriously distorted.

In order to avoid becoming ensnared in assuming responsibility for the alcoholic's sobriety or lack of it, the counselor should strive not to become ego-involved in the outcome of the counseling process. If there is any kind of counseling in which a success drive on the part of the counselor is detrimental, it is in work with alcoholics. If the alcoholic senses that the counselor has too great a stake in his getting sober, he has acquired a weapon to use against the counselor in periods of hostility and anti-dependency. The alcoholic unconsciously senses that he can frustrate him by not moving toward sobriety. The counselor who tries too hard and thus reveals that he must prove himself by succeeding as a counselor conveys a lack of concern and respect for the person in and of himself. The alcoholic with his low self-esteem catches this feeling of being manipulated and reacts to the counselor in the same way that he would to a mission worker who gives the alcoholic the impression that he is interested in him as an opportunity to save a soul. Otis Rice once warned against the attitude of those clergymen who enjoy "collecting spiritual scalps"; this warning has its relevance for counselors of alcoholics.

The counselor should not give the impression that the alcoholic's lack of sobriety is the counselor's defeat, nor that the alcoholic's success is a victory for the counselor. Thus, he respects the alcoholic's right to drink or not to drink, and he keeps the initiative where it must be if he is to stop. How does a counselor achieve this attitude? It is not easy, for it requires a high degree of self-esteem not to need to prove one's self or to be threatened by the alcoholic's lack of success. Most of us achieve this attitude only to a limited degree. It helps some to recognize that if an alcoholic becomes happily sober, it is because he, the alcoholic, has achieved sobriety with the help of God. The counselor, at best, is only a catalytic agent. As one seasoned worker with alcoholics observed, "If an alcoholic with whom I've been working gets sober, I try to remember that it may be that it occurred in spite of what I did." The same can be said, of course, about the alcoholic who does not make the grade to sobriety. Any counselor who is worth his salt has a genuine concern for his counselees and their welfare. The point that has been emphasized in this section is that the concern should be for *them* and not mainly for the gratification of his own need for success. A discussion of this whole matter, which could be read with profit by the minister, is found in an article by Giorgio Lolli entitled "On 'Therapeutic' Success in Alcoholism." [17]

The counselor should use great caution in deciding to do anything that might have the effect of protecting the drinking alcoholic from the normal consequences of his irresponsible behavior. Seldom is it constructive to intervene with an employer, a spouse, or the law, to ask for special concessions on the alcoholic's behalf. Such interventions may prevent immediate consequences such as loss of a job, but the long-range results are usually negative in that they deprive the alcoholic of his right to experience the pain which might bring him to the point of openness to help. Such overprotection, as we have mentioned, has been called "cruel kindness." It appears to be kind, but its effects are usually cruel in the long run.

A psychiatrist who was connected with a sanitarium treating alcoholics described an alcoholic who had been going on periodic binges for a number of years, using the sanitarium as a drying-out place. It was only when, through a prearranged plan, the man's wife told him she was leaving if he didn't follow through on getting help, his employer announced that he was through unless he got help and stopped drinking, and the psychiatrist informed him that he would not be accepted as a patient unless he agreed to stay long enough to allow for effective therapy, that the man admitted he was licked and needed help. Before this, he had been shielded from the consequences of his behavior by the sizable allowances that significant people in his life had been making. It was when they stopped making these allowances, and meant what they said, that he was forced to face reality.

In most cases, it is not necessary to use such a calculated approach to "withdrawing the props" which have been supporting the alcoholic's denial of reality about his drinking. If the overprotectors in his life can get out of the way and stop blocking the normal consequences of his immature behavior, a tipping of his inner motivational teeter-totter toward accepting help will often occur. In effect, the overprotector sits on the wrong end of the teeter-totter, delaying the person's "hitting bottom." By withdrawing the dependency shields and allowing the alcoholic to experience the pain of being "clobbered by reality," the relative or counselor allows the teeter-totter to tilt toward getting help.

## Nonaddictive Excessive Drinking

The counselor should be alert to the possibility that an excessive-drinking counselee is *not* an alcoholic in the sense of being *addicted* to alcohol

(Jellinek's Gamma, Delta, and Epsilon types). Many problem drinkers (Alpha alcoholics) do not respond to AA or other alcoholism treatment methods because they are actually not addicted. Instead, their heavy drinking is a direct response to the pain of a disintegrating marriage, a severe loss, frustration of a cherished dream, or a temporary depression. The drinking may, of course, worsen the marriage relationship, thus producing a vicious cycle. But, if the person has not yet moved into the zone of progressive "loss of control," the appropriate therapy is that which is aimed at lessening the pain for which the alcohol is being used as a self-prescribed anesthetic. For example, the minister may recommend marriage counseling (or offer it himself, if he is so trained), help the person work through his grief, or refer him for medical assistance with his depression, as the person's needs may indicate. If the person is not addicted, his drinking will diminish as the pain is alleviated. However, if he is addicted, the attempts to reduce the pain will usually fail. The person will not respond to marriage counseling. If the person is addicted, the heavy drinking will tend to continue, even if the pain is reduced, since the drinking is the result of a self-perpetuating inner process and not just a response to the pain.

On the subject of diagnosis, it is well for the counselor to have in mind the possibility that a person who appears to be addicted actually may be suffering from quasi-alcoholism. Ernest A. Shepherd, head of the Connecticut State Alcoholism Program, has pointed out that some persons who are psychotic, mentally deficient, prepsychotic, or psychopathic personalities drink excessively but are not addicted.[18] The drinking pattern appears to be that of an alcoholic but when confined where alcohol is unobtainable, they do not experience the withdrawal symptoms and craving characteristic of an alcohol addict. Actually, their excessive drinking is almost entirely a symptom of the major pathology from which they suffer and which needs treatment. There are, of course, persons in all the above mentioned categories of pathology who are also addicted to alcohol. If a minister suspects that he may be dealing with a person suffering from a major mental disturbance or mental deficiency, whether or not he is addicted, the appropriate action is to refer him as soon as possible for a psychiatric evaluation.

## REFERENCES

1. *Psychological Reflections* (New York: Pantheon Books, 1953), p. 73.
2. See H. J. Clinebell, Jr., *Basic Types of Pastoral Counseling* (Nashville: Abingdon Press, 1966), chapters 1-4.
3. *The Vital Balance* (New York: The Viking Press, 1963), p. 352.
4. This is Ernst Ticho's phrase; quoted by Menninger in *The Vital Balance*, p. 350.
5. "Pastoral Counseling of Inebriates," *Alcohol, Science and Society*, p. 454.
6. Workshop on "Therapy with Alcoholics," Yale Summer School, 1949.

7. "Pastoral Counseling of Inebriates," p. 451.

8. Paul Tillich, "The Theology of Pastoral Care" in *Clinical Education for the Pastoral Ministry*, Proceedings of the Fifth National Conference on Clinical Pastoral Education, Ernest E. Bruder and Marian L. Barb, eds. (Published by the Advisory Committee on C.P.E., 1958), p. 5.

9. "The Pastor's Resources in Dealing with Alcoholics," *Pastoral Psychology*, April, 1951, p. 18.

10. (New York: Harcourt, Brace and World, 1933, Harvest Book edition, p. 234.)

11. Quoted by Wayne E. Oates in *Religious Factors in Mental Illness* (New York: Association Press, 1955).

12. Edith S. Lisansky, "Alcoholism in Women: Social and Psychological Concomitants," *QJSA*, XVIII (December, 1957), No. 4.

13. Held at Fort Worth, Texas, 1949.

14. From a paper "Criteria for Assessment and Motivation of the Alcoholic in Early Contacts," presented by Sam E. Wilson at the Utah School of Alcohol Studies, June 21, 1962.

15. Several of these are from a lecture by Gordon Bell at the Utah School of Alcohol Studies, June 18, 1963.

16. Presented at the Annual Meeting of the National Council on Alcoholism, March 18, 1955. Dr. Feldman is now with the Department of Physical Rehabilitation, Stanford University.

17. *QJSA*, XIV (June, 1953), No. 2.

18. *Pastoral Care*, J. R. Spann, ed. (Nashville: Abingdon Press, 1951); see the chapter entitled "Alcoholics," by Shepherd, p. 175.

# 10

# The Process of Counseling with Alcoholics: Moving Toward Recovery

The four operational goals of alcoholic counseling were outlined in Chapter 8. In the chapter just concluded, the achievement of the first and most difficult of these goals was explored—helping the alcoholic to accept the fact that his drinking per se is a problem with which he requires assistance. It was shown that the process is one of reaching and helping to mobilize his inner motivation to accept help. The heart of this approach is the establishment of a trustful relationship which then becomes the instrument by which the alcoholic is helped to face reality with reference to his drinking. One aspect of the process is the educative dimension of counseling aimed at increasing the person's understanding of his addictive illness. Although the pastor may be the key person in working with a resistant alcoholic, the help of an AA member or understanding physician who can "talk turkey" in ways that reach the alcoholic may be needed to complement the minister's efforts.

### Recognizing Openness to Help

Here is a segment from a counseling session involving a minister and an alcoholic:

Mr. B.:  I didn't mean to get drunk last week. It was the first time in a month that I'd had anything to drink. I was worried about a few things at the office that weren't going well. I decided I'd walk around a little, and I passed by this beer joint—well, you know, the first thing I realized I was inside drinking. I didn't want to, but I just couldn't help it.

Pastor:  You thought that getting drunk would solve all your problems. Did it help?

Mr. B.:  No, it only made things worse. I broke my promise to you and God—and I feel terrible. I'm sick, I tell you. I've got to have some help!

239

*Pastor:*   You feel sick because you broke your promise and got drunk.

*Mr. B.:*   I—don't know. Maybe that's the reason. Maybe it goes beyond that. I guess I'm all wrong inside.[1]

This interaction illustrates the difficulty which a counselor may have in hearing an alcoholic's cry for help when he begins to utter it. In his first statement, Mr. B. apparently seemed to the pastor to be giving a rather lame excuse for beginning to drink again. (The pastor responded with a statement which may or may not be the way B. felt, and an obvious and finger-pointing question that must have felt rejecting to the alcoholic.) What the minister missed was the possibility that B. was really expressing *his fear and desperation at finding himself drinking against his conscious intention.* This should have been explored by the minister, beginning with a response such as: "How did you feel when you realized you were drinking in spite of your decision not to?" or "Somehow you felt as though things were beyond your control?" This might have opened B. to talk about his awful feelings of weakness and of being trapped by his compulsive drinking and distorted thinking. If he is beginning to experience the panicky fear of not being in control and of the destructive consequences of his drinking, he is probably becoming open to help. The last two sentences of B.'s second response and his third response support the view that he is feeling desperate and is crying out for help. In the pastor's second response, he again misses the alcoholic's desperate plea for help, focusing instead on B.'s guilt feelings related to the broken promise. These feelings are certainly within the legitimate concern of counseling, but focusing on them at this point distracts the process from the crucial issue—B.'s reaching out for help. The pastor's second response might well have been a recognition of his feeling, such as, "The situation feels desperate to you, and the need for help is very pressing." The pastor could then say, "You mentioned that you feel sick. Tell me more about how you see this and what kind of help you feel you need." This would give the minister some grasp of B.'s perception of his problem and the required treatment. By moving in this direction, the pastor could eventually introduce the idea of getting help from AA or such other resources as seem appropriate.

## Obtaining Medical Help

The second goal of counseling is to get the alcoholic to a physician who can, if necessary, facilitate detoxification and treat the physical consequences of prolonged inebriety, as well as decide whether brief hospitalization is needed; if the physician is oriented psychiatrically, he may be of assistance in identifying cases of severe underlying psychopathology. Medical treatment is often required long before the alcoholic hits bottom psychologically. Many alcoholics require repeated hospitalizations before their motivational teeter-totter tilts decisively and they determine to accept treatment for the addiction per se. In such cases, it is essential that the alcoholic and his family know that simply treating the physical effects of excessive drinking, as important as this can be, does not constitute treatment of the addiction. Some persons erroneously believe that "unsuccessful treatment" of alcoholism has occurred when actually only the preliminary stage of treatment—"drying out" and physical rehabilitation—has taken place.

Alcoholics who are obviously in need of medical attention, who have the "shakes" or other withdrawal symptoms, and those who say that they feel "sick" (Mr. B., for example) will usually not resist seeing a physician to get relief from their pain. It is wise for the minister to encourage even those who are feeling relatively well to have a physical checkup to ascertain if there are less obvious organic problems which need treatment. The minister's role is to assist the alcoholic to "connect" with a doctor who accepts alcoholics as patients, knows the latest methods of treating the problems associated with alcoholism, and is appreciative of the contributions of AA and pastoral counseling. A physician who does not understand alcoholism and AA can, by his attitudes, unwittingly push the person deeper into his addiction and away from the help he desperately needs. To illustrate, the statement by a trusted family doctor to an alcoholic patient, that he "is not an alcoholic but simply drinks too much and should cut down," can petrify that man's resistance to seeing his problem for what it is. The doctor's statement usually reflects a Skid Row stereotype of "the alcoholic." On the other hand, because of the status of physicians in our society, an accurate explanation of the nature of alcohol addiction and a recommendation that the help of AA be sought can carry special weight with some alcoholics.

What is the minister's role during the period when an alcoholic counselee is hospitalized? He should maintain a supportive pastoral relationship, showing his continuing interest by visits and phone calls to the alcoholic and to his family. In addition, he has an opportunity to encourage carefully selected AA members to establish a relationship by visiting the alcoholic in the hospital (with the permission of the person and his doctor). Al-Anon members can do the same for the spouse and other family members.

If the minister is contacted by an alcoholic or the family of one who has been on a prolonged bender, it is crucial to make sure that he gets medical attention. As indicated in Chapter 8, withdrawal symptoms such as delirium tremens and alcoholic convulsions can be very dangerous, even fatal. The danger is compounded if the person has been combining alcohol and barbiturates ("goof balls"), since each tends to enhance the depressive effects of the other. The alcoholic may have been taking barbiturates without the family's knowledge. The only safe course is to make certain he gets medical help.

### Interrupting the Addictive Cycle

The third goal of counseling is to help the person learn how to avoid reactivating his compulsive-addictive chain reaction of drinking. Early in the process of working with an alcoholic, it is helpful to discuss the fact that he has an uphill battle against an insidious illness, and then to spell out what is involved in winning the battle. Gordon Bell, a physician who directs an addiction treatment center in Ontario, Canada, has an effective way of describing to the alcoholic the task he faces. Bell explains to the person that his body has burned out its ability to handle the chemical (alcohol) which he has been using to cope with stress. He then points to that person's symptoms of loss of this ability, such as, getting drunk on less, having blackouts, and so forth. Next, he stresses the fact that the person must, for health reasons, learn other ways of handling stress—by "people methods" rather than chemical methods. Finally, he tells the person that he is caught in a self-perpetuating process in the interruption of which there are two phases. The first is "turning off the physical motor" by getting the alcohol out of his body (thus interrupting physical craving), and second, "turning off the mental motor," which means terminating obsessive thinking about alcohol (mental craving) and the response of automatically turning to alcohol to handle any stress.[2] This general outline is useful in pastoral counseling with the alcoholic.

The focus of counseling, in this stage, is on the drinking pattern itself and the need to learn how not to take the first drink. A part of this learning consists of identifying and interrupting the rationalization process which leads to the first drink. (For instance, "One glass of beer can't possibly hurt me. After all, I've been stone sober for three weeks.") The alcoholic should be helped to see that although his heavy drinking may have begun as a symptom of other problems and may continue to be aggravated by them, the drinking itself has now become a problem which must be treated in its own right if the person is to recover. The late Harry M. Tiebout likened the "runaway symptom" of the alcoholic's out-of-control drinking pattern to the dangerously high fever of pneumonia. The fever is a *symptom* of the underlying infection, but unless it can be lowered, the person may die of the "symptom." As Tiebout pointed out, the direct treatment of the alcoholic's "runaway symptom" is essential, and it consists of methods by which the cycle of drinking to overcome the effects of previous drinking is blocked.

Counseling procedures, in this stage, should deal primarily with behavior and only secondarily with feelings. The counselor should not allow himself

242

to be diverted into extensive discussion of why the person drinks excessively, whether this discussion is in terms of attempts to understand his inner conflicts, early life experiences, or current external pressures. Searching for causes, in whatever direction, is usually unproductive with respect to the alcoholic's problem of highest priority—how to keep the addictive cycle from being reactivated. The "causes" which are discovered may be used by the alcoholic to avoid responsibility for changing his present irresponsible (self- and other-damaging) behavior. Instead of searching for the why of his drinking, counseling should focus on the facts about his drinking and its consequences, and on how he can avoid taking the first drink and thus increase his ability to be more responsible in other areas of his life.

The alcoholic's other problems can become accessible to handling and help only if he learns how to avoid the first drink. For example, a counselee makes a statement such as, "If I didn't feel so depressed, it would be easier to stay off the bottle"; or "If my wife hadn't left me . . ."; or "If I didn't have to live in one room . . ."; at this point the counselor can point out that although there is certainly some truth in his statement, his first problem is to stay off alcohol. This is his first problem in that its solution is a prerequisite to getting at the others. Even though he feels depressed, misses his wife, and abhors living alone in one room, he doesn't have to drink. The choice is still within his power to make. Furthermore, his wife's leaving was a consequence of his drinking, and his chances of getting her back are contingent on interrupting the drinking. If a person continues to put other problems ahead of sobriety, it may be an indication that he is still fighting acceptance of the fact that he is an alcoholic. A frank discussion of this issue is in order in the counseling session.

The most widely available means of keeping the addictive cycle broken while new coping patterns are learned is AA. The minister should do whatever is required to help the person establish a strong relationship with a local AA group. When the pastoral counselor senses that an alcoholic is evidencing some receptivity to help, he should ask: "How would you feel about talking over your situation with someone who has been through the same problem and has found an answer that works for him?" If the person agrees, the minister can make a phone call while that person is present to arrange for a three-cornered talk involving the two of them and an AA member. (The AA member should be of the same sex, general age, and socioeducational group as the person, if possible.) After explaining that the person they will be talking with is an AA member, the pastor should inquire what the alcoholic knows about that fellowship. This may reveal blocks to successful affiliation with AA, which the person needs to work through in counseling. When asked what she knew about AA, a woman responded, "Am I that badly off?" Behind her question was the misconception that

243

AA is designed to help only those in advanced alcoholism. Another alcoholic responded to the minister's suggestion that he try AA with the information that his alcoholic uncle had stopped on his own by simply deciding to quit drinking. The message the person was communicating was two-pronged— discomfort at the thought of identifying himself with a group of self-acknowledged alcoholics and the feeling that he should, like his uncle, be able to gain sobriety without outside help.[3]

In describing why the person should go to AA as well as participate in counseling, it is well to stress that making the grade to stable sobriety is a difficult accomplishment in which several forms of help are often needed. The AA fellowship will give group support that the person will need in addition to what he derives from counseling. Although the minister knows that the person will receive a multitude of benefits from AA beyond group support, it is better for him to restrain his enthusiasm and avoid seeming to oversell the AA program.

If the three-cornered meeting goes well, communication will be well-established between the AA member and the counselee before it is over. When this has happened, the pastor may decide to excuse himself, thus encouraging the two of them to develop their relationship without his presence. The typical outcome of such a meeting is that the AA member invites the alcoholic to come with him to an AA meeting.

The counselor should encourage the alcoholic to attend as many AA meetings as possible during the early phases of his recovery, whether or not his reactions are entirely positive. If the person continues to expose himself to the AA philosophy and group *élan*, he may begin to identify with AA, almost in spite of himself. The sense of belonging which exists in most AA groups is a powerful magnet. The counselor can help the person deal with any blocks to full identification which may arise during the early stages of AA attendance, by inquiring regularly about the person's reactions to AA.

Many alcoholics are now encountered who have dabbled in AA, or tried it seriously but unsuccessfully. Some seem to be "vaccinated" against it by having attended a few meetings when they were in a highly defensive state. To help such persons, the counselor can first explore the nature of the resistance to AA. Does the resistance reflect the limitations of a particular AA group or the person's reluctance to admit his need for help? Second, the counselor can recommend strongly that he try AA again, perhaps going to a different group or to several, if they are available in the vicinity. Third, the minister can arrange for him to get acquainted with an experienced and accepting AA member who may serve as a bridge to feeling at home in an AA group.*

* In a study of factors which produce "readiness" for affiliation with AA, Harrison M. Trice discovered that alcoholics with the following characteristics tend to relate effectively

With those alcoholics who will not attend AA or do not respond to it, the minister's role is to assist them in finding other help. Referral to an alcoholic clinic or to a physician for Antabuse may supply the help that is needed to break the addictive cycle and achieve stable sobriety. Such a referral is also appropriate in the case of alcoholics who are continuing to work at the AA program but seem to need additional help. If an alcoholic counselee suffers from a severe underlying personality disturbance, he will probably require psychiatric and other medical treatment, in addition to AA, in order to keep the addictive cycle broken. Disturbed persons sometimes use alcohol to deaden their overwhelming anxiety. Abstinence, without psychiatric help, may cause them to deteriorate psychologically.[4]

Many alcoholics have one or more "slips," particularly in the first year or two of their serious efforts to keep the addictive cycle broken. It is important for the counselor to handle these in such a way as to make them opportunities for insight—concerning the rationalization process, the buildup of resentments, or the pattern of staying away from AA meetings, which tend to precede a return to drinking. The alcoholic may avoid the minister after a slip because of his guilt feelings. Under such circumstances, it may be wise for the minister to take the initiative in reestablishing contact. Otherwise, his opportunity to help the alcoholic may be terminated. It is particularly salutary for a person with alcoholism to discover that *a clergyman is not judging him* or angry at him because he had a slip.

The pastor's tolerance of failure and his not becoming ego-involved in the outcome of counseling (as discussed in Chapter 9) are extremely important in counseling with alcoholics because of the practical fact that he will fail so often. The process of such counseling is often slow and characterized by many setbacks. The counselor must be content with "little successes" in many cases. For example, counseling is a relative success if a person who has had an average of five binges a year is able to cut the number to two or three. Counseling with alcoholics is difficult and often frustrating to the counselor. It can also be deeply satisfying when the counselor senses that he has been an instrument in helping a person who has been engaged in slow suicide to move into a new and constructive chapter in his life.

### The Resynthesis of Life

The fourth goal of counseling is *to help the person develop a new way of life to replace his alcohol-centered way of life*. To reintegrate his life

to AA: Before contact with AA, they often shared troubles with others, had lost drinking friends, had heard positive things about AA, had no relative or friend who had quit through willpower. These and other findings of Trice's research can be useful to the counselor in his efforts to reduce the resistance of an alcoholic to affiliation with AA. (See: "A Study in the Process of Affiliation with Alcoholics Anonymous," *QJSA*, XVIII [March, 1957], No. 1, 39-54.)

without alcohol, he must find new, satisfying values and new, effective ways of coping. The recovering alcoholic must find nonalcoholic means of satisfying the needs he formerly satisfied or attempted to satisfy through drinking —reduction of anxiety, closeness to others, psychological "vacations" from painful reality, a sense of adequacy, experiences of transcendence, and euphoria. Permanent sobriety and productive living are contingent on finding such satisfactions in relationships—with fellow AA members, family, and, in many cases, a "higher Power."

The rebuilding of one's values and relationships is obviously a long-range objective. Its achievement involves clearing up the debris in one's inner life, striving for constructive relationships, surrendering one's self-centeredness, finding a place to make one's life count for something, discovering a sense of meaning in existence, learning to draw on the help of other people and also to be of help to them, and finding some transcendent resource for coping with the burdens and anxieties of existence.

For many, AA's Twelve Step recovery program is an invaluable means of stimulating precisely these types of personal growth. As was evident in Chapter 5, the AA group and program are designed as a means of facilitating the particular kinds of continuing growth which are necessary to undergird productive sobriety.

The clergyman-counselor can contribute significantly to helping the alcoholic move toward the goal of reconstructing his life without alcohol. During the early stages of recovery in AA or in an alcoholic treatment facility, the minister's role is mainly a supportive one. The primary responsibility for learning to avoid the first drink is the alcoholic's, and his major resource for accomplishing this is AA (or other treatment approaches). His main source of emotional support (often hour-by-hour) during the first difficult days and weeks are his fellows in AA.

The minister's role is to give pastoral care, to maintain a warm, caring relationship with as much support as the person needs and to be easily available for counseling if the alcoholic desires it. Without being possessive or prying, the pastor should show interest in the person's experiences in AA or in treatment. Dropping by for a cup of coffee, phoning to express interest in "how things are going," occasionally attending the open meeting of his AA group—these are some of the ways the minister can keep in touch with the early-stage recovering alcoholic. He should express his pastoral interest and support without "hovering" over the person or seeming to check up on him. As the alcoholic identifies more closely with AA, he may need to withdraw some of his emotional ties with the pastor. This is a part of his growth. In many cases, the alcoholic eventually moves beyond this and chooses to relate to his minister on a new and close basis.

There are at least three points at which the minister's counseling skills can be particularly helpful to the recovering alcoholic, after he achieves a reasonably stable interruption of his drinking cycle and begins to strive for a resynthesis of his life. The first is in assisting the alcoholic who requests it with the "moral inventory" steps in AA (4 through 10).

> AA member:  Pastor, I've talked these things over with my sponsor, and it helped, but it seems like it would be a good idea to discuss them with you, too. There are a couple of points in my inventory where I really felt hung up—and still do. The guilt and resentments just won't seem to go.

A minister who is trained in counseling is equipped to help the alcoholic take his moral inventory *in depth*, to look below the surface behavior to some of the sources of resentment, self-pity, guilt feelings, and self-rejection which feed the behavior and push the person toward drinking.

In his discussion of the minister's role in assisting the alcoholic with the moral inventory, John E. Keller states:

> The inventory procedure needs to be talked about in a positive way, pointing up the value of taking such an inventory. Hopefully he will benefit by being able to: (1) Get to know himself better; (2) Become more keenly aware of how he needs to change; (3) Recognize danger signals to his sobriety before he takes the first drink; (4) Live more comfortably with himself and others; (5) Have the door opened for a more personal and meaningful relationship with God.[5]

Helping AA members with their moral inventories can be a means of engaging them in an ongoing counseling process through which the hard, cold lumps of guilt which immobilize growth and block relationships can be melted. An indispensable part of the inventory process is making amends to the persons one has harmed (steps 8 and 9). The counselor should encourage this follow-through, in spite of the pain involved. Otherwise the recovery process is short-circuited. By taking action to assume some responsibility for past irresponsibilities, guilt is reduced, self-acceptance enhanced, and relationships improved. As the alcoholic makes a list of those he has harmed, one person in particular should not be forgotten. As Keller put it: "Essential also is to put himself on the list and make amends with himself. He may have hurt a lot of people, but no one quite as much as he has hurt himself." [6] During fourth step counseling, the minister can help the person see that self-forgiveness and forgiveness of others are always linked and that the way one makes amends to himself is to live in those ways that fulfill one's personhood and potentialities.

A second area in which the clergyman can help the alcoholic reconstruct his life is by being easily available to counsel with him regarding his problems of coping constructively with responsibilities and relationships. Such counseling, usually at the alcoholic's request, can complement the help the person receives as he continues to work at the AA program. By the time the alcoholic achieves sobriety, his marital, parental, vocational, and social relationships frequently are in shambles. Interrupting the drinking cycle is a prerequisite to rebuilding these vital relationships, but it does not automatically accomplish it. The permanency of his sobriety may be dependent, to some degree, on the revitalization of these shattered relationships or their replacement if they are beyond repair. The counseling process here is relationship-centered, helping the person change those attitudes and behavior patterns by which he gets in his own way as he attempts to relate to others. Marriage and family counseling is the most important form of such counseling help.

The minister who is well trained in counseling and psychotherapy may help the alcoholic whose inner conflicts and residual feelings from early relationships make his hold on sobriety tenuous. Earthquakes from the cellar of the person's psyche shake the house of his present relationships so continuously and violently that some form of psychotherapy is essential. The minister who is trained in pastoral psychotherapy and has the time and inclination to do so can render a significant service to such alcoholics. However, these considerations should be kept in mind. First, exploration of depth feelings and early-life relationships can be very disturbing and should be attempted only after other forms of help have proved inadequate and only after sobriety has been reasonably stable for several months or longer. Second, looking at the past can become a substitute for responsible coping with the demands of the present, and over-focusing on feelings can become a way of evading responsible action. To minimize this second danger, it is well to keep a four-pronged focus in psychotherapy with alcoholics—on the past *and* the present; on feelings *and* actions in relationships.

### The Spiritual Dimension of Recovery

A third way in which the minister's counseling skills can be useful to the recovering alcoholic's resynthesis of his life is *in helping to further his spiritual growth*. The discussion of philosophical and religious factors in the etiology of alcoholism (Chapter 2) and of the psychodynamics of a religious approach to alcoholism (Chapter 6) emphasized the following points: Alcoholism is a spiritual illness (as well as an emotional, physiological, and cultural illness). It is a spiritual illness in two senses: There are spiritual factors among its causes, and full recovery depends on the discovery of a philosophy of life and/or a religious experience that can satisfy the alcoholic's fundamental religious needs.

248

As one who is professionally trained to be a *spiritual growth enabler*, the clergyman can fulfill a unique role in helping alcoholics. When a recovering alcoholic comes to him for help with his religious problems or with the "spiritual angle" in AA, he has an opportunity to contribute to the creativity of that person's new way of life. The goal of counseling in this area is to help the alcoholic develop a meaningful relatedness to the vertical dimension of life—the dimension of values including the ultimate value which is called God. In counseling with alcoholics, one discovers that problems in the vertical dimension are always intertwined with problems in the horizontal (person-to-person) dimension. Spiritual and interpersonal difficulties, and growth are actually two sides of the same reality—the reality of one's relationships. Anything that enhances the quality of one's relations with one's fellows will tend to improve one's relationship with God, and vice versa. Conversely, blocks in relationships with one's spouse, children, and friends have their counterparts in blocked relatedness with God. The skilled counseling pastor should be able to move in both dimensions with equal facility and to help the alcoholic see the connections between them. It is noteworthy that again and again in AA, as an alcoholic reconstructs his relationships, his spiritual life gradually becomes more meaningful to him.

A major block in the spiritual life of the drinking alcoholic, which often continues as a barrier during his sober life, is a magical understanding and use of religion. Until this changes, the channels of a more vital relationship with the spiritual universe seem to remain blocked. Typically, if the drinking alcoholic has any religious life, it reflects his narcissism and his unresolved inner conflict between autonomy and dependence.

He often expects God to take care of him in infantile, magical ways. He tries to use God as an overprotective grandmother whose main function is to extricate him from alcoholic scrapes scot free. He makes impossible demands, expects a special set of rules-of-the-game, and then feels rejected when God does not "come through" according to his demands. His religion both reflects and enhances his narcissistic self-worship and his dependency conflict. Rather than allaying anxiety it increases it because it operates in the same manner as his neurosis. The underlying meaning of much alcoholic atheism seems to be, "All right, if you won't take care of me like a child, I'll show you! I'll destroy you by the magic of thought —by not believing in you!" [7]

Thus, during active alcoholism, as the person is cut off from nurturing relationships including his relationship with God, he is forced into a kind of idolatrous position in which he is his own god. His grandiosity and feelings of being above needing others are a part of his defense against deeper feelings of isolation, vulnerability, and fear of closeness.

Some drinking alcoholics come to ministers seeking easy, magical solutions to their complex problems. The pastor must not comply and seem to sanction their expectations. Many recovered alcoholics tell of praying "until they had calluses on their knees" during their drinking days, to no avail. Generally their prayers are of the magical, manipulation-of-reality type described above. The minister should work with persons who have such orientations to help them see that problems of their relationships with God are directly related to problems in their human relationships, and to guilt-producing living. The counseling process should first aim at interrupting the addictive cycle and straightening up human relationships; then it is appropriate to turn to overtly spiritual problems, which are interrelated with all of the alcoholic's other problems.

The counselor can help the recovering alcoholic gain the inner strength to let go of his tendency to defeat his own spiritual quest by his manipulative style of relating to God and the universe. The AA approach provides a sound model for the counselor in helping the alcoholic move toward a reality-respecting religious life. Step eleven of that program says, "Praying only for knowledge of His will for us and the power to carry it out." If the "will of God" is understood as a symbolic way of saying "the way things are" (the nature of reality in an orderly, cause-and-effect universe), the profound significance of this step becomes clear. The alcoholic is asking for the knowledge and ability to line up his life with reality rather than expecting (as in his drinking days) that reality should adapt itself to him. The recovering alcoholic thus is striving to develop a relationship with God which is almost the exact opposite of that of his pre-sobriety days. In doing spiritual counseling with a person having a magical, immature faith, the aim is not to deprive him of that faith (which he may need to hold his world together), but to help him outgrow it and replace it gradually with a more mature faith.

### Surrender and Recovery

To understand the psychodynamics of recovery and particularly the role of spiritual growth in this process, the concept of *surrender*, as explored by the late Harry M. Tiebout,[8] is illuminating. The phenomenon which he described has been observed by various workers with alcoholics, including the author. Surrender occurs on different levels at progressive stages of recovery. The first and most decisive surrender is the alcoholic's illusion that he can handle alcohol. To take step one of the AA recovery program—"We admitted we were powerless over alcohol, that our lives had become unmanageable"—the alcoholic must let go of that factor in his self-image which makes him need to feel equal to whatever comes. Another surrender is required by step three: "Made a decision to turn our will and our lives over to the care of God as we understood him."

Tiebout observed that when an alcoholic really surrenders, there is a dramatic shift in his inner life. His self-deceiving "alcoholic thinking" is replaced by openness and honesty. He stops fighting life and begins to cooperate with it. Feelings of inner peace, acceptance, and genuine humility replace his guilt, tension, isolation, defiant-grandiosity, and self-idolatry. Surrendering seems to be letting go of a terrible burden—the unsuccessful attempt to play god. It is significant that step eleven states that a "spiritual awakening" occurs as a result of the previous steps—the surrender and moral inventory (and restitution) steps. This sequence can serve as a guideline in the counselor's work with alcoholics on their spiritual blocks. Tiebout stated the matter this way:

A religious or spiritual awakening is the act of giving up one's reliance on one's omnipotence. The defiant individual no longer defies but accepts help, guidance and control from the outside. And as the individual relinquishes his negative, aggressive feelings toward himself and toward life, he finds himself overwhelmed by strong positive ones such as love, friendliness, peacefulness.[9]

Surrender, as used here, is not a negative giving-up. It is a turning away from a futile, self-defeating orientation and toward a reality-accepting way of feeling and coping. By accepting his weakness and finitude, the alcoholic finds relatedness and strength for coping constructively with his problems.

Mark M., age 40, came to his minister because his marriage was on the verge of disintegration because of his alcoholism. He made it plain to the counselor that he wanted no part of AA. He had tried that approach, he said, and felt that he was too intelligent to need that kind of help. He expressed the view that he could handle his drinking himself and that he just wanted a few tips on "how to keep the little woman off my back." During the first three weeks of counseling, he maintained this mask of defiant self-sufficiency, tinged with superiority feelings. He kept the minister at a distance. His view of his problem was that all would be fine if his wife would nag less and be more appreciative of his good points. Nothing significant was accomplished in counseling, and he continued to come only because he was afraid his wife would leave him if he stopped. His drinking was undiminished.

After a two-weeks break in the counseling, Mr. M. appeared at the minister's study door for a counseling session with a strikingly different look on his face, which caused the minister to exclaim, "What happened?" Mr. M. replied, "I don't know, but I guess I've given up my I-ism." He described a family crisis, during the past two weeks, involving the tragic death of a child. Instead of joining with other family members in giving the mutual support that everyone desperately needed, he had gone on a binge to end all binges. Following this, his guilt and remorse were intense. It was in the midst of this painful self-confrontation that Mr. M. "hit bottom." His smug mask of self-sufficiency, denying his problem and blaming others, was jarred loose by the awareness that he had been living a self-

251

centered lie. His alibis and his compulsion to "run the show," as he put it, collapsed. His defensive pride crumbled, and he experienced the self-disgust that was behind it. After a while, this began to pass, and he felt more relaxed, self-accepting, and grateful for life than he could have imagined before this happened.

Mr. M. reported that he had gone back to AA after letting go of his I-ism; he said that that it was a new experience, as though he had not been to AA before. He said that he felt closer to his wife and children than ever before. Even the colors in nature seemed more vivid to him.

In counseling, Mr. M. showed a new openness. He began searching for ways of making his marriage more constructive. The focus of counseling was on this and on how he could keep his I-ism from returning, which was one of his major concerns. Reflecting on his drinking, he said, "When my I-ism increased, I drank more, and the more I drank, the stronger my I-ism became." Gradually he learned to recognize the danger signs of regression into I-ism—the ego-centric, self-pitying, demanding superiority feeling that always seemed, in retrospect, to precede a drinking bout.

How can we understand the surrender experience? The I-ism which Mark described seems to be derived from infantile narcissism. Alcohol facilitates psychological regression to this position of magical power and grandiose self-sufficiency. Narcissism is a defense against deeper feelings of powerlessness and fear of death.[10] But the regression to the psychological position of the infant exposes the person to the giant anxieties of that period of development. As alcoholism progresses, these produce "nameless fears"; the illusion of special power becomes more and more difficult to maintain in the face of increasing failure in the various areas of one's life.

The surrender experience seems to have at least two components. First there is the unconscious renunciation of the path of regression to infantile narcissism, which no longer gives satisfactions to offset its disadvantages. David A. Stewart, in *Thirst for Freedom*, describes the operation of the alcoholic's narcissism as "the little dictator," an unconscious complex of magical thinking, false pride, fear, anger, lack of insight, and resistance to facing one's need for outside help. When surrender occurs, the little dictator is deposed,[11] and the self-damaging defense of narcissism is given up.

The second component in surrender is a desperate leap toward trustful relationships to fill the void left by the now-empty pattern of distance from people and self-centeredness. One alcoholic gave this description of the experience: "It's a leap of fear. You leap from the chasm blindly, not knowing what's on the other side. Fear is pushing you, and hope is pulling you." During his drinking days, the alcoholic often saw the world as peopled with depriving mother figures. Having taken the leap toward trust, he discovers (in AA, for example) that trustworthy relationships are possible *for him* and that he can participate in the *give* as well as the *take* of life. For many alcoholics, this is a strikingly new experience. By his leap toward trust, the alcoholic breaks the vicious cycle in which he has been trapped, the cycle of spiraling anxiety, isolation, anger, and grandiosity. Thus, as one alcoholic put it, "he rejoins the human race."

As a direct result of this positive surrender to life, the person begins to develop feelings of genuine self-esteem (the opposite of narcissism), rooted in trustful and mutually nurturing relationships. New and effective ways of coping with anxiety are discovered within these relationships. The alcoholic has let go of his narcissistic need to play god. Because of this and because of his involvement within a group (AA) which incarnates and communicates the accepting love of a higher Power, the alcoholic begins to develop a relationship with God as he understands him. As this relationship grows, it reinforces his ability to trust people and to become a giving person himself. By remaining in a dependent relationship with the higher Power, he is helped to retain his humility and to resist the temptation to regress to narcissistic self-idolatry and to drinking. Equally important, a trustful relatedness to God gives him an effective way of facing and handling his existential anxiety, depriving it of its terror and making it a stimulus to creative living. As Tillich holds, it is only when existential anxiety is confronted and taken into the person's self-affirmation that it enriches rather than diminishes life. The alcoholic who has developed trustful relationships—with himself, others, and God—is able to "die living rather than live dying," as one put it:

Yet the surrendered alcoholic must continue to exercise vigilance to avoid losing his humility. The underlying problem of infantile narcissism is not resolved but instead is walled off in the experience of surrender. When deep-seated anxieties are aroused by threats to his self-esteem or by failure to grow spiritually, the old temptation to regress to his primitive defense and curse still remains. This accounts for the necessity which most AA members feel to "work the program" continually, even though their sobriety has been stabilized for years.[12]

### Counseling and Surrender

Surrender represents a profound reorientation at a depth level of the psyche. It seems to occur when an alcoholic "hits bottom," i.e., is faced by the bankruptcy of his old way of life. It usually follows a long and painful struggle within the person. Although it involves a person's consciously letting go of old self-damaging patterns of living, it is not a simple matter of deciding to surrender. Since it occurs at least in part at an unconscious level, it involves a more than conscious intention to change.

The counselor can help to create the conditions under which surrender is most likely to occur by utilizing the methods of "elevating the alcoholic's bottom," described in the last chapter. In particular, these conditions can be created by: (a) Avoiding and helping others avoid protecting the alcoholic from the consequences of his self-centered behavior. Mr. M. was not shielded from the reality of his wife's intention to leave unless he changed, nor from facing the fact that he responded inappropriately to the death in the family. (b) Providing an accepting relationship which will stimulate the alcoholic's hope and encourage him to take the leap toward trust. (c) Helping the person see that his I-ism is the cause of his inability to accept help and the source of his agonizing loneliness. (In some cases, discussion of the "little dictator" or an opportunity to read Harry Tiebout's or David Stewart's discussions of surrender may help develop awareness of the nature of their trapped condition.) (d) Helping the person see that his denial of reality is depriving him of the very things he wants out of life. (e) Avoiding strengthening his defensive grandiosity by not becoming engaged in a futile power struggle with him. The alcoholic may feel that he must outwit the counselor or in other ways prove that he is smarter than the counselor. If he can lure the counselor into a position of taking responsibility for his sobriety, giving him advice, or making decisions for him, he can "defeat" the counselor by getting drunk, or proving that the advice or decisions were not sound. (f) Exposing him to a group such as AA in which the contagion of genuine self-acceptance is present because many of the members have experienced surrender. Spiritual growth occurs most readily in a group committed to spiritual values. In such a group a stimulus to growth is caught from others who are growing spiritually.

### The Alcoholic's Basic Religious Needs

Every human being has certain fundamental needs which can be satisfied adequately only within some religious (philosophical, existential, or spiritual) context. These include: (a) *The need for an experience of the transcendent and the numinous.* Anthropologist Ruth Benedict referred to the belief in "wonderful power" which was found to be ubiquitous among the cultures she studied. Abraham Maslow describes the "peak-experiences" which are the raw material of religions.[13] (b) *The need for a sense of meaning, purpose, and value in one's existence.* Viktor Frankl calls this the "will-to-meaning" [14] and sees it as more basic in man than Freud's will-to-pleasure or Adler's will-to-power. (c) *The need for a feeling of basic trust and relatedness to life.* Maslow uses the phrase "oceanic feeling" in his discussion of the self-actualizing person to describe the experience of being a part of the whole universe. (d) *The need for an "object of devotion,"* to use Erich Fromm's phrase. Each person needs something that transcends himself to which he may give devotion and in which he may invest oneself. (e) *The need to share a common philosophy of life and object of devotion with a group of one's fellows.*

The minister's distinctive contribution to helping alcoholics is in the spiritual dimension of recovery. It consists of assisting them in discovering effective ways of satisfying the fundamental religious needs listed above. This is particularly crucial since many alcoholics suffer from spiritual longing and emptiness, which they have been attempting to fill by a pseudoreligious means: alcohol. Only as they are successful in developing spiritually vital lives can their religious needs be met in a satisfying way. The renewal of "basic trust" (Erikson) and the filling of the "value vacuum" (Frankl) are indispensable to full recovery from alcoholism.

The minister has several resources for use in this work, in addition to his counseling skills. One is the church fellowship. Many recovering and re-covered alcoholics find help in the supportive relationships of a person-centered church. The spiritually feeding experiences—worship, religious festivals, communion, fellowship groups, service opportunities—help gratify dependency needs, renew basic trust, and strengthen the alcoholic's sense of meaning and purpose in life. The clergyman-counselor can help the person discover which small groups within the church help to satisfy his particular spiritual needs and stimulate his spiritual growth. The counselor must avoid pushing the alcoholic toward involvement in the church before that person is ready for this experience. Often considerable spiritual growth in AA must precede such readiness to participate in the more heterogeneous church group.

Increasing numbers of churches are establishing personal growth and counseling groups under a variety of labels.[15] Their aim is to stimulate growth in relationships, including one's relationship with God. As increasing numbers of alcoholics are sober for extended periods, the desire for study and growth experiences beyond AA becomes more prevalent. In some cases, this desire is the result of a flare-up of underlying personality problems, often after a decade or more of sobriety. In other cases, it is simply the result of an inner push to move ahead in one's spiritual growth, building on what has occurred in AA. Whatever its source, this desire represents a growing opportunity for the churches. In small (usually twelve or less) spiritual growth groups, people with a variety of problems can assist each other in moving toward more authenticity in relationships and a richer, more meaningful faith.

The new way of life of the recovering alcoholic is a path along which he moves rather than a static goal which he achieves. David Stewart describes five stages of sobriety:

*Initial sobriety:* Physical health regained; preoccupation with sobriety, reduction of guilt and anxiety; increased self honesty.

255

*Learning sobriety:* Loss of freedom (to drink in moderation) accepted; give and take of real personal relations replaces grandiose behavior; regains acceptance of family and friends; sense of humor replaces self-pity; learning to cope with anxious or depressed states.

*Accepting sobriety:* Loss of desire to drink becomes lasting; thinking, feeling, and ethical perception improves.

*Creative sobriety:* Freedom from alcohol deeply appreciated; religious desires centered on new way of life; appreciates need for help from others; uses new freedom in other activities.

*Pleasurable sobriety:* At peace with oneself and the world; anxiety and shyness diminish in genuine interpersonal relations; enjoys sobriety; rewards of sobriety clearly exceed tough times.[16]

However one conceptualizes the stages of sobriety as a new way of life, it is clear that it is a process. The role of the clergyman and the church in stimulating spiritual growth varies from person to person and from stage to stage. In general, the *spiritual* growth factor becomes more crucial as one moves ahead in the process. The aim of the counseling minister should be to contribute to each person's spiritual growth by helping him meet his spiritual hungers at his particular stage of growth.

## The Use of Religious Resources

A natural question which arises in the mind of a pastor is this: Shall I use prayer, sacraments, or scripture in counseling with the alcoholic? There are no fixed answers to this question. The general principle is to use such religious resources only after rapport has been established and the minister has an understanding of what they will probably mean to the particular counselee. Even then, they should be employed with extreme care and in moderation. One reason why some alcoholics are reticent about going to talk with a clergyman is the fear that they will be "prayed over." Even those who come to clergymen may feel some hostility toward religion and God. So the minister whose tendency is to pray at the drop of a hat should restrain himself where alcoholics are concerned. It is well to remember that it is sometimes necessary to avoid the outward symbols of religion in order to preserve the relationship with the alcoholic which can become religious in the deeper sense of being a channel for the healing power of God. As AA's are fond of saying, the spiritual angle often has to slip up on an alcoholic.

Marty Mann has a valuable suggestion concerning work with an alcoholic about whose religious attitudes the pastor is not certain. "If he is not sure of the alcoholic's attitude, he would be wise to understate the spiritual aspects, not only of AA but of his own interest in the case." [17] This is

256

important because, if the pastor presents AA as a spiritual approach, he may prevent the alcoholic from going to it for help.

The establishing of a strong counseling relationship should always precede the use of religious tools. Only within such an interpersonal context can they be used meaningfully. One of the Yale ministers put it well: "In some cases I have had prayer. The patient must be well chosen and must understand that the minister understands him before prayer can have the right psychological results. A lot of pious phrases from a minister can leave a sense of guilt that may send him out to get drunk again." If one does pray, it is well to reflect the feelings of the alcoholic in the prayer (showing him that one regards his feelings, however negative, as acceptable to God). It is also well to avoid any phrase which might be construed to mean asking for a magical solution, to emphasize the idea that God stands ready to help us when we actively participate in using his help, and to point to the fact that help comes through a revitalization of our own inner resources. The "faith without works is dead" philosophy is a healthy emphasis in counseling with alcoholics.

It is true that an alcoholic who comes to a minister may want something different from what he wants when he goes to a psychiatrist. He may want the strength and help of religion. Satisfying this need may or may not involve the use of overtly religious tools or resources. The clergyman should remember that whatever he does will register as religious in the sense that he represents the spiritual dimension of life and the religious community to the alcoholic. It is well for the pastor to adopt the Emmanuel philosophy that healing by any means involves the action of God. On the other hand, if prayer and scripture reading are familiar and natural, and they seem to have value for the particular person, they should be used. Ernest A. Shepherd expresses an important caution in this matter when he writes: "Every clergyman should be warned against using these means as ways to make himself feel more useful, regardless of the effect on the parishioner." [18]

In deciding whether or not to use religious resources in a counseling relationship, the minister may ask himself the question of whether such use will contribute to the person's sobriety and to his development of a more mature faith. Will such use increase or lessen the possibility that the person will move toward the experiences of surrender and spiritual awakening? Will it stimulate spiritual growth or contribute to the neurotic misuse of religion that contributes to spiritual cripplings. Only when the pastor is reasonably sure that such use will not block growth and may stimulate it should he employ traditional religious symbols and practices. In counseling with the drinking alcoholic, such resources are apt to be experienced in a distorted fashion by the alcoholic. In contrast, the person who has achieved stable sobriety and is searching for a deepening of trust may find the use of such

257

resources, by the minister and in his own personal devotions, exceedingly helpful.

## Counseling Homeless Alcoholics

Most ministers, especially those with downtown churches, are frequently confronted with the perplexing problem of how to deal constructively with the homeless alcoholic who comes to the door. He may be one of the "town drunks" or a part of the great mass of homeless men who live on an itinerant basis.

The homeless alcoholic usually comes to the minister for an "easy touch," since he regards a minister as a "live one." Of course hitting a minister for a "loan" is not confined to derelict alcoholics. Many alcoholics, particularly those who have not yet reached the lower levels of the disease, are extremely ingenious in concocting stories as to why they need money. Most ministers acquire a protective skepticism concerning hard-luck stories from strangers— a skepticism based on disappointing experiences when they were more naïve.

What about giving money to alcoholics or to persons one suspects are alcoholics? The best rule is *almost never do it.* No matter how convincing the story, the minister should follow the procedure of all social agencies and investigate. For example, if the person says that he is down on his luck because of a prolonged illness, ask for the name of the physician and check with him before giving any monetary help. If the person is an alcoholic, he will usually develop his story in such a way as to make it seem imperative that he have some money at once. This is the bait which the clergyman sometimes takes, to his subsequent regret. A wise procedure is to say, "I'm sorry but it is my policy never to give financial help without investigating first. If you will come back this afternoon, I'll be able to tell you whether or not I can loan you the money you need." After the person leaves, the pastor can check the address given and any other facts in his story. If the person is not on the level, he will usually not return. If his story is factual and his need legitimate, he will return.

But does not this procedure mean missing many opportunities to give real help to sick persons? No, because an opportunity usually does not exist. If an alcoholic's only motive in coming is to get money for drinking, the odds are great that he is not open to real help at that point. I recall once giving a "town drunk" type alcoholic some money on the theory that he might return when he became open to help. The hope proved illusory. In spite of the fact that I gave him no more money, I was plagued for several years by return visits motivated only by his desire for a "loan." Each time he came he looked more like the shadow of death, but he showed no desire for basic help. It is probable that, by giving him money, I had blocked rather than opened the way to real counseling.

The type of alcoholic who makes his living by panhandling has an inner contempt for those he exploits. Underneath his surface show of gratitude he is sneering at the sucker he has duped and reveling in his own superior cleverness in having accomplished the duping. By giving him money one is contributing to his neurotic, exploitative orientation, as well as helping to push him a little further into the morass of alcoholism.

Even if an alcoholic shows what appears to be a genuine desire for recovery, it is not wise to give him more than a little money. AA experience has shown that it is better for a newcomer to work his way up from the bottom. This forces him to rely on his own resources and if he succeeds, it is his victory. Second, it helps to keep him from becoming overly dependent on the helper. This is particularly true because of the fact that money is a symbol of power and independence in our culture. The alcoholic cannot tolerate the dependence of being too indebted. Third, it tends to help him face the fact that his problem is not the lack of money, which has been one of his favorite rationalizations, but staying sober.

If a person says he is hungry, give him food, not money. If he needs clothing, give him some that has little pawn value. If he needs shelter, it would be better to make direct arrangements for it rather than give him money for a room. If he has a legitimate and pressing need for a little money (for example, for carfare to get to work), let him work for it. This will keep him from feeling weak and dependent as well as test the legitimacy of his need.

In assaying the available resources a pastor will need to visit the local Salvation Army center and/or mission. By discussing the work of the institution with the leaders, one can determine the basic philosophy and procedure, and discover whether constructive handling is likely. If the Salvation Army men's service center has an AA group connected with it, the pastor is fortunate insofar as referral of homeless alcoholics is concerned. It means that the alcoholics will have an opportunity to get help through either the evangelistic or the AA approaches; it also indicates a broader philosophy on the part of the leadership.

However hard or well he tries, the minister should not expect to succeed in a very large percentage of cases of homeless alcoholics. For, as we said in Chapter 3, one is dealing, not with just one problem but with two. To the problem of alcoholism is added the psychosocial problem of homelessness. For this type of alcoholic, homelessness often is a way of life that fits his psychological eccentricities with the least pain.

Detroit attempted to do something constructive about the problem by establishing a "counseling center" in a storefront adjacent to the main Skid

Row area. In addition to the counseling proper, the center was also equipped to arrange for food, lodging, and employment. Out of the original group of 770 men who were counseled, only 70 were judged successful.[19] Even with optimum resources, success is not high in this type counseling.

It might be helpful to a minister in sizing up a counseling situation to know about certain factors which were found to be linked with success in counseling homeless alcoholics in the Detroit project. It was found that the chances of success were greater if (a) a homeless man had been married, (b) his occupation was clerical, skilled, or professional rather than unskilled, (c) he recognized that he was an alcoholic, (d) he did not ask for money, and (e) he attended church during and after the counseling.

There are several rays of hope on the horizon in the treatment of homeless alcoholics. One is the enlightened approach of the Men's Service Center of Rochester.[20] The director is Thomas B. Richards, a clinically trained minister with broad experience as an institutional chaplain. He has transformed the center from a conventional evangelistic mission to an institution which is pioneering in a combined religious and scientific approach. An AA group meets there, and a new philosophy of social service for homeless alcoholics has been developed. There is also a halfway house to which those who are motivated to stop drinking can go. Pilot experiments such as this may, it is hoped, provide both the pattern and the inspiration for other cities to take constructive action in relation to their Skid Row problems. The cost of such rehabilitative work is undoubtedly less than a city spends for the police-jail-public shelter approach to alcoholism which is essentially futile.

Another ray of hope (mentioned in Chapter 3) is the work that AA has done and is doing with low-bottom alcoholics. In the early days of AA a high percentage of members had spent time on Skid Row. This fact shows that AA is often effective in helping such alcoholics. In some areas, AA groups have made special facilities available for contacting and helping homeless alcoholics, by providing physical help as well as the basic AA program. One reason why AA is able to help many who have lived on Skid Row is the fact that a considerable portion of these men have not accepted the homeless life as a permanent state. They are there only temporarily while they are on a binge. These who are not resigned to permanent homelessness still have the psychological resources to identify with an AA group.

This leads to the suggestion that in cases in which a homeless alcoholic seems to have even an embryonic desire for help, it may be wise to discuss the matter with an AA member who has himself lived on Skid Row, rather than referring the person directly to the Salvation Army. The AA member will be able to size up the situation rather accurately. Having lived on Skid Row, he will be better able to establish rapport with the homeless man.

One of the few helpful discussions of an effective pastoral approach to homeless alcoholics is in an article by Thomas B. Richards, who was mentioned earlier; it is entitled "The Minister and the Bum." His discussion reminds me of the all too accurate definition of a city as "the place where people are lonely together." Richards writes:

> The city minister, busily engaged in church activities and active in all manner of worthy civic causes, may forget the fact that for many, many people a city is a cold, lonely place. In his preoccupation with the obligations of a clergyman in a big city he may overlook the growing multitude of those who are friendless and alone on the city streets, in the hospitals, and in the institutions that are within a stone's throw of his church.

On the basis of this, Richards suggests an area of special opportunity for the city pastor:

> If his basic interests are with people . . . he will discipline himself to the point where he *will* be able to find the time to follow through on those whom he refers to the expert for professional care.
>
> There is need, heart-breaking need, for his intelligent interest and friendly concern. He can supply the personal touch, the time to listen, and the patience to understand, which the institutional officials are too busy to give. They are inundated by sheer weight of numbers, tired out and pressed down by the masses of those in any institution who await their professional care. . . .
>
> Herein lies the minister's greatest opportunity. The harassed institutional official will welcome his help. This does not mean that he is to "meddle" in the diagnosis or attempt his own particular "cure." *It does mean, however, that his intelligent interest and friendly concern for the individual involved will be of tremendous importance in the entire healing process.*

This is the "team" approach discussed earlier. Richards puts it well when he writes: "The minister who readily assumes that the doctor, the psychiatrist, or the social worker have no need for him, or that they resent his presence, is too easily dissuaded from his 'high calling,' or else he is allowing himself to rationalize an unpleasant responsibility." [21]

The development of "halfway houses" for homeless alcoholics, in various parts of the country, is another bright spot in a generally dark picture. Such facilities provide a temporary residence, halfway between life on Skid Row and the demands of living as a part of a family in a normal community. Having a bridge of this sort helps some men make it across a gigantic social chasm. Halfway houses are sponsored by a variety of agencies including Councils on Alcoholism, churches, municipalities, and groups of AA members. The most effective houses are small (not more than twenty-five clients), have simple rules, maintain an atmosphere of homelike informality, and employ staff counselors who are recovered alcoholics, often former Skid Row-ers.[22] In June, 1966, the Association of Halfway House Alcoholism Programs of North America [23] sponsored a significant conference involving the directors of such programs.

A number of hopeful programs are underway using a combination of medical, psychiatric, and vocational therapies. Most workers in this field agree that some form of institutional care is an essential ingredient in the treatment of Skid Row alcoholics. The program at Boston's Long Island Hospital has been in operation for over ten years. Only volunteers are accepted for treatment. After a careful social, psychiatric, and physical evaluation, the man is put on Antabuse, given psychiatric help and "religious counseling" to deal with some of his emotional problems as he begins to work and attempt to reestablish relationships in the community. AA is an integral part of the program. A three-year follow-up study of one hundred men who had attempted the program showed that twelve had achieved complete sobriety and had reestablished themselves with their families; forty-two showed improvement in their drinking patterns but remained dependent on the structured hospital community; and the remaining forty-six had changed little if any in their drinking or social patterns, in spite of all the help offered them.[24]

New York's "Operation Bowery" is a multifaceted program of action, research, and community planning. With an interdisciplinary staff of fourteen full- or part-time persons, the project maintains a diagnostic and treatment center where homeless men receive medical and psychiatric examinations, psychological testing, group or individual psychotherapy, vocational counseling, and Antabuse. A "Fellowship Center" at the Men's Shelter provides lay counseling services. A pilot detoxification center for drying-out, treatment, and referral is planned. Operation Bowery helps to interrupt the futile "revolving door" practice of the police and courts, with its repetitive arrests of homeless alcoholics—"life imprisonment on the installment plan." [25] When attorneys of the Legal Aid Society began to represent homeless men arrested on "disorderly conduct" charges, convictions dropped from 98 to 2 percent. A second blow to the revolving door system came in 1966 when the Federal Court of Appeals ruled, in effect, in the Driver and Easter cases, that public intoxication per se is not a crime. Columbia University's Bureau of Applied Social Research carries on sociological studies of homelessness under a contract with Operation Bowery.

A Philadelphia project has as its goal the relocation and rehabilitation of Skid Row inhabitants so that the Row could be terminated (as a part of Urban Renewal) without creating new ones elsewhere. Phase one consisted of organizing the cooperation of the City Council and social welfare agencies, and of publicizing a casework-oriented program. Phase two was a careful census and sociological study of Skid Row, involving 2,278 interviews.

In the third phase a diagnostic and relocation center was established, located near Skid Row, staffed by professionals and a research team as well as former Skid Row residents, and offering to a systematic sample of the men diagnostic, recreational, therapeutic, vocational-counseling and housing-relocation services, including training in social as well as occupational skills.[26]

## A Model for Counseling with Alcoholics

To maximize his counseling effectiveness with alcoholics, the minister should have a clear picture of the style of counseling which has proved to be most functional with alcoholics. The author has described such a "revised model" of pastoral counseling elsewhere,[27] contrasting it with the client-centered or Rogerian model. In brief, the revised model has these characteristics:

(1) It emphasizes short-term, crisis counseling methods aimed at helping the person cope constructively with his current situation rather than exploring the past extensively. It uses supportive rather than uncovering methods. It focuses directly on assisting the person in increasing the constructiveness of his behavior. (2) It emphasizes helping the person face reality and function more responsibly. (3) It seeks to help the person enhance the constructiveness and mutual satisfaction of his relationships, rather than to aim at intra-psychic changes. Increase in self-esteem and the reduction of guilt are seen as the *results* of improved relationships.

In the early stages of an alcoholic's recovery, counseling with him is essentially *crisis counseling*. The insights and methods of psychiatrist Gerald Caplan and his associates are highly useful in this phase.[28] Several key insights emerge from experience in crisis counseling. First, one does not need to know how a fire started in order to put it out, in most cases.[29] To illustrate, it is usually unnecessary to discover *why* an alcoholic became an alcoholic in order to help him to recover. In fact, the search for "causes," while the crisis is whirling, often produces a worsening of the drinking problem. Second, the personality is like a muscle—it atrophies with disuse and is strengthened with exercise. While an alcoholic is drinking, his personality resources are increasingly immobilized. Interrupting the addictive cycle and beginning to cope with responsibilities such as holding a job, lead to the strengthening of the coping "muscles." Third, facing and handling a crisis constructively give the person new resources for coping with future crises. Each crisis that is handled in a reality-oriented way makes the alcoholic stronger and better able to handle the next crisis.

As mentioned in Chapter 5, the drinking alcoholic becomes increasingly like a car with the engine racing but the clutch disengaged. His personality is "out of gear"; he is not going anywhere. Breaking the drinking cycle puts his personality back in gear; he can now use his personality resources for handling adult responsibilities and rebuilding fractured relationships. The more he uses his "engine" to move in these directions, the stronger it becomes. In this way, many alcoholics can recover and live constructive lives without any pressing need to rebuild the engine (through psychotherapy). This is not true of the alcoholic who is deeply disturbed.

The orientation of William Glasser's "reality therapy" [30] is close to the revised model for counseling alcoholics. A central emphasis of this approach is on responsible living in the here and now. By "responsible," Glasser means satisfying one's needs for love, self-esteem, and identity, within the realities of one's relationships, and doing so without depriving another of the satisfaction of his needs. Glasser's therapy consists of establishing a relationship with the troubled person, diminishing self-defeating (reality-denying) behavior, and then helping the person "learn to fulfill his needs in the real world" of human relationships.[31] Glasser's approach is similar to what AA has been doing to help alcoholics for some thirty-plus years. Along with the other "action therapies," it can help balance the emphasis on feelings in pastoral counseling.

## REFERENCES

1. N. S. Cryer, Jr., and J. M. Vayhinger, eds., *Casebook of Pastoral Counseling* (Nashville: Abingdon Press, 1962), p. 221.

2. Lecture at the University of Utah Summer School of Alcohol Studies, June 18, 1963.

3. If a person feels strongly that he can do it without help, the counselor should wish him success but then add that, should things not work out well, he should bear in mind that help will still be available.

4. See E. M. Pattison, "A Critique of Alcoholism Treatment Concepts," *QJSA*, XXVII (1966), 61-62.

5. *Ministering to Alcoholics* (Minneapolis: Augsburg Publishing House, 1966), p. 119.

6. *Ibid.*, p. 57.

7. H. J. Clinebell, Jr., "Philosophical-Religious Factors in the Etiology and Treatment of Alcoholism," *QJSA* XXIV (September, 1963), 484.

8. Tiebout's writings on surrender include: "Surrender Versus Compliance in Therapy, with Special Reference to Alcoholism," *QJSA*, XIV (1953), 58-68; "The Ego Factors in Surrender in Alcoholism," *QJSA*, XV (1954), 610-21; "Alcoholics Anonymous—an Experiment of Nature," *QJSA*, XXII (1961), 52-68.

9. "AA and the Medical Profession" (AA Publishing Company, 1955), p. 24.

10. For a more comprehensive discussion of how this operates see: Clinebell, "Philosophical-Religious Factors in the Etiology and Treatment of Alcoholism."

11. (Toronto, Canada: The Musson Book Co., 1960), Chapters 3 and 6.

12. Clinebell, "Philosophical-Religious Factors in the Etiology and Treatment of Alcoholism," p. 486.

13. *Religions, Values, and Peak-Experiences* (Columbus: Ohio State University Press, 1964).

14. *The Doctor and the Soul* (New York: Alfred A. Knopf, 1955).

15. See H. J. Clinebell, Jr., "Group Pastoral Counseling" in *Basic Types of Pastoral Counseling*, pp. 206-21.

16. This description of the five stages is abbreviated from Stewart's *Thirst for Freedom*, pp. 273-75.

17. "The Pastor's Resources in Dealing with Alcoholics," *Pastoral Psychology*, II (April, 1951), 18.

18. *Pastoral Care*, p. 178.

19. For a report on this project, see W. W. Wattenberg and J. B. Moir, "Factors Linked to Success in Counseling Homeless Alcoholics," *QJSA*, XV (December, 1954), 587-94.

20. *Pastoral Psychology*, VI (May, 1955), 6, 65, 66.

21. This series of quotes is from Thomas B. Richards, "The Minister and the Bum," *Pastoral Psychology*, VI (May, 1955).

22. Earl Rubington, "Halfway Houses," a lecture presented at the Alumni Institute, Summer School of Alcohol Studies, Rutgers University, July 18, 1966.

23. 334 Mounds Boulevard, Saint Paul, Minnesota 55106.

24. For a description of this project, see David J. Myerson, "Rehabilitation for Skid Row: The Boston Long Island Hospital Rehabilitation Program for the Homeless Alcoholic," *Fifth and Sixth Annual Institutes on the Homeless and Institutional Alcoholic* (New York: National Council on Alcoholism, 1960-1961), pp. 1-5.

25. "Dedication to Human Restoration, Operation Bowery" (Annual Report, September 3, 1965–September 2, 1966), p. 1.

26. Leonard Blumberg et al., "The Development, Major Goals and Strategies of a Skid Row Program: Philadelphia," *QJSA*, XXVII (June, 1966), 257.

27. *Basic Types of Pastoral Counseling*, Chapters 2 and 9.

28. Gerald Caplan, *Principles of Preventive Psychiatry* (New York: Basic Books, 1964), pp. 26-55. For a discussion of pastoral crisis counseling see Clinebell, *Basic Types*, Chapter 6.

29. This apt figure of speech is from William Menninger.

30. *Reality Therapy* (New York: Harper & Row, 1965).

31. *Ibid.*, p. 60.

# 11

# Helping the Family of the Alcoholic

My husband is an alcoholic, but will not ask for help. He thinks he can work it out for himself. He's not doing it, but what can I do? Is there anyone in the world who can help us or will try to? Please, for God's sake, can you help me? [1]
—Letter from the wife of an alcoholic

This letter came to the clearinghouse for the Al-Anon family groups which are an outgrowth of AA. The words are familiar to a pastor—words that he hears when the spouse of an alcoholic comes in despair seeking help.

## A Major Pastoral Opportunity

The average parish pastor has considerably more opportunities to help members of families of alcoholics, than he has to help alcoholics. There are two reasons for this. One is the numerical factor. There are usually several people in the circle of chaos and concern clustered around an alcoholic. This means that around the five and one-half million alcoholics there are probably at least twenty million with a direct concern for them. One authority puts her estimate of the size of this group at twenty-five million.[2] When we recall the variety of types of relationships represented by those close to alcoholics who have come—in my case for instance this includes a husband, wife, daughter, son, mother, father, fiancée, nephew, sister-in-law, neighbor, intimate friend— we realize that this estimate may not be far from accurate.

The other reason why the pastor has more opportunities of this kind is the fact that members of the family are often accessible to him when the alcoholic is not. Frequently, they are more open to help by a minister. Deterioration often hits the home before other areas of the alcoholic's life. Because the family is less defensive than the alcoholic himself, they are more likely to come to the minister before the final stages of the illness have developed. Work with the family, therefore, represents an opportunity for prevention through early detection. One of the Yale ministers reported, "Families ordinarily will work with the minister to better advantage than the alcoholic himself." This has been the experience of many clergymen.

Working with the families of alcoholics represents multiple opportunities. It is sometimes an indirect way of helping the alcoholic. One of the Yale ministers told of helping to sobriety an alcoholic whom he had never had an opportunity to see, by helping the wife to change her attitudes toward him. It is probably not very often that an alcoholic problem can be completely solved through a relative, but such an approach can certainly contribute to a solution. Although it is important for the family to see their role in the situation which produces alcoholism, they should usually not be led to believe that they alone can lead the person to sobriety. This expectation would only complicate the interpersonal relations of the family and lead to guilt when they fail. Another side of the pastor's opportunity lies in the fact that members of an alcoholic's family often need understanding counsel as much as the alcoholic. Anyone who has not lived with an alcoholic can hardly appreciate the shame, loneliness, and despair that develops in such an atmosphere. Truly, as is often said, "Alcoholism is a family disease." What is more, studies have shown that the mates of alcoholics are often almost as disturbed, anxious, and in need of treatment as the alcoholic. For example, at the Cornell University Medical College, New York Hospital, alcohol research project, the psychiatrists found it as essential to treat the families as it was the patients themselves.[3]

The various facets of the clergyman's opportunity in helping the family could be summarized as follows: (a) Bringing the hidden alcoholic's family out of hiding. This may be accomplished by using the same methods as those described in Chapter 8 for bringing the hidden alcoholic out of hiding. (b) Sustaining and guiding the spouse and children during the period before the alcoholic seeks help. (c) Increasing the likelihood that the spouse's way of relating to the alcoholic will hasten rather than retard his becoming open to help. (d) Helping the spouse respond constructively during his treatment. She can help or hinder his chances of success. (e) Educating the congregation to fulfill its pastoral care function in relation to the alcoholic's family. It is clear that this dimension of ministry is a rich and challenging one.

## Preparation for Counseling the Family

One's general preparation for counseling alcoholics is also useful in counseling the families of alcoholics. In addition, an understanding of the dynamics of the interpersonal relationships in the alcoholic's family and the effects of alcoholism on these relationships is important. Fortunately, there are a number of articles written by social scientists on the subject. Several of these are listed in the references at the end of this chapter.[4]

Beyond this a pastor will need to have an acquaintance with what has been written concerning helping the families of alcoholics to meet their problems constructively. Here is a list of books and pamphlets which will be useful in this regard. Those with an asterisk are suitable for loaning to the family.

*Living with an Alcoholic, with the Help of Al-Anon* (New York: Al-Anon Family Group Headquarters, 1960). This is a basic book for the family and for the pastor in helping the family. It is for the family what the Big Book of AA is for the alcoholic. Included is a series of illustrative case histories of families who found help.

*Al-Anon Faces Alcoholism* (New York: Al-Anon Family Group Headquarters, 1965). This book contains statements about Al-Anon and the family problems created by alcoholism. The statements are by professionals who work with families of alcoholics and by "those who live with the problem." The working principles and history of Al-Anon are also included.

*The Dilemma of the Alcoholic Marriage* (New York: Al-Anon Family Group Headquarters, 1967). This is a guidebook for the alcoholic spouse. It includes a chapter on applying the Twelve Steps to marriage problems.

*New Primer on Alcoholism* by Marty Mann, in a chapter on "What to Do About an Alcoholic," has sections entitled "If You Are the Wife of an Alcoholic" (206-13), "If You Are the Husband of an Alcoholic" (213-17), "If You Are the Son or Daughter" (217-19), "If You Are a Friend" (219-21), and "If You Are the Employer" (221-24).

*"The Alcoholic Husband, A Message for Wives" and "The Alcoholic Wife, A Message for Husbands" are two pamphlets produced by AA. They seek to help the person understand the problem of alcoholism, AA, and how he may help get his alcoholic mate into AA. The Big Book of AA has a chapter on "The Family Afterwards" (122-35).

*These pamphlets are produced by Al-Anon: "Al-Anon, You and the Alcoholic," "Al-Anon Family Groups at Work," "How One AA Wife Lives the Twelve Steps," "Alcoholism, the Family Disease," "To the Mother and Father of an Alcoholic." Alateen pamphlets include: "It's a Teen-Age Affair," "Youth and the Alcoholic Parent," "Operation Alateen," and "For Teen-Agers with an Alcoholic Parent." (Al-Anon and Alateen literature is available from Al-Anon Family Group Headquarters, P.O. Box 182, Madison Square Station, New York, New York 10010.)

These resources are useful for the person counseling with the family of alcoholics: *Pastoral Psychology*, Vol. 13 (April, 1962), No. 123, special issue on "Counseling with the Family of the Alcoholic"; John E. Keller, *Ministering* to Alcoholics, Chapter VI, "Counseling the Spouse," pp. 124-37; Thomas J. Shipp, Helping the Alcoholic and His Family (Englewood Cliffs, N.J.: Prentice-Hall, 1963), Chapter 12, "Helping the Alcoholic's Family," pp. 120-32.

In his preparation for helping the family, it is important for the minister to acquire a firsthand understanding of how Al-Anon and Alateen groups function. It is also helpful, for purposes of referral, to become well acquainted with several key Al-Anon members. The most efficient method to prepare oneself in both of these ways is to attend Al-Anon meetings with regularity for several months. The time and place of nearby meetings can be ascertained by calling the number listed in the phone book for "Alcoholics Anonymous." [5]

## Alcoholism as a Family Crisis

It is important for the pastor to have an appreciation of the manner in which the nightmare of alcoholism engulfs an entire family. Joan K. Jackson, formerly a research sociologist, department of psychiatry, University of Washington School of Medicine, did a three-year study of the wives of alcoholics, the results of which are reported in "The Adjustment of the Family to the Crisis of Alcoholism." [6] In this article she gives a picture of the cumulative nature of the family crisis, as it develops from stage to stage.

Stage 1: Incidents of excessive drinking begin and, although they are sporadic, place strains on the husband-wife interaction. . . .

Stage 2: Social isolation of the family begins as incidents of excessive drinking multiply. The increasing isolation magnifies the importance of family interaction and events. Behavior and thought become drinking-centered. Husband-wife adjustment deteriorates and tension arises. The wife begins to feel self-pity and to lose her self-confidence as her behavior fails to stabilize her husband's drinking. There is an attempt still to maintain the original family structure, which is disrupted anew with each episode of drinking, and as a result the children begin to show emotional disturbance.

Stage 3: The family gives up attempts to control the drinking. . . . The disturbance of the children becomes more marked. There is no longer an attempt to support the alcoholic in his roles as husband and father. The wife begins to worry about her own sanity and about her inability to make decisions or act to change the situation.

Stage 4: The wife takes over control of the family and the husband is seen as a recalcitrant child. Pity and strong protective feelings largely replace the earlier resentment and hostility. The family becomes more stable and organized in a manner to minimize the disruptive behavior of the husband. . . .

Stage 5: The wife separates from her husband if she can resolve the problems and conflicts surrounding this action.

*Stage 6:* The wife and children reorganize as a family without the husband.

*Stage 7:* The husband achieves sobriety and the family . . . reorganizes to include a sober father and experiences problems in reinstating him in his former roles.[7]

This developmental scheme is important to the pastor because his approach as a counselor will depend in large measure on what stage of deterioration or reconstruction the family is in when he encounters the situation. He will usually encounter them when they are in Stage 2, 3, or 7. Should it be Stage 1, the family will be absorbed with attempts to deny that a problem exists. In Stage 2, the effort will be to hide the problem from the outside world, coupled with desperate efforts on the part of the family to control the alcoholic's drinking by any and all means. Stage 3 represents family disorganization in which a spouse begins to adopt a "What's the use?" attitude. In Stage 4 the wife, mother, or husband may become protective and masochistic in a way that makes the relationships unhealthy for all concerned, including the alcoholic.

If one omits the happy ending of Stage 7 (which Joan Jackson could include because her study was done in an AA wife's group), and translates the language of the social scientist into the parlance of everyday living, one has a picture of the starkest interpersonal tragedy. The picture includes the family's attempt to adjust to a person who lies and is least responsible when he most needs to be, who is unbearably irritable and egocentric, who embarrasses them in front of friends and spoils their holidays by being on a binge, who spends money they need for necessities on whiskey, and who seems completely oblivious to their welfare or their pleadings. The picture includes the dark spiral of drinking, nagging, drinking, remorse, promises, drinking ad infinitum. Fear pervades the entire picture—fear of violence to herself or the children, fear of loss of family status, fear that others will find out, fear of insanity, fear that she will return home to find him drunk. Sexual relations within the picture, reflecting the interpersonal conflict, are usually very unsatisfactory. Heartbreak hangs over the picture like a dark cloud. In the midst of the chaos and insecurity is the crowning tragedy of what is happening in the emotional life of the children. Into this picture of sick horror the pastor is sometimes able to bring a ray of light.

In one sense, the family crisis of alcoholism is more difficult than a crisis such as bereavement because it is an unstructured crisis. When death strikes a family circle, there are socially prescribed patterns of behavior and feeling which help the persons involved cope with the crisis. Alcoholism, in contrast, is a crisis for which there are no socially structured responses. In this way it is like mental illness and death by suicide. All are forms of social deviation which do not elicit community support of the family. Since most of us do not expect them to happen to our families, we are unprepared emotionally for their rude intrusion. The family response is to feel alienated, baffled, and stigmatized.

## Getting Inside the Family's World [8]

When the spouse of an alcoholic ventures out of hiding, it is important that she[9] experience a high degree of empathic understanding. The more the pastor can feel *with* her, the more he can share the agony of her inner world, the better are the chances that she will stay out of hiding and in the helping relationship.

Here is a fragment of a pastor's first session with Mrs. John R., a middle-aged parishioner:

*Mrs. R.:*  I'm not sure I should be here talking about this problem, pastor. But I've tried everything to help John, and nothing seems to work. He says that his drinking is nobody else's business, including mine. (*Pause*) It's started to affect the older boy's schoolwork. (*Pause*) I feel I just have to help John, but everything I do seems to backfire and make his drinking worse.

*Pastor:*  It wasn't easy to come, but your situation is getting so difficult you decided you had to seek some help. I'll be glad to help in any way I can.

*Mrs. R.:*  I thought perhaps you could tell me how to approach John so as to help him see what he's doing to himself and his family. If I even mention his drinking, he flares up and stomps out of the room. I don't think he's an alcoholic, but he's been coming home drunk several times a week lately, and he often can't make it to work on Mondays. One of these days his manager is going to get wise to his excuses.

*Pastor:*  The drinking is getting heavier and affecting his work, but he's so sensitive about it you can't discuss the matter with him.

*Mrs. R.:*  I thought when he changed jobs last fall and got out from under some of the pressure that things would get better. But he seems to be worse. Last night he came in after midnight. First he insisted on waking up the children to give them a bawling out about leaving their bicycles in the way in the garage. Then he got sick and made a mess right in the middle of the living room—in front of them. He's home sleeping it off today. I can't understand it—he's so different. All he thinks about is himself and liquor.

*Pastor:*  It's hard on you and the children when he is so inconsiderate.

*Mrs. R.:*  Yes, (*eyes filled with tears*) his temper is terrible when he's drinking, and he seems to pick on the older boy especially. I try to protect him, and John gets furious. (*Pause*) I try to keep the kids from irritating John, but you know how children are. Whatever I do seems to be the wrong thing.

*Pastor:*    It gets very frustrating when you feel blocked whichever way you turn in trying to help.

Four facets of Mrs. R.'s inner world are evident in these opening statements. First, she communicates *some of her feelings about coming for help.* It was important for the pastor to recognize and respect these feelings. Otherwise the person may be reluctant to trust the minister with other painful feelings. It usually suffices to say, as this minister did, "It wasn't easy to come."

A second aspect of Mrs. R.'s inner world is her picture of *what constitutes her problem.* As she now sees it, her husband's drinking is the problem. Closely related is the question of why she came for help now—the crisis the night before. The pastor was probably correct in not following the lead presented by her reluctance to apply the label "alcoholic" to her husband. Her understanding of the nature of his problem will be an important goal of subsequent counseling, but the early part of the first interview is not the time to explore or educate. It is the time for the counselor to concentrate on disciplined, intensive listening.

The third facet of her inner world is her picture of *the kind of help she needs and wants.* Wives are usually at one of three stages when they seek help: (a) "Do something to help my husband." (b) "Help me to help my husband with his drinking problem." (c) "Help me with my problems and those of the children." In my experience, 90 percent are at stages one or two. To Mrs. R., the purpose of counseling is to help her help her husband. She does not think of herself as being in need of counseling for her own sake. Her limited picture of what kind of help she needs is an expression of her frantic desire to change her painful situation and a defense against her guilt. She cannot realize, at this point, that her obsession to help her husband makes her do the very things that allow him to excuse his drinking. Because she feels so responsible and guilty, she will be threatened by even a hint that what she fears is true—that she is contributing to her husband's problem and that she is also disturbed and needs help.

Yet Mrs. R. *does* need help in her own right. She *is* disturbed, in spite of her façade of competence. Whatever personality problems she brought to the marriage (and these may be great or small) have been magnified tremendously by the family trauma of alcoholism. She needs help with these problems and in coping with the impact of Mr. R.'s drinking. She needs this help for her own sake and for the children's sake, whatever Mr. R. does or does not do about his problem. Furthermore, Mrs. R.'s chances of relating helpfully to her husband also depend on her learning to handle her own inner problems more adequately.

The fourth aspect of Mrs. R.'s inner world is *her own painful feelings and experiences connected with the family crisis of alcoholism.* In his third re-

272

sponse, the pastor encouraged her to ventilate these feelings. (A somewhat better response would have been, "It must be very hard for you and the children in such a situation.") This process continued in his fourth (and subsequent) responses. In this way the minister helped her move toward an awareness of her own need for help. If a wife is reluctant to turn in this direction, it is usually because she is sitting on a volcano of explosive feelings which she fears may erupt embarrassingly and expose her as the weak person she feels she is. The façade of self-sufficiency, however, is a burdensome defense. After a tearful torrent of pent-up resentment, fear, and confusion came gushing forth in a dark tide, one wife said: "I've felt I had to be so strong because he was so weak. I didn't dare let myself go before." The safety of the counseling relationship had allowed her to relax her defenses.

Through sensitive listening and responding, the minister encourages the wife to ventilate her feelings concerning the private hell in which she has been living. This helps to accomplish four things: (a) Rapport is established through significant communication on a feeling level. She knows that the pastor is with her in her nightmarish problem. As in other counseling, the quality of the relationship is the essence of helping the alcoholic's family. (b) She experiences relief from the pressure of her mountainous burden of negative and frightening feelings. (c) This unburdening enables her to cope with her life situation more constructively. Her anger toward her husband will not distort her relationships with him and the children so severely because she has worked out part of it through counseling. (d) Through sensitive listening, the pastor forms a tentative picture of the nature of the problem. His diagnostic impressions should include his clinical hunches concerning whether he is dealing with true addictive alcoholism or with nonaddictive problem drinking. It may be that Mr. R.'s drinking is mainly a response to the pain of a deep, but hidden problem in the R.s' marriage relationship. If so, and if he has not yet lost his *ability* to control his drinking (become addicted), skilled marriage counseling may allow him to return to moderate drinking by healing the source of pain in the relationship. If the minister suspects, in the light of his discussion with Mrs. R., that this may be the case, he should recommend marriage counseling, though probably not in the first interview. Should R. be addicted (as the initial facts about his drinking seem to suggest), changes in his marriage will either not occur or, if they do, they will not reduce his drinking significantly.

When the alcoholic's or problem drinker's wife comes to the minister, *his first job is to help her and through her, the children.* He may never have an opportunity to counsel with her husband, but she is there in his study pouring out her problem. But she sees her "real problem" as her husband. Somehow she must be helped to make the difficult transition from the role of "helper" to that of one who is also being helped. By gently encouraging her to look at her own feelings and reactions, the pastor can help her become aware of how her own needs as a person are not being met. By allowing her to experience a helping relationship, he may assist her in coming down from her lonely pedestal of "helper" to accept help for herself.

## Ascertaining the Alcoholic's Motivation

During the early phases of counseling with the spouse, the question of her husband's degree of openness to help should receive attention. Obviously the kind of help she needs depends in part on whether or not he can be helped at this point. Equally important, an inquiry about the husband is a way of connecting with the "presenting problem," as seen initially by the wife. If, unlike Mrs. R., a wife does not volunteer information about the husband's view of his problem, a simple question such as, "Does your husband feel he has a problem with alcohol?" will open up this area. While the wife should realize that wanting help is a precondition to receiving it, she also needs to see that wanting help is usually mixed with a degree of *not* wanting it.

In sizing up the husband's motivation, it is wise for the minister to remember that the wife may be unaware of certain of his feelings, because of his defensiveness toward her. If it is possible to see the husband, the pastor may be surprised to discover openness to help which is hidden from his wife. The husband will reveal these feelings to the minister only if he sees the minister as genuinely concerned for him and not primarily as the wife's representative.

## Supportive Crisis Counseling

Suspecting that Mr. R. might be more open to help than Mrs. R. thought, the minister contacted Mr. R. by phone. It should be emphasized that this was done only after receiving permission from Mrs. R. to make the call and say that she had been in for a talk concerning her relationship with her husband, about which she was worried. The minister offered Mr. R. an opportunity to come in for a talk, if he wished to do so. Mr. R. rejected the invitation curtly, saying that he felt they could handle their family problems themselves.

Counseling with the spouse or other relatives of an alcoholic who is not yet open to help, is essentially crisis counseling. Its method should be primarily supportive-adaptive (following the "revised model" described in the last chapter) rather than insight-oriented. Helping Mrs. R. with her problems in coping does not mean attempting to dig for insight concerning the subsurface levels of neurotic interaction with her husband. She is too disturbed by the destructive emotional tornado in which she is living, and too threatened by awful feelings of failure, to look deeply within herself. To try to do one-sided

274

marriage counseling with a drinking alcoholic's wife is something like attempting to discuss the redecoration of his living room with a person whose house is on fire. The living room may need redecorating, but the discussion is ill timed. The realistic and constructive goal of pastoral care with the family of a drinking alcoholic is *to help them deal constructively with the runaway family crisis in which they are emotionally entangled.*

Just as alcoholism is best approached as a "runaway symptom" (Tiebout), the family's problem is approached most effectively when seen as a *runaway adaptation to the crisis of alcoholism.* As in the case of alcoholism, the very mechanisms which came into being in response to the crisis tend to intensify it. For example, the family increasingly isolates itself, as alcoholism develops, in an effort to protect itself from social disapproval. But this very isolation produces intense feelings of alienation and even greater fear of "what others will think." Supportive-adaptive counseling aims at reversing this out-of-control adaptive mechanism which has become maladaptive to the family's coping with the crisis. They are cut off from supportive and perspective-giving relationships with friends and relatives, at precisely the time they need them most. By encouraging the family to reestablish social relationships—with Al-Anon, Alateens, and with the fellowship of the church—the pastor can help them interrupt the vicious cycle of isolation, at the same time he helps them increase their supply of interpersonal satisfactions.

The supportive-adaptive approach is based on the premise that there are only certain kinds of "insights" that a person in crisis can use. In the case of Mrs. R., these include an understanding of the nature of alcoholism (as it eventually became clear that Mr. R. is an alcoholic), the futility of her attempts to coerce him to stop drinking, and the importance of her changing her assumption that any improvement in the family situation is totally dependent on his sobriety.

One important aspect of supportive crisis counseling is to help the wife cope with the pressing practical problems that face her and threaten to overwhelm her. Enabling her to handle acute problems constructively will usually help her to reassemble her shattered self-confidence. By assisting her in reducing the pressures of her external situation, her inner crisis is lessened and her resources for coping released. As one wife put it, "I feel that my head is above water and I can swim now, even though I'm still in the whirlpool."

This phase of counseling often is closer to first aid than basic therapy. But, as in a battle or accident situation, first aid sometimes can be a life-and-death matter. Even when it is not, it may save the person from much suffering and prepare him for other therapies.

When Mrs. B., a woman in her early thirties, phoned, the pastor sensed that he must arrange to see her at once. In the interview, he learned that Mr. B.

had become increasingly destructive and violent during his sprees in recent months. The day before, his cruelty toward his wife and children had included brandishing a gun in a threatening manner. Mrs. B. was nearly paralyzed with fear and indecision. The minister saw his role as that of helping her face the implications of what she already knew—that she and the children were in a dangerous situation. As she began to think more clearly, with the support of the minister's understanding, she was able to examine the alternative courses of action, as she saw them. She finally decided that a legal separation, coupled with moving temporarily to a relative's home in another city, was the safest approach.

The spouse often needs such help in making decisions and in planning direct action to meet practical problems realistically. Effective counseling often involves referral to specialized community agencies which complement and supplement what the minister is equipped to bring to the situation. The counselor needs to know the mental hospital commitment procedures in his state to help the family of an alcoholic with severe mental disturbance. But he will also need to help the family see commitment as a step toward rehabilitation rather than a "betrayal" of its loved one.

Where there is no immediate danger to life and limb, it is wise to encourage the spouse to postpone a decision about leaving her husband until she has had an opportunity to get a broader perspective on her situation through counseling. It is well to remind a wife who faces cruelty that no one really has to put up with such behavior. When an alcoholic understands that his wife means business about calling the police or taking other direct action, he will usually desist (unless he is psychotic or has a severe character disorder).

### Knowing and Facing the Facts

If the wife is to halt the runaway family crisis, it is essential that she become acquainted with the facts about alcoholism. The educational phase should begin in the second half of the first interview or as soon as the minister is reasonably sure that he is dealing with alcoholism. The wife's understanding of alcoholism provides a solid foundation for realistic decisions and attitudes on her part. The matter can be introduced by saying, "It will be helpful to you in handling your situation to learn all you can about the problem." A primary goal in exposing her to the facts about alcoholism is to help her accept the fact that her husband is suffering from a compulsive-addictive illness of which she is not the basic cause. The sickness conception, if accepted, has tremendous guilt-reducing potential. It is not easy for most families to accept this conception as applied to one of their members. It seems to be a blow to the family's self-image to think of one of their number as an "alcoholic" and as one who is not fully in control of his behavior. The counselor's task is to help them work through their emotional resistances to accepting what is, for them, a distasteful fact.

When the family comes to face the fact that their member has a chronic, progressive illness, they will be in a position to insulate themselves to a degree against some of its destructive effects. (As long as they cling to the futile hope that "maybe he'll lick it by himself this time," they are vulnerable to bitter disappointment.) Acceptance of the facts will prepare them to relate to the alcoholic in ways that may eventually contribute to his becoming open to help.

Certain kinds of knowledge are especially useful to the family. For example, it helps to know that the alcoholic's almost unbearable egocentricity and dishonesty are really desperate attempts to cope with deep feelings of chaos, fear, and worthlessness. As one wife said, "It takes some of the sting out of his obnoxious behavior." Knowledge that his symptoms such as blackouts, nameless fears, and secretive drinking are common among alcoholics often has a reassuring effect. To know that alcoholism is incurable but highly treatable is important in that it revives realistic hope. The pastor should acquaint the family with AA and other treatment resources that are available so that, if and when the alcoholic becomes open to help, they may know how to proceed. Timing is important, and the family, being on hand, can sometimes be the key if they are alert for an opening on the alcoholic's part and know the resources for help. A visit to an open AA meeting may help to prepare the family to contribute to his rehabilitation through understanding.

The sickness conception should not be presented too early in the first interview, since its effect may be to cut off the wife's catharsis of resentment and anger. The danger that this conception will stimulate the wife's maternal impulses leading to pampering can be minimized by frank discussion of the danger. When a counselor raised the question of possible overprotection, one wife responded, "After all, if Frank had pneumonia, I would make all kinds of allowances for his actions." To counter this faulty analogy, the pastor can point out that alcoholism (and other emotional illnesses) is different from pneumonia in that one of the surest ways of keeping the person from becoming open to help is to reward his illness by pampering him.

At the close of the first interview, the educational phase of the counseling can be expedited by lending the wife one of the books or pamphlets listed earlier, or a copy of *Alcoholics Anonymous*.[10] New windows of understanding often open between sessions. The person may return with a comment such as, "I feel as though I have a solid foundation under my feet for the first time. Things are beginning to make sense."

277

## "Releasing" the Alcoholic

As suggested in Chapter 9, the most salutary thing the wife of a drinking alcoholic can do is to "release" him. A member of Al-Anon said, "When I got out of the driver's seat, it took a terrific load off of me." She told how her determination to get her husband sober had become a passion into which she had poured herself. The more she failed, the more frantically and obsessively she tried. Somehow her sense of worth as a person had become bound to her husband's sobriety. He sensed this, and it gave him tremendous power over her. Finally, after years of futile struggle, she gave up, accepting the fact that nothing she could do could *make* her husband get sober. In a real sense, she "hit bottom" and "surrendered." For the first time in years, she felt a sense of inner serenity. (There is a remarkable parallelism between this kind of experience and the surrender experience of the alcoholic.)

Facilitating this kind of surrender is a major goal of pastoral care of the alcoholic's spouse. This surrender invariably produces beneficial results in the lives of the wife and children, insulating them emotionally from much of the destructiveness resulting from the alcoholic's drinking. Frequently it produces a positive turning point in the alcoholic's openness to help. One wife reported: "My husband told our minister that he had to join AA to figure out what had happened to me in Al-Anon." What had happened was that she had succeeded in releasing her husband.

Releasing the alcoholic means letting go of him emotionally, giving up all attempts either to control his drinking or protect him from its consequences. A wife is able to release him because she has had a surrender experience and because she recognizes the futility of her attempts at control. She has, in effect, cut the power which he had over her by no longer needing or attempting to control him. The change in her responses to his behavior often shocks the alcoholic by changing the interdependency pattern in their relationship. Her surrender may hasten and facilitate his surrender.

The alcoholic's psychic economy often depends on perceiving his wife as a mother figure. The more he regresses into alcoholism, the more he needs to keep her in that role. He sees her less and less as the "good mother" who gives and cares for him, and more and more as the "bad mother" who controls and deprives. This seems to him to justify his angry drinking. By thus attacking her, he maintains his grandiose illusion of self-sufficiency. The more the wife attempts to "help" him, the more she reinforces his conviction that she is a bad, controlling mother. When she is able to release him, this neurotic interaction pattern is interrupted. He is deprived of his method of avoiding responsibility for his behavior by blaming his wife.

Put in terms of Eric Berne's structural and transactional analysis, what is interrupted by the wife's release is a Parent-Child game.[11] The wife gives up parenting her husband, which upsets his half of the game. Often he will try frantically to force her back into the parent role by acting even more irresponsibly. An insightful portrayal of the dynamics of an alcoholic marriage was in the movie *Country Girl*, which many readers may recall. It showed clearly the manner in which each person fed the neurotic needs of the other. The alcoholic, being immature, craved mothering. The wife, having a dominant, protective personality, fell naturally into the mothering role. The more she accepted the responsibility for running the family, the more dependent and irresponsible he became, as well as resentful and alcoholic. The more irresponsible he became, the more she felt she had to manage everything for the family. Thus a vicious, self-perpetuating cycle developed.

The general principle which should guide the family is this: *Avoid both punishing and pampering*. On the one extreme, some families make the mistake of attempting to coerce the alcoholic by continual threats and recriminations. This succeeds only in giving the alcoholic an additional rationalization for his drinking. By taking the nagging, punishment approach, the family only brings more suffering on itself. Tactics such as pouring the liquor down the drain or hiding it from the alcoholic are forms of parenting which are no more effective than trying to hide all water from one with a hand-washing compulsion. The alcoholic's craving is so powerful at times that nothing short of actual incarceration will keep him from getting alcohol. Furthermore, he responds to parenting attempts to control his behavior with childish rebelliousness which produces increased drinking.

An even greater error, at the other extreme, is protecting the alcoholic from the painful consequences of his drinking, which is a form of "cruel kindness." In such cases, the pastor's greatest service is to help the wife discover the specific ways in which she is coddling the alcoholic, often without realizing it. The way to do this is by examining in detail a particular drinking crisis and how she responded to it. By "withdrawing the props" which protect him from reality, she may help him to hit bottom and become open to help. The pattern of overprotection is difficult to break because the spouse is usually protecting herself, the children, the family reputation, and perhaps the family income, as well as the alcoholic. She reasons: "If I don't take care of him, he'll cause me more embarrassment, heartache, and expense." It is not until the wife realizes that as long as she protects him from the consequences of his behavior, he will have little incentive to accept help, that she may be willing to release him in this way. Seeing release as an act of concern rather than rejection may also help her release her husband. Furthermore, it is important for her to see that this may be of help in protecting her children from the worst emotional damage of their father's illness.

The book *Alcoholics Anonymous* contains an example, written by the wives of early members, of how a wife might avoid overprotecting the alcoholic:

Frequently, you have felt obliged to tell your husband's employer and his friends that he was sick, when as a matter of fact he was tight. Avoid answering these inquiries as much as you can. Whenever possible, let your husband explain. . . . Discuss this with him when he is sober and in good spirits. Ask him what you should do if he places you in such a position again.[12]

The pastor's goal in counseling with the family is to encourage any tendency in them, however weak, to make the alcoholic face the reality of adult life and of his drinking. In order to be helpful, the family must be firm with the alcoholic, walking the middle ground between recrimination on the one hand and pampering on the other. This is something like walking a tightrope, and they will need all the help they can get both from the pastor and from Al-Anon. Walking the middle ground is possible only if the spouse has released the alcoholic to an appreciable degree and resists the temptation to slip back into the mothering role.

It is possible for the minister unwittingly to block rather than facilitate the wife's release of the alcoholic. In the play *The Pleasure of His Company* by Samuel Taylor and Cornelia Otis Skinner, Mackenzie Savage is asked by his daughter, "You were never very happy with mother, were you?" He replies, "Your mother was a saint who made our home an outpost of heaven. It's why I spent so much time in saloons." The message of this fictional fragment—that behind the alcoholic is a wife who subtly "drives him to drink"— is a common theme in the folklore of our culture. It is a feeling that both the minister and the alcoholic's spouse (as well as the alcoholic) have somewhere within them. The minister's knowledge of certain research findings may confirm this feeling for him. In her review of the professional literature on alcoholism and marriage, Margaret Bailey concludes: "Most students of the problem have found in some or all of their cases this interactive pattern of the dependent, inadequate alcoholic male married to a dominating woman who is usually seen as maintaining a semblance of adequacy only at his expense." [13]

The effect of this influence on the minister is to tempt him to make the focus of counseling the wife's hidden neurotic needs which allegedly find satisfaction in the husband's continued alcoholism. This approach tends to block rather than facilitate her releasing of her husband. She already suspects that she is somehow driving him to drink. For the minister to imply that she has unconscious needs which contribute to his drinking increases her guilt and her frantic, futile struggling to change things or change her husband so that he won't drink as he does.

There is little doubt that *some* wives find neurotic satisfactions in being married to weak, dependent, drinking alcoholics. One study showed that when marital bonds are dissolved by death or divorce, the wives of alcoholics frequently marry another alcoholic.[14] Some wives of alcoholics hold tenaciously to their masochistic, martyrish, controlling postures. I recall one case where separation from the alcoholic husband was clearly indicated in order to protect both the wife and the children from physical and emotional harm. The wife consistently refused to consider leaving him. Her reasoning was simply, "How would he get along without me? Someone has to take care of him when he's drunk." In some cases the spouse or parents of an alcoholic justify overprotective behavior on religious principles—"going the second mile" —failing to see that such cruel kindness is anything but redemptive in its effects. Various psychological studies have shown that the presence of a mothering figure in his immediate interpersonal world is one of the most characteristic aspects of the alcoholic's picture. This is often the most difficult factor in helping the alcoholic, and it may be the key to helping the family help him. If the wife of the alcoholic derives satisfactions from her power as head of the family while he is drinking, she will have ambivalent feelings about his getting sober. In extreme cases, wives of alcoholics have developed psychosomatic or psychological illnesses after their husbands achieved sobriety.

Being alert to the possibility that *some* wives may attempt to sabotage their husbands' sobriety does not mean that one should use this as a general approach to helping the family. There are tremendous differences among alcoholics, their wives, and their marriages. For many wives, factors which militate against the husbands' sobriety are either practically nonexistent, or they are offset by other needs for strength in their husbands. Let us assume that a particular wife does have self-punishing and controlling tendencies which contribute to her mothering behavior with the alcoholic. Focusing on her neurotic tendencies or searching for their causes will usually make such a person guiltier and more anxious, and therefore more self-punishing and controlling. This will make releasing her husband more difficult for her. To be able to release him, she must be helped to feel less responsible and guilty, not more so. *If she can release him, the influence of her neurotic tendencies will be neutralized* to a considerable extent; this is because the neurotic interaction which strengthens these tendencies will be interrupted.

As studies by Joan Jackson have shown, the personality disturbances of many wives come directly from the runaway crises in which they are caught. In counseling, the minister should proceed on the assumption that the wife's disturbance *is the result* of the crisis. What appears to be a marked personality disorder may clear up as the husband gets treatment or the wife neutralizes the impact of his behavior by releasing him. In any case, it is therapeutically unproductive to try to correct deep inner problems in the midst of a crisis.

Here are some implications of this approach, by way of summary: (1) Focusing on why the wife married an alcoholic or a potential alcoholic is definitely contraindicated. This kind of awareness is available only through long-term psychotherapy in depth. Her crisis will be intensified, in most cases, by attempts to search for such insight. (2) It is equally unwise to encourage her in her futile search for the magic key to handling her husband so as to stop his drinking problem. This is parenting, and the opposite of release. The futility of the "home treatment"—pleading, threatening, moralizing, coercing, nagging—should be emphasized. (3) The counselor should emphasize the medical nature of the problem of alcoholism, pointing out that if her husband had diabetes she would not feel an obligation to cure him. This approach often helps reduce her exaggerated, unrealistic, and unproductive sense of responsibility for her husband's drinking problem. By reducing her irrational guilt, it can help her release him. (4) The counselor should describe the meaning of "releasing" and help her work though the feelings of guilt and inappropriate responsibility that keep her from moving in this creative direction. He can point out that release does not necessarily mean separating from the alcoholic, since it is a psychological process, although in some cases it may be well-nigh impossible without a separation. (5) The pastor can help the wife discover ways in which she can make real progress in handling her problems, in spite of the husband's continued drinking. At the same time she is told that she can't do anything to reform her husband, she must be helped to see that there is something very important that she can do: to work on her own attitudes and problems in living. After she has released the alcoholic and gained some sense of serenity, usually she will begin spontaneously to look into the adequacy of her own life as a person.

## Developing the Family's Maximum Potentialities

A vital ingredient in the release process is the refocusing of the spouse's energy on increasing the adequacy of her own inner life and of her relationships with her children and friends. In order to do this, the wife must have relinquished her assumption that any improvement in the family is dependent on her husband's achieving sobriety. Her holding to this assumption, in effect, makes it true. Only when she lets go of it and begins to develop her own potentialities and those of the family does she discover its fallacious nature. The Big Book of AA recommends to wives of still-drinking alcoholics:

Be determined that your husband's drinking is not going to spoil your relation with your children or your friends. They need your companionship and your help. It is possible to have a full and useful life, though your husband continues to drink. We know women who are unafraid, even happy under these conditions. Do not set your heart on reforming your husband.[16]

Developing her own potentialities as a person helps to make life more satisfying and her self-esteem more robust. Both of these factors help make it possible for the wife to function more adequately as a need-satisfying parent. They also help her to tolerate the inevitable frustrations of her husband's drinking and the inadequacy of the marriage.

The long-range role of the church in this process can be vitally important. Once the minister has helped the family over the crisis stage, his function broadens from pastoral counseling to the more inclusive function of pastoral care. He maintains a steady, dependable relationship which helps to sustain them through what may be an extended period of time before the alcoholic becomes open to help; this makes the minister readily available for additional counseling when crises recur. Much of the sustained-supportive ministry to the family is provided by the corporate worship and group life of the church. The pastor should encourage the family members to find group relationships that are satisfying to each of them. If a *pastoral care team* [16] has been selected and trained by the minister, these laymen can be invaluable allies to him in providing the ongoing supportive ministry to the alcoholic's family. Certainly every team should include at least one male and one female Al-Anon member. These persons will have a special entrée to the alcoholic's family and can therefore be of help in relating the family to both the church and to Al-Anon.

### Abundant Use of Al-Anon

Early in the counseling relationship with the alcoholic's spouse, the minister should recommend that she visit the local Al-Anon Family Group. Helping her work through her fears and resistances to attending Al-Anon and then arranging, with her permission, for a stable Al-Anon member to take her to a meeting are strategies for helping her to relate to this excellent helping resource. Attendance at Al-Anon should parallel pastoral counseling in most cases. It is, for the family member, what AA is for the alcoholic. In order to coordinate these parallel therapies, the pastor should take an active interest in her Al-Anon experiences.

There are now over three thousand Al-Anon groups with more springing up each month. "Purposes and Suggestions for Al-Anon Family Groups," published by the Al-Anon Family Group Headquarters, describes the groups as follows: "The Al-Anon Family Groups consist of relatives and friends of alcoholics, who realize that by banding together they can better solve their common problems. Both before and after the alcoholic joins AA, there is much that the families can do to help the alcoholic, and themselves." The primary focus of the groups is to encourage each person to apply the Twelve Steps of AA to *his own problems in living.* Any two or three relatives of alcoholics can start a Family Group. Most groups begin in the living room of the wife of an AA member and are conducted somewhat like AA closed meetings (for instance, centering on the discussion of how one of the Twelve Steps has helped or might help the persons present). The groups follow the principle of allowing no criticism of an alcoholic partner in the meetings. Instead, newcomers are encouraged to make friends with more experienced members with whom they can discuss their personal difficulties in private.

The Al-Anon group can serve a valuable function both before and after the alcoholic is in AA. Fellow Al-Anon members give massive emotional support to the wife during the lonesome, dreary days when the alcoholic refuses help. They have the special empathy of those who have "lived in the same squirrel cage." Like AA members, they are bound together by the common crisis through which they have all gone or are going. Al-Anon participation will bring the wife out of her lonely, frightened shell and help her to a *feeling-level* acceptance of her husband's illness. It will encourage those attitudes which make possible her surrender and the emotional release of her husband. (The term "release" was coined by Al-Anon members out of their experience.) Her fellow members will help her identify the subtle ways in which she is overprotecting her husband; they will help her learn how to handle all sorts of practical problems by sharing their own experiences. Participation in Al-Anon will stimulate personal growth and self-awareness through the application of the Twelve Steps to her own life. After she has released her husband, she will be able to look at her own life and the changes she needs to make in the marriage without its stimulating inappropriate guilt and controlling behavior. The Twelve Steps will assist her in maintaining her release of her husband— through the first step in which she admits she is powerless over his use of alcohol. Most important, practicing the Twelve Steps in Al-Anon will help her find spiritual resources, through relationship with a higher Power, which she will need in coping with her problems in living and her existential anxiety.

### How the Family Can Help the Alcoholic Accept AA

For a wife to nag her husband to go to AA is an almost foolproof method of keeping him away. Because of the hostility in their relationship, resulting in his need to thwart her, she has given him another reason for not going. Even if a wife is successful in getting her husband to AA under duress, the chances are that he will not "get the program." In fact, most of the interviewees, in my study who had had a time gap of more than a year between contact with AA and active participation in it were those who had been pushed in by well-meaning but misguided relatives.

A wife or other relative often can help the most by keeping a hands-off attitude or by working indirectly. Clifford Earle gives an example of how this was done in one case:

A lawyer whose wife showed unmistakable signs of alcoholism included several AA pamphlets and other suitable literature in a stack of papers on his desk at home. Then he had his secretary phone her for information she could get only by going through the things on her husband's desk. In this way he was able to get her to read selected literature on alcoholism that she would have resented and rejected if he had given it to her directly. The method was devious but successful.[17]

The technique of leaving AA literature around where the person will find it, without making it seem that it was planted, is a subtle way of informing him concerning the help that is available, without threatening his ego. Some pamphlets which are useful for this are: "Is AA for You?" "This Is AA," "AA, 44 Questions and Answers About the Program of Recovery from Alcoholism," "Medicine Looks at Alcoholics Anonymous," "AA for the Woman," "Young People and AA." All are obtainable from a local AA group or from the General Service Office of AA, 305 East 45th Street, New York, New York 10017.

If an alcoholic has a trustful relationship with his physician, it is sometimes possible for the family to enlist his help in getting the alcoholic to AA. The family members may describe the problem, as he sees it, to the doctor and ask if he would broach the subject with the alcoholic, should the opportunity arise. This approach is effective only if the doctor is favorably disposed toward AA.

The use of any indirect method should be considered only if a frank, above-board approach has failed or is nearly certain to fail. The weakness of indirect methods is that they are manipulative. Even if such a method does not backfire (as it will if the alcoholic discovers what is occurring), it tends to compromise the openness and mutual trust that should characterize marriage and family relationships. The fact that such a method is used usually indicates that such trust and openness do not exist in the relationship. The question that must be asked in such cases is whether the end (getting the person in contact with AA) justifies the means.

The family's fundamental contributions to helping the alcoholic accept help from AA or any other treatment resource consist of *releasing him*, as described previously, and of *accepting the sickness conception themselves*. A psychiatrist, speaking at the Yale Summer School of Alcohol Studies, declared: "I've very seldom convinced an alcoholic that he has a disorder until I have convinced the family that he has a disorder." [18] Until the emotionally significant people in his life accept the sickness conception and apply it to him, it is difficult for the alcoholic to do so. Until he does accept it, he is unlikely to become open to the kinds of help he needs.

There is, of course, no reason why the spouse should hide her desire that the alcoholic get help. A part of the firmness of attitude, which is neither pampering nor punishing, is the attitude on the family's part that lets him know that they expect him to get treatment and what will happen, as far as they are concerned, if he does not. This should be done without nagging and certainly without empty threats. The tone should be that of holding up reality, emphasizing particularly what steps the family intends to take if the alcoholic's self- and other-destructive behavior continues. In this way the spouse and other family members can exert a steady pressure on the alcoholic to accept treatment. Unless the marital relationship is thoroughly disintegrated, such reality pressure can help to motivate the alcoholic. This is an additional source of pressure, along with the pressure that results from external circumstances to which the alcoholic is exposed when the family stops "covering" for him.

A discussion which may prove helpful to a person who is attempting to interest a mate in AA is that written by the wives of the first hundred AA's. Derived as it is from their experiences, it includes many practical suggestions as to how one may approach alcoholics who are in different stages of the illness and who have varied attitudes toward getting help. This discussion is in Chapter 8 of the AA book and is entitled "To Wives."

### Helping the Family During Treatment

The attitudes and behavior of the wife can constitute either a barrier or a bridge to sobriety for the alcoholic who is in the early stages of treatment. The counselor's goal is to help her make these attitudes a bridge. He can do this in several ways. First, the wife who has not been in contact with Al-Anon prior to her husband's entry into AA should be encouraged to affiliate with Al-Anon and to attend open AA meetings with her husband. This will help her understand the AA approach and support his striving for sobriety. Second, the pastor can sometimes help the wife by interpreting what is happening in the particular treatment program (AA or otherwise) in which her husband is receiving help. Third, the pastor can emphasize the importance of letting *him* make the decisions concerning what shall be told friends and neighbors about his problem. Closely related is the importance of not attempting to "protect him from temptation," which, like other forms of overprotection, usually backfires. He must learn to live in a world where liquor is available. It is unrealistic for the wife to believe that she can really protect him in this way, and, more important, the recovering alcoholic usually resents being treated in this manipulative and subadult fashion.

If the pastor senses that a wife is unconsciously blocking her husband's attempts to get help, he has the difficult task of trying to help her see what she is doing. I recall one wife who consistently planned for her husband to do something else on the night when AA met in their town. This was in spite of her conscious eagerness for him to achieve sobriety. It was not until her unconscious sabotaging was explored and diminished that she was able to support his participation in AA.

The pastor should stay close to the entire family during the early stages of treatment for other reasons also, including supporting them if the alcoholic slips. By helping the spouse understand the uphill struggle her husband is going through, he will enhance her appreciation of his progress and cushion her disappointment at the occasional setbacks. Emphasizing the importance of patience has a salutary effect on the family. It can be pointed out that it took the husband an extended period of time to develop his addiction and it may require several years for him to achieve stable and productive sobriety. The AA motto "Easy Does It" is good advice for the family.

The "suggestions for newcomers" in an Al-Anon brochure can be used by the pastor with families of alcoholics. Here are some of them:

Remember that the alcoholic is an emotionally sick person. Try to stop nagging and causing scenes.

Take a personal inventory of your own faults and make a sincere effort to overcome them.

Try to learn all you can about AA and alcoholism.

Cooperate actively with the alcoholic in his or her AA work. But do not push. The alcoholic has a far better chance when the family really understands and follows along.

Be gracious about the alcoholic's closed meetings and 12th Step work. To overcome the alcoholic obsession will require an equally strong AA obsession.

Some alcoholics are much sicker than others. Don't be discouraged if progress is slow. The AA seed has been planted. Growth is slower in some soils than others.

When AA's assume an attitude of superiority, don't be dismayed. This is a perfectly natural reaction from their previous tragic inferiority . . . spiritual growth usually levels off this attitude. Then real partnership becomes possible, for there will be neither superiority nor inferiority.

Above all don't expect too much too quickly. Because of distorted relationships, directly or indirectly resulting from drinking, both you and your AA partner will have many personal problems to solve.

Finally, have faith in the AA member of your family. The AA program has been successful in thousands of cases. So it can be in yours.[19]

## The Family After the Alcoholic Is Sober

If all the troubles in the family of an alcoholic were the direct effects of alcoholism, it would be reasonable to assume that, given a certain period of time after sobriety, most of these troubles would disappear. As a matter of fact, they often do not, and the pastor does well to keep close to a family even after the alcoholic member has achieved sobriety. It may be that he will be able to render valuable help during period of readjustment.

We have already mentioned the wife's personality problems as one cause of interpersonal difficulty when the husband is sober and attempting to assume the normal role of an adult male in the family. On the alcoholic's side of the problem is the fact, emphasized by sociologist Selden D. Bacon,[20] that the same kind of personality problems which tend to make one susceptible to alcoholism also give rise to marital discord. Merely removing the inebriety does not solve these problems. Rather than thinking of the problems of an alcoholic family as entirely the *effects* of alcoholism, it is well to remember that an inadequate marital adjustment can be as much a *cause* as an effect of inebriety. For example, the immature male who cannot accept the demands of his role as husband and father, may retreat into alcoholism to escape the anxiety of adult responsibility. His inadequacy and the attendant problems are aggravated by alcoholism, but the basic problems are there when inebriety is removed.

All this makes it doubly fortunate that AA is, in a real sense, a family program. Long before there were Al-Anon Family Groups the wives of AA members were taking an active interest in the program. Beginning with Lois W., wife of co-founder, Bill W., AA wives have shared the sense of belonging and the resultant resocialization of the AA group. Very early they realized that they could well apply the Twelve Steps to themselves. In the chapter "To Wives" in the original edition of the Big Book, the wives of the first hundred AA's wrote to the wives of other alcoholics: "If God can solve the age-old riddle of alcoholism, he can solve your problem, too." [21] The husband and wife who together try to live the AA program will have a great advantage in the business of solving their family problems. One of the valuable functions of the Al-Anon Family Groups is that of giving wise counsel concerning the problems of adjustment after sobriety. Further, these groups fill an important need by helping to resocialize the mate, giving her a strong sense of belonging similar to that provided by AA. This is especially important for, as the Family Group brochure puts it, "When your alcoholic partner goes on AA business, Family Group activities will cure that lonely and left-out feeling."

One of the most helpful descriptions of the marital problems that beset the alcoholic family after sobriety and how they can be met, is in the Big Book, Chapter 9, entitled "The Family Afterwards." The pastor who has occasion to counsel with such a family will do well to read and absorb the insights of this chapter which was written by alcoholics.

This chapter suggests, among other things, that the family may be helped in its readjustment by establishing or reestablishing their connections with a religious organization. By encouraging the family who have gotten away from the church during the nightmare of alcoholism to reenter the Christian fellowship, the pastor can render valuable service to them and to his church. He can help them try their new social wings in a nonalcoholic circle and can put them in touch with all the resources and opportunities for service represented by the church. On the other hand, as the Big Book puts it, in discussing the alcoholic who returns to church, "He and his family can be a bright spot in such congregations. He may bring new hope and new courage to many a priest, minister or rabbi." [22] All this is contingent on the willingness of a congregation to accept an alcoholic and his family into the fellowship, without reservations. Sad to say, this is not always the case. But where it is, the pastor will find that a vital resource for helping the families of alcoholics is very near at hand—in his own church.

If involvement in AA, Al-Anon, and the church program do not suffice in helping the alcoholic and his wife make the marital adjustments which will undergird productive family life, the pastor should help them obtain marriage counseling. If he is trained in marriage counseling and has the time to invest in this function, he may decide to offer his help to them. If not, his role is to help them find a competent marriage counselor. One of the most encouraging methods of helping alcoholics and their spouses with marital problems is that of *group marriage counseling* in which five or six couples meet under the leadership of a group counselor or, in some cases, two co-counselors.[23]

## Helping the Children of Alcoholics

In its advanced stages, alcoholism crushes the interpersonal relations of family life like a heavy boot on a delicate spider web. It is in the intricate interdependencies of the family that the agonies of alcoholism are devastatingly felt. Family life is the most intimate and therefore the most demanding of all human relationships. The very qualities which make possible a growth-producing family—tenderness, compassion, emotional maturity in parents—are in short supply or are early casualties of the illness of alcoholism. It is not surprising, therefore, that few, if any, children of alcoholics escape without emotional scars. The dependable supply of emotional nutrition which children need to grow strong, resilient personalities is not available in most alcoholic families.

The damage to the children varies, depending on a number of factors—the strength of the nonalcoholic parent, the age of the child at the onset of the most destructive phases of the illness, the nature of the relationship with the alcoholic parent, and the social class level of the family. On this last point, middle-class, status-seeking families seem to be disturbed the most deeply by parental alcoholism. In families where the father is the alcoholic and the mother has received help, damage can be minimized. Where the mother is the alcoholic, damage is often deep. One husband told of the response of his young son to finding his mother in an alcoholic stupor. He said, "Mommy is dead." Emotionally, she was dead to him, in that she was nongiving and non-available to him when he needed her. The child's involvement in the husband-wife conflict was reflected in these words to his father: "We don't like Mommy, do we?"

There are at least four factors in the alcoholic family which are disturbing to children and teen-agers:[24]

1. *The shift and reversal of parental roles in an unpredictable and confusing way* is the first factor. When the father is drinking, he abdicates his parental role which is taken over by mother. This distorts her functioning in her unique role as mother. During periods of sobriety, the whole family tries to adjust. The lack of a strong male with whom a son can identify and thus achieve a sense of his own emerging maleness is a serious deficiency. The same can be said for the lack of a male figure who is both loving and strong with whom a daughter can discover a sound way of relating to males. When the mother is the alcoholic, the identity problems are reversed, and they are compounded by the limitations of the alcoholic mother's ability to give to her children.

2. *The inconsistent, unpredictable relationship with the alcoholic* is the second disturbing factor. The alcoholic may be alternately cold and rejected, and sentimentally overindulgent for reasons that are not apparent to the child. Attempts by the child to grasp the pattern of how to relate to the parent so as to obtain the security, approval, and affection he needs are continually frustrated by the unpredictable nature of the alcoholic's responses.

3. *The nonalcoholic parent is unable to relate in a need-satisfying way with the child* because of her disturbance. The wife is obsessed with her husband's drinking and filled with fears which make parenting roles very difficult. Her own needs are not being met in the marriage, thus leaving her lonely and frustrated. This makes it increasingly difficult for her to satisfy the emotional needs of her children. One response to loneliness may be to exploit the children by attempting to derive emotional satisfactions from them which she should be getting from the marriage. She may unwittingly use the children in her struggle with the husband. Divisive alliances—mother-son vs. father-daughter—are frequent and damaging to the emotional health of the children.

4. *Increased social isolation of the family* is the fourth factor. The family turns in upon itself; interaction is too intense. The family loses the supportive relationships with friends and community which are so vital to its health. Family morale rises and falls with the alcoholic's drinking behavior. The child's peer relationships are distorted or eliminated. He feels, "I can't bring my friends home because Dad might be drunk and embarrass me in front

of them." He may withdraw from peer relationships in an effort to protect himself from the discovery by his peers of the family stigma. The more the family turns in upon itself, the more its problems feed upon themselves and grow.

What can the minister do to help the children? The most important way of helping the children is by helping their parents. Even if the alcoholic parent resists treatment, the nonalcoholic spouse can, through the approach described in this chapter, change the emotional climate of the home and make her relationship with the children more need-satisfying.

In addition, the pastor can do these things to provide direct help to the children: He can encourage them to stay actively involved in the church school and youth groups within the church, resisting the temptation to withdraw into protective but harmful isolation. Church school teachers, adult advisors to the youth groups, or youth within the groups can be enlisted as allies in the effort to surround the children of alcoholics with a supportive network of relationships. This must be done without breaking the confidences which the family may have with the pastor about the nature of their problems.

The minister can encourage the adolescent sons and daughters of alcoholic parents to participate in an Alateen group. These groups help the teen-ager to understand the nature of his parent's illness, to experience the group support of peers who share many of the same problems, and to apply the Twelve Steps to their own problems of living in an alcoholic home. The opportunity to talk openly about painful experiences that were formerly kept in secrecy surrounded by feelings of shame has an unburdening effect; feelings of self-confidence are strengthened by group acceptance. In these and other ways, Alateen groups do for the adolescent what AA does for the alcoholic and Al-Anon does for the spouse.

If the children show signs of serious disturbance—either the inward retreat of withdrawal or the outward attack of aggression and delinquency—the minister should recommend and assist the parent in obtaining professional help for the children at a child guidance clinic. If the alcoholic is still drinking, the nonalcoholic spouse may have to handle making these arrangements; but certainly the alcoholic should be informed that his children are disturbed and why. If the family is intact, it may be that some form of conjoint family therapy [25] will prove to be the most efficient way of helping the disturbed child by alleviating the disturbance in the total family of which the child's problems are expressions. Marriage counseling for the parents, conjoint family therapy for all the members of the family, or psychotherapy for the disturbed child and the parents at a child guidance clinic—all these can be effective ways of healing the emotional wounds suffered by children in the chaos of the alcoholic home.

A final way in which the clergyman can help the children is by establishing

291

a strong, accepting relationship with them himself. This does not require large investments of time, in most cases. What is required is for the pastor to be interested in them and to express warmth and caring in his contacts with them. Such relationships between a pastor and children can have a qualitative meaningfulness, on both sides, that far outweighs the investment of time. To the extent that a relationship of this kind helps satisfy the child's need for stable, loving adult identity figures, it is a long-range investment in the child's future mental and spiritual health.

## REFERENCES

1. Jerome Ellison, "Help for the Alcoholic's Family," The Saturday Evening Post, CCXXVIII (July 2, 1955), 48. Used by permission of the author.

2. Marty Mann, New Primer on Alcoholism, p. x.

3. Joseph Hirsch, The Problem Drinker (New York: Duell, Sloan and Pearce, 1949), p. 111.

4. S. Futterman, "Personality Trends in Wives of Alcoholics," Journal of Psychiatric Social Work, XXIII (1953), 37-41; T. Whalen, "Wives of Alcoholics. Four Types Observed in a Family Service Agency," QJSA, XIV (December, 1953), 632-41; S. D. Bacon, "Excessive Drinking and the Institution of the Family," Alcohol, Science and Society, pp. 223-38; Margaret B. Bailey, "Alcoholism and Marriage, A Review of Research and Professional Literature," QJSA (March, 1961), pp. 81-97; D. E. Macdonald, "Mental Disorders in Wives of Alcoholics," QJSA, XVII (June, 1956), 282-87; K. L. Kogan, W. E. Fordyce, and J. K. Jackson, "Personality Disturbance in Wives of Alcoholics," QJSA, XXIV (June, 1963), 227-38; "Some Concomitants of Personality Difficulties in Wives of Alcoholics and Nonalcoholics," QJSA, XXVI (December, 1965), 595-604; K. L. Kogan and J. K. Jackson, "Stress, Personality and Emotional Disturbance in Wives of Alcoholics," QJSA (September, 1965); R. G. Ballard, "The Interaction Between Marital Conflict and Alcoholism as Seen Through the MMPI's of Marriage Partners," The American Journal of Orthopsychiatry, XXIX (July, 1959), 528-46; M. B. Bailey, Paul Haberman, and Harold Alksne, "Outcome of Alcoholic Marriages: Endurance, Termination or Recovery," QJSA, XXIII (December, 1962), 610-23.

5. If no number is listed, AA and Al-Anon meetings can often be located by contacting a clergyman who has been in the area for several years. Information about the nearest Al-Anon group and about the Al-Anon program in general can be obtained by writing the Al-Anon Family Group Headquarters, P. O. Box 182, Madison Square Station, New York, New York 10010.

6. QJSA, XV (December, 1954), 562-86. See also Jackson's article, "Alcoholism as a Family Crisis," Pastoral Psychology (April, 1962), pp. 8 ff.

7. "The Adjustment of the Family to the Crisis of Alcoholism," pp. 568-69.

8. Much of the material in this and subsequent sections of this chapter is adapted from the author's article, "Pastoral Care of the Alcoholic's Family Before Sobriety," Pastoral Psychology, XIII (April, 1962), 19-29.

9. Since there are at least four times as many wives as husbands of alcoholics, the words "she" and "wife" will be used generally throughout this discussion. However, much that is said will apply to other close relatives of alcoholics who seek help—husbands, parents, grown children, etc.

10. (New York: Alcoholics Anonymous Publishing, 1955).

11. For a discussion of Berne's Parent-Adult-Child ego states, see his book Transactional Analysis in Psychotherapy (New York: Grove Press, 1961). The game of

"alcoholic" is discussed in Berne's book *Games People Play* (New York: Grove Press, 1964), pp. 73-81.

12. *Alcoholics Anonymous*, pp. 115-16.

13. "Alcoholism and Marriage," p. 85.

14. From a report read by Gladys Price at the Cleveland Symposium on Alcoholism, reprinted in the first issue of *QJSA*.

15. *Alcoholics Anonymous*, p. 111. Used by permission of AA General Service Headquarters.

16. For a description of how such a team can be selected and trained, see Clinebell, *Basic Types of Pastoral Counseling*, pp. 287-91.

17. *How to Help an Alcoholic* (Philadelphia: The Westminster Press, 1952), p. 61.

18. Lecture by William Wade, Yale Summer School, 1949.

19. From "Purposes and Suggestions for Al-Anon Family Groups." Used by permission of Al-Anon Family Group Headquarters.

20. *Ibid.*

21. *Alcoholics Anonymous*, pp. 129-30.

22. *Ibid.*, p. 132.

23. For a description of one approach to group marriage counseling see Genevieve Burton, "Group Counseling with Alcoholics and Their Nonalcoholic Wives," *Marriage and Family Living*, XXIV (February, 1962).

24. A relevant paper on "The Effect of Parental Alcoholism on Adolescents" was presented by Herman E. Krimmel and Helen R. Spears at the National Conference on Social Welfare, Los Angeles, California, May 26, 1964.

25. For a discussion of the application of family group therapy in pastoral counseling, see Clinebell, *Basic Types of Pastoral Counseling*, pp. 120-30.

12

# The Prevention of Alcoholism

*The church's most important task, in relation to the problem of alcoholism, is prevention.* In this area it has a tremendous mother lode of practically untouched opportunity. Organized religion has direct contact with over half the people in the country. This is more than any other nongovernmental organization. If a substantial share of the religious organizations in our country would undertake an enthusiastic and realistic program of prevention, America's fourth largest public health problem could be brought under control and hundreds of thousands of persons would be protected from becoming alcoholics.

Prevention is the only real solution to the problem. As things are now we are like Alice in Wonderland, running as hard as we can to stay at the same place. (Actually we are falling behind.) Alcoholics are being created wholesale while all the therapeutic agencies together are able only to treat them retail. As the great Japanese Christian, Toyohiko Kagawa, once put it regarding the problem of slums, this is like building a rescue station at the bottom of a cliff to help those who have fallen over, without working at the top of the cliff to keep others from falling.[1] There are 5½ million alcoholics in the country, and AA has approximately 375,000 members. This means that AA, with its amazing effectiveness, has been able to reach slightly less than one out of every fifteen alcoholics in the country. That it has been able to achieve this in thirty years makes it a near miracle, but it is not the complete answer to the problem. Too many are falling over the cliff into the morass of the sickness of alcoholism each year. Somehow we must build a fence that will reduce the number of new alcoholics.

But what kind of fence is effective in preventing alcoholism? What constitutes real prevention? We must have an answer to this before we can expect to approach the problem of prevention realistically. Our effort to point toward an answer will be divided into three categories. In Chapter 2 it was shown that the various causes of alcoholism operate on three levels:

(a) the "soil of addiction," (b) symptom selection, (c) perpetuation of the addictive cycle. A comprehensive program of prevention can and should operate on each of these three levels of the alcoholic sickness. The three corresponding levels of prevention are: (a) prevention at the "grass roots," (b) prevention through the influencing of symptom selection, (c) prevention through early detection and treatment.

## Prevention at the "Grass Roots"

The place where grass roots prevention must ultimately take place is at the point where alcoholism begins—in the home. By exerting its educational influence in terms of the type of parent-child relationship that will satisfy the emotional needs of the child, the church can cut the roots of alcoholism. This is, of course, a long range program. . . . Some within the church will prefer to continue to engage in the less time-consuming business of manipulating symptoms—for example, by attempting to shield people from becoming *compulsive* drinkers by making them compulsive non-drinkers.

The church is primarily concerned with making the life of abundance—of full psychological and physical need satisfaction—a reality in the lives of men. If it is successful in its primary task, it will help to deal the death blow to the status of alcoholism as a major area of human tragedy.[2]

As we saw in Chapter 1, approximately 6 percent of those who drink are vulnerable to alcohol addiction. In Chapter 2 we found that this 6 percent seems to be people who, because of inner conflict and anxiety, have an abnormal craving for the anesthetic effects of alcohol. Their personality problems and emotional immaturity constitute their Achilles' heel which renders them vulnerable to alcoholism. Conversely, those who are fortunate enough to have relatively mature and well-integrated personalities have a much smaller chance of becoming alcoholic. Whatever the church can do, then, to promote mental, emotional, and spiritual health helps to prevent alcoholism at the grass roots. The prevention of alcoholism is thus related to the prevention of all other forms of social pathology.

Prevention of alcoholism at the grass roots is a gigantic task. Just how gigantic becomes clearer when one sees alcoholism as a symptom of the large areas of social malignancy within our culture. Leslie A. Osborn has said, "Big as it is, the problem of alcoholism opens into vastly bigger difficulties of our tangled and complex civilization."[3] The late Christopher Morley stated the same truth in another way when, in commenting on *The Lost Weekend*, he wrote: "It becomes almost the history of a whole era of frustration."[4] One can understand the depth and complexity of alcoholism, and therefore its prevention, by seeing it as a "tragic response to areas of tragedy in our culture."

We have seen that alcoholism is rooted in personality conflicts. In her illuminating discussion of inner conflicts, the late Karen Horney wrote: "The kind, scope and intensity of such conflicts are largely determined by the civilization in which we live." [5] The civilization or culture into which an infant is born is channeled to him through the mothering adult in the early period of his life. The aspects of the culture, harmful or beneficent, which she is able to focus on the infant are determined in considerable measure by the way in which the culture was focused on her. Each culture tends to develop what Ruth Benedict has called its "configuration," [6] a certain pattern of attitudes and practices which control individual and group behavior and produce a nucleus of personality shared by most members of the culture. One configuration may make for emotionally satisfied and secure individuals who develop to a high degree their personality potentiality. Another culture's configuration may produce patterns of child rearing, family life, interpersonal relations, social and economic life which produce a high degree of frustration and emotional warping in its members. The latter would lay the groundwork for maladjustments of all kinds. It would prepare the soil of addiction of which we have spoken above.

Our cultural configuration seems to provide amply for the conditions which cause the traumatization and emotional deprivation of personality. Because of the wide individual differences which are seen in any culture, these destructive attributes are focused with greater force on some than on others. The chart on page 297 is a summation of factors found to be the most common in the parents of the alcoholics interviewed by the writer. It attempts to show the following in schematic form: column A, three cultural attitudes which are prominent in our "configuration" and in the personality patterns of the parents of the alcoholics; column B, the effect that these cultural attitudes have on the parents; column C, the way in which these effects tend to deprive the child of the satisfaction of certain vital needs; column D, the relationship between this deprivation of satisfaction and the psychological characteristics which are typical of alcoholics.

A child's basic emotional need is for adequate love. This includes a sense of being wanted, of approval, of achievement, of belonging, of emotional warmth, acceptance, and nearness or relatedness to security-giving adults. Adequate love also includes the satisfaction of the child's need for increasing autonomy, self-direction, and individual self-fulfillment. This implies accepting the child's individuality, his physical drives, and his feelings. The maintenance of the balance between the child's need for security and his need for independence is essential for emotional growth. David Roberts has written: "The child's foremost need is an adequate supply of wise love. By 'wise' I mean steady and natural, instead of sporadic and forced; unsentimental and geared to growing autonomy instead of plaintive and smothering." [7]

If a child gets enough "wise love," love that is as free and accessible (and as important) as the air he breathes, he will become a healthy, loving, and self-reliant person, a person who does not need to use alcohol as a personality crutch. *The three cultural attitudes mentioned on the chart—authoritarianism, success-worship, and moralism—all tend to impair the parent's ability to give the child wise love.* Thus they help produce the soil of addiction.

## THE WAY OUR CULTURAL ATTITUDES PRODUCE THE "SOIL OF ADDICTION"

| A<br>Cultural Attitudes Common<br>in Parents of Alcoholics | B<br>Effects of These Attitudes<br>on Parents |
|---|---|
| 1. *Authoritarianism.* Dominance-submission patterns throughout our culture. Worth of person judged by his power and prestige. | 1. Feelings of inferiority, producing need to dominate others; directly—policeman type, or indirectly—by over protection. |
| 2. *Success-worship.* Individual judges worth of self and others in terms of property and position, thinking of himself as a commodity. | 2. Impossible goals resulting in inevitable frustration, i.e., perfectionistic goals projected on child. Child is valued for the "success" he achieves for parent. |
| 3. *Moralism (Puritanism).* Sex and all negative or aggressive feelings are regarded as evil. Body is seen as in conflict with the spirit. Good and bad entirely a matter of willpower. | 3. Guilt, emotional frigidity. Extreme moral demands. Unable to give child early body love. Rigidity, moralism, and pharisaism. |

| C<br>Needs in Child Which Are<br>Deprived Satisfaction by<br>These Effects | D<br>Alcoholic Characteristics<br>Produced by This<br>Deprivation |
|---|---|
| 1. The need for self-fulfillment and autonomy, plus whatever needs are threatening to the parents' ego demands. | 1. Inferiority, shyness, feelings of inadequacy, anxiety, defensive grandiosity, and isolation. Ambivalence toward authority and responsibility. Need to dominate. |
| 2. The need for self-direction and autonomous growth. The need for unqualified love and acceptance (which doesn't have to be earned or won). | 2. Extreme ambition coupled with fear of both success and failure. Perfectionism. Compulsiveness. Defeats himself to defeat parents' image in him. |
| 3. The need for self-acceptance of the whole person, including body and emotions. The need for love not contingent on moral excellence. The need for bodily enjoyment. | 3. Guilt about sex and aggressive feelings or behavior. Emotional inadequacy and self-hatred. Feelings of isolation from others. |

Unfortunately, Protestant churches have unwittingly contributed to the cultural configuration which has produced emotional damage. These past mistakes give Protestantism an added responsibility to contribute to those attitudes which produce emotional health. A group of chaplains of the Council for Clinical Training, men who have unusual opportunities in their work in mental hospitals and correctional institutions, to observe the mistakes of Protestantism, puts it this way:

American Protestantism has frequently made critical and tragic errors in its presentation of the Christian religion—errors which have contributed to the emotional and spiritual conflict and immaturity in our people. Most of these errors find a focus in a stern, legalistic, absolute and Pharisaical moralism which is the characteristically American form of Puritanism. . . . Churches have had too little concern for understanding why people behave as they do and have been most relentless in their condemnation of acts contrary to social standards, with the result that many have responded with intense guilt feelings. . . . The guilty feel a sense of fear, loneliness and rejection and the result is various degrees of emotional disturbance.[8]

The report goes on to point out that the churches and their leaders have often propagated an unhealthy authoritarianism, resulting in fear, submissiveness, and immature dependence. Further, they have often made the mistake of saying directly or indirectly that sex is morally wrong.

We might add that the church has erred in that it often has made religion and the vitalities of life seem as opposites. Further it has often failed to create a healing fellowship which would attract people because it met their deep emotional needs. In his poem "The Little Vagabond," William Blake describes his contrasting feelings concerning what the church and the tavern have to offer in this respect:

Dear mother, dear mother, the church is cold
But the ale-house is healthy and pleasant and warm.[9]

If the church had more often offered a fellowship that was "healthy and pleasant and warm" to children, youth, parents, and families, it might have done much more than it has toward preventing emotional ills, and it would have been unnecessary for persons to find their fellowship in taverns.

The chaplains quoted earlier go on to point out that the unhealthy attitudes and practices do not represent the "deepest and best in the Christian tradition or in the contemporary church." They state that the errors represent a departure from the spirit of the life and teachings of Jesus who was non-authoritarian in his dealings with people, understanding and not condemnatory to those involved in sin, and who reserved his anger for the legalists and moralists of his day.

The church's first contribution to the prevention of alcoholism at the grass roots, by helping to prevent emotional conflict and illness, is to examine its own message and approach to people to make sure that they are in conformity with the principles of mental health and the best in the Christian tradition.

A church that is concerned about human values has no business allowing itself to be an agent in the perpetuation of harmful attitudes in the culture.

But it must go further than simply avoiding the doing of harm. It can put the weight of its educational program solidly behind the movement which aims at disbursing to people in general the precious discoveries of the social sciences in the area of healthy personality growth. The leaders of the Emmanuel Movement called for a "preventive psychiatry" which could help parents prevent the "wounds of childhood." Herein lies a tremendous educational opportunity for the church, with its natural entrée to families.

Let us see how this applies to alcoholism. The most cogent psychoanalytic explanation of alcoholism indicates that the emotional damage involved probably occurred in the very early life of the person—during the period when the child's primary way of relating to the outside world is oral. During the very early months of life the baby not only ingests food but also absorbs security and love through his body, and especially through his mouth. Several authorities in this field have indicated their conviction that alcoholism represents an attempt to return to the so-called oral stage of life. Whether or not this is true—and the essential orality of alcoholism would suggest that it is —the important fact is the one on which child-development authorities agree, that *it is during the first six years that the foundations of personality are laid.*

What would happen educationally if the church would face the implications of the fact that the first six years are the most important years of a person's life from the standpoint of character structure and personality? Would it not embark on a comprehensive program of parent education as a central focus of its work, making the discoveries of the psychologists concerning the emotional hungers of children, from the very dawn of life on, easily available to all its parents? Through such a program parents could come to see that healthy personality is "homemade" and that an ounce of mother is worth a pound of psychiatrist. Such parent education should put particular emphasis on helping the parents of infants to satisfy their babies' oral needs, the babies being allowed abundant sucking and given cuddling as well as generous amounts of "t.l.c." (tender loving care). By helping parents to do that which they basically want to do but often cannot—namely, raise children who are mentally, emotionally, and spiritually healthy—the church would help to prevent alcoholism at its very roots.

Fortunately, an increasing amount of attention is being directed to the resources for enhancing mental health within the program of the church. For example, the author's *Mental Health Through Christian Community* [10] was written to assist a local church in enhancing its ministry of growth and healing by releasing the mental health potentialities within its many-faceted activities. Each dimension of a church's program—worship, preaching, social action, the church school, church administration, small groups, family life, counseling, and the ministry of the laity—has untapped possibilities for helping children, youth, and adults move toward greater personhood. Mental health seems to be "an idea whose time has come." Churches should be playing an increasingly vital role in the surge of interest in this area. As they do, they will be making a significant contribution in the area of prevention. These developments are completely consistent with the central concern of the church—the growth of persons in ways that develop their God-given potentialities. It is well to remember that the words "health," "hale," "whole," and "holy" all come from a single Anglo-Saxon root.[11]

In discussing the role of the church in relation to alcoholism, several of the Yale ministers wrote some insightful words concerning prevention. Two of them pointed to the social dimension of the sickness when they wrote: "The Church's job, I think, is to shed the searchlight of the Gospel on the causes of human misery of which alcoholism is a symptom"; and "We can prevent it by helping people learn how to live in a complex world." And a third wrote: "The best preventive measure for alcoholism is developing normal, wholesome personalities in tune with God."

As a matter of fact, the church through the years has made a real though unmeasurable contribution to the prevention of alcoholism at the grass roots. To the extent that it has succeeded in its objective of helping people to a sense of acceptance and belonging, to love and be loved, to find meaning in life and a faith for meeting death, it has prevented people from needing to escape into the pseudoworld of alcoholism. No one can know how many people might have become alcoholics but didn't because of the faith and fellowship which they found in their church. By utilizing the newer insights of the mental health movement, the church can make a much larger contribution in this area in which it has long been serving.

## Prevention Through the Influencing of Symptom Selection

Some will say that attempting to prevent alcoholism at the grass roots is so large an undertaking as to be almost Utopian in nature. There is some truth in this point of view, and we should never allow our concern with the long-range and fundamental program of prevention to deter us from also working to attain the nearer preventive goals. As a matter of fact, there is a danger from the educational standpoint involved in the grass-roots approach. The danger is that, having heard that "emotionally healthy people don't become alcoholics," the individual will assume that he is not a potential candidate for the sickness. Consequently, he will become overconfident in his relationship with alcohol.

In order to counteract this danger, it is important to emphasize certain facts as we push for grass-roots prevention: First, that *one need not be aware of severe neurosis or emotional instability to become an alcoholic.* Many of our deep psychological problems are hidden and disguised even from ourselves. The emotional damage which underlies alcoholism seems to have happened at a very early age, in many cases, and has been overlaid by many strata of comparatively normal personality adjustment. Alcohol seems to reactivate these buried problems. Few, if any, of the people who become alcoholics think that they are neurotic or prealcoholic before they enter their addiction. *Second, at the present stage of psychological knowledge it is impossible to predict with any degree of accuracy just which six people out of any one hundred drinkers will become alcoholics.* Until it is possible, it is wise to accept the warning contained in the title of a pamphlet which came to my desk, "You, Too, Can Be an Alcoholic."

We know that there are factors other than the possession of healthy personalities which help prevent some people from becoming alcoholics. We know, from Chapter 2, that even very neurotic people will usually not become alcoholics if they live in a subcultural group which makes drinking or drunkenness unattractive. We know that if a person lives in a group that encourages the use of alcohol to excess and as a means of interpersonal adjustment, he may become an alcoholic even if he has a relatively adequate personality. It is clear that the culture factors which control inebriety have definite implications for the prevention of alcoholism.

Robert Straus, Sociologist on the faculty of the University of Kentucky Medical School, has said regarding alcoholism, "Those who drink constitute the 'exposed population' from an epidemiological standpoint." [12] It is true, as those who advocate total abstinence hold, "If you don't drink you won't become an alcoholic." Let us evaluate the strengths and limitations of total abstinence as a means of preventing alcoholism. If an individual decides that it is smarter not to drink, he is detaching himself from the "exposed population" so far as the sickness of alcoholism is concerned. One may well make this decision in the light of these facts:

1. One person in fifteen who drinks will become a problem drinker. If one is a male, the risk is much higher. (Approximately 80 percent of all alcoholics are males.) This is the realistic danger that all drinkers should face.

2. No one really knows whether or not he is a potential alcoholic.

3. Even if one is not a potential alcoholic, abstinence may prevent one from having an adverse influence on others who may be. This is especially applicable to influence on children and youth.

On the other hand, it is well to recognize the limitations of the abstinence position, if it is regarded as the only approach to the prevention of alcoholism. For one thing it does not provide protection for the majority of people who do not hold to this position and who are not likely to be persuaded in the foreseeable future. The Mulford Study (see Chapter 2) showed that only 37 percent of Protestants and 11 percent of Catholics practiced total abstinence. Of the 15,747 college students surveyed by Yale, 74 percent use beverage alcohol. In spite of the abstinence teachings of their church, 70 percent of Methodist students drink. Of the 26 percent who abstain, slightly less than one third do so because drinking is contrary to religious or moral training.[13] These facts do not, of course, invalidate total abstinence as a tenable position, but they do show that it cannot be the only approach to the problem.

Secondly, if it is assumed that, so far as alcohol is concerned, there are only two groups ethically speaking—drinkers and nondrinkers—an unfortunate splitting of the ranks occurs. Those who hold very strongly to the abstinence position often forget that there is another group who are as opposed to excess as they are and who might be allies in developing sanctions against drunkenness. From our study of the Jewish culture we know that such sanctions are extremely effective in preventing alcoholism. We also know that unified sanctions against drunkenness do not exist in American life in general, and that their absence contributes to the high rate of alcoholism. Those who are compulsive in their espousal of abstinence tend to drive the real moderationists—whose existence they do not recognize—into identifying themselves with those who use alcohol to excess.

Even the churches tend to divide ranks along these lines. The churches in the temperance tradition have tended, on the one hand, to regard their position as the only "Christian" one, to misunderstand the nature of alcoholism, to divide all persons into two groups—drinkers and nondrinkers. They have tended to ignore the more fundamental problem in alcoholism—the sick personality—which should have been their primary concern as Christians. On the other hand, the nontemperance churches, partly as a reaction to the temperance churches, have tended to overlook the realistic dangers of the use of alcohol in our neurotic culture, to treat drinking as if there were no moral problem involved, and to ignore the seamy side of drinking. Both sides have oversimplified the ethical complexities of the problem. Thus the churches, which should have been helping to form unified cultural sanctions concerning the use of alcohol to excess, have contributed to the confusion.

From the standpoint of potential alcoholics, the abstinence position if compulsively held has another limitation. This is the "forbidden fruit" atmosphere which can be especially dangerous for young people who are in the rebellious period of adolescence. A considerable number of the alcoholics I interviewed had come from rigidly prohibitionist homes and attributed their early excess in part to a reaction against the taboos of their early lives. It was apparent that Prohibition affected some prealcoholics in the same way.

J. H. Skolnick, using data from the College Drinking Survey,[14] compared the drinking behavior of students of various religious affiliations. He devised a "social complications" measure, to ascertain the amount of problem behavior connected with the drinking of each group. He found that 39 percent of Episcopalians, 34 percent of all male students in the College Drinking Survey, and only 4 percent of Orthodox Jewish students reported social complications related to their drinking. In contrast, 50 percent of the Methodist students and 57 percent of the nonaffiliated (with any religious group) students from abstinence backgrounds reported social complications.[15] (All percentages are of *drinking* students in a particular group.) The Jews had the highest proportion of students who drink at home and whose most frequent drinking companions are their families. The Methodists had the highest occurrence of initial drinking experiences in automobiles or bars and current drinking in commercial establishments among small male groups.

The crucial issue of why the abstinence orientation seems to promote problem drinking behavior is explored by Skolnick. He concludes, "Abstinence teachings, by associating drinking with intemperance, inadvertently encourage intemperance in those . . . who disregard the injunction not to drink." [16] The fact that the students from abstinence backgrounds frequently begin drinking outside their homes, without their parents' knowledge and in opposition to their religious teachings (which would tend to arouse guilt), and with no ethical guidelines from their churches to distinguish responsible from irresponsible drinking, also may contribute to the high incidence of problem drinking behavior.

Parents who choose personal abstinence will help their children most by doing so in a matter-of-fact manner, without making it a great issue. A study of the drinking habits of college students showed that the most important factor in determining these habits is parental example. Many, but of course not all, of the young people were found to drink (or abstain) like their parents. What the parents taught on the matter was of little importance compared with what they actually did.[17] The study suggested that conflicts in sanctions in the home concerning the use of alcohol is a factor which seems to encourage incipient alcoholism in young people.[18] Further, the attitudes and practices of the parents were much more influential on the young people's thinking and action than were the teachings of their schools or churches.

The Jewish culture can provide valuable insights concerning the prevention of alcoholism through influencing symptom choice. In Chapter 2 we saw that most Jews drink, that very few become alcoholics, even if they are emotionally disturbed. This is an example of the control of cultural sanctions against drunkenness. What can we apply from the Jewish situation to American drinking patterns in general? It is not realistic to say that all that is needed to prevent alcoholism is to do as the Jews do. The Jewish attitudes and sanctions are a part of the total milieu of the religiosocial community which is Judaism and which is the product of many centuries of historical development. It is not possible to transplant one segment of this and expect it to thrive in a different environment. Cultural sanctions have deep roots, and it is not possible to create them by any short-term educational procedure.

It *is* possible to learn from the Jewish group the effectiveness of unified sanctions against drunkenness. It is also possible for individuals and institutions —in this case, the church—to exert their influence in the direction of a gradual growth of such sanctions in American life. The sickness conception of alcoholism is the best foundation for such a development. If it were generally recognized that habitual drunkenness is a symptom of a disease that is both personally and socially devastating, and if it were generally accepted that frequent use of alcohol as a means of interpersonal adjustment can lead to alcoholism, a new climate of public opinion would come into being. Instead of accepting and even encouraging drunkenness, cultural attitudes would exert pressure against it. More of this in the third section.

Closely related with this is the matter of deglamourizing drinking. Of course this is much easier said than done. But the fact is that people, especially young people, do not have an opportunity to make a free choice about drinking. On every side drinking is presented as an indispensable part of gracious and fashionable modern living. Their choice is made under pressure from their normal desire to partake of this living. One need not believe in the prohibition of all drinking or even in abstinence for oneself to be concerned about reducing this pressure, which undoubtedly causes many who cannot handle it to use alcohol through social conformity. A candid look at America's drinking patterns reveals a measure of truth in the quip, "If alcoholism is a sickness, a lot of people are trying to catch it." The unrestricted, high-pressure advertising of a product which will produce untold tragedy for 6.7 percent of those who use it has ethical implications which our society must face. Related to this are the pressures in American life which associate ability to drink and "hold one's liquor" with masculinity and being "in." These pressures have an unfortunate effect on teen-agers and are one reason why many alcoholics have trouble accepting the truth about their sickness so that they can get help.*

The late E. M. Jellinek did a cross-cultural comparison of the relation between drinking practices and alcoholism rates in 25 countries. His findings demonstrate the relation between the two types of prevention described above. The following diagram delineates his major conclusion: [19]

* The Cooperative Commission on Alcoholism, in an illuminating discussion of prevention, makes these proposals for modifying drinking patterns and thus lowering the rates of alcoholism: First, reduce the emotionalism associated with drinking; second, clarify and emphasize the difference between acceptable and unacceptable drinking; third, "discourage drinking for its own sake and encourage the integration of drinking with other activities"; fourth, "assist young people to adapt themselves realistically to a predominantly 'drinking' society." (See *Alcohol Problems, A Report to the Nation,* pp. 136-52.)

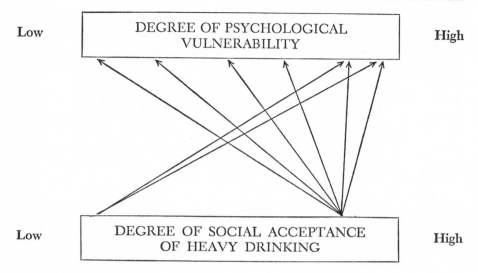

The top bar represents the degree of psychological disturbance in the individuals in a given population, producing vulnerability to alcoholism. The grossly disturbed persons are represented by the "high" (right) end of the continuum, the mentally healthy by the "low" end of the bar. The lower bar represents the degree of acceptance of heavy drinking as "normal" behavior in a particular culture or subculture. The "high" end represents societies in which heavy drinking is viewed as normal (for instance, France); the "low" end those societies or groups in which normal behavior is seen as including only abstinence or extreme moderation (for instance, the Jews).

As the arrows indicate, Jellinek found that in cultures in which there is non-acceptance of heavy drinking, persons who become alcoholics tend to be drawn from those in the population suffering from a high degree of psychological disturbance. In contrast, in cultures in which heavy drinking is seen as normal behavior, some persons from all degrees of mental health or illness (i.e., all degrees of psychological vulnerability) become alcoholics.

Jellinek summarized his study in what he described as his "working hypothesis":

In societies which have a low degree of acceptance of large daily amounts of alcohol, mainly those will be exposed to the risk of addiction who on account of high psychological vulnerability have an inducement to go against the social standards. But in societies which have an extremely high degree of acceptance of large daily alcohol consumption, the presence of any small vulnerability, whether psychological or physical, will suffice for exposure to the risk of addiction.[20]

305

The importance of the implications of this study for an understanding of prevention cannot be overemphasized. If one lives in a culture or closely knit social group in which there are strong sanctions against heavy drinking and drunkenness, the chances of becoming an alcoholic are relatively small, even if one is markedly disturbed psychologically. Conversely, if one lives in a heavy-drinking culture or group, one can become an alcoholic with relatively minor psychological problems. Thus, alcoholism can be prevented by reducing the degree of general psychological vulnerability in a population (prevention at the grass roots) and/or by education which reduces drinking, especially heavy drinking and drunkenness (prevention through influencing symptom selection).

## Prevention Through Early Detection and Treatment

In spite of the many new resources for helping alcoholics, countless sufferers from this illness are reaching treatment only after they have wasted what should be the most productive and creative years of their lives. Thousands of others are dying without ever reaching or becoming receptive to effective treatment for their total problem. Any seasoned minister could give examples of such tragedies from his pastoral experience. *Somehow we must devise better means of early detection and motivation-to-treatment of the majority of alcoholics whose problem is still hidden.* The importance of early treatment is highlighted by the now well-established fact that those who have treatment while they are still holding jobs and with their families have significantly higher recovery rates than do those who have lost these key incentives to recovery. In Chapter 8, certain methods of bringing hidden alcoholics to help were explored. The importance for prevention of the utilization of such techniques cannot be overemphasized. To use them with maximum effectiveness, one must understand the forces which tend to keep alcoholics in hiding and away from the help that is available.

In Chapter 2 we saw that one group of etiological factors operates on the level of perpetuating the addiction once it is established. It is these factors that make it necessary for the sickness to grind on and on through years of agony before the person is open to help. To the extent that these factors can be altered and early treatment instituted, the alcoholic will be prevented from having to go through the terminal period of suffering. What are the factors and what can be done about them? In many cases it is a combination of a lack of knowledge concerning the early signs of alcoholism, plus the voluntaristic, moralistic attitude toward alcoholism still prevalent in our culture which allows the sickness to go so long untreated.

The fact is that alcoholism slips up on many people. The loss of control is usually insidiously gradual and therefore difficult to recognize, particularly in oneself. Everyone has at least a little magic in his attitude toward himself—magic of the "It can't happen to me" type. This, plus the power to rationalize, so that one gives normal reasons for one's abnormal behavior, causes many to fool themselves for years about alcoholism. A contributing factor in this process is widespread ignorance concerning the danger signals of early alcoholism. How often the alcoholic or his relative says in retrospect, "If I had only been aware of the early symptoms, I could have looked for help rather than trying to fight it through myself." Overcoming this ignorance is an educational task in which the church should play a part.

Let us review some of the danger signals. A person is in the early stages of alcoholism or is in serious danger of entering them:

1. If he uses alcohol rather than his personality resources as a persistent means of solving his problems.

2. If alcohol holds a prominent place in his thinking and the planning of his activities.

3. If he uses alcohol as a persistent means of gaining social confidence or courage.

4. If he spends money for alcohol which he really needs for the necessities of life.

5. If he is defensive about how much or when he drinks.

6. If he gulps drinks, or drinks in secret.

7. If he drinks in the morning to cure a hangover, or to "pep up" for the day.

8. If he has blackouts when he is drinking.

9. If his drinking behavior is in defiance of the drinking standards of his important social or fellowship group.

10. If he begins to feel "normal" only when he has alcohol in him.

11. If his drinking interferes with his homelife, his job, his social life, or his health.

Early detection and treatment are dependent on more than simply the knowledge of early signs. They depend even more on whether the person can apply his knowledge to himself. Even if a person has accurate knowledge about the early signs, he can still rationalize and say: "These don't apply to me. I have very good reasons for my drinking behavior. I can quit when I want to." The fact is that when an alcoholic can stop, he usually doesn't want to stop, and when he wants to stop, he can't. What is involved, then, is a change in basic attitudes toward the problem.

Why does the alcoholic rationalize and resist the idea that he might be an alcoholic? One of the chief reasons is because he lives in a culture that traditionally has regarded inebriety largely as a matter of morals and willpower, and still does to a considerable degree. The survey cited in Chapter 2 showed that a majority of Americans accept the fact that alcoholism is in some sense an illness. However, in the thinking and feeling of a large proportion of these, an underlying moralism still blocks full acceptance of the sickness conception. In spite of all that has been written and said about alcoholism being a compulsive illness and an addiction, many Americans still think of it in moralistic, willpower terms. This lack of deep-level acceptance of the sickness conception is naturally internalized by the alcoholic in his thinking about himself.

As long as the alcoholic thinks of his trouble as essentially a matter of willpower, he will tend not to seek help. To do so would be an admission that he is weak or morally corrupt. But as soon as he accepts the sickness conception and applies it to himself, he will tend to take action appropriate to a sickness—get help. Those whose attitudes help perpetuate the moralistic conception of alcoholism are thus unwittingly responsible for pushing alcoholics deeper into the dark morass. As Marty Mann puts the matter:

> Up to now the alcoholic has been made to feel shame if he could not handle his drinking *by himself*. Our goal must be to reverse that: to make him feel shame at not seeking help for his illness. If he himself really comes to believe that he has a disease, the chances are greatly enhanced that he will seek treatment for it. Thousands of cases have proved this.[21]

That alcoholism is an illness has been known for a long time. Ulpian, a Roman jurist who lived in the second century, urged that inebriates be treated as sick persons. In a paper published in 1785, Benjamin Rush, a signer of the Declaration of Independence and foremost physician of his day, referred to alcohol addiction as a disease. In 1804 a Scottish physician, Thomas Trotter, wrote a doctoral dissertation in which he said: "In medical language, I consider drunkenness, strictly speaking, to be a disease." [22] Around the year 1820, Lyman Beecher sat beside the bed of a young parishioner, a chronic alcoholic who was dying. Later Beecher said, "I indulge the hope that God saw it was a constitutional infirmity, like any other disease." [23]

In spite of Beecher's early recognition and that of some others like him in the church, there has been considerable resistance on the part of religious leaders to the sickness conception. This has been especially true among the temperance denominations. Until the sickness conception is generally accepted, realistic prevention on a large scale will be very difficult. If a religious group helps to foster the general acceptance of the conception, it promotes the following constructive conditions: (1) Community pressures are mobilized in the direction of motivating the alcoholic toward help rather than away from it, in the early stages of his illness. (2) A major obstacle to early treatment is removed from the mind of the alcoholic himself. (3) He will have community support rather than rejection during and after his treatment. (4) Society at large will come to recognize that it is to its advantage to provide adequate facilities for treating the alcoholic.

If one has doubts about the effectiveness of a wide dissemination of realistic knowledge about alcoholism in encouraging earlier treatment, he has only to look at what has happened in AA. Each year from almost the beginning, the average age level seems to have declined in AA. The reason for this seems to be that AA itself, by its dramatic success based on the treatment of alcoholism as an illness, has had a tremendous educational impact. Through its influence, many younger alcoholics came to recognize their trouble and seek help. The existence of "Thirty-five and Under" groups and the AA pamphlet "Young People and AA" are both indications of what has happened. AA has and will continue to have a leavening influence on our whole society, so far as a more enlightened view of alcoholism is concerned.

Prevention through early detection and treatment is directly related to a fourth form of prevention—*prevention through helping the children of alcoholics.* In Chapter 2, a study by Jellinek was cited as evidence of the fact that many alcoholics have alcoholic parents. It is probable that between 20 and 30 percent of children of alcoholics eventually become alcoholics because of the emotional damage inflicted on them in their early lives. Since children of alcoholics have a high degree of vulnerability to the illness, they constitute an important target group for prevention! Such prevention may take one or more of three forms. First, early treatment of the alcoholic parent prevents the extreme emotional trauma to the children of the advanced stages of the illness. Second, helping the nonalcoholic spouse cope more effectively with her parental role, using methods described in Chapter 11, can diminish the emotional malnutrition suffered by the children. Third, direct help of the children, by pastoral counseling, Alateen group participation, and the other means described in the last chapter can enhance their mental health and thus make them less vulnerable to alcoholism a decade or so hence. These forms of direct and indirect help for the alcoholic's children are ways of preventing the various personality illnesses and social deviancies to which such children are prone. As a focus of preventive activities, it combines prevention at the grass roots and prevention through early treatment.

## REFERENCES

1. E. O. Bradshaw, *Unconquerable Kagawa* (St. Paul, Minn.: Macalester Park Publishing Co., 1952), p. 90.

2. H. J. Clinebell, Jr., "American Protestantism and the Problem of Alcoholism," *Journal of Clinical Pastoral Work*, II (Winter, 1949), 214-15. Used by permission.

3. "New Attitudes Toward Alcoholism," *QJSA*, XII (March, 1951), 60.

4. Charles Jackson, *The Lost Weekend* (New York: The New American Library, 1949), Preface.

5. Karen Horney, *Self-analysis* (New York: W. W. Norton & Co., 1942), p. 27.

6. Ruth Benedict, *Patterns of Culture* (New York: Houghton Mifflin Co., 1934).

7. *Psychotherapy and a Christian View of Man*, p. 65.

8. "American Protestantism and Mental Health," *Journal of Clinical Pastoral Work,* I (Winter, 1948). Used by permission.

9. Quoted in Charles Clapp, Jr., *Drinking's Not the Problem, How You Can Help a Potential Alcoholic* (New York: Crowell and Co., 1949), p. 62.

10. (Nashville: Abingdon Press, 1965).

11. Paul B. Maves, ed. (New York: Charles Scribner's Sons, 1953), p. 1.

12. From a paper presented at the annual meeting of the National Committee on Alcoholism, March 18, 1955.

13. Harold A. Mulford, "Drinking and Deviant Drinking, U.S.A., 1963," p. 637. The Yale survey of college students is reported in Straus and Bacon, *Drinking in College.* See pp. 46 and 65 for the facts mentioned.

14. Conducted by the Yale Center of Alcohol Studies, 1949–1951.

15. J. H. Skolnick, "The Stumbling Block: A Sociological Study of the Relationship between Selected Religious Norms and Drinking Behavior," Yale University Thesis, 1957.

16. J. H. Skolnick, "Religious Affiliation and Drinking Behavior," *QJSA,* XIX (1958), p. 470.

17. *Drinking in College,* p. 85.

18. Report by R. Straus in a speech before the annual meeting of the National Committee on Alcoholism, March 18, 1955.

19. This diagram is similar to the one which Jellinek used to illustrate the lecture in which he reported on this study at the Yale Summer School of Alcohol Studies, 1961.

20. *The Disease Concept of Alcoholism,* pp. 28-29.

21. *New Primer on Alcoholism,* pp. 198-99.

22. Taken from a history of the sickness of alcoholism by H. W. Haggard and E. M. Jellinek, *Alcohol Explored* (Garden City: Doubleday & Co., 1942), p. 142.

23. F. W. McPeek, "The Role of Religious Bodies in the Treatment of Inebriety in the United States," *Alcohol, Science and Society,* p. 406.

# 13

# An Alcoholism Strategy
# for the Congregation

*The spirit of the Lord is upon me . . . to proclaim release for prisoners and re-
covery of sight to the blind; to let the broken victims go free.*

*—Luke 4:18 (NEB)*

Those who are concerned about alcoholism and who also believe that the
church has a significant role in the second half of the twentieth century long
to see it take a more dynamic role in the solution of this gigantic problem.
Local congregations, viewed collectively, represent a sleeping giant of influence
and help to the burdened, so far as their potential contributions in this area
are concerned. Many individual clergymen are providing valuable services
in alcoholism education, working with local Councils on Alcoholism and
helping alcoholics and their families. But most local churches, as total congregations, have hardly scratched the surface of their potential opportunity to
be the "servant church" in the area of alcoholism.

The clergyman should set the tone of concern and help provide leadership
for his church's ministry in this area. His job is to catalyze interest, motivate
key laymen, work with them to plan strategy and train a task force to implement it, and be available as a knowledgeable resource person. In the contemporary understanding of the church, ministering is a function of the entire
congregation. The clergyman is a pastor of pastors, a teacher of teachers, a
counselor of counselors.[1] His role is to inspire, train, coach, and work alongside the lay ministers who composed the congregation, in their ministering to
persons in need (and to the needs of society through social and political
action). This approach reflects a recovery of the New Testament understanding of the nature of the church and the Christian life.[2]

Every member of a congregation has a job to do in the healing-redemptive
ministry of his church. It is his unique job—only he can do it. Only as increasing numbers of us catch this vision and accept this challenge—to be
where the action is in the church—can our congregations become redemptive
communities, centers of help and healing. Only thus can they be gardens and
hospitals, places of growth and healing, rather than museums.

311

One of the challenges-to-service to which some members of every congregation should respond is the problem of alcoholism. Think of five and one-half million alcoholics and twenty million family members caught in a gigantic web of suffering. What an opportunity to make one's life count in helping to meet human needs in the name of the Great Physician!

Implicit in the preceding chapters has been the belief that the minister and his congregation have many strategic opportunities in the area of alcoholism. The purpose of this final chapter is to discuss a five-pronged approach by which a local church can fulfill its opportunities and release its potentialities for good in this area. This chapter will be an overview of a plan and strategy for the church. As such, it will summarize some of the salient points in the chapters of Part III.

The five areas in which important contributions can be made by a congregation are: Education, prevention, community outreach, helping the alcoholic, and helping the family.

## I

*Alcoholism education aimed at developing a climate of understanding and acceptance.* A church has an opportunity to help build the solid foundation of *informed* concern on which any effective approach to the problem must be based. Taken together, the churches and temples have the widest educational contact with adults of any institutions in our society. Over 121 million Americans belong to a church. Each week, forty or fifty million adults and many young people in the formative years listen to a spiritual leader speak on something which (hopefully) touches people where they live. Each week some three million teachers function in church programs of religious education for children, youth, and adults. Through these channels, the churches have an unrivaled opportunity to help develop understanding of alcoholism at the grass roots of our population. To take advantage of this opportunity, the church's lay and ministerial leadership should plan and carry out a sustained, systematic educational effort to reach all ages from junior high up with the basic facts about alcoholism.

Education is concerned with aims, target groups, content, and methods. Choice of content and methods will be determined, to a large extent, by the aims or objectives of the educational program and the target groups one hopes to reach. In addition to its broad target—reaching the entire congregation with a message that will help them understand alcoholism—the church has a number of more limited and strategic target groups: teen-agers and pre-teens who are making or are about to make decisions about alcohol; parents who are searching for ways to prepare their children to cope constructively with alcohol and to avoid alcoholism; alcoholics and their families who need help but are afraid to come out of hiding (see Chapter 8). In addition, there are in nearly every congregation employers who have alcoholics in their businesses or plants, workers who know of untreated alcoholics in their unions, professional people with alcoholics among their clients or patients, public schoolteachers and opinion molders who through social prestige, political leadership, or involvement in the mass media help to create new images of public problems. By reaching target groups such as these with an enlightened view of alcoholism, church leaders can help key people in the community think, write, speak, and act more creatively on this problem.

Alcoholism education ought to be integrated into the church's ongoing program of education on social problems in general, including other problems of alcohol and problems of mental health and illness. Whether one's goal, so far as drinking is concerned, is abstinence or moderation, it is wise to approach education concerning alcoholism via the sickness conception and AA. Educationally these provide the best entrée to the interest of the average person. Nearly everyone, I have found, is interested in the dramatic story of AA, and this is a natural point of departure for a discussion of alcoholism. In this post-Prohibition era there are many people who are "allergic" to the usual temperance approach, but who will listen with rapt attention when alcoholism is presented as an illness to the danger of which one exposes one's self when he drinks. Many young people find it almost impossible to conceive of taking a drink as a major moral issue, but they can readily understand the danger of getting a disease. Speakers from AA, Al-Anon, and Alateens often make an unforgettable impact on church groups by personalizing the problems and the recovery from alcoholism.

Whatever is taught about alcohol and alcoholism should be put in the context of a *positive* view of the good life as seen from the religious perspective. Emphasis should be placed on what the church is *for* rather than on what it is against. An important aspect of the unique contribution of a church is to provide a context for alcoholism education—a view of life as a glad adventure and a gift from God. Within this frame of reference, decisions about all matters including alcoholism can be made, and an understanding of the congregation's mission to the burdened, including the alcoholic, can be gained.

Alcoholism education in churches, schools, and families should have two phases. The first has as its objective *head-level understanding*. Rigorously accurate presentation of the facts about alcoholism is the method of helping people move toward this objective. Information about the nature, causes, and treatments of alcoholism now available, plus an emphasis on the importance of knowing the warning signs of approaching addiction, are germaine to this phase. The new hope which now surrounds the problem should be highlighted, perhaps by describing the spiritually refreshing AA program and other treatment resources. The atmosphere of hopelessness which still attaches itself to "alcoholic" in the minds of many people is no longer appropriate to or in conformity with the treatability of the illness. Particular emphasis should be put on the inaccuracy of the Skid Row stereotype of "alcoholic," so far as the great majority of actual alcoholics are concerned. It is important, of course, to avoid oversimplifying the enigmatic complexities of the problem and to avoid painting an overoptimistic picture which ignores the dark realities and the unsolved problems which still exist in abundance.

Phase two of alcoholism education should move beyond head understanding to *heart understanding* of the persons suffering from the problem. This objective is much more difficult to achieve than the first. It involves modifying attitudes and feelings about alcoholics, increasing compassion toward them and their families, saying "yes" to them as persons of worth, whatever their problems in living. What is required is *education in depth*.

There are at least two things that seem to be crucial in changing attitudes. First, attitudes are changed *in relationships* and through *experiencing* something new that does not fit one's old images and biases. One way of approaching this is to ask all the teachers in the church school to attend two open meetings of AA as a part of their preparation for teaching in the general area of alcohol and alcoholism. A schedule of nearby meetings should be provided with the suggestion that no more than two go to a given meeting. It should also be suggested that they stay after the meeting and get acquainted over coffee with some of the members. Person-to-person contacts with recovered and recovering alcoholics in AA have probably done more to lessen punitive attitudes toward alcoholics than any other influences. Such contacts will allow the teachers or pastoral care team members to discover that recovered alcoholics are not only people; they are frequently fine and likeable people.

The second thing about attitudinal change is that, although relatively little of it occurs in most formal educational procedures, it does take place spontaneously when people get involved in constructive action on a problem. Laymen should be encouraged to serve on local Councils on Alcoholism, work as volunteers in enlightened treatment facilities and halfway houses, both because such help is often needed and because the experiences will help to modify relationship-blocking stereotypes concerning alcoholics. A congregation's own program for alcoholics can be invaluable for the same two reasons. Somehow people who are to be effective in this area must be helped to get beyond their fears of alcoholics and their anger toward them, to a warm fellow-feeling which makes possible a joining of hands in mutual acceptance.

The basic attitudinal climate in a congregation with respect to alcoholism provides either a bridge or a barrier to its work with alcoholics and their families. If it is to be a bridge, so that the congregation can use its potential helping resources creatively, then somehow the hard lumps of judgmentalism which linger in our psyches, even when we wish they would go, will have to be melted by compassion. Only thus can a person become a channel of that acceptance of others which is the healing force in religion. The ultimate test of a church's redemptive concern is its ability to accept the socially unacceptable, including the alcoholic.

The blocks to fuller acceptance of others are within the individual; they have to do with his lack of self-acceptance and his inability to accept God's acceptance. In small personal growth and spiritual discovery groups, some laymen and pastors are discovering how to remove these inner blocks. They may discover, for instance, that it is because alcoholics and other social deviants threaten them psychologically that they become anxious and therefore hostile in their attempts to relate. Working through to a living experience of grace in group relationships can heal the inner alienation that keeps us alienated from others.

Some church people are troubled by the sickness conception of alcoholism, believing erroneously that it denies that there are ethical issues involved. Since the sickness conception is the only sound place to begin, in either prevention or therapy, this is a serious dilemma for them. Wrestling with the issues raised in Chapter 7 may help resolve this dilemma. It should be emphasized that to say that alcoholism is an illness does not necessarily imply that there are no ethical dimensions to the problem. An alcoholic is simply a *person* with a condition called alcoholism. His behavior, like yours and mine, is composed of a complex mixture of sin and sickness, compulsiveness and freedom, accountability and drivenness. The point is how one handles the ethical aspects of the problem. To moralize, as indicated earlier, is utterly futile. To treat the alcoholic as a person who has the capacity to become more responsible is close to the heart of both sound counseling and the AA approach. The point is that the sickness conception need not be seen as amoral in order to be an instrument of acceptance in the relationship.

There is a growing body of useful materials in the area of alcoholism education.[3] Sources of pamphlets, films, books, and teaching guides include local Councils on Alcoholism (or the National Council,[4] if there is no local affiliate), state alcoholism agencies, and denominational social problems agencies. An excellent, brief film for introducing a program or series is "To Your Health," produced for the World Health Organization.

## II

**Prevention.** As indicated in the previous chapter, this is probably a church's most important contribution in the struggle to conquer alcoholism. It is obvious that one of the chief channels of prevention is the program of alcoholism education. Prevention and education overlap, but they are not identical.

A congregation needs a *strategy* for prevention which is a part of the larger strategy for preventing the broad spectrum of individual, family, and community problems. One of the mistakes that many churches have made in the past was to conceive of the prevention of alcohol problems on one level—in terms of persuading people not to drink. The most important point in the last chapter was that the prevention of alcoholism can and should occur on several different levels simultaneously. Since prevention was discussed in detail in that chapter, the consideration here will be limited to illustrations of how a congregation can contribute to prevention on two of the four levels.

*Prevention at the grass roots* includes the whole range of activities in the program of a local church, which contribute to the development of wholeness in persons and the vitalizing of families so that they satisfy the basic interpersonal hungers of children, youth, and adults. A marital enrichment group, a family camp, a child-study group, a youth fellowship, a preparation-for-retirement group, a nursery program, a senior citizen club, premarital counseling, marriage counseling, pastoral care in bereavement, parent-child counseling, and the entire spiritual growth and educational thrust of the church—all these are examples of resources which are designed to stimulate the growth of personality toward the realization of each individual's potentialities. To the extent that a church program succeeds in this, it helps to prevent alcoholism and other forms of personality illness at their source. The church's role in presenting its message in pro-life ways, and in changing cultural attitudes such as moralism and success worship, is another contribution to grass-roots prevention.

*Prevention through influencing symptom selection* is accomplished through alcoholism education which actually leads to either abstinence or the prevention of drunkenness. In a society in which a majority of adults not only use alcohol but attach considerable social significance to drinking, it is safe to assume that the majority of persons who are now children and youth will eventually decide to drink. Since this is the case, it is essential that a part of their preparation for living constructively in the adult world be to learn to distinguish responsible from irresponsible drinking. (The ethical distinctions, for example, between drinking as a part of a relaxed evening at home and drinking prior to operating a car or other piece of potentially lethal machinery, need to be seen clearly by a young person.) There are gradations of social responsibility and irresponsibility involved in a wide variety of drinking situations. With reference to the prevention of alcoholism, it is important to help young people see that the *why* of drinking is directly related to whether or not a person moves into problem drinking and that frequently intoxication or use of alcohol to cope with personality problems is dangerous and therefore irresponsible. It is at the point of failing to help youth develop ethical controls on the extent, occasion, and reasons for drinking that the one-track abstinence approach to alcohol education fails to prepare them for life in a society where the majority of them will probably drink.

The church's role in *prevention through early detection and treatment,* and *prevention through helping the children of alcoholics* has been discussed adequately in the previous chapters.

### III

*Community outreach and leavening.* The church that is isolated from the problems of its community (which extends from the local to the world community) is not being true to its mission to become the "light of the world" and the "salt of the earth." Ministers and laymen should see involvement in community alcoholism programs as an expression of their religious dedication. What is needed is for churches to devise imaginative ways of getting more of the hundreds of thousands of dedicated laymen directly involved as trained volunteers in projects to deal with all kinds of personal and social problems, including alcoholism.

One of the encouraging aspects of the present picture is the amount of preventive educational work that is being done by individual ministers in their communities. The 146 Yale ministers had almost all been very active in this field. As we have said, five of them had helped to organize local Councils on Alcoholism. Another was engaged full time as the director of a state alcoholism program; still another reported that he was executive officer of a state "pilot experimental project" which included an information and rehabilitation center for alcoholism. Three respondents told of the following significant work on the community level:

1. Facilitated some friendly contacts between AA and a judge of the municipal court as well as the personnel manager of a large industrial firm.

2. Behind-the-scenes attempt to get the city welfare association to begin the educational approach to the problem in the community.

3. Tried to promote consideration of alcoholism as a public health problem with local council of social agencies and state council of social welfare.

Almost all the ministers reported giving talks on alcoholism to all manner of youth and adult groups in public schools, youth camps, AA groups, and various community organizations. Twelve had written one or more articles on alcoholism. The impressive contributions which this particular group of ministers is making in the educational and community leavening areas are evidences of what can and is being done. What they are doing is but a small fragment of the total contribution of thousands of ministers over the country.

These men are convinced, for the most part, of the validity and importance of the scientific-therapeutic approach to alcoholism. They are rendering yeoman's service in helping to spread the kind of knowledge in their communities that will bring hidden alcoholics to help and lead gradually to the prevention of the disaster of alcoholism. It is hopeful that their number is increasing and that many of them are beginning to involve their laymen in this work.

Here are illustrations of what some churches are doing, usually through their social action committees, to implement an outreach ministry in alcoholism:

Many churches have invited AA, Al-Anon, and Alateen groups to use their fellowship halls. This is often a mutually enriching and enlightening experience, particularly if church members take the initiative in getting acquainted and expressing interest by occasionally attending open meetings, and by inviting speakers from these groups to address church groups.

Churchmen have worked with others to establish alcoholism inpatient and clinic facilities. A survey of clergymen conducted by Benson Y. Landis showed that a majority "expressed the opinion that the local church should help other community agencies establish special clinics to treat alcoholics." [6] Public clinics for alcoholics are right from the humanitarian and therapeutic standpoints. (They are also less expensive than the present "public care" system in which local governments spend millions each year on court, police, and jail facilities.)

Church members have helped establish local Councils on Alcoholism and have served as volunteers to "man" the information centers. Alcoholism is too big and complex a problem for any group to handle alone. Dedicated, knowledgeable churchmen have often seen the need to join forces with others in sparking a community-wide action program, coordinated by an Alcoholism Council.

Working to help open local hospitals to accept alcoholics as any other sick person is an important form of community outreach. It is particularly ironical when church-related hospitals have a policy (written or simply understood by the admissions staff) of not accepting alcoholics. Effective action can be taken by working through hospital boards.

Mobilizing moral support for state alcoholism programs is another way in which concerned churchmen can be an influence for good in this field. Unless public support is evident to state legislators, the programs may suffer from budgetary strangulation.

Many churches have had a role in backing alcohol education in public schools. The crucial issues are that it include alcoholism education and that it be sound in method and objective in content.


## IV and V

*Help for the alcoholic and his family.* It is not valid to assume that, since there are now numerous specialized agencies engaged in alcoholism treatment, the church can properly relinquish all responsibility for direct services to alcoholics. For one thing, many alcoholics are not being reached in time with help by any of the community agencies. Alcoholics are very different and their treatment needs varied. An approach that suffices with one may not with another. Many require a combination of treatment resources to achieve recovery. For this reason, we need a diversity of approaches so that as many as possible may be helped. Equally important, the church has unique contributions which it can and should make to the helping process. Therefore, it is not appropriate to say, "Let AA and the local alcoholic clinic do the total job."

A church ought to support (with volunteer time, interest, and, if needed, money) the community's alcoholic treatment programs and agencies. It should use them as often as appropriate to make referrals. Where needed community treatment resources are lacking, the clergyman and his lay leaders should help to spearhead efforts to provide them. But, at the same time, a *church should be engaged in some one experimental approach by which it seeks to develop (1) ways of bringing a unique service to the helping of alcoholics and their families, and/or (2) new ways of reaching and motivating hidden alcoholics to accept help.* Just what project a particular congregation should choose to do depends on the unmet needs of its community and the resources of the members who are available to help.

The following are examples of what various churches are doing. They are presented to suggest the wide variety of possibilities open to a congregation, possibilities limited only by the needs of the community and the resourcefulness of a church's leaders.

An East coast church is sponsoring an experimental program in alcoholic rehabilitation for men on probation because of alcohol problems. The weekly meetings alternate between AA speakers and mental health or alcoholism education films.[6] A Southern California church sponsors "Sunday Night with Recovered Alcoholics" for these two purposes:

(1) To create an occasion and an atmosphere in which members of the clergy and other professional people may learn more about alcoholism and observe the recovered alcoholic through his own story. And, to give the recovered alcoholic a similar opportunity to listen to members of other disciplines who are interested and knowledgeable in the problem of alcoholism. (2) To give recovered alcoholics the means of better learning about the eleventh step, namely, "to seek through prayer and meditation to improve their conscious contact with God."[7]

Recovered alcoholics and professional people, in approximately equal numbers, are invited to these weekly meetings.

The Cleveland Center on Alcoholism has set up a series of afternoon discussion sessions at a church in a marginal economic area for wives of men with drinking problems. Since women from this particular area seldom come to the Center for help, it was decided to take the Center to them. The women could walk to this meeting place, which was in familiar surroundings, and their children could be left under supervision in the church's recreation room. This is an illustration of a church cooperating with a community agency in a new pattern of service to families of alcoholics. There is no reason why a local church could not take the initiative in setting up a similar type of group, calling on whatever community resources are needed to provide the desired program.

On the West coast a halfway house for alcoholic men is sponsored co-operatively by several churches of one denomination. A church of another denomination, in the same area, is developing plans for a halfway house for alcoholic women. In such projects, it is important to train a group of laymen within the church for the various roles which they may fill.

A refreshing example of direct, congregational involvement in working with homeless alcoholics is a Church of the Brethren program. About a dozen congregations have "sponsored" alcoholics released from mental hospitals and prisons with no place to go. Sponsorship is similar to that accorded refugee families. The sponsors are responsible for helping the person find a job, obtain housing, and bear expenses until his first paycheck. A group within the congregations is trained to receive and relate to the alcoholic. Their assignment is to assist him in any way that may help him to adjust to living outside the institution. The educational impact of this program on the congregations—in terms of their understanding of alcoholism and their acceptance of alcoholics—has been a valuable by-product. A staff member from the office of Social Welfare of the denomination provides the preparatory training for the congregation, secures the alcoholic, and is available for follow-up guidance as problems arise. The first alcoholic to be sponsored by a congregation had four slips in that many years, but since then has had some eight years of complete sobriety. That one church has sponsored eleven other alcoholics. The most important thing a congregation must give a recovering alcoholic is a sense of acceptance in the fellowship. Such direct involvement in helping deeply troubled people forces a congregation to test the reality of its dedication to loving God and neighbor.

The use of personal growth groups as an aid in the spiritual development of recovered alcoholics was suggested in Chapter 10. Many of the depth Bible study, prayer fellowship, and koinonia groups which now function in many churches can serve alcoholics (and others) as means of stimulating growth which they desire in the vertical dimension of their lives. Frequently these groups are led by spiritually mature laymen who have had special training and preparation, including extensive small group experience.

The pastoral care team was mentioned in Chapter 11. This is a task force composed of those committed to pastoral care as their primary focus of lay ministry. Carefully selected and trained, this group works under the minister's guidance, supplementing and broadening his work with the troubled. To help alcoholics effectively, the team should include stable AA and Al-Anon members of both sexes, and a physician who is acquainted with current medical approaches to the problem. The team should meet regularly for in-service training. Team members serve at the minister's discretion, as "befrienders" [8] of those in crisis and those bearing heavy loads.

## Organizing for Action

Alcoholism programs in local churches, which have been effective, seem to have gone through certain general steps:

1. *Someone who is a "self-starter" and is concerned about alcoholism took the initiative.* In some cases this was the minister. If a layman is the initiator, it is important for him to discuss the matter with the minister and get his support. Most clergymen are delighted when a layman takes active leadership in beginning such a project. The key point here is that in almost every case of a successful action project, one person started the ball rolling.

2. *A group (usually small) was selected or recruited to share the responsibility.* This can be an already-established committee on social action or a committee on alcohol problems. In some situations it is better for an ad hoc task force to be recruited to do a particular job. In any case, the responsible group must be brought in on the planning of the project as well as the implementation phase. Unless something of their thinking goes into the planning, it is probable that their motivation will be minimal.

3. *The needs of the local situation were studied and a decision made by the responsible group concerning which unmet need should have top priority.* In some cases, the minister or someone else had already decided what he felt needed to be done, and a group was invited to help in doing it. This may work, if the project has obvious merit and the group has some voice in deciding how it will be carried forward. But, in general, the earlier the working group can be included in the decision-making and strategy-devising activities, the stronger will be their motivation to invest themselves in the project.

Careful study, by all members of the action group, of the recommendations of the Cooperative Commission on the Study of Alcoholism, should precede the decision- and strategy-making steps. The Commission's major report (*Alcohol Problems, A Report to the Nation*) is an invaluable resource for any clergyman or lay church leader who is searching for fresh insights and directions in the church's approaches to alcoholism. Church groups have an opportunity to help implement its salient recommendations in cooperation with other groups at both the local and national levels.[9]

4. *Plans were formulated on how to proceed on the chosen project, and*

*work was begun.* It is important for a group to concentrate its efforts on one project at a time, to have frequent evaluation sessions on the progress of the project, and to draw in such resource people as may contribute to achieving the goal of the project. One aspect of planning is for task force members to consult with others who have attempted similar projects and to read relevant reports and other literature. A congregation considering a ministry to alcoholics and their families, for example, might well read the summary of the seminar on "The Pastoral Care Function of the Congregation to the Alcoholic and His Family." This seminar was sponsored by the Department of Pastoral Services of the National Council of Churches.[10] Sources of literature and guidance include local Councils on Alcoholism, the National Council on Alcoholism, and denominational social problems agencies. It is encouraging that several of the major denominations have developed plans and resources in the areas of alcoholism education, community action, and rehabilitation.[11] It may be productive for a minister or task force member to write to several denominational agencies, in addition to his own.

The five-pronged approach described above for use by a local church can also be used advantageously by denominational and ecumenical groups in their planning of alcoholism strategy. There is a need for each denomination to develop its own unique style and contribution, but there is also a need for much increased cooperation by religious groups across denominational, faith, and national lines. This is the place where ecumenical bodies such as the National Council of Churches and the World Council of Churches (perhaps in cooperation with the World Health Organization) have a major opportunity to provide coordination and joint strategy designing.

If the influence of church groups is to make a contribution in relation to the federal mental health and alcoholism programs (in the U.S.), it will have to be expressed through ecumenical channels. In the light of this, it is fortunate that a foundation for joint action was laid in a statement adopted by the General Board of the National Council of Churches in 1958. Here are some excerpts:

> The churches share a pastoral concern for alcoholics, problem drinkers and their families. . . . Alcoholics are persons in need of diagnosis, understanding, guidance and treatment. They are especially in need of pastoral care and the divine love which the church can bring them. . . . Ministers and churches should not be content merely to direct alcoholics to treatment centers.
> The concern of the churches for alcoholics and their families is being shared increasingly by the community as a whole. We look to the member churches of the National Council to encourage the establishment and maintenance of clinics and other appropriate therapeutic facilities when competently conducted, for the victims of alcoholism. . . . The churches should disseminate such sound information as is now available concerning the understanding and counseling of persons with

alcohol problems. The churches have a special responsibility to assist pastors to become more effective counselors in this field.[12]

### The Key—The Helper's Personality

If a minister or layman desires to maximize his effectiveness in any dimension of the alcoholism field, he must become competent in both skills and knowledge about the illness. But there is one factor which is more important than either of these: his personality and particularly his feelings about himself in relation to alcoholics and other deeply troubled persons. To the extent that he possesses a *therapeutic attitude* toward himself and others, he will be able to use his knowledge and skill. This attitude will be reflected in his relationships with alcoholics and their families. It will show in his tone and manner as he participates in alcoholism education. His approach to prevention and alcoholism action projects will be colored by it. In short, his ability to implement strategies in all five areas—education, prevention, community outreach, helping alcoholics and their families—will be influenced by the relative presence or absence of the therapeutic attitude.

The nature of this basic personality orientation has been illuminated by research in the field of counseling and psychotherapy. A study reported by Carl R. Rogers points to three components which are a part of what I am describing as the therapeutic attitude: *Congruence, empathic understanding,* and *unconditional positive regard*.[13] Congruence means genuineness as a person. Rogers declares, "The most basic learning for anyone who hopes to establish any kind of helping relationship is that it is safe to be transparently real." [14] Congruence involves knowing one's feelings and owning them. The most important thing a person brings to any helping or teaching relationship is *himself*—unhidden and real. Congruence is particularly important in working with alcoholics. They are hypersensitive to its absence—"being a phoney" or "putting on an act."

Empathic understanding means being able to "tune in" on the inner world of feelings and meanings of another person. It means being *with* him in terms of what really matters to him behind his façade. In relating to an alcoholic, empathic understanding means that one is able to understand, to an appreciable degree, the chaotic complexity of his fears, guilt, despair, and hopes. This understanding, which is a thing of the heart as well as the head, is crucially important because of the alcoholic's feeling of haunting aloneness in a bizarre world and his belief that others could not possibly comprehend.

Unconditional positive regard means warm, human regard for the individual as a person of unconditional worth. With his fragile self-esteem (hidden by his defensive grandiosity), the alcoholic desperately needs positive regard. He hungers like a starving man for the acceptance he cannot give himself. The alcoholic's emotional immaturity causes him often to react in ways that are selfish, irresponsible, and impulse-ridden. This makes it difficult for a helping person to remain accepting and nonjudgmental. It helps to remind one's self that he is the way he is, in large measure, because of some inadequacy in his early relationships which blocked his emotional growth. The thing that Longfellow said about our enemies is equally applicable to the alcoholic: "If we could read the secret history of our enemies, we should find in each man's life sorrow and suffering enough to disarm all hostility." The link between empathic understanding and unconditional positive regard is very direct.

Acceptance of the alcoholic is dependent, as has been suggested, on the helping person's acceptance of the reality of the illness from which he suffers. This is the basic reason for the emphasis which has been placed on the sickness conception of alcoholism throughout this book. A prerequisite for any constructive approach to the problem is the recognition that alcoholism is not an isolated problem, but a part of the total sin and sickness of our society—a *sin and sickness in which all of us are participants*. The problems of the alcoholic are the problems which all of us share in differing degrees and with varying symptoms. This sense of involvement in the total cultural problem, of which alcoholism is one painful expression, and an honest recognition of our complicity in the kind of world which produces alcoholics are the points at which we must begin. This was where Lyman Beecher began over a century ago when he wrote concerning alcoholism, "For verily we all have been guilty in this thing." [15] We can choose no better starting point today.

The recognition by the helping person that he has a basic kinship with the alcoholic, that he is not better but only luckier that his symptoms are different, helps him to accept the alcoholic without condescension. This is the application of Tillich's "principle of mutuality," mentioned earlier. Deep inside himself, the helping person must be aware of the fact that the alcoholic is not essentially an alcoholic. He is essentially a *human being* with alcoholism. This affirms the alcoholic's humanity and provides a link with the humanity of the helping person. To be able to establish this link the person must be aware of his own dark side, his own inner conflicts, dishonesties, anxieties, compulsions, and grandiosities. The surrender experience is as important for the minister or lay worker as it is for the alcoholic.[16] It is also equally important that they be aware of the grace and acceptance of God in their own lives. Otis Rice put the matter in this way, in a talk to a group of ministers: "More than anything else we need to learn to love the alcoholics. The only way I know to do this is to remember that God loves them, and to remember how much he puts up with in order to love us." The words of Tolstoy come to mind at this point: "Only he who knows his own weakness can be just to the weaknesses of others."

The therapeutic attitude begins to dawn as the helping person senses, in the presence of the alcoholic or of his spouse, that "there but for the grace of

God go I!" It exists more fully as he moves beyond even this to the deflating awareness—"*There go I!*" This fellow feeling lowers the walls which block the flow of healing forces in the relationship.

Retaining this fellow feeling is very difficult for most of us. To identify with the essential humanness of the despairing threatens our fragile defenses against our own despair. To recognize that the [alcoholic in D.T.s] is more like than different from oneself shakes the very foundation of our defensive self-image. To accept this truth at a deep level is possible for most of us only to a limited degree. It requires an inward surrender of subtle feelings of self-idolatry and spiritual superiority. One student referred to this as "getting off the omnipotence kick." Even a partial surrender of one's defensive superiority feelings helps to open the door to mutually redemptive relationships. Somehow it melts a hole in the icy barrier of pride that freezes real self-esteem and keeps people—especially disturbed people—at a distance.[17]

The helping person's own religion can help him maintain the therapeutic attitude. He knows that he is only a finite and fallible instrument, through which the healing, growth-producing forces of life can, at times, operate. He is aware of the fact that, at best, he is an imperfect channel for the flow of these God-given forces. Because of this he is better able to accept the fact that there are many people he cannot help or whom he can help only in very limited ways, no matter how hard he tries. This awareness makes it easier for him to avoid the false humility of unproductive self-blame when he fails, and to look honestly at his approach to discover weaknesses or mistakes which need not be repeated. Because of his own experiences of growth, reconciliation, and healing, he has a confidence in the power of the divine forces in every person which makes these experiences possible. This faith helps to prevent him from applying the easy label "hopeless" to the people he cannot help.

The therapeutic attitude includes a realistic awareness of one's limitations as an instrument of growth and health; *but it also includes an awareness of one's potentialities as such an instrument.* A certain alcoholic had been drunk nearly every night for five years. During his drinking he considered himself an agnostic. Finally, he came into AA, and at the time I heard him speak, he had been sober for three-and-a-half years. Here is what he said about how he was helped by a minister:

For the first seven months in AA I was dry on conceit and ego pride. I had nothing to do with the higher Power, and no support from the outside. I stayed sober, but it's a hell of a way to stay happy. At the end of that time my wife told me, "You're just as drunk in your mind as you ever were." I went to have a talk with a member of the local clergy. That day I saw the grass, the buds, the sky in a way I'd never seen them before. I've never lost the experience I had that day, and I now have a speaking acquaintance with Someone greater than myself.

325

We do not know what the minister did or said in his meeting with this man. But it is safe to assume that, whatever it was, it occurred within a relationship to which the minister brought the precious ingredient which I have called the therapeutic attitude. The results of the encounter were more immediate than is usually the case in working with alcoholics (or others). But the helpfulness of the contact is not atypical.

In this meeting of two human beings, decisive events occurred which changed the direction of a man's existence—turning him toward life, opening his eyes to the world around him, and beginning his relationship with "Someone greater than myself." Ministers and other persons of religious dedication can be instruments in such a life-transforming process. This is the challenge and the satisfaction of working with the alcoholic and his family.

## REFERENCES

1. H. R. Niebuhr et al., *The Purpose of the Church and Its Ministry* (New York: Harper & Row, 1956), pp. 83 ff.

2. See Clinebell, *Basic Types of Pastoral Counseling*, Chapter 16, "The Layman's Ministry of Pastoral Care and Counseling."

3. Here are a few of the many resources available for use in alcoholism education: The two basic books are Raymond G. McCarthy, ed., *Alcohol Education for Classroom and Community, A Source Book for Educators* (New York: McGraw-Hill Book Co., 1964); and Margaret E. Monroe and Jean Stewart, *Alcohol Education for the Layman* (New Brunswick, N.J.: Rutgers University Press, 1959). The latter is an annotated list of library materials—books, pamphlets, articles, films, and filmstrips—for use in alcohol and alcoholism education. The Association for the Advancement of Instruction about Alcohol and Narcotics produces a newsletter which contains useful material. Background books include: the AA and Al-Anon books; Marty Mann's *New Primer on Alcoholism*; Arnold B. Come, *Drinking: A Christian Position* (Philadelphia: The Westminster Press, 1964); Wayne E. Oates, *Alcohol In and Out of the Church* (Nashville: Broadman Press, 1966).

4. 2 East 103rd Street, New York, New York.

5. "A Survey of Local Church Activities and Pastoral Opinions Relating to Problems of Alcohol," *QJSA*, VIII (March, 1948), 636-56.

6. Robert E. Bavender, "Rehabilitation in Brentwood," *The Methodist Story*, November, 1964, pp. 39-40.

7. From a leaflet describing the program.

8. This is the term used by the "Samaritans," laymen who staff crisis counseling centers in the British Isles and elsewhere, to describe their work.

9. Another resource for the action group is a report entitled *Alcohol and Alcoholism* (Public Health Service Publication No. 1640), produced by the National Center for Prevention and Control of Alcoholism, Chevy Chase, Maryland 20203, in 1967. It gives a brief survey of present scientific knowledge concerning the causes, treatment, and prevention of alcoholism; describes present research and that which is needed; and outlines the national alcoholism program. For a survey from the international perspective, see "Services for the Prevention and Treatment of Dependence on Alcohol and Other Drugs: Fourteenth Report of the WHO Expert Committee on Mental Health" (Geneva: World Health Organization Technical Report Series, No. 363, 1967). This report summarizes the WHO approach to drug dependence and describes treatment, education, training, and research programs in various countries.

10. This seminar was held at Columbus, Ohio, October 12-14, 1962.

11. The Episcopal and Methodist Churches have done pioneering in this area. The North Conway Institute, which meets in New Hampshire each summer, provides a chan-

nel for interdenominational collaboration and discussion of the problem of alcoholism. On the international scene, it is noteworthy that one of the sections of the Twenty-Eighth International Congress on Alcohol and Alcoholism (held in Washington, D.C., September 1968) was on "Religion and the Church."

12. Statement adopted February 26, 1958, at New York City.

13. *On Becoming a Person*, pp. 47-49.

14. *Ibid.*, p. 51.

15. F. W. McPeek, "The Role of Religious Bodies in the Treatment of Inebriety," *Alcohol, Science and Society*, p. 406.

16. For an illuminating discussion of this point, see John E. Keller's *Ministering to Alcoholics*.

17. Clinebell, *Basic Types of Pastoral Counseling*, p. 297. (The words "alcoholic in D.T.s" substituted.)

# Index

AA. *See* Alcoholics Anonymous

Absenteeism, 23, 39, 204

Abstinence, 62, 82, 88, 89, 98, 99, 183, 188, 189, 190, 191, 207, 214, 232, 301, 302, 303, 313, 316, 317

Acceptance, 49, 50, 51, 88, 117, 137, 145, 151, 158, 159, 160, 161, 162, 174, 176, 199, 202, 219, 227, 233, 251, 254, 256, 284, 291, 296, 300, 312, 314, 315, 323, 324

Addiction, 26, 31, 32, 44, 68, 74, 176, 178, 189, 190, 206, 207, 208, 209, 237, 241, 287, 295, 308

Addictive cycle, 107, 111, 129, 144, 150, 191, 205, 209, 242-45, 248, 263, 295

Addictive pattern, 28-36

Adler, Alfred, 111, 254

Age level and drinking, 67

Aggressiveness, 64, 89, 162, 251

Al-Anon family groups, 139, 191, 196, 233, 241, 266, 268, 269, 275, 278, 280, 283, 284, 287, 288, 289, 291, 313, 318

Alateen groups, 196, 268, 269, 275, 309

Alcohol

anesthetic quality of, 31, 32, 57, 59, 208, 210, 221, 237, 295

attitudes toward, 62, 74

availability of, 60, 68, 74

as a cause of alcoholism, 43, 44, 60

as a means of adjustment, 20, 58, 82, 73

as a neurotic "solution," 31, 58, 69, 159

pharmacological properties of, 44-45

as a substitute for religion, 36, 73, 104, 154, 158, 255

and religion, 154-69

Alcoholic convulsions, 241

Alcoholic hallucinosis, 205

Alcoholic personality types, 59

Alcoholics

age of, 24

characteristics of (psychological), 53 ff., 193, 215, 296

childhood of. *See* Childhood

definition of, 19, 26

high-bottom, 23, 27, 36

homeless (*see also* Skid Row), 79-103

identifying, 19-26

low-bottom, 22, 23, 27, 36, 79, 80, 100, 102, 260

manic-depressive, 176, 208

periodic, 23, 25, 26, 27, 112, 236

personality change in, 34

religious need of, 29, 34, 254-56

resistance and receptivity to help. *See* "Hit bottom," Motivation

steady, 23, 26, 27, 112, 236

uniqueness of each, 22, 24, 27, 29, 59

Alcoholics Anonymous (AA), 18, 19, 21, 23, 54, 55, 79, 91, 95, 99, 112, 114, 115, 119-53, 158, 159, 163, 169, 173, 174, 179, 180-83, 185, 191, 192, 193, 196, 197, 199, 200, 201, 204, 206, 208, 210, 211, 218, 221, 225, 232, 234, 236, 239, 241, 243, 244, 245, 249, 250, 252-62, 277, 278, 284, 285-89, 294, 309, 313, 317, 318, 325

beginner's meeting, 138

Big Book (*Alcoholics Anonymous*), 125, 127, 130, 137, 143, 193, 277, 279, 282, 288

blocks to affiliation with, 243-45

closed meetings, 94, 131, 283

clubhouse, 128, 139, 197

dynamics of, 127-44, 149

effectiveness of, 144-52

family groups. *See* Al-Anon

General Service Office, 126, 197

Pastoral care, 185, 186, 204, 225, 246, 267, 275, 278, 283, 320, 322
Pastoral care team, 283, 320
Pastoral counseling, 192, 194, 195, 211, 213, 218, 241, 242, 248, 281, 283. *See also* Counseling, Minister's approach
Peabody, Richard, 106
Perfectionism, 51, 53, 55, 58, 143, 297
Periodic alcoholics. *See* Alcoholics
Personality change, 114, 144, 148
Personality problems and alcoholism, 24, 38, 48, 56, 57, 60, 74, 115, 143, 201, 205, 209, 240, 245, 255, 296, 305, 306
Philosophical and religious factors in alcoholism. *See* Causes, philosophical
Philosophy of life, 71, 72, 160, 248, 255
Physicians, 17, 18, 21, 27, 106, 167, 181, 189, 191, 195, 196, 197, 201, 207, 239, 240, 241, 242, 245, 258, 261, 285
Physiological factors in alcoholism. *See* Causes, physiological
Pittman, David J., 64, 81, 83, 102
Plateau alcoholic, 26, 37. *See also* Alcoholism, Delta
Plaut, Thomas F. A., 76, 188, 204
Prayer, 84, 88, 106, 107, 110, 138, 152, 250, 256, 257, 320
Prevention, 42, 63, 70, 202, 204, 266, 272, 294-310, 315-17, 321, 323
  at the grass roots, 295-300, 316
  by influencing symptom choice, 300-307
  by helping alcoholic's children, 309
  through early detection and treatment, 306-9, 316
Problem drinking, 25, 26, 27, 65. *See also* Alcoholism, Alpha; Nonaddictive excessive drinking
Prohibition, 23, 60, 63, 183, 184, 302, 313
Protestants, 44, 80, 297, 298, 301
Psychiatry (psychiatrist, psychiatric therapy) 51, 57, 93, 97, 99, 106, 112, 194, 195, 201, 204, 208, 210, 211, 236, 245, 257, 261, 262, 263, 267, 285, 299
Psychoanalysis (psychoanalytic), 56, 68, 107, 108, 114, 115, 116, 117, 162, 208, 299
Psychodynamics of religious approaches to alcoholism, 154-63
Psychological causes of alcoholism. *See* Causes, psychological
Psychology (psychologist), 42, 48, 113, 117, 151, 172, 194, 195, 211
Psychopathic personality, 33, 55, 176, 237, 276
Psychosis, 25, 36, 49, 60, 93, 106, 190, 207, 208, 237, 270, 276

Psychotherapy, 91, 107, 113, 143, 145, 151, 171, 173, 174, 175, 189, 194, 196, 197, 204-11, 248, 264, 281, 291, 323
Puritanism, 52, 55, 157, 176, 298. *See also* Moralism

Rapport in counseling, 182, 216, 217, 254, 273
"Rat experiment," 69, 227
Rationalization, 31, 36, 70, 141, 211, 231, 232, 242, 245, 259, 279, 307. *See also* Alibi system
Reality, confrontation with, 220, 230, 232, 233, 236, 239, 254, 263, 280, 286. *See also* Counseling, confrontation in
Recovery process, 230, 231, 244, 250
Referral, 181, 192, 196-204, 245, 259, 269, 276
Regression, 159, 162
Rehabilitation, 83, 195, 206, 277, 322
Reik, Theodor, 215
Rejection, 50, 52, 55, 56, 151, 157, 176, 216, 247, 279
Relationship, therapeutic. *See* Counseling, relationship
"Releasing" the alcoholic, 233, 234, 278-82, 284
Religion and alcohol, 61, 70, 71, 73
Religion, dynamic function of, 154-63
Religion, magical, 249, 250, 257
Religious affiliation and drinking, 67, 301, 302, 303
Religious approaches to alcoholism, 79-163, 248-58
Religious ecstasy, 88, 113, 122, 146, 156, 157, 161
Religious experience, 88, 89, 145, 248
Religious group, 89, 158, 159, 160
Religious needs, 155, 223, 248, 255
Religious resources. *See* Counseling
Remorse, 21, 23, 28, 35, 82, 86, 140, 218, 223, 270. *See also* Guilt
Repression, 58, 71, 91, 108, 116, 149
Rescue mission approach, 80, 83-93, 94, 95, 110, 146, 157, 168, 196, 259
  conception of alcoholism, 90
  effectiveness of, 90-93
  goals of, 86
  psychodynamics of, 86-89
Research on alcoholism, 18, 25, 42, 44, 47, 64, 130, 195, 197, 202, 203, 204, 211, 262, 263, 321
Resentment, 28, 32, 141, 149, 211, 224, 227, 233, 245, 247, 269, 277
Resocialization, 136, 151. *See also* Counseling, resynthesis of life